New Vistas in Indian Performing Arts

No. 1 Hindustānī Music and the Aesthetic Concept of Form by Anjali Mittal (ISBN 978-81-246-0134-1)

No. 2 Hindustani Sangeet and a Philosopher of Art: Music, Rhythm and Kathak Dance — *vis-à-vis* — Aesthetics of Susanne K. Langer by S.K. Saxena (ISBN 978-81-246-0180-8)

No. 3 Speaking of Dance: The Indian Critique by Mandakranta Bose (ISBN 978-81-246-0172-3)

No. 4 Performing Artistes in Ancient India by Iravati (ISBN 978-81-246-0207-2)

No. 5 Ritual as Ideology : Text and Context in Teyyam by T.V. Chandran (ISBN 978-81-246-0275-1)

No. 6 Tantra — Mantra — Yantra in Dance : An Exposition of Kathaka (ISBN 978-81-246-0268-3)

No. 8 The Art of Tablā-Rhythm — Essential, Tradition and Creativity by Sudhir Kumar Saxena (ISBN 978-81-246-0368-0)

No. 9 Kathaka — The Tradition: Fusion and Diffusion by Ranjana Srivastava (ISBN 978-81-246-0473-1)

No. 10 Elements of Hindustani Classical Music by Shruti Jauhari (ISBN 978-81-246-0799-2 Hb) (ISBN 978-81-246-0800-5 Pb)

No. 11 Khyāla Vocalism: Continuity within Change by Deepak Raja (ISBN 978-81-246-0481-6 Hb) (ISBN 978-81-246-0482-3 Pb

New Vistas in Indian Performing Arts, no. 7

Hindustani Music

A Tradition in Transition

by
Deepak S. Raja

Foreword by
Pandit Shivkumar Sharma

Introduction by
Lyle Wachovsky

PRINTWORLD
Publishers of Indian Traditions

Cataloging in Publication Data — DK
[Courtesy: D.K. Agencies (P) Ltd. <docinfo@dkagencies.com>]

Raja, Deepak S., 1948 -
Hindustani music : a tradition in transition / by Deepak S. Raja: foreword by Shivkumar Sharma ; introduction by Lyle Wachovsky.
p. cm. (New vistas in Indian performing arts, no. 7)
Includes bibliographical references (p.)
Includes index.
ISBN 13: 9788124608067 (Hbk)
ISBN 13: 9788124608074 (Pbk)

1. Hindustani music — Theory. 2. Music — India.
I. Title. II. Series : New vistas in Indian performing arts, no. 7

DDC 780.954 21

ISBN 13: 978-81-246-0806-7 (Hbk)
ISBN 13: 978-81-246-0807-4 (Pbk)
First Published in India in 2005
Second impression in 2007
Third revised edition 2015

Published and printed by:
D.K. Printworld (P) Ltd.
Regd. Office: *Vedaśrī*, F-395, Sudarshan Park
(Metro Station: Ramesh Nagar), New Delhi - 110 015-11
Phones: (011) 2545 3975; 2546 6019; Fax: (011) 2546 5926
e-mail: indology@dkprintworld.com
Website: www.dkprintworld.com

To

my mother

Smt. Kamlini Raja

who gave me my love of music

and of literature

and so much else!

FOREWORD

CHANGE is the only permanent reality in music. Even the music of the same *gharānā* changes from generation to generation. No musician can be a perfect xerox of his *guru*. This is the way it has been, this is the way it will remain, and this is the way it should be. It is this process that allows new styles to emerge, and new genres of music to be created. If classical music does not change constantly, it will stagnate, and become irrelevant to society.

Along with accepting the permanence of change, we have to acknowledge that, in music, as in other fields, each generation is attuned to certain values based on the environment in which it has been brought up. Because of their conditioning, a majority of people tend to develop firm notions about what is good and what is bad, or what is right and what is wrong, and find change difficult to accept. Their initial response to anything new is often rejection, and even condemnation. It is only gradually that society begins to discover the elements of truth in the newer manifestations of human endeavour, and concedes legitimacy to them.

To develop an intelligent approach to change and diversity in music, we have to recognize that classical music, like any other art form, evolves in society in response to the changing socio-economic realities, and sustains itself by fulfilling the cultural needs of society. Its evolution is the result of an interaction between musicians and their audiences and reflects the quality of the relationship they wish to forge between them.

In our own era, say a little before that, performances of classical music were confined to the courts of the *mahārājā*s and *nawāb*s. Outside this circle, concerts took place primarily in private gatherings. They were either *jumme-kā-takiyā* (Friday evening gatherings) or special occasions where either a musician's son was getting married, or some musician was hosting a commemorative concert for a deceased father or relative. Sometimes, a local aristocrat hosted these concerts. In most cases, the organizers and the audiences were either musicians, or close friends and relatives of musicians — in short, people of considerable discernment in matters of classical music. The event had virtually no financial implications for anyone. This was the chamber-music stage of evolution of our tradition. Considering the context of these gatherings, the music of the era was naturally of a very high standard, very intellectual, very competitive, and perhaps even intimidating.

In the second quarter of the twentieth century, music came out of the chamber-music context into the public arena. These were also the sunset years of British rule and the era of *mahārājā*s and *ndawāb*s as patrons of music. That was the time when scholars like Pandit V.N. Bhatkhande, and enthusiastic patrons like Jeevanlal Mattoo in Lahore and Lala Babu in Calcutta (now Kolkata) started organizing music conferences. At that stage, musicians were still poorly paid; and audiences were not large — maybe 500 or 700 people at the most. But, musicians got an opportunity to acquire a following, and create a market for their music. Around the same time, the radio and the gramophone record also started taking music all over the country. So, there was an opportunity as well as an attraction for reaching out to audiences — of shaping a career in music. From this stage onwards, the receptivity of audiences became an important determinant of the quality of music that was performed.

I am sure that, out of audiences 500 or 700 strong in that era, 100 per cent of the listeners were not knowledgeable about the intricacies of music. The proportion of audiences who understood, for instance, the nuances of the *gāndhār* of Darbārī was probably not much higher than it is today. From that stage to present times, audiences have become larger, their profile has changed, their expectations from music have changed, and the media for exposure to music have grown in number and reach. But, as a percentage of the total population, I doubt if classical music audiences are much larger today than they were fifty years ago. I also doubt if the ratio of the discerning to the rest is very much smaller today.

I am driving at two points here. First, that music has changed much more because society has changed, and not as much because the discerning audiences have been reduced to a small minority. Second, despite dramatic changes in the quality of music, which some regard as signs of decay, the musicians who enjoy stature along with popularity today exhibit the same values as those of the early twentieth century, whom we mention with reverence. And this quality is what I call the "Musician's Truth".

The "Musician's Truth" touches the mind, heart, and soul of audiences irrespective of their level of discernment. This truth goes beyond *rāga*-grammar, and aspects of music theory. People relate to music in a million different ways, and it is futile for a musician to think that he can tailor his music to specific audience profiles and needs. The only thing he can rely on is a steadfast commitment to the "Musician's Truth". and help his audiences to become receptive to it. He may not accomplish this in a year, or five years, or even ten years. But, abandoning it is no solution to his relevance as a musician. If this element of "Truth" is missing from a musician's art, even the undiscerning listener will be uneasy, though he may not be able to tell you why he is uneasy. If it is present, even the total ignoramus will go home happy, and will return for more. In the short run, a musician may be able to create a niche for himself without the "Musician's Truth". But, he will find it impossible to retain that position without a secure grip over it.

The foundation of the "Musician's Truth" is sincerity and seriousness of purpose. This is reflected in several facets of music, which have remained, and will remain, fundamental to our music. A musician's intonation should be perfect. Whatever his interpretation of a *rāga*, his exposition of it should be consistent and coherent. He should organize his musical material neatly and logically. There should be a reasonable balance between the melodic and rhythmic elements in his music. While a degree of partiality to either melodic or rhythmic elements is acceptable in our tradition, an obsession with either of them at the cost of the other deprives the music of its aesthetic value. These qualities qualify as good music by any yardstick of value.

The "Musician's Truth" has exhibited amazing resilience for over a century now, and I have no doubt that it will continue to attract musicians in sufficient numbers for the tradition to survive. However, I am concerned about the threats that have emerged in the last decades of the twentieth century. The threat comes from two recent developments — the tidal wave of consumerism, and the "commoditization" of music.

It takes ten or fifteen years of rigorous training to groom a classical musician, and another ten to twelve years of concert experience for him to reach his peak level in the profession. A life in classical music requires the musician to defer his economic aspirations until he is about 40. This is asking for a lot of self-denial from a musician who sees a successful pop singer achieve a glamorous lifestyle at the age of 20 or 25.

This reality may, or may not, shrink the inflow of top class talent into classical music. But, it will certainly encourage classical musicians to think in terms of a "strategy", in which the "Musician's Truth" becomes the first casualty. With the growing impatience of musicians to live well, and an environment that offers ample opportunities for exposure, we now find a large number of talented musicians struggling — somehow, and even anyhow — to create a comfortable niche for themselves. This tendency is crowding the music market with a lot of dishonest classical music.

However, there is no reason to be pessimistic about the future of Hindustani music. I believe so because a few of the musicians struggling in the "somehow–anyhow" circuit might stumble upon the "Musician's Truth", even if inadvertently. Moreover there will always be musicians outside this circuit who have the *junūn* (passion/commitment) to pursue the "Musician's Truth" irrespective of the financial consequences. The number of such musicians has always been small, and will remain small.

The task before the community of musicians and music-lovers is to make the world of Hindustani music more receptive to the "Musician's Truth", which will continue to shine forth, though almost certainly in less homogeneous and more unfamiliar manifestations. This requires us to rise above our conditioning, and open our minds to change and variety. It also requires us to drop the arrogance of the classical music world, and appreciate the manifestations of the "Musician's Truth" in other forms of music — semi-classical, folk and even popular.

It is in this context, that I commend Deepak Raja's book *Hindustani Music: A Tradition in Transition* as a panoramic, and serious, review of the Hindustani music tradition in the post-Independence era. Deepak is an author with a keen analytical mind, imbued with a scientific approach. His chapters on *rāga* grammar, *rāga* authenticity, *rāga* chemistry, and his introductory essays on *dhrupad, khyāl, ṭhumrī* and *ṭappā* can be of immense value to music students and scholars. His essay on the time-theory of *rāga*s is a thought-provoking piece of writing, which deserves the attention of the music fraternity in view of the changing context of music performance and enjoyment. I may not personally agree with all his views on the current trends in Hindustani music. However, I acknowledge them as representing those of his generation of hard-core *rasik*s, who find themselves in a minority today.

I sincerely hope that this book will be widely read, and will encourage serious discussion and debate on different facets of Hindustani music. I wish Deepak success in his endeavours as a student of Hindustani music and as an author.

16 May 2004 **Shivkumar Sharma**
Mumbai

PREFACE
TO THE SECOND EDITION

It is heartening that after more than nine years since the release of this book, it continues to engage the attention of serious music lovers. The book has brought me in touch with some of the finest scholars and connoisseurs of Hindustani music in India and abroad. Their reactions and comments have suggested to me those facets of our music, which readers would like me to explore more comprehensively.

Two segments of this book appear to have engendered the widest interest. The most important, not surprisingly, is the phenomenon of *rāga*. A close second is the coverage of musical instruments. Both subjects are inexhaustible. An attempt is, however, made in this edition to enrich the contents of these two sections of the book.

On the subject of *rāga*-ness, I have added two new chapters reflecting my current understanding and concerns. To the original chapters, I have added post-scripts where I thought they were warranted. To enlarge the coverage of musical instruments, the book includes chapters on *tānpūrā*, violin, *bāṅsurī*, *pakhāwaj* and *tablā*, and harmonium, which have appeared in my recent book, *Hindustani Music Today* (D.K. Printworld, 2012).

I trust these additions will make this book significantly more valuable to my readers.

Mumbai
Vijaya Dashami, 2014

Deepak S. Raja

PREFACE
TO THE FIRST EDITION

THIS book is a collection of essays written between 1996 and 2003. Some of them have appeared in *Sruti*, the performing arts monthly published from Chennai; some are papers published in other journals or read at seminars; and the rest are backgrounders forming part of my commentaries on recordings produced by India Archive Music Ltd. (IAM), New York.

The moment this book was envisaged, the sub-title, "A Tradition in Transition" acquired a degree of inevitability. This meta-theme pervades the essays featured in this book, and has been central to my efforts at interpreting the Hindustani musical tradition. The theme also reflects the very essence of Indian culture, with its infinite propensity for change without losing its intrinsic character.

The book begins with a Prologue, which sets out the perspectives that have guided my writings on music up to this stage. The main body of the book is divided into six parts.

Part I deals with some important societal, cultural, economic and technological drivers of Hindustani music in the contemporary context. These facets of our musical culture have received some attention from Western musicologists. Although I have no quarrel with alien perspectives, the emergence of an Indian viewpoint on them is, I hope, helped by my consideration of the issues.

Part II deals with musical forms and structures. In this part, I have dealt with issues pertaining to architectural and sculptural, rather than stylistic aspects of Hindustani music, and some presentation formats. The limited choice of subjects for this part could reflect merely the urgency with which the Hindustani music community, I feel, needed to take cognisance of present-day tendencies.

Part III deals with the world of *rāga*s. The papers in this part attempt to give the reader a feel for the notion of *rāga*-ness, understood intuitively by cultivated Indian listeners, but an enigma for uninitiated, though enquiring, audiences. However, the number of connoisseurs who found these essays informative has surprised me.

Part IV presents backgrounders on the four major genres of Hindustani vocal music — *dhrupad, khyāl, ṭhumrī,* and *ṭappā*. They attempt to outline the historical, structural as well as aesthetic aspects of these genres.

Part V consists of backgrounders on the major solo melodic instruments of the Hindustani tradition. The specific recordings for which they were originally written have determined the thrust of these backgrounders. For this reason, they might appear to lack the uniformity of format and coverage evident in the backgrounders on the vocal genres. However, they do uniformly highlight the essential as well as the little-known facets of the instruments, and have been appreciated widely by lovers of Hindustani music.

Part VI presents a glossary of words in italics, a list of suggested readings, and an index. The list of suggested readings includes sources I have relied on, but is intended, in general, for the relative beginner and the cognoscenti of music, rather than for scholars.

This book makes no claims to scholarship. Nor is it a journalistic endeavour. It is writing that has secured the support of the most demanding editors outside academia and deserved the attention of some astute lovers of Hindustani music in several parts of the world. Explicitly, it addresses music lovers of above-average familiarity with Hindustani music, and curiosity about its inner workings. Incidentally, it may also prove useful to other writers on music, and to scholars.

Whatever its merits, this book would have almost certainly not been in your hands, but for the Foreword written by Pandit Shivkumar Sharma, amongst our most learned, popular, and respected musicians. I have no words to thank him for helping me to reach you.

10 December 2004 **Deepak S. Raja**
Baroda

CONTENTS

PART V
The Major Instruments

ACKNOWLEDGEMENT

I ACKNOWLEDGE the blessings of, Śrī Vighneśvara who permits this endeavour to reach fruition, and Śrī Naṭarāja and Mātā Sarasvatī who allow me access to knowledge of music.

My lifelong quest for knowledge of music has been guided by outstanding *gurus*, to all of whom I express my deepest gratitude (in chronological order): Shri Chandrakant Pandit (Gandharva), Shri Usman Khan Abdul Kareem Khan, late Shri Pulin Behari Deb Burman, Pandit Arvind Parikh, and Pandit Dhondutai Kulkarni.

In the mid-1960s, my Professor of Philosophy at Hindu College, Delhi, Dr. S.K. Saxena, offered to oversee my grooming as an aesthetician. His aspirations for me have remained unfulfilled. However, when I was ready with the manuscript of this book, he introduced me to Shri Susheel K. Mittal of D.K. Printworld, and made this book possible. I cannot thank him enough for his inspiration, kindness and affection.

In the 1970s, well before I became a professional journalist, three friends allowed me to test my abilities as a writer on music: Vinod Mehta as Editor of *Debonair* magazine, Umaima Mulla-Phiroze, as Managing Editor of the *Taj* Magazine, and M.J. Akbar, as Editor of *Sunday* magazine. I seek the compassion of the above-named for the juvenility of my responses to the glimpse they gave me of destiny.

For launching me as a writer on music with negligible proof of competence, I acknowledge my debt to Lyle Wachovsky, Managing Director of India Archive Music Ltd., New York. Since March 1996, he has kept me fully involved in his missionary task with rewarding work, unmatched friendship, and great depth of understanding. He has also given me a *carte blanche* for including any part of my work done for him in this book, and waived all copyright claims in my favour. For all his support, I remain most grateful.

My intensive and extensive exposure to recordings of India Archive Music Ltd. triggered off perspectives on several aspects of modern and contemporary music. In converting these into readable text, I have received invaluable encouragement from Kishor Merchant, Publisher of the *Mumbai Rasika*, and the late Dr. N. Pattabhiraman, Editor of *Śruti*. Almost half of this book is a direct result of their encouragement and the access they gave me to their columns.

My attempts at interpreting Hindustani music have drawn immeasurable inspiration from the writings of the late Shri Vamanrao Deshpande, whom I acknowledge, in all humility, as my intellectual guide.

As a writer, my search for superior wisdom has led me repeatedly, and always fruitfully, to three mentors (in order of seniority): My Guru, Pandit Arvind Parikh, the renowned musicologist, Prof. Ashok Ranade, and my learned friend, Dr. Suvarnalata Rao. For their magnanimity and affection, I am deeply indebted to them.

In addition to these, I express my heartfelt thanks to all the musicians whom gave me interviews while I was attempting to interpret the music they have recorded for India Archive Music Ltd. Their contribution to my understanding of music, and to the writing of this book, is considerable, even if it is not identifiable.

My evolution as a writer has benefited greatly from the encouragement of a few friends, many of whom I have never met and will, perhaps, never meet. Because of their friendship, I have the satisfaction of having real people to address when I write. Else, I would have been vulnerable to the writer's risk of addressing an assumed audience, the like of which may not exist anywhere on earth.

Amongst these, I owe a special debt of gratitude to Ailsa Mathiesen and Alessandro Dozio for previewing the manuscript of this book, and to Eric Landen for a nuts-and-bolts surgery on it. Each of them has brought a different perspective to the scrutiny of this work, and enriched the final product.

"An Introduction to Dhrupad" in this book is reproduced, though in edited form, from the 1999 issue of the *Journal of the Indian Musicological Society*, with the kind consent of the Secretary General of the Society. The paper titled "Architecture in Modern Hindustani Music" is reproduced from *Sangeet Natak*, journal of the Sangeet Natak Akademi with permission. The paper titled "An Introduction to Ṭhumrī" relies substantially on the work of Prof. Peter Manuel of the City University of New York. I acknowledge, with gratitude, the prior consent of each of these authors/publishers for their waiver of copyright claims in my favour.

In preparing the manuscript of this book for acceptance by a publisher, I have received immensely valuable and affectionate help from my friend and graphic designer, Smt. Malti Gaekwad, and her associate, Shri Chetan Boda of Datasafe, Baroda. Without their inputs, this book might still have been waiting for a publisher.

The most fruitful contribution to this book has been that of Shri Susheel Kumar Mittal of D.K. Printworld, and his team. Without their professionalism, this book would not have been in your hands. I am deeply indebted to them for the trust they have reposed in my capabilities and for what they have contributed to my acceptability to a discerning audience.

I admit, without hesitation, that your willingness to open this book could have been influenced decisively by Pandit Shivkumar Sharma's Foreword, and the Introduction contributed by Lyle Wachovsky. Without their endorsement, this book could have remained largely unsold and unread.

My journey to this point would have been inconceivable without the support of my wife, Meena. She married a business executive, but ended up with a writer on music for a husband. I remain indebted to her for accepting the unpleasant surprises of life most gracefully.

For all those — named or otherwise — who have made this book possible, I wish the satisfaction of having supported a worthy beneficiary.

Deepak S. Raja

KEY TO TRANSLITERATION

अ *a* (but)	आ *ā* (palm)	इ *i* (it)
ई *ī* (beet)	उ *u* (put)	ऊ *ū* (pool)
ऋ *ṛ* (rhythm)	ए *e* (play)	ऐ *ai* (air)
ओ *o* (toe)	औ *au* (loud)	ळ* ḷ
क *ka* (skate)[1]	ख* *kha* (blockhead)[1]	ग *ga* (gate)[1]
घ *gha* (ghost)[1]	ङ *ṅa* (sing)[1]	
च *cha* (chunk)[2]	छ* *chha* (catch him)[2]	ज *ja* (john)[2]
झ *jha* (hedgehog)[2]	ञ *ña* (bunch)[2]	
ट *ṭa* (start)[3]	ठ* *ṭha* (anthill)[3]	ड *ḍa* (dart)[3]
ढ* *ḍha* (godhead)[3]	ण* *ṇa* (under)[3]	
त *ta* (path)[4]	थ *tha* (thunder)[4]	द *da* (that)[4]
ध* *dha* (breathe)[4]	न *na* (numb)[4]	
प *pa* (spin)[5]	फ* *pha* (philosophy)[5]	ब *ba* (bin)[5]
भ *bha* (abhor)[5]	म *ma* (much)[5]	
य *ya* (young)	र *ra* (drama)	ल *la* (luck)
व *va* (vile)	श *śa* (shove)	ष *ṣa* (bushel)
स *sa* (so)	ह *ha* (hum)	क्ष *kṣa* (*kṣatriya*)
त्र *tra* (*trishūl*)	ज्ञ *jña* (*jñāni*)	

अं (˙)*ṁ* (*saṁskṛti*) *ṁ anusvāra* (nasalisation of preceding vowel)

अः *ḥ* (*prātaḥ*) *ḥ visarga* (aspiration of preceding vowel)

* No exact English equivalents for these letters.

[1] guttural [2] palatal [3] lingual [4] dental [5] labial

PROLOGUE

THIS prologue was an afterthought. It was conceived as an Epilogue, but finds itself at the beginning of the book because referees of superior wisdom wanted it so. They felt that the book, although a collection of essays, has a uniformity of perspective — perhaps even a world-view — running through it, and that this needs to be crystallized, up-front, for the benefit of readers. They wanted me to be explicit about whom I am addressing, and what I hoped to achieve by this enterprise. This was a fair demand, and deserving of compliance.

By a conspiracy of circumstance, my writing on music has come to address cultivated listeners of Hindustani music — the connoisseurs. My endeavour has been to enhance their insights into the inner workings of modern and contemporary music. For this purpose, it is hardly necessary to distinguish between different categories of connoisseurs. For, irrespective of their level of discernment, and almost by definition, they seek to achieve a better understanding of what they hear, and of the forces that shape their musical experience.

These tasks are worthy of attention because understanding is an important pathway to enjoyment. Higher levels of understanding and enjoyment also bestow upon connoisseurs higher status and influence in the community of musicians and music lovers. And, by virtue of the status and influence that connoisseurs acquire, they fortify the cultural mechanism — nebulous though it might be — which ensures that art-music retains the features that distinguish it from other forms of music, especially entertainment.

Our society has been starved of periodical media to serve the special needs of connoisseurs. Academic journals, which might partially address these needs, are largely beyond their physical as well as conceptual reach. At the other extreme, we have the lay media, which are habitually oriented towards personalities and events, and do not serve the connoisseur's purpose either. The Internet has begun to serve the connoisseur in recent years. But, its use, especially in India, is not yet widespread. It is primarily the writers of books who have performed the task of strengthening the forces of discernment. Not surprisingly, after working through a few other media, and rejecting untested options, I have gravitated to the same medium — the book — for making this contribution to the cultural process.

Not by Accident Alone

Although I apparently became a writer on music by accident rather than deliberate design, it seems as if destiny had prepared me for this from childhood. Nature gave me the basic equipment for involvement with music. Thereafter, destiny took charge. It took me through several decades of training in music with outstanding *gurus*, representing the most respected lineages of Hindustani music. This training even enabled me to enjoy a short stint as a performing musician. It encouraged me to build up a sizeable library of significant recordings and books, and to invest a large part of my leisure in its study. It brought to me several friends amongst archivists, who generously shared their resources. It gave me several assignments in journalism, which matured my skills as a communicator in print. It allowed me a formal education and a professional trajectory, which honed an analytical ability, and enabled my observations to be made with a degree of confidence. This combination of influences has equipped me to decipher some facets of the Hindustani music tradition with a reasonable degree of satisfaction.

The ability to share this understanding with fellow connoisseurs was tested and cultivated on the job. In March 1996, when Lyle Wachovsky of India Archive Music Ltd. (IAM), New York, asked me to write a commentary (sleeve notes) for a CD he had produced, I had a reasonable reputation as a writer on media, marketing, and finance, but virtually no experience as a writer on music. He liked what I wrote, and that turned out to be a turning point in my life. It gave me my fourth profession. Between then and now (July, 2004), I have studied over 100 *rāga*s recorded for him by over forty-five musicians, representing eight instruments, and all the genres of vocal music. Based on my understanding of this music, I have written commentaries of 8,000 to 18,000 words on each of them, with the total wordage now approaching a million.

For these commentaries, I interviewed as many of the musicians as was possible, and developed valuable insights into the relationship between the artist and the art. To acquire a perspective on their styles, I located recordings of their *guru*s, and attempted to identify elements of continuity as well as change between two consecutive generations. In order to understand the *rāga*s they performed, I studied authoritative texts as well as several recordings of the same *rāga*s by other contemporary and recent musicians. As this activity grew into a full-time occupation, the focused efforts, originally aimed at understanding and explaining *rāga*s, genres, lineages, and musicians, began to yield a bigger picture of what Hindustani music is, and where it is heading.

The Bigger Picture

It was this bigger picture, which triggered off my column for *Śruti*, the monthly magazine on music and dance, published from Madras (now Chennai). When I sent the first essay for publication in 1998, I hesitantly asked the Editor if he would consider more contributions from me. I got a telegraphic reply: "Keep sending". And, that is what I did. The result was a series of essays published in *Śruti* many of which have found a place in the present book.

My writings for *Śruti* owe their content, character and inspiration to several sources. The first, of course, was my reading of what was happening to the world of Hindustani music, and the different forces shaping it. The second was the editorial environment of *Śruti*, with its bias in favour of Carnatic music. Because of this, I felt the need to deal with several issues in Hindustani music, which could help widen the appreciation of Hindustani music amongst audiences not greatly cultivated in the tradition. The third source was the set of ideas that had arisen from my involvement as a repertoire analyst for IAM. The fourth source was the thinking stimulated by the occasional papers I wrote for seminars and academic journals on music.

The *Śruti* and IAM associations have worked beautifully together. Although their audiences are different, and so is the context in which I address them, each has gained immensely from the other. Both would have been poorer in the absence of the other in my literary life. Considering that I started late in this profession, their simultaneous presence has enabled me to grow faster than I might otherwise have done.

Amongst the audiences of these media, I have acquired a few friends in several countries, all of whom are exceptionally astute musical minds. They established contact with me after reading my work, and thought it worthwhile to develop a regular correspondence on musical matters. I now habitually check out my writings with several of them — in addition to my referees closer to home — before I publish them. Their views and concerns have now become an important trigger for enlarging, deepening, and sharpening my understanding of music, and guided my writing in terms of content as well as style.

The Language Issue

It is also because of these two involvements that my work on music came to be written in English, rather than Hindi, the only language with which I am equally comfortable. My mentors amongst scholars have, in fact, pointed out that because my writings have forced me to think in English, I might have done less than justice to some Indian musicological concepts, which do not lend themselves to effective communication in English. They have even suggested that I should do all my writing first in Hindi, and then translate it into English.

I accept these comments as embarrassingly valid. Despite my comfort with English, I have struggled often to communicate certain concepts effectively. However, I have reason to believe that the outcome of my struggle has benefited my readers, though probably not in a manner that my scholarly friends would approve. In many cases, I have had to invent an expression in English to represent a complex idea, originally expressed in Sanskrit. This "invention" has often redefined the original in a contemporary conceptual framework. And, to the extent that the expression is consistent with my analytical approach, without being necessarily discordant to the original idea, it probably makes a small contribution towards making its logic accessible to audiences outside India, and even Indian audiences who think in English. I record this possibility with the support of several scholarly readers abroad, who have valued the access I have given them, for the first time, to certain concepts in Indian musicology.

I cannot, however, be satisfied with making a virtue out of an obvious weakness. My writings must move towards a more accurate expression of Indian musicological ideas in English. To this end, I must expose myself more extensively and intensively to significant writing in the Indian languages. Until then, the readers of my writings in English will have to bear with approximations, which might occasionally represent a conceptual refinement.

Predictably, along with admiration, my writings have also brought me my share of criticism. And, it seems proper that I deal with the issues that have exposed me to it.

Issues of Objectivity

In my efforts at understanding and interpreting Hindustani music, I have encountered, and dealt with, two basic phenomena — the unity within diversity, and the continuity within change. As cultural phenomena, the two are inseparable because diversity at any given point in time carries within itself the germ of change over a period of time. Both are expressions of the pluralistic and dynamic culture of a vibrant, multi-racial, multi-lingual nation.

I have sought to do justice to these features of our culture by adopting a descriptive–analytical stance, as free from a judgemental tendency as is possible. In this spirit, I have treated every piece of music, every genre, every lineage and every trend, as legitimate, as long as it claims an audience. My endeavour has been to place each of these manifestations of our musical culture in a historical perspective. Towards this end, I have sought constantly to isolate the elements of unity from those of diversity, and elements of continuity from those of change, and to proffer plausible hypotheses for the relationship between them.

Evidently, I have not been very successful in this regard. Hardliners of different schools of thought have accused me of being excessively lenient on diversity. The "Young Turks" of the music world have labelled me a rabid reactionary, while conservatives have charged me with a liberalism verging on permissiveness. These criticisms suggest either that a descriptive–analytical perspective is not particularly palatable to connoisseurs of Hindustani music, or that I have not been objective enough. The first implication, if true, I can only lament. But, the latter implication, even if only remotely valid, I must address forthrightly.

I neither command, nor claim, sufficient scholarship to establish the legitimacy or inevitability of every tendency I have observed. When a phenomenon is observed without being explained in terms of its causation, there is a likelihood of a judgemental suggestion creeping into its recording. Such possibilities arise from the musical values I have acquired in my formative years. These values are represented by the music of a few twentieth century giants — Ustad Vilayat Khan and Ustad Ali Akbar Khan amongst instrumentalists, Kesarbai Kerkar and Ustad Ameer Khan amongst *khyāl* vocalists, and Ustad Nasir Aminuddin and Nasir Moinuddin Dagar amongst *dhrupad* vocalists. I study their recordings for the sound principles of music-making they represent, but not without my critical faculties on full alert.

I am obliged to accept that, collectively, these mid-twentieth-century principles might function as a yardstick against which I judge all music. I see no reason to be apologetic about the identities of the musicians whom I regard as models. Whether this automatically establishes me as a reactionary, I do not know. But, I trust this disclosure will at least protect me against the charge of weak discernment and poor taste.

The Writer's Role

More fundamentally, however, I distrust the proposition that a yardstick of musicianship militates against a writer's role in the cultural process. A writer is, after all, nothing but a connoisseur who has decided to share his understanding with other connoisseurs. And, as such, he is a part of the watchdog mechanism, which keeps art faithful to its elevating ideals. My task, as a writer, is to help connoisseurs interpret their musical experience. Such an interpretation is inconceivable without a benchmark of quality musicianship and artistic endeavour. And, the benchmark will inevitably be one as understood by my generation of music lovers. However, I am obliged, by the ethics of my profession, to be conscious of my biases, to prevent them from intruding surreptitiously upon my observations, to respect alternative benchmarks as equally legitimate, and to recognize that no yardstick is perennially relevant. In fact, it is a part of my duty to make my readers aware of alternative benchmarks, and changing yardsticks. If I have succeeded in doing this, I will be read. If I have failed, my work deserves to gather dust on the shelves of the bookstores.

Another criticism levelled against my writings is the preponderance of commercial reasoning in the interpretation of some trends evident in the music world. I have even been charged with desecrating Hindustani music by treating audiences as consumers, recording companies and impresarios as intermediaries, and musicians as service providers in the leisure industry. My critics on this count do not challenge either my reasoning or my conclusions. Their reaction almost accuses me of having exposed some conspiracy of theirs — a conspiracy of silence on the subject.

Their discomfiture is, I suspect, rooted in collective guilt. They seem angry with me for having proven, often tellingly, the extent to which money has come to drive classical music. They are aware that societies do have a choice in the extent to which they surrender any activity to the operation of market forces. Civilized societies have found ways of insulating activities related to the life of the spirit — the soul, if you like — from the operation of market forces, and protecting them against a drift towards populism and degeneration. Most civilized societies have given such protection to religion, and many have also granted it to their performing arts traditions. As enlightened members of the community, my critics feel guilty about having neglected what they know to be their responsibility towards Hindustani music. My failure, if any, is that of having touched a raw nerve, and having evoked anger, rather than action.

This brings me to the next criticism I have encountered. I have frequently been accused of adopting a provocative, and even strident, stance in my writings in the periodicals media. My critics feel that this might deny my arguments a fair chance of being evaluated on their merits. Their observation is valid, while the consequences, if as predicted, would be unfortunate.

Towards Connoisseur Activism

The provocative titles and lead-ins to my essays are, in most cases, honest to the original provocation that suggested a topic to me, and triggered off a chain of ideas which demanded verbalization with a sense of urgency. Sharing such provocations with readers is a journalistic device appropriate to the periodicals media. It is useful for flagging the target audience, drawing the reader into the writing, focusing his attention on the subject of the text, and making the writer's position on it clear at the outset. The device is particularly suitable for a magazine like *Śruti*, whose readership is oriented predominantly towards Carnatic music. When I write for a clearly journalistic medium, I am guided by my perception of the role of the connoisseur in the cultural environment, and my desire to persuade, and even exhort, him into performing that role effectively.

Until well into the twentieth century, Hindustani music was a chamber-music art, hosted by the aristocracy, with access limited to connoisseurs, and only by invitation. Audiences were small, but their depth and width of knowledge was sufficient for the fate of musicians to depend on their approval. They performed a quality control function efficiently enough to give us the era now described as the Golden Age of Hindustani music.

In the post-Independence era, technological, political, and economic changes enlarged the size of audiences, and dramatically altered the relationship between them and the musicians. The cognoscenti amongst audiences were steadily outnumbered by the *innocenti*. The connoisseur now constitutes a hopeless minority, unable to hold the musician accountable for the quality of the artistic endeavour. He is frustrated and, understandably, angry. He is angry not only with the fact of being marginalized, but also with anyone who cares to remind him of this fact. His anger arises from a sense of helplessness, which leads to a paralysis.

Consider this piece of information provided a few years ago by the Director General of All India Radio (AIR) at a closed-door meeting with the Music Forum in Bombay (now Mumbai). When the AIR discontinued the nightly broadcast of classical music on the FM channels because it was generating no advertising revenue, the national broadcaster received one solitary letter of protest. On reasonable reckoning, these FM broadcasts would have had at least 100,000 regular listeners in a population of about 30 million affected by the decision! Whether a 100,000 protest letters would have averted this event, is a debatable point. But, the ridiculous minuteness of the protest is indicative of the paralysis that has seized the connoisseurs of Hindustani music. And, it is this that I hope to address through the provocative stance I have adopted in my writings.

By virtue of his knowledge and involvement, the connoisseur will always remain one of the pillars of Hindustani music. Having been outnumbered as a member of the audience, he can no longer perform his quality control function effortlessly by just being a listener. His responsibility as a watchdog has now grown several fold, and his task has become more difficult. If he wishes to prevent the dawn of a Stone Age in Hindustani music, he needs to make his voice heard above the din that supports the opiates of the masses.

There could yet be hope for the connoisseur's cause, and I therefore offer no apology for attempting to jolt his conscience into activism. I may not have yet achieved the perfect balance between persuasion and provocation required for this purpose. However, at this stage of life, I cannot possibly harbour delusions of being able to change the course of cultural history.

Clarity of Purpose

What drives me is the search for a better understanding of the Hindustani music tradition — ascending the ladder of connoisseurship. Professionally, I have drifted into sharing this enterprise with others. However, reaching out beyond my professional orbit is incidental to my objectives. I explain things as I understand them, but I admit I understand them a lot better when I share what I think I understand. I will continue to enlarge my own sphere of understanding; but I will wish to share my knowledge only as long as I have readers who find my efforts rewarding.

My professional work revolves around assignments from IAM, a recording company that services a global market and is inspired and given a direction by Hindustani music enthusiasts whom I have befriended through the IAM connection, primarily products of western cultures. This orbit defines my priorities for study and writing, and could easily bias my writings for periodicals and books towards a "Western" way of understanding music.

The risk of distorted priorities seems negligible because those whom I address are guiding my attention towards the more uniquely Indian aspects of our musical tradition. And, I find that their priorities seem to be entirely consistent with my own. The risk of a bias towards a "Western" way of interpreting music — whatever that might imply — probably exists. How great this risk is, I cannot tell. But, it would have been much greater if I had been conversant with Western classical music. Since this is not so, my writing works much harder at translating Indian ideas into concepts that are intelligible to alien audiences.

This effort, as it turns out, has received an encouraging response also from Indian audiences, who have encountered some of the contents of the present book either in *Śruti*, or in other media or *fora*. This would suggest that Indian connoisseurs who read English are not very different from alien enthusiasts who read English. And, if there is any damage being done to the distinctive "Indianness" of musicological ideas, it is the English language that is doing it, and not the ethnicity of the audiences I address — either explicitly or otherwise.

This hypothesis gave me the confidence to place this book in your hands, without any need to alert you in advance about its greater value either to alien or Indian audiences. This also gives me the confidence to continue writing in English as long my readers feel I am making sense. But, some day, I would like to be able to write on music in Hindi, too, even if only to capture some of the cultural meaning which probably escapes me when I write in English.

INTRODUCTION

THE Indian classical music tradition, and writings on it, can be traced back to the pre-Christian era. Since then, the melodic structures, the presentation formats and the instruments, have evolved in fits and starts, and available documentation leaves us with only a patchy picture of their evolutionary path. The systematic organization of knowledge of the various facets of the Hindustani tradition gained momentum towards the end of the nineteenth century. Significantly, that period also witnessed a great flowering of the performing tradition, often described as the Golden Age of Hindustani music. Today, at the dawn of the third millennium, the tradition is experiencing yet another efflorescence — though of an entirely different kind — and is accompanied, once again, by literary activity aimed at interpreting its content and significance.

Deepak Raja's volume — *Hindustani Music: A Tradition in Transition* — is a welcome overview of the post-Independaence trends in Hindustani music. It provides a panoramic, rather than encyclopaedic, appraisal of important developments in Hindustani music, and confronts us with the problems that Indian classical music faces today. At the same time, Raja has a very definite point-of-view and argues it passionately. The consistency of his viewpoint may, at times, seem questionable. He acknowledges this in his Prologue by disclosing that conservatives as well as liberals have, on different occasions, had reason to criticize his writings.

The book also has very definite structural underpinnings. It is linear, in that he begins with a series of chapters providing a contemporary overview of Hindustani music and moves towards dealing with more and more specific aspects of the presentation of the music, ending with chapters on the genres of vocal music and on instruments used in presentation. It is circular in that it begins with an assessment of the effects of populism and globalism on Indian classical music and ends with acceptance of possibly the most "populist" of instruments, one introduced very recently to Indian music from outside India, the Hawaiian slide-guitar.

Raja sets out the underlying approach of his argument in the very first chapter of the book. Indian classical music has suffered from a "major discontinuity" imposed upon it, as an unintended consequence, by Indian Independence. The sudden end to the royal/feudal patronage of great musicians terminated the era of music as an economically secure and hereditary profession. The depth of musicianship previously cultivated by musicians gave way to competent artistry, even as musicians became somewhat of a commodity controlled by "market forces". The concurrent evolution of a mass market involved a concomitant dumbing down of the audience. This has left the connoisseur — amongst whom Raja counts himself — and connoisseur-quality music in a state of decline and disadvantage.

Raja, as noted, is a passionate connoisseur. He accepts the obvious fact that the continuation of the circumstances that enabled the music he cherishes is an unrealistic expectation. Great musicians and music validate themselves only in, and through the environment and means that produce them. How to achieve a return to a high standard of musicianship and artistry in a world driven by commercial considerations is the author's main concern. Although, as he acknowledges, "art-music" comprises only 2 per cent of the commercial recordings market, he sees no reason why contemporary music has necessarily to be qualitatively inferior to pre-Independence music.

Part I of Raja's book deals with the identification of the problems and their causes, which the author finds to be at the root of the dilution and mediocrity that now confront Indian classical music. The first chapter outlines the overall problem — times have changed. The traditional patronage model, which produced the greatest musicians and music, is no longer viable. Social and economic forces have caused the acceptance of a new paradigm — the mass marketplace as the arbiter of taste. Indian classical music, which thrived in the narrow upscale patronage market of music-knowledgeable *rājās* and *zamīndārs*, is now in the position of being controlled by the need to earn a living in the musically unsophisticated mass market — concerts, recordings, and teaching.

On the other hand, Indian classical music and musicians are thriving. Over the past fifty years, there has been a veritable explosion of concerts, recording companies and students. The market for Indian classical music is now larger, and no longer only Indian, but worldwide. And, there has even been minimal corporate support (e.g., the ITC-sponsored Sangeet Research Academy), and government support (e.g., Madhya Pradesh-sponsored Dhrupad Kendra). The problem, Raja finds, is the quality of the music being produced.

Raja notes, "In the totality of the scenario, the bottom-line is positive for all participants, except the *rasik* (the connoisseur)". And he lays part of the problem squarely at the door of *rasik*s themselves, whose value system he explicitly questions: they are unwilling to pay for what they want. While noting that a *rasik* will hand over Rs. 2,000 to his children for a ticket to an American pop icon's concert, he will grudgingly pay only Rs. 200 for a ticket to a concert by a "superstar" Indian classical musician. On the other hand, he finds that, adjusted for inflation, at the top end, contemporary classical musicians are paid 200 to 500 per cent more per concert than were their counterparts in the 1940s. Raja explains: "Because he is in a hopeless minority, it suits everyone to ignore him (the *rasik*) and reach out to audiences at a lower level of discernment". How much money and how many connoisseurs are needed to effect a change? There are no easy answers.

The author has considered the roles of two major emerging players in the classical music market: the government and the corporations. And, while holding out hope for help from these two sources, he, more or less, dismisses both possibilities, as, realistically, the business model for corporations and the patronage model for government are both based on principles of quantitative rather than qualitative results.

Raja then considers the musicians' point of view towards achievement in the music world and the value of producing connoisseur-quality music. The author is sympathetic with the problems of today's musicians in carving out a career. But, he is critical of the fact that many fledgling musicians promote their stature by giving themselves honorifics such as *paṇḍit* or *ustād*, whose merits audiences are not qualified to judge. Having done so, they perform to the level of their audiences' understanding, often the only level they know. Evidently, this phenomenon increases the risks of music as a profession, and provides little motivation for artists to maintain or achieve connoisseur-level abilities. The author believes that artists can, themselves, correct the ensuing inequity in the rewards system.

He acknowledges the extinction of the old model in which an artist had limited options — either to be a *paṇḍit* or an *ustād* who found royal patronage, "or a nobody with his next meal being uncertain". He advocates a new price-value relationship model, which allows a collective of musicians, rather than the audiences, to validate a musician's status. The author suggests the formation of a musician's guild that could act as a body to protect each member of the profession: an aspect of which would be a grading system for musicians, that also links fees to accomplishment levels. At the same time, he acknowledges that the profession lacks either the enthusiasm or the leadership for such a movement.

In a significant chapter dealing with the place and value of archival recordings, in raising both audience and musician standards by providing easy access to music from the past, the author also analyses the phenomena of acoustic and aesthetic obsolescence in music, and the value of digital restoration technologies. The author sees great advantage to young musicians in that "the archival movement partially corrects a significant discontinuity . . . the growing shortage of competent teachers. . . ." On the other hand, he infers, interestingly, that commercial availability of archival recordings might have a significant impact on the sales of recordings by contemporary musicians. The essay ends by acknowledging that the overall benefit of archival recordings are subject to the commercial considerations of the recording companies, which might release these recordings: "If faster or sharply focused results are desired, the music community will have to take the initiative in converting the rewards of technology into a trigger for a veritable renaissance."

Continuing the exploration of continuity and change, the book addresses the rapid loss in the last half of the twentieth century of the individuality and variety that characterized the pre-Independence and pre-technological Indian musical world. *Gharānā* uniqueness, an individuality of presentation style, was previously a musician's "wealth". Unrestricted access to this wealth, and its dilution by various socio-economic changes has fostered a homogenization of styles. The author admits to the paradox here: that the greatest vocalists of the twentieth century broke through *gharānā* barriers, and many musicians considered authentic *gharānā* stylists had actually received training from multiple *guru*s representing a multiplicity of *gharānā*s. The *gharānā*s, so it would seem, took care of continuity along with diversity, while everything else took care of itself. Excellence was not either directly or necessarily dependent on the restrictive facet of the *gharānā* system. The author concludes that we are moving towards a new model or models of "the balance between continuity and change and, between homogeneity and diversity, (which) will be decided by how audiences want art-music to relate to the world around them, and to their inner worlds".

The book has an important Part dealing with specific avenues of Indian classical music presentation and understanding. The structural aspect of modern Hindustani music receives astute consideration in a chapter that deals with the logic of progression. Music, like any other language, needs commonly agreed upon structure to be understood. The contemporary trend towards shortening or truncating some aspects of structure and progression and entirely doing away with others, leads towards a situation of enjoying music — or listening to music — on the basis of vague familiarity with a phrase or theme. Without specific structural and progression formats, which are also meant to open up expansive creative possibilities, exactly the opposite will happen and is happening — performances are shorter, the content less complex, enriching, and rewarding.

With specific reference to instrumental music, the author explores the shortcomings of the trend towards widening individual instrumental idioms by borrowing from others in search of novelty, which sadly tends to result in a dilution, if not denial, of the idiom. He appears to accept the traditional notion of hierarchy in the musical arts, which accords the highest status to the vocal expression. This yardstick also determines his notion of hierarchy within the instrumental segment. By his argument, instrumental music validates itself either by getting closer to the experience of vocal music, or by exploiting the distinctive features of the instruments. After providing examples of stylistic innovations he approves of — by his yardstick — and those he questions, the author argues that as a tendency, drifting towards an "inferior" idiom in search of novelty risks creating *apaṅga* (crippled) music. His answer is not to lose sight of *auchitya,* which he defines as "a sense of propriety, of balance and moderation". His is a cry of anguish as he acknowledges that: ". . . Hindustani instrumentalists, including some of the most successful ones, might be answerable for the results of their innovative zeal."

In his chapters on *jugalbandī* and *tihāī*, the author has his say on the contemporary tendencies on the part of both musicians and promoters towards excitement, newness, and entertainment as substitutes for music of substance, and the problems of the enthusiastic public embrace of these cheap shots at art and artistry. In recent years, *jugalbandī*, far from being at its best — the intermingling and meshing of two distinct musical personalities in a way that made the sum greater than its parts — has become a promotional tool hyped as ground-breaking, innovative, refreshingly different, experimental and, rarely, if ever, rising to the level of musical promise that promoters imply or suggest as possible.

The *tihāī*, once a spontaneous, subtle, and highly improvised structural tactic, used by vocalists and instru-mentalists alike as an occasional means of achieving contrast and surprise, has come to be a replacement for improvisation, as a crowd-pleasing means of conveying rhythmic excitement and titillation, easily grasped by and appealing to today's unsophisticated audiences.

Part III of the book is, literally and figuratively, the heart of this book. In this Part, the author presents and analyses in depth the basics upon which the melodic framework of Indian classical music is structured in theory and in performance: what a *rāga* is, what its characteristics are, what makes it identifiable and intelligible, what differentiates one *rāga* from another, the centrality of the emotional expression to the *rāga*'s aural experience. The author considers the basic components, which identify and distinguish one *rāga* from another, and how these components are used creatively to innovate compound *rāga*s that mesh in a manner that creates a distinctive new entity/*rāga*.

The association of each north Indian *rāga* with a time of day and/or season of the year is a conjunction that is unique. The author acknowledges the traditional basis and longevity of this convention and its overall value in that it further informs or refines or defines the emotional content of each *rāga*. However, he plainly confronts the fact that the entire context of performing and delivering music to audiences has changed. Today, it is entirely possible that to many listeners, *rāga*s may seem associated with other times or seasons than those with which they were originally connected, or have no specific time or seasonal association at all.

The chapter entitled "The Experience of Melody" provides a compact, although panoramic, overview of how past vocal genres, and then various instruments and their genres have defined an approach to melody that has, in Raja's estimation, become progressively more fragmented and atomized. Raja starts with the relationship between "literature, melody and aesthetics" that was integral to the vocal *dhrupad* genre as expressed in the writings of Tansen, the legendary musician at the court of Akbar in the late sixteenth century. The author then takes us through the introduction of the *khyāl* genre, its structural links with the *dhrupad* genre, and the ensuing partial liberation of melody from poetry, through the progressive fragmentation of melody by mid-twentieth-century sitārists and sarodists, to the ultimate "atomization" of melody in the music played on the *santūr*.

In the penultimate section, the author provides brief histories of the development of the *dhrupad, khyāl, ṭhumrī,* and *ṭappā* genres and outlines the formal structures and vocal techniques of each genre, as we experience them today. In the course of each essay, the author is careful to include and credit the contributions and innovations of those artists primarily responsible for bringing each genre to the contemporary fulfilment of its purpose.

In the last Part, the author reviews the historical usage, and physical development and construction of most of the major musical instruments in current use, except the *bāṅsurī* and the percussion instruments, and the development of the individual genres of expression unique to, and uniquely suited to, each instrument. The Part also analyses the efforts to adapt the various genres and formats of vocal music to each instrument as was best suited to their abilities for expression.

Raja's book ends with a chapter on the Indian classical slide-guitar. This brings him full-circle back to his initial discourse on populism and globalism, their influence and value, as he muses on the future of the Indian classical guitar: ". . . its future could well be shaped as much by the global music market as by the Indian mainstream."

1 June 2004 **Lyle Wachovsky**

PART I

Culture, Technology and Economics

1.1

POPULISM AND RIVAL FORCES

POPULISM has been the most widely noticed tendency in post-Independence Hindustani music. While it has, without doubt, shaped the music-scape in the latter half of the twentieth century, it has also acquired rivals. And, it is these rivals, which are driving Hindustani music into the twenty-first century. Populism, by its very nature, is easily understood. The operation of its rivals is, however, relatively opaque. It is therefore necessary to examine populism, along with its rivals, so that we may acquire a clearer picture of the direction that Hindustani music is taking.

Independence imposed a major discontinuity on Hindustani music. The disappearance of feudal patronage exposed it to market forces, and converted something that provided a secure way of life for the truly great, into a high-risk self-employed profession for all.

As a result, classical music suffered a depletion of talent, along with a decay in the process of grooming the subsequent generations into the art. The great music disappeared along with the giants of the early twentieth century. As a legacy, what most of them left behind was not much more than the bonsai of a banyan tree — very few competent disciples, and commercial recordings, mostly of three-minute duration.

Technological advances soon enabled the creation of a mass-market for art-music. By this time, however, there were neither enough musicians with strong moorings in the tradition, nor audiences with a well-defined yardstick for judging what was being dished out to them.

These forces gave rise to strong populist tendencies in Hindustani music. These tendencies have, in turn, triggered off a conservationist reaction, which insists on the sanctity of the dividing line between art and entertainment. In the fortification of this barrier, the conservationists have found an ally amongst Hindustani music enthusiasts and scholars in the US and Western Europe.

Hindustani music is now set on a path of irreversible globalization, and has raised fears of its "de-culturation". The Indian aesthete must now come to terms with this new reality.

The Emergence of a Market

By the mid-1970s, most of the towering musicians of the twentieth century had departed. Musicians with inadequate grooming in the music of the great *gharānās* invaded the stage. From then on, musicians have been marketing their respective brands of music in a competitive, multi-media environment. The financial rewards of a career in music experienced a significant boost when, in the mid-1960s and 1970s, Europe and the US opened up in response to pioneering efforts by some of India's greatest musicians.

The post-Independence Hindustani musician now addresses an international market of considerable size and diversity. Today's market for classical music consists of 80 per cent "innocenti", and only 20 per cent cognoscenti. The rewards of addressing only the cognoscenti are now beyond the reach of most musicians, while the risk of ignoring the innocenti has become unaffordable. Hindustani music now finds it profitable to address the lowest common denominator by keeping itself accessible, intellectually undemanding, and familiar. This reality defines contemporary classical music more comprehensively than most professional musicians will care to admit.

Dimensions of Populism

For the uninitiated, instrumental music is easier to handle than vocal music because audiences are not required to come to terms with the quality of the voice delivering it, or to grapple with the poetic element. In the 1960s and 1970s, the formidable musicianship of Ustad Bismillah Khan, Pt. Pannalal Ghosh, Ustad Vilayat Khan, Pt. Ravi Shankar and Ustad Ali Akbar Khan overtook the giants amongst their vocalist contemporaries in terms of popularity. In the 1980s and 1990s, Pt. Shivkumar Sharma, Pt. Hariprasad Chaurasia, Pt. Brijbhushan Kabra and Ustad Zakir Hussain consolidated this trend. This is reflected in the growing disparity between the concert fees of the leading vocalists and instrumentalists of comparable stature.

The decline of vocal music threatens not only vocal music, but all of classical music. This has to be so because vocal music is the principal originator of all musical ideas, and also its most authentic exponent. When the originator and the most authentic exponent ceases to attract the best talent, the art-form risks losing its ability for self-generating growth.

Partly because of the ascendancy of instrumental music over vocal music, classical music is also undergoing a melodic simplification. This trend also permits wider reach to a more diverse and less discerning audience profile. Fewer and fewer *rāga*s are now heard — from all musicians collectively, and even from each musician individually. Even in the presentation of common or popular *rāga*s, there is a tendency to simplify, compress or truncate the form of the traditional, and often complex, compositions. The principles of systematic and comprehensive *rāga* exposition have also been thrown to the winds.

The same shrinkage of variety and richness is discernible in the choice of *tāls*. *Ektāl* and *tīntāl* now dominate vocal music. The *baḍā* (slow tempo) *khyāls* in *jhūmrā*, *tilwāḍā*, *rūpak* and *jhaptāl* are threatened by extinction. In instrumental music, the variety may be a little richer. However, there too, *dhamār*, *chautāl*, and *ektāl* have virtually disappeared from the concert platform. The enigmatic *ādā chautāl* is now a rarity in instrumental as well as vocal renditions.

The galloping populism of classical music is evident also in the changing role of the percussion accompanist. He is no longer in a supportive role to the process of music making. Under the guise of securing full-fledged participation in the process, he expects the freedom to intrude upon it to justify his presence. It is in the nature of rhythm to titillate and benumb the mind. Rhythm binds; melody liberates. Musicologist Ashok Ranade has often argued that if this were not true, why would martial and disco music be heavy on rhythm and flimsy on melodic and poetic content?

It would be difficult for anyone to argue that the new celebrity status for *tablā* players is based on a superior public understanding of the intricacies of the *tablā* idiom. If this were so, it would have shaped a substantial market for *tablā* solos. In fact, just the reverse is true. In the 1940s and 1950s *tablā* exponents like Ustad Ahmed Jan Thirakwa and Ustad Ameer Hussain Khan could make a living primarily as soloists and teachers. Such careers are virtually inconceivable today. With no demand for the comprehensive art of the percussionist, it could perish at the altar of audience titillation.

Musicians and their percussionists are finding it profitable to engage in a musical strip tease, unashamedly orgasmic in its aesthetic intent. Instrumentalists — more than vocalists —

are now exploiting the undiscerning majority of audiences by selling Rolls Royce bodies, fitted with Volkswagen engines. Music fit for the discos now seeks the respectability of the classical platform, and gets it.

Rāga presentations now habitually accelerate to a tempo at which neither the melodic contours of the *rāga*, nor the accentual structure of the *tāl*, can retain their respective distinctive characters. Crossing the limits of a culturally defined musicality now merits handsome rewards in terms of thunderous applause and concert engagements.

The Hindustani music scene is hurtling towards the familiar, the predictable, and the titillating. The content of music is fast falling prey to the machinations of expression. A great deal of classical music now challenges the dividing line between art and entertainment.

The Conservationist Reaction

Like all socio-cultural trends, these trends too have triggered off their own corrective mechanism. The tussle between populism and conservationism has commenced.

The populists argue that cultural change is an inevitable response to changing audience profiles and aesthetic values. It is, therefore, futile to question its validity. In the present context, conservationism has to be distinguished from conservatism. Conservationism does not resist change per se and is not, therefore, reactionary in its inclinations. The conservationists contend that all change is answerable to a yardstick of "propriety"; and the test of propriety neither begins, nor ends, with public acceptability. The notion of propriety, according to them, is founded on a society's concern for orderly and evolutionary change. It assumes a discernible link of continuity between the past, the present, and the future. They see their task as one of restoring the quality control mechanism which has been greatly corroded in recent years, of giving the performing art the benefit of the scholarship that led to the twentieth-century renaissance in Hindustani music, and of protecting the tradition against the consequences of discontinuity.

Attempts at re-injecting continuity into the cultural process have to contend with the absence of the early twentieth-century giants groomed under conditions, which are now, in retrospect, regarded as ideal. The near-impossibility of reviving the traditional systems of hereditary musicianship and highly personalized tutelage is also a fait accompli. Despite these limitations, the Sangeet Research Academy (SRA) in Kolkata has proven the possibility of creating an environment conducive to the perpetuation of the distinctive stylistic traditions even in an environment unfriendly to the forces of continuity. Another significant experiment was launched in the early 1980s, when the Government of Madhya Pradesh sponsored the Dhrupad Kendra at Bhopal to revive the medieval genre threatened with extinction. This institution has by now produced quality musicianship in significant numbers, and helped *dhrupad* to return to the mainstream concert platform.

There are, indeed, divergent opinions about the SRA and the Dhrupad Kendra as models for building institutions for replacing the traditional pedagogical model. However, the success of these institutions — whatever the magnitude — has stimulated discussion amongst musicians, musicologists, and scholars on the whole issue. This is a significant development in the field of art-music.

Another important phenomenon is the receding famine of concert-length recordings of the great masters. The restoration of old, poor-quality recordings has now become feasible and economical. Priceless old music is now hitting the market on a significant scale. Its popularity is encouraging recording companies to pursue this segment more avidly.

Individual as well as institutional archivists, who have hitherto been possessive and secretive about their collections, now realize that their treasures will have no aesthetic or commercial value as soon as the present fifty-plus generation of listeners departs. They have very little time in which to get any kind of price for their labours of preservation. This realization is persuading them to surrender their gems to the recording companies for commercialization. These archives can serve as a substitute, however limited, for quality training, which has all but disappeared. More significantly, contemporary music can now be held answerable to a demanding yardstick of musicianship, which refuses to go away.

Archives, as restorers of continuity, have often been pooh-poohed on the pretext that there is no such thing as timeless music; and therefore, it is impossible to respond meaningfully to music, especially art-music, from a substantial distance in time. This argument, however, underestimates the highly creative and complex process by which the enquiring musical mind absorbs and utilizes old ideas to generate new ones.

The education of audiences is gaining momentum. In this endeavour, cultural organizations are increasingly holding public seminars, lecture demonstrations, music appreciation courses, and workshops at different levels of sophistication. These are attracting a progressively larger number of participants.

The conservationist movement is now showing signs of becoming galvanized. This phenomenon is best reflected in the activities of The Music Forum, an informal body representing all the significant segments of the classical music community in the major cities. The movement was launched in Mumbai at the initiative of the scholar-musician, Arvind

Parikh, and Shanta Gokhale, the Arts Editor of *Times of India*, with the objective of creating a healthier climate for the evolution of classical music in the city. The Music Forum movement has now spread to Kolkata, Chennai, and Delhi, and could, one day, become a formidable voice of sanity in the classical music world.

Despite isolated success stories, the magnitude of this endeavour may not be able to keep pace with the growth of the audience population and the dilution of audience discernment. The sheer magnitude of the task is sufficient to condemn it to failure.

The Unlikely Ally

The conservationists at home have, in recent years, forged an interesting alliance with Hindustani music enthusiasts in the US and Europe. The Western markets for Indian classical music might still be numerically small. But, it has a considerable presence of serious scholars within it, and even the less initiated members approach Hindustani music with respect for the seriousness of its music-making process. This sensibility is able to express itself — to some extent — in their preferences because the size of the populace involved in Hindustani music is not large enough to trigger off the dynamics of a market. If there is no "market", there is no incentive for the product to pander to the lowest common denominator. In such an environment, art has a better chance of remaining true to its ideals.

In this context, the Indian Music & The West Seminar held in Mumbai in 1996 was a very significant event. Over thirty Western scholars and musicians presented papers and performances. The understanding and respect they exhibited for the essentials of Hindustani music could have embarrassed many an Indian musician and scholar.

The superiority of Western scholarship surprises nobody. The real surprise is the credible challenge posed to Indian musicians by Western performers. Several foreign performers of Hindustani music are steadily becoming household names amongst Indian connoisseurs, especially the Swiss sarodist Ken Zuckerman, the American flutist Steve Gorn, and the Italian *dhrupad* vocalist Amelia Cuni.

The track record of the international recording companies in producing Hindustani music is even better. The Rotterdam Conservatory of Music researched an authoritative contemporary anthology of *rāga*s, and Nimbus, a British label, published it. Navras Records, the leader in the Hindustani recordings market, is a British company, though owned by non-Resident Indians. India Archive Music Ltd. and Raga Records Inc. (both in New York), Chhanda Dhara of Stuttgart (Germany), and Makar Records (France) have emerged as serious specialist producers of Hindustani music. Some of these companies have virtually no distribution in the Indian market. Despite the small size of the market they service — US, and Western Europe — their standards, across the board, can make Indian recording companies blush in embarrassment.

However, these are developments at the most serious end of the Indophile movement in the US and Europe. Qualitatively, what the Western "market" for Hindustani music contributes by its seriousness is largely set-off by the undeveloped state of discernment amongst audiences, and the isolation of the music from cultural meaning. It is, no doubt, significant that the commitment of some developed countries to a serious multi-culturalism should provide a strong impetus to the sustenance and growth of Hindustani music. John Naisbitt's "Global Paradox" is with us already. But, it is not clear whether this represents utopia.

India, an uncompetitive exporter of most tangible products, now takes pride in the successful and profitable globalization of its classical music. This pride is tinged with the anxiety about the paradox inherent in the situation. Hindustani music, as we understand it, is unlikely to survive without ceasing to belong exclusively to the people of Hindustan. It has become dependent on the West for economic sustenance, discerning audiences and scholarly inputs.

A significant manifestation of this phenomenon is the number of brilliant young musicians who have become so busy and successful in USA and Europe, that they have neither the time, nor the economic necessity to cultivate Indian audiences for their art. Isolated from an active engagement with the cultural meaning of their music, many of them are evolving a musical idiom that recalls the signs outside many establishments during the colonial era — "For whites only: Indians and dogs not allowed".

Under these circumstances, the anxiety about the "deculturation" of Hindustani music would be natural and, many believe, legitimate. But, if this process is irreversible, it really does not matter whether these concerns are legitimate or not. How, then, must the Indian aesthete come to terms with this reality?

Responsible musicologists often cite the example of Western classical music, which is tending to stagnate and become excessively intellectual because it has remained insular and parochial. Against this backdrop, they see the globalization of Hindustani music as a sign of its vitality, and a guarantee of its survival. This view appears to have the support of history. Hindustani music survived the second millennium because it adapted itself to the tastes of its new patrons from the Middle East, by assimilating Perso-Arabic influences.

It is inevitable that economics will drive the content and form of Hindustani music, as of every other aspect of society's artistic expression. Economically, Hindustani music is now being driven by populism at home, and elitism abroad. In both these tendencies, the performing arena allows the music to evolve free from accountability to the Indian connoisseur, who constitutes the principal element of the quality control mechanism in Hindustani music. Compared to the financial muscle of the audiences that sustain Hindustani music, the salutary presence of the conservationist forces at home will remain too miniscule, feeble and disorganized to influence Hindustani music in a substantive manner.

Of the two diversionary forces, globalism is perhaps the more insidious because it wields greater financial clout and is also pregnant with a "de-culturation" of Hindustani music. The impending divorce of music from cultural meaning, and the burgeoning presence of alien musical ideas in Hindustani music are almost a foregone conclusion. If this is the case, the Indian aesthete should derive some satisfaction from the fact that, in India as well as the Western markets, there exists a serious conservationist force, however small, to set-off alarm signals, however inaudible, when warranted.

An enlightened view of the scenario should certainly lament that the great *gharānā*s of Hindustani music have now merged into the "cocktail Gharānā". But, this view should also permit pride in the emergence of a "Rotterdam Gharānā", and a "San Rafael-Senīya Gharānā", whose commitment to excellence might revitalize Hindustani music, even if it does so in ways we cannot foresee, and in ways some may not readily approve.

1.2

IF PEANUTS IS WHAT YOU PAY

DISCERNING listeners of Hindustani classical music, the *rasiks*, are an unhappy lot. They find that music no longer matches up to their standards of excellence, and that they have been reduced to a minority unable to hold music providers accountable for the quality of music in circulation.

The *rasik*'s reduction to a minority has been caused by a steady decline in the price of music to the consumer, and the resulting explosion in the size of the market. Explosive numerical growth has been accompanied, predictably, by a dilution in the discernment levels of audiences. The result of this process is a brand of music that fails to qualify as sound classical music, as understood by discerning audiences.

The process of "commoditization" of high art is not unique to India. Post-war developments in the technologies of storage and distribution have made it a global phenomenon. In the West, classical music was insulated from the forces of market-driven populism by great institutions with substantial government and corporate funding. But, a substantial contribution towards the sustenance of high art was also made by the willingness of audiences to pay exorbitant rates for a face-to-face encounter with classical music.

In India, neither government support nor corporate patronage have had any significant conservationist impact. The onus of preserving thoroughbred music has therefore been substantially on the *rasik*. Not realizing this, he became an unwitting accomplice in the process that has driven quality music out of circulation, perhaps forever.

The Changing Context

For today's *rasik*s, the benchmark is the music that was performed between 1940 and 1950, the tail-end of the period often described as the Golden Age of Hindustani music.

In that era, the concert platform was the primary interface between musicians and audiences. The penetration of radio was below 10 per cent of urban households, while the gramophone record had perhaps not reached more than 5 per cent of them.

Other than the patron–employers of the musicians, it was the aristocracy in the major cities, which typically hosted concerts. Audiences attended free, and by invitation. The size of the audience rarely exceeded 350/400. This could be partly because amplification acoustics were scarce, and partly because selectivity based on aesthetic cultivation was an integral part of the musical culture of the era.

If this describes the "Golden Age" of Hindustani music, we would also need to accept that it offered ideal conditions for the creation of music we consider great. The music world has changed substantially since then.

With the fading away of aristocratic patronage, audiences have started paying for attendance. But, the concert platform has itself ceased to be the primary interface between musicians and their audiences. This shift has been caused by the explosive growth of the electronic media — first the radio and, later, pre-recorded music, especially after the advent of the audio cassette. If we consider the totality of these trends in terms of cost of music to consumers, we find that they are getting their music cheaper by the year.

The Economics

Let us first look at the **cost of concert admissions**. According to my information, the system of audiences contributing, in an organized manner, began in the early 1950s, when concerts moved out of private gatherings into large auditoria and open-air *paṇḍāls*. The highest level of concert-admission was around Rs. 100 per seat in 1961, Rs. 150 in 1971, Rs. 200 in 1981, Rs. 250 in 1991, and has settled down at Rs. 500 at the end of the last century.

If we apply an inflation-adjustment factor to these figures, we find that a front-row seat of Rs. 100 in 1961 is worth Rs. 2,100 in current rupees. Against this, we are today paying only Rs. 500 for front-row seats. If we plot a long-term trend-line on inflation-adjusted data, we conclude that the real cost of concert-admissions has been falling by 40/50 per cent every ten years.

Although the average durations of concerts have also been shrinking, they have certainly not shrunk at the rate of 40/50 per cent every ten years. To this extent, it can be proved that even the cost-per-hour of concert music has been falling significantly.

Now consider recorded music. Here, of course, the cost per unit of time has to be applied to fully understand the economics.

The 78-RPM record, with 7 minutes of music, cost Rs. 3.5 in 1958, or Rs. 0.5 per minute. The inflation-adjusted price of that record today would be Rs. 12.62 per minute.

Then came the long-playing record with 44 minutes of music at a price of Rs. 22 in 1963-64. The inflation-adjusted price of the LP today would be Rs. 9.96 per minute.

This was followed by the audio-cassette with 60 minutes of music at Rs. 20 around 1968-69. The inflation-adjusted price of that music works out to Rs. 4.12.

Then consider the present scenario of CDs with 74 minutes of music at an average of Rs. 295, and a considerable volume of quality classical music available on CDs for as little as Rs. 90. This brings the price of the contemporary CD to Rs. 1.20 per minute of music at the lower end, and Rs. 4.92 at the average.

Thus, from the 78 RPM record, which sold music at the present-day equivalent of Rs. 12.62 per minute in 1958, the cost of music on a CD has come down to Rs. 4.92 per minute in the year 2000-01 at the average, and as low as Rs. 1.20 per minute at the lower end.

What about musicians' fees? If the consumer is paying less and less for his music, is this hurting the musicians? This does not appear to be the case. According to reliable reports, in 1945, Ustad Faiyyaz Khan, and Kesarbai Kerkar, the highest-paid musicians of that era, were paid Rs. 750/Rs. 1,000 for a concert. Adjusted for inflation, this works out to about Rs. 85,000/110,000 at current prices (*c.* 2000-01).

These figures are shocking considering that — according to industry figures — the highest-paid vocalist today is paid 250 to 300 per cent of this amount, and the highest-paid instrumentalists receive as much as 500 per cent of this amount. While this data only establishes a comparison at the top end of the scale, it is indicative of the overall rise in remunerations of musicians, disproportionate to the basic level of inflation.

How reliable are the numbers? I have reconstructed the price history of concert admissions and prices of recorded music from my own memory, and the memories of senior observers of the music scene. For inflation adjustment, I have used the time-series data of the Wholesale Price Index, as published by the Reserve Bank of India. Neither of these is a perfect solution to understanding the trends in the economics of the music market. However, a similar reconstruction of history by any other raconteur, submitted to an alternative inflationary adjustment, is not likely to lead to very different conclusions. The orders of magnitude could, of course, be less dramatic.

The consumer pays less and less, while the musician gets more and more. How do the sums add up? Who makes the arithmetic work?

The sums add up because of the role of the two dominant intermediaries in the music market: the recording companies, and concert sponsors. They are both playing a progressively larger financial role in the music market — without having either the need or the desire to promote quality music.

Consider the recording companies first. Their expertise lies in making a profit on volumes. Their strategies are guided by the logic of the popular music market, which is essentially price-sensitive. They have allowed the same logic to work in the classical music segment because they have found it profitable. It is understandable that they should have no provocation to adopt a different strategy for this small market — reportedly less than 2.0 per cent of the total recordings market.

By treating the two segments similarly in their marketing strategy, they have encouraged the quantitative expansion of the classical music market. But, in so doing, they also diluted the discernment profile of listeners accessing the music, and thereby, the quality of music that would be delivered through the pre-recorded media.

Now, consider the concert sponsorship situation. Sponsorship is increasingly being offered by corporate entities for the promotion of corporate and brand personalities. To a smaller extent, this function is also being performed by government organizations towards cultural or tourist promotion. The rewards sought by a corporate or government sponsor are unrelated to the quality of music that is delivered. Their motivations would logically tilt more strongly towards quantitative reach, than the qualitative criterion.

None of the major participants in the market has had any reason to consider the qualitative dimension of the cultural process. While the classical music market is not defined by economic status, it can be argued that music is more likely to attract truly dedicated and discerning audiences when it demands an economic sacrifice, than when it is subsidized. As a corollary, when audiences pay a fair price for their music, they do not need to surrender the right to select the music to an unworthy intermediary.

The Bottom Line

In the totality of this scenario, the bottom-line is positive for all participants, except the *rasik*. Because he is in a hopeless minority, it suits everyone to ignore him and reach out to audiences at a lower level of discernment.

While the tyranny of technology and economics tends to be irresistible, the community of *rasik*s cannot consider itself blameless. It had the opportunity of creating a market segment that demands quality music and is willing to pay for it. This community of *rasik*s happily gave its kids Rs. 2,000 to attend a Michael Jackson concert, but felt no pangs of guilt while paying only Rs. 200 to hear Ustad Vilayat Khan. It also loved the idea of paying less and less for concert-length recordings of Pt. Bhimsen Joshi, along with the convenience of listening to them in the comfort of home. In the process, it surrendered the right to choose the music to unworthy intermediaries.

And, now that the consequences are upon them, they are complaining. Audiences get the music they deserve; but they also get the music they pay for. To quote Peter Drucker, amongst the wisest men of our times, "If peanuts is what you pay, monkeys is what you get".

1.3

GOVERNMENT, BUSINESS AND CLASSICAL MUSIC

FOR several decades now, the state and the corporate sector in India have tried to convince us that they have efficiently taken over the patronage of Hindustani classical music from the aristocracy of the pre-Independence era. Unfortunately, such a development is neither a fact nor a foreseeable possibility.

The reasons for this are complex and fundamental. Modern governments and businesses are both managed through a bureaucratic decision-making process, which is, in its very nature, inconsistent with the demands of the patronage function. This reality operates even more mercilessly against the classical arts because their audiences constitute a microscopic minority of the population. The rewards of competent patronage of classical music, therefore, cannot enhance the legitimacy of the repositories of power and money.

If Indian society has substantial funds to divert towards the promotion of classical music, as it evidently has, it will have to find more intelligent and less destructive means of channellizing them than it has so far done.

The Traditional Patronage Model

To appreciate the issues, it is useful to identify the salient features of the traditional model of aristocratic patronage, against which we might evaluate the credentials of modern institutions.

1. *Patron Profile*: The traditional patron was a highly cultivated and discerning listener of classical music. In many cases, he was a trained, and even accomplished, musician. He was the sole and unquestioned decision maker with respect to the disbursement of his largesse — whether to musicians or to other beneficiaries.

2. *The Patronage Relationship*: The relationship between the patron and the patronized musician was a personal one, in addition to being based on a discerning admiration of the maestro's music. In many cases, the patron was a formally accepted disciple of the maestro. The economics of the relationship were designed to free the maestro from all anxieties related to the comfortable maintenance of his personal establishment, which included family and disciples.

   This guarantee was implicitly available not only to individual musicians during their lifetimes, but also to their descendants, as long as they lived up even reasonably well to the promise of heredity. Since such support was available to several musicians in the same court, it resulted in a spirit of healthy competition and sharing of musical ideas between musicians from different stylistic backgrounds. In addition, the patron granted "court musicians" the freedom to perform outside the patronage orbit and to get remunerated for it.

3. *Motivations of the Patron*: The patron was motivated by two desires. By way of personal satisfaction, the patron sought the unrestricted access to the music of the

maestro, perhaps including training from him. By way of public satisfaction, he sought the prestige and prominence within a community of connoisseurs through the vicarious ownership of the maestro's art-asset.

Benefactor Qualifications

With the backdrop of this patronage model, it is possible to assess how, if at all, the modern democratic state or business enterprises might qualify as a replacement for the traditional patron, whose support shaped the "Golden Age of Hindustani music".

Let us first consider the ***benefactor/patron profile.***

The State and business are both handicapped in the performance of the patronage function by the fact that they are not individuals but impersonal entities, operating under conditions of multiple-participant decision-making. While individuals can be highly cultivated and discerning listeners or students of classical music, organizations cannot. Even a hypothetical organization consisting only of connoisseurs would not nullify this argument because all modern organizations are, in their nature, bureaucratic.

A bureaucracy is, by definition, an organization wherein decision-making is distributed, impersonal, and result-neutral in terms of the identities of the beneficiaries. In such organizations, no individual can have unfettered authority over the commitment of resources. The multiple decision-maker process cannot function with a unified yardstick of discernment. As a result, the modern organization — whether the state or a business house — cannot either be an efficient judge of artistic merit, or commit corporate resources as whole-heartedly as the patronage function demands.

Let us now consider the ***benevolence/patronage relationship.***

Neither the state, nor business houses, can possibly establish any personal relationship with musicians. This is so mainly because personal relationships can only be established between individuals. But, this is also because the basis for the establishment of this specific relationship is a high level of discernment in music, accompanied by a passionate admiration for an individual maestro's art. Such a basis is inconceivable in the context of an impersonal institutional entity such as the state or a business house.

The institutional or corporate benefactor of classical music also fails to fulfil the economic criteria of the traditional patronage model. He may be lavish in his support of specific public appearances of leading musicians; but he does not guarantee to the beneficiary a life-long maintenance of his personal establishment at a decent level of comfort. As musicologist Ashok Ranade has argued (Proceedings of the Seminar on Content and Expression, Sangeet Research Academy, Mumbai, 8-9 December 2000), the sponsorship of events is not to be confused with patronage. Concert sponsorship is contractual and event-specific, while patronage is unconditional and permanent. Event sponsorship is a business deal, while patronage is a passionate commitment. The absence of passion in decision-making is essential to the character and success of the state and business organizations. This very feature makes them incapable of matching up to the traditional patronage model.

And, finally, the ***patron's/benefactor's motives***. Neither the state nor business organizations can seek any personal satisfaction for benefaction because they are impersonal entities. Their motivations have, therefore, to be understood purely and solely in terms of public satisfaction. On this dimension as well, the two institutional types have similar perspectives.

The arithmetic of public opinion prevents governments, especially in a democratic society, from adopting a stance that genuinely addresses the needs and concerns of aesthetes who are, by definition, a small minority. The best they can do in this regard is to pay lip service to such concerns, while allowing the opinion of the masses to dominate its substantive actions.

Even in the process of acknowledging "conservationist" concerns, democratic governments are forced to justify the commitment of resources on quantitative rather than qualitative considerations. A music-festival, which costs government Rs. 5,00,000 in sponsorship, is more successful if it draws a crowd of 5,000 ignoramuses than another, which cost the same amount, but attracts only 500 cognoscenti. In order to achieve numerical targets, state sponsorship is obliged to support music that caters to the lowest common denominator in public taste.

The perspective of business houses is not much different. Every business house — including its product — is a "brand" which seeks a premium position in the public mind. The objective of achieving such a position is to enable an easier commercial exploitation of the "market" so accessed. The sponsorship of a cultural event is, in effect, an exercise in "co-branding" in which a premium is created for corporate brand by associating it with a "cultural brand".

If the "cultural brand" has an appeal limited only to the cognoscenti, the co-branding exercise achieves only sub-optimal results. An encashable co-branding exercise is obviously one that maximizes its quantitative reach, independently of qualitative considerations of aesthetic cultivation. Here again, the lowest common denominator in musical values is the more obvious path to success than music to satisfy the cognoscenti.

In essence, the modern democratic state, as well as the corporate benefactor of classical music, has a lot to gain by "buying" the image of high culture, but a lot to lose by making a substantive commitment to it. If their motivations are at variance with those of the traditional patronage model, the results of their benevolence cannot possibly be compatible.

Reconfiguring Benefaction

The traditional patronage model has faded into history, and is impossible to reconfigure. In its present-day *avatār*, benevolence acts without the discernment of the traditional patron. But, being genetically handicapped in the area of discernment, it is obliged to legitimize itself by promoting the notion that the interests of classical music are best served by "popularizing" it. Nothing more self-defeating is conceivable. An art form meant for audiences of high aesthetic cultivation cannot possibly be served by driving it towards populism.

If the experience of the West in handling such issues is any indication, our unseemly benefaction scenario is probably just one stage in the maturation of the cultural process. The West has successfully created great, autonomous institutions like conservatories, opera houses, and philharmonic orchestras which function as centres of discernment and channellize the benevolence of the state and corporate benefactors towards a close approximation to the traditional patronage model. Although these institutions were spawned in the feudal era, they have made a successful transition into becoming vehicles for modern society's commitment to cultural values.

Such developments have, by and large, escaped India. The only significant attempt to address the substantive issues under present-day conditions is the Saṅgeet Research Academy sponsored by ITC Ltd. In a different sort of way, the Dhrupad Kendra in Bhopal, established by the Government of Madhya Pradesh, is also a significant experiment. The success of these experiments, whatever the scale, has certainly sparked off serious discussion about the ideal institutional framework for the preservation and promotion of classical music. The debate has highlighted the need for a constructive alliance between the repositories of money and power on the one hand and forces of discernment on the other.

There are several hurdles to the proliferation of such alliances.

From the point of view of the state and corporate benefactors, classical music is only one amongst several competing demands on the treasury, all of which are more popular, and in the short run more rewarding. In addition, these institutions feel no need to question their belief that they are, in fact, making a positive contribution to classical music. It is therefore necessary for the community of musicologists, professional musicians, and the specialist media to pressurize the contemporary Indian benefactor into maturing at a faster rate.

How does one educate, coax, cajole, pressurize, chastize and seduce a benefactor, all at the same time, without risking his disinterest, displeasure and even alienation? This is a task demanding rare diplomatic skill; and the music community has to find leaders who possess it.

1.4

PAṆḌITS AND USTĀDS APLENTY!

WHAT does it take to become a *paṇḍit* or an *ustād* of Hindustani classical music today? Some audacity and a visiting card with an honorific prefix! A large number of aspiring musicians in India labour under this illusion and achieve only laughable results. In reality, the plight of such musicians, as well as their audiences, deserves sympathy. A lot of it is good talent, having no way of claiming musicianship above the ordinary, except through an absurdity. And, here are audiences, looking for good musicianship, not necessarily of superstar quality, and having no way of finding it except by risking disenchantment.

All this boils down to one simple conclusion. The collective mentality of the classical music community, in this respect, is still a prisoner of a bygone era. It has not understood that we no longer live in a world where a musician was either an *ustād* or *paṇḍit* enjoying the security of royal patronage, or was a nobody with his next meal being uncertain.

To use an automobile industry metaphor, today's music market has a place for Mopeds, Fiats, and Hondas, as well as Rolls Royces. It is also a market that allows Mopeds to grow into Rolls Royces. What the market needs is a structuring of the different segments — providing the means by which each level of excellence can be brought in contact with its prospects to conduct a transaction satisfactory to both.

Classical music is now a profession. Every profession has a market, which consists of intermediaries and consumers. The profession relates itself to its market through a graded system of value and price. The more realistic this system of grading, the more efficient the functioning of the market.

All India Radio (AIR) attempts to administer precisely such a graded system of price–value relationships. The AIR system might have become a formidable force in the classical music market had AIR not decided to engineer its own irrelevance by diluting standards and insulating itself from the world outside. Today, it is possible to shape a successful career in classical music without having qualified as an AIR artist. The concert and recording markets are the bread-and-butter markets for the musician. And, it is in these markets that the forces of demand and supply require skilful management.

Today's musician is marketing a service to a complex market. The intermediaries in the market include concert and festival organizers, corporate sponsors, and the recording companies. The customers are music lovers who access the musician's art through the intermediaries. As in any other market for services, the supplier (musician) is always vulnerable to exploitation by the intermediaries. The only way to avoid exploitation is for the profession to organize itself for credibility amongst consumers.

The value of a grading system is obvious. It becomes an indication of the value that the members of the profession deliver, and justifies the prices they command in the market. From the point of view of intermediaries and customers, this becomes an indication of the value they are buying and, of how much it should cost.

From the point of view of musicians, the advantages are even greater. Once they have achieved a grade that relates to a certain market value, and the credible authority of a profession backs them, they can avoid having to negotiate rates for every engagement, and concentrate instead on cultivating their art. A graded system also becomes a ladder, ascending which becomes a worthwhile motivator towards greater effort.

As an indirect pay-off, such a system will replace the informal and inefficient quality control mechanism in today's Hindustani classical music with a formal and more efficient one. Such a formalized system of accountability for standards of musicianship must necessarily elevate standards across the board. This is the only way for musicians, as members of a self-employed profession, to protect their interests while seeking higher standards of excellence. It also happens to be the most efficient way of protecting the interests of consumers. This convergence of interests is logical because nothing promotes the interests of a profession as efficiently as protecting the interests of its clientele.

The financial clout of an organized profession can also be formidable. The collective bargaining power of a musicians' guild with respect to financial services such as loans, insurance, and medical risk cover, can be powerful incentives for concerted action. Considering the profession-related, and other benefits, many musicians will agree that musicians need to organize themselves.

Many might hope that a government body will take the initiative. If the functioning of the government's cultural institutions is any indication, this thought deserves to be dismissed summarily. Ultimately, musicians will realize that the only people competent to set up and administer such a system are professional musicians themselves. They will also realize that the unity of the entire profession backing each graded member offers the best security for the interests of all musicians.

To the extent that government support, or blessings, might be desirable, an organized community of musicians will obtain it far more easily and effectively than an unorganized one.

Consider, for instance, the legislation that gave statutory recognition to the profession of Auditors or Company Secretaries. Both these professions organized themselves into strong bodies before they were chartered by an Act of Parliament.

In the field of Hindustani music, it may seem as if nobody knows where to start. The task is, indeed, daunting. Establishing and administering such a system will require a professionally manned organization for which the members will have to pay in relation to their respective stakes in the profession. In effect, the stars and superstars will be subsidizing and supporting the rank and file of the profession, as happens in all organized professions. Every difficulty and complexity of the endeavour justifies itself by the rewards.

Today, individualistic sports like tennis, golf and even chess are lucrative professions precisely because the professionals organized themselves, and took charge of their own grading, and the sharing of spoils. These professions did not get organized after the big money came to them. The big money came after, and because, they got organized and hired the finest managerial talent to attract the money.

If musicians do not organize themselves into a guild, they will remain vulnerable to exploitation by intermediaries. If musicians shy away from defining the yardsticks of musicianship, some modern-day Aurangzeb sitting in *sacivālaya* or unqualified journalist or TV chat-show host, will start defining them. Media-savvy and well-connected musicians of questionable accomplishment will continue to promote themselves as *paṇḍits* and *ustāds* and invite ridicule towards the entire profession.

An organized profession with graded membership will, no doubt, make many musicians uncomfortable. Many will insist that in art, there cannot be any objective yardstick of accomplishment. Many will seek shelter under the argument that an organization means politics, a much-maligned and misunderstood reality. The truth, of course, is that an unorganized profession is more unfair to its members than an organized profession. The very purpose of organizing the profession is to eliminate the rewards, which the unworthy are reaping from the disorganized state of the profession.

It is fair to ask why the necessity of organized professionalism has not witnessed any concrete action. The main reason for this lapse might be that many of our senior musicians, whose mindset still dominates the music world, grew up in the era of feudal and aristocratic patronage. A booming mass market, along with the growing power of intermediaries, are unfathomable realities for them. If they are comfortable, they see their success as a triumph of their art. If they are uncomfortable, they blame it on the failure of personal relationships — the anonymous enemy called "politics".

They are attuned to seeing their peers within the profession as rivals. It is not easy for them to start seeing their peers as potential allies, aligned in a commonality of commercial interests. To them, the notion of an audience as a market, and a concert host or sponsor as an intermediary, is alien, and perhaps even revolting.

Although our pre-Independence stalwarts and post-Independence superstars may not see the advantages of a guild organization in obvious terms, they in fact, have the most to gain. Once the floor-level of remuneration to guild members has been stabilized at a respectable level, the rewards of the seniors and the stars will accrue in higher multiples.

The stalwarts and superstars ought to encourage the post-Independence generation of promising musicians to set the ball rolling in this direction. For a variety of reasons, the young ones are more likely to provide the leadership for such a movement. The youngsters seek success in a cruel world, and are better equipped to comprehend its complexities. They understand and deploy both competition and cooperation as parts of a career strategy. When these developments will crystallize, nobody can predict. But, thanks to the alarm signals set-off by an audacious few, it could happen faster than most people imagine.

1.5

ARCHIVAL MUSIC AND THE CULTURAL PROCESS

OVER the last decade, Indian recording companies have made large investments in the acoustic re-engineering and marketing of archival Hindustani music. The activity in this market is accelerating. It is important, at this stage, to understand the cultural implications of the additional lease of life granted to archival music by the technology of acoustic restoration, and the large-scale commercialization of archival music.

Vintage music has long been available to serious seekers who could worm their way into the charmed circle of collectors and archivists. What makes this access a significant cultural phenomenon now is the commercial scale on which it has become feasible, and the acoustic quality of the product that can be delivered to the market — both results of technological advances in sound processing and storage media technologies.

I am treating 1975 as an approximate and notional bridge between archival music and the contemporary musician. This is justified by several considerations, the most important being the passing away, in 1974, of the vocalist Ameer Khan, who has emerged as the single most formidable force in the archival music market. This was also the time when two trailblazing vocalists, Pt. Kumar Gandharva, and Smt. Kishori Amonkar, spearheaded what the learned musicologist, Vamanrao Deshpande describes as the Romantic Movement in Hindustani music.

Around the same time, the first generation of post-Independence musicians emerged on the professional scene. As a watershed in the cultural life of the country, Independence is important because it is only at that point and after that the electronic media enabled, and encouraged, musicians to cultivate audiences as a replacement for the patronage-based relationship typical of the pre-Independence era. This transition was fundamental enough to alter the musician–audience relationship and the music that was on offer to audiences.

With this perspective, I refer to music recorded before 1975 as "archival music", and musicians emerging on the professional circuit after 1975 as "contemporary musicians".

Obsolescence in Recorded Music

Music, once recorded, is susceptible to two types of obsolescence with the passage of time — acoustic obsolescence, and aesthetic obsolescence.

By acoustic obsolescence, we mean the fact that every recording incorporates acoustic values as captured and reproduced by the audio technologies available at the time. These values are, presumably, acceptable to audiences of that time. But, with new developments in recording and reproduction technology, these values become progressively unacceptable to audiences accustomed to the acoustic output of later technologies. With the passage of time, therefore, the decline in the perceived quality of older recorded music can reach a stage, which denies it an audience.

By aesthetic obsolescence, we mean the fact that every piece of music represents musical values prevalent at the time when the music was recorded. The music of each era addresses audiences of that era; therefore, the aesthetic values inherent in it can be assumed to be most acceptable when the music was recorded. With aesthetic values in music responding to socio-cultural changes over time, all recorded music will inevitably drift towards unacceptability.

These two notions of obsolescence are, of course, connected. Acoustic obsolescence progressively depletes the size of audiences willing to expose themselves to a piece of recorded music. Aesthetic obsolescence progressively depletes the size of audiences able to relate to the aesthetic values incorporated in a piece of recorded music. There is a numerical relationship between the willing and the able. If we enlarge the number of people who are willing to hear a piece of archival music, we also enlarge — even if not in the same proportion — the number of those who are able to appreciate its aesthetic values.

By utilizing restoration technologies, which enable us to delay acoustic obsolescence, we are potentially also delaying the onset of aesthetic obsolescence. We accept, of course, that the technological life of a piece of recorded music is at least theoretically unlimited, while its aesthetic life is finite. Even a total nullification of acoustic obsolescence, if such is conceivable, cannot ever wish away the reality of aesthetic obsolescence.

The Archival Music Market

Archival restoration and commercialization activity today covers all segments of the art-music legacy since commercial recordings came to India in 1902. 78-RPM recordings, EP recordings, LP recordings, and pre-1975 audio-cassette productions are being re-marketed on a significant scale after being acoustically upgraded/restored. As an aesthetic force, however, the most significant segment of this activity is the commercialization of concert recordings from the pre-1975 period. By virtue of being concert-length, and by virtue of having been recorded during a face-to-face interaction with an audience, these recordings come closest to the "real thing", and therefore have the potential to exercise an aesthetic influence over contemporary tastes and musicianship which neither shorter, nor studio-made, recordings can exercise.

Art-music reportedly constitutes less than 2 per cent of the total recorded music market in the country. It is too small a segment to deserve a differentiated marketing strategy. Therefore art-music is marketed through the same volume-driven strategy as popular music. Given this reality, the large investments in the revival of vintage music would be justified only if it had begun to start selling in much larger numbers than has done for many years hitherto.

This conclusion suggests a structural change in the generational composition of the music market. This suggestion is supported by the observation that the music industry is now investing even more feverishly in the revival of vintage popular music than it is investing in vintage art-music. Obviously, music lovers above the age of 45 today, who were below 20 in 1975, have now become a large, fast-growing, and profitable market.

Life expectancies of the Indian population are growing and re-defining the market for cultural products, along with other markets. According to one estimate, the 45+ population is projected to become about 24 per cent of the population by the year 2025. If we focus these estimates more sharply towards the urban middle class, which has better access to health care, the 45+ age group could be heading for becoming one-third of the Indian population by 2025. This estimate can be sharpened further, even if only on a speculative basis, to support the hypothesis that as much as half of the classical music market could soon be above 45.

In any event, the 45+ age group is the natural hard core of the market for art-music for two reasons. The meditative-contemplative character of Hindustani art-music will tend to appeal primarily to audiences who have outgrown the need for frivolous music. In addition, it takes several years, indeed decades, of exposure to develop a level of comfort with Hindustani art-music. These facts automatically define the generational profile of the art-music segment as predominantly middle-aged and above.

The recent emergence of a youth market might have marginally corroded this dominance. But, the youth segment is unlikely to outnumber the "grey" segment in the near future. The importance of the "grey" market is enhanced further by its superior knowledge and discernment, which enables it to influence the preferences of the younger generations of audiences. This market would justify a product range that enables its members to grow old with the music with which they grew up. In both segments — classical and film/popular — the recording industry could be encashing the same nostalgia of the middle-aged for their youth, and the accompanying sclerosis of aesthetic values.

Generations as "Markets"

A musician does not consciously address any particular generation of audiences. However, by virtue of belonging to his/her generation, he/she represents its aesthetic values along with the values inherited as a part of the artistic tradition. The process by which these values interact to acquire a significant constituency for an individual musician's art is mysterious and variable. However, it can be argued that the constituency of every musician — no matter how popular — will be limited to a certain generational profile. At every stage in his/her performing career, a musician will inevitably fail to address, and will thereby forfeit access to, a substantial part of the art-music audience, which is either too young, or too old.

This proposition is a little easier to enunciate from the point of view of audiences. It can be observed that, in Hindustani music, audiences relate most intimately to the music that dominated their music-scape between the time they were about twenty, up to the time when they are about fifty. They remain loyal till the end to aesthetic values of music absorbed during these three decades of their lives, and find it difficult to relate to music that represents earlier or later aesthetic values.

This could be the defining paradigm of the current phenomenon. Because people are now living longer, a large volume of archival music, with a substantial residue of aesthetic life, is seeking to encash its commercial potential by enhancing its acoustic acceptability to match, or at least approximate, contemporary standards.

While this might define the commercial aspect of the present phenomenon, the issue of generations as markets, and the finite aesthetic life of music, is far less cut-and-dried than I might have appeared to suggest. In the case of music, perhaps more than other artistic expressions, artistic values are not disseminated entirely, or even largely, through direct voluntary exposure. Secondary and involuntary exposures, and even referrals and prestige suggestions, play a significant role in enhancing receptivity and creating preferences.

The osmotic potential of obsolescent aesthetic values is aided by the foundation of continuity in Hindustani music. This foundation consists of the *rāga* and *tāl* systems, and the accompanying architecture (*rāga* presentation protocol), all of which ensure that, within limits, any recording of Hindustani music, from any era, has a decent chance of evoking willingness to exposure amongst contemporary audiences, provided its acoustic standards are acceptable. The archival music phenomenon could, therefore, be more significant than merely a technological answer to the commercial opportunity in servicing the "nostalgia" market.

Continuity and Change

Having been triggered off by demography, and made viable by technology, the archival phenomenon now participates actively in the complex interplay between continuity and change in three important ways. First, it is providing competition to the recordings of the post-Independence generation of musicians. Second, it is reviving, in a demonstrable way, a yardstick of musicianship, which would have departed with the creators of this music, were it not for the possibility first of recording, and later, of restoration and commercial scale marketing. And, finally, it is providing valuable study material for future generations of musicians, scholars and researchers. We may now look at each of these individually.

The Challenge from the Graveyards

Pre-recorded music has taken over, from the concert platform, the primary function of delivering art-music to its audiences. On approximate reckoning, an average listener of art-music spends at least ten times as many hours a year listening to music recordings as he spends in concert halls. According to music industry reports, recording fees now function increasingly as a lump sum multiple of an artist's rating in terms of concert fees, rather than a sales-based royalty. It would therefore appear that in geometric proportion to their market rating, contemporary musicians depend substantially on recording fees for their livelihood.

If this is true, the contemporary musician must increasingly reckon with competition from archival music on the shelves of the music stores. The challenge is more severe because recording companies have tended to sell contemporary music and archival music at the same price, and often even at lower prices. In addition to such commercial disadvantages, the contemporary musician is denied the "nostalgia premium" of the "grey" (45+) market, and its influence over the purchasing decisions of the younger generations of audiences. While it is possible that the flood of re-engineered archival music is expanding the art-music market as a whole, it is almost certain that it is also eating into the sales potential for the music of contemporary musicians.

The dead are, indeed, leaving less breathing space for the living. With a shrinking market share of the recordings market for contemporary music, the big contemporary names will inevitably consolidate their hold over the market, restrict the growth of the most promising second-liners, and impede the entry of fresh talent. Even if this pressure does not convert itself into a depletion of revenues in the short run, it will do so in the medium term. This is inevitable because, fundamentally, the contemporary musician is competing for the discretionary time of the music lover, and not merely for his purchasing power. Art-music is not Muzak. It is a "leisure consumption" product, and requires undivided attention — it cannot be listened to as "background music". For any given customer, the discretionary time available for art-music will always be finite. To this extent, any a priori preference for archival music will deny an opportunity of exposure to contemporary music. Because of this, even if the strugglers amongst contemporary musicians manage to sell more copies of recordings, this does not guarantee them proportionate exposure to further their careers.

Market access for struggling contemporary talent is being restricted not only by deceased musicians, but also by the recordings of the ageing stalwarts of contemporary music made during their peak performing years. The releases of such recordings have now emerged as valuable "retirement plans" and "pension schemes" for the ageing stalwarts of contemporary music.

The disadvantage to contemporary talent may also be aggravated by the fact that today's environment permits the exceptionally talented to access the recording and concert markets very early in life, even before their music has matured fully. In the pre-recorded market, therefore, their hesitant individuality has to struggle for acceptance in comparison with the authoritative solidity of archival music, recorded mostly during the peak performing years of the old masters.

This prognosis for emerging talent is justified by the burgeoning importance of pre-recorded music to the art-music business in its totality. To today's musician, the commercial recording is his/her advertisement, his/her "sample pack", as well as the product itself. It has now replaced the radio as the basic launch vehicle for art-musicians, and also functions as the primary builder of a national and even international presence. Without such a presence, a musician cannot develop the concert market; and without a significant presence in the concert market, he/she cannot either develop or sustain the interest of the commercial recording market, which is his/her primary source of income.

Without the spiralling effect of this interactive relationship between the concert market and the pre-recorded music market, struggling talent is tempted to gatecrash somehow, even anyhow, into the concert market, and entice the recording companies through an established concert-market presence. Such gatecrashing has to be engineered through the mass media — the undiscerning media, such as the lay press and television. This route to success requires musicians to exploit those facets of their personalities that are unrelated to their competence as art-musicians, and to invest a major part of their energy into "marketing" themselves as "brands", leaving less and less energy for their growth as musicians.

Admittedly, the relationship of the living with the living is a tough barrier for the dead to penetrate. Contemporary music therefore, can never be completely swamped by archival music. The dead cannot compete with the living for a presence on the concert platform and in the lay media. Nor can the dead reshape their music for superior acceptability with present-day audiences. But, the dead can now put the living under pressure by claiming a substantial and growing share of the purchasing power and time resources of the audience. From this perspective, archival music is now restructuring the market largely, though not solely, along generational lines. In the short run, it is putting contemporary music under economic pressure. In the long run, however, it will inevitably affect the yardstick by which audiences distinguish between good and bad music.

The Yardstick of Musicianship

Hindustani music is an improvisation-dominant art-form. The role of the pre-composed element has been shrinking steadily for over two centuries now, with its current durational share being as low as 10-15 per cent in the totality of a rendition. This, too, is only a notional ratio because the relationship of the pre-composed element to the improvised element is unique to each rendition. A piece of Hindustani music, as rendered, is therefore is a totally unique event, impossible to recreate, most of all by the musician himself. If it is true that the validity of any art is entirely contextual, it is true of Hindustani art-music more than any other major art-music tradition.

The continuity-and-change model of Hindustani music is inherent in its continuation as an aural tradition. The tradition has never either intended, nor attempted, to preserve even an approximate record of performed music either for replication or as a pedagogical device. And, the utility of whatever documentation was done could never go beyond an aid to memory. The aesthetic and musical values of this tradition were always intended to be transmitted from one generation to another only through what a musician performed, and what he taught during his lifetime. Having passed them on, the individual musician disappeared from the scene, allowing the interaction between future generations of musicians and audiences to shape their own musical relationship.

This model of continuity and change, "appropriate" for an individualistic and improvisation-dominant art-form has now been "distorted" by technology. Aesthetic values of a bygone era are now acquiring a relevance unsupported by the contemporary socio-cultural environment. That era cannot be considered either superior, or inferior, to contemporary conditions in terms of any objective yardstick. It was simply different, and cannot be recreated. But the parameters of musicianship which it enabled have now been given an additional, and if you like, "unnatural", lease of life — first by recording technology itself, and then by the technology of acoustic re-engineering of archival recordings. Consciously or otherwise, contemporary audiences could now begin to hold contemporary musicians accountable to these parameters of musicianship that are holdovers from a previous era.

The "yardstick" notion has two dimensions. First, it refers to the phenomenon of something acquiring a priori value merely by virtue of having once been lost. It is not subjected to critical evaluation before it is accorded a premium. It is considered valuable merely because it cannot be revived or replicated, and is beyond reach. Second, we are dealing with the unstated assumption that everything in this world is drifting away from being "as it was intended to be", and the farther back you go into the past, the closer you are to "things as they were intended to be". By implication, therefore, whatever is closer historically to the "original" is assumed to be closer to the ideal.

With a substantial co-existence of archival music along with contemporary music on the shelves of the music stores and in our homes, this generalized "nostalgia premium" acquires a power beyond the validation of personal experience. This extra-experiential racial nostalgia operates through the agency of the 45+ age group of audiences, who wield great influence over the tastes of the younger listeners, and validate musical values that go much farther back into history.

As an operative reality in the cultural process, this premium to antiquity, divorced from the socio-cultural context of music, has been made possible by the acoustic acceptability of vintage music to contemporary audiences. As a result of this intervention of technology, the contemporary listener is willing to give vintage music an equal chance of shaping the values that enable the mind to distinguish good music from bad. Consequently, the balance between the forces of continuity and the forces of change is being tilted in favour of the former.

The "Virtual Guru"

Perhaps the most significant facet of the phenomenon under review is the emergence of archival music as study material for aspiring musicians. In this role, archival music is filling — even if only partially — the large vacuum in the availability of competent *gurus*.

It is obvious that recorded music cannot function as a total substitute for a competent *guru*. It can only provide a stylistically coherent model of performed music. It cannot inculcate, in the student, either the ideation process or the principles of music-making which make that music possible. Under ideal conditions, therefore, archival music should be a supplementary source of guidance, complementing the efforts of a real-life *guru*.

The optimal use of archival music as study material might require a quality of personalized guidance even rarer than a traditional *guru*. Such a revolution in the process of grooming Hindustani musicians is inconceivable for quite some time to come. Therefore, archival music will influence the music of future generations driven largely by the individual predilections of aspirants. This scenario might appear pregnant with highly unmusical consequences. However, the results may not be uniformly unseemly.

The most obvious results of such a situation could be the mushrooming of xeroxes, and even laughable caricatures, of the great musicians of the past. Such tendencies are already visible with respect to the influence of some of the modern masters, who are no more. This is not too frightful a prospect.

The *guru–śiṣya paramparā* in Hindustani music was not very different from a reliance on pre-recorded music in its explicit intent. In that system of aesthetic indoctrination, a substantial amount of teaching and learning energy was invested in shaping the *śiṣya* as a decent xerox of a *guru*. Mercifully, the endeavour failed in most cases because of three human imperfections: imperfect perception, imperfect retention, and imperfect reproduction. Because of these imperfections, the traditional system became an effective instrument of continuity within change. Because of the possibility of repetitive exposure, a pre-recorded archive removes some of these imperfections, and enhances the risk of producing xeroxes and even caricatures.

With a much larger volume of each departed musician's archive being commercially available, there is bound to emerge a breed of musicians which can adopt, from archival music, the principles of music-making, and evolve an expression without the need to ape the archival cliché. Even if this prospect did not exist, this risk need not bother us because the Hindustani tradition has always refused to grant any credibility to xeroxes. Moreover, for every hundred xeroxes, the tradition would still be capable of producing one brilliant original.

The other obvious consequence of the emerging scenario is the possibility of aspirants indiscriminately absorbing a multiplicity of stylistic influences from archival sources. This has the potential for shaping music that is no more than an incoherent patchwork of clichés, lacking in substance. But, since we cannot wish away the onslaught of technology, we might look at the more acceptable possibilities arising from it. History will bear witness that the Hindustani tradition has consistently produced great originals who could integrate diverse influences into an aesthetically coherent whole. Indeed, the greatest names in pre-Independence music were, almost without exception, disciples of multiple stylistic lineages.

The intervention of technology in effect enables the Hindustani tradition to resume the transmission of aesthetic values and the skills of musicianship, disrupted for over two generations because of a growing shortage of competent *gurus*. Even if the conditions for the exploitation of archival material as a pedagogical device are not ideal, its availability on a commercial scale constitutes a definite empowerment of every aspiring musician.

Optimism about the intelligent, rather than mindless, utilization of the archival resource is justified by the emerging profile of musicians. Increasingly, professional musicians belong to highly educated families, and have acquired significant academic credentials, though not necessarily in music. They have the intellect, and the keenness, to establish an interactive relationship with scholarship in the field of music, and to acquaint themselves with its output. Such a profile greatly reduces the risk of absurd results.

The Big Picture

Essentially, the archival revival movement corrects a significant discontinuity imposed on the Hindustani music tradition by the growing shortage of competent teachers in the post-Independence period. In the cultural process, the forces of continuity have now been strengthened through an infusion of a powerful source of traditional aesthetic values. As recording companies encash the commercial opportunities opened up by the demographic patterns of the market, Hindustani music could now be revitalized by the restoration of the continuity, which was lost during the second half of the twentieth century. Contemporary musicians may now find it possible, and even necessary, to forge a stronger link between the music of the present and the music of the past. Such a link may become a prerequisite to establishing their credibility amongst the influentials of the music market. The forward march of romanticism and post-modernist tendencies could now be arrested, at least for the moment. These pressures are primarily the creations of the technologies of acoustic restoration of archival recordings, and the feasibility of their low-cost commercialization and distribution on a national scale.

This phenomenon also has larger implications for the contemporary music-scape, which the contemporary musician should welcome, rather than fear. The present music scene reveals three categories of impoverishment in comparison with the pre-Independence era. The variety of genres represented by quality musicianship has shrunk drastically. The pre-modern *dhrupad* and the semi-classical *ṭhumrī*, for instance, stand considerably depleted. Within each genre, there is a diminution in the variety of *gharānā*s represented by quality musicianship. And, across genres and *gharānā*s, the total number of *rāga*s and *bandiśe*s being performed on the concert platform, or available on pre-recorded media, is dwindling.

All these losses may be partially recovered by the return of vintage music to the shelves of the music stores.

A serious musician, at any level of accomplishment, remains forever a student of music. He seeks and values a "reference library" that aids the ideational process, and enables him to enrich the musical product that he delivers. To this extent, the accelerated commercialization of archival music can be expected to enrich the totality of the environment for Hindustani music through its influence on listeners as well as contemporary musicians.

What we are witnessing today is a market-driven phenomenon. The logic of the recording companies will necessarily be different from that of those who are concerned about the preservation and revival of the artistic tradition. The music community can, therefore, expect only limited and slow benefits from the initiatives of the recording companies. If faster or sharply focused results are desired, the music community will have to take the initiative in converting the rewards of technology into a trigger for a veritable renaissance.

1.6

A REQUIEM FOR THE GHARĀNĀS

OVER the last half a century, stylistic pedigree and genealogy have emerged as the least clearly understood, and the most insidiously exploited facet of our musical culture. The truth or otherwise of *gharānā* claims made by individual musicians is not the issue, because these are verifiable in every case. The issue is whether the claims carry any substance in terms of musical value, and what we may legitimately infer from *gharānā* linkages in the contemporary context.

What Is a Gharānā?

The word *gharānā* is used to denote a distinctive style of rendering *rāga*-based music in the modern genres of Hindustani music. The *gharānā* system or tradition is most clearly defined in the *khyāl* genre of vocalism, and has been a formidable force in shaping Hindustani music for two centuries. The *gharānā*s had their forerunners in the four *bānī*s (literally, dialects) of medieval *dhrupad* music, which ruled Hindustani art-music between the fourteenth and eighteenth centuries. But, even pre-*dhrupad* music recognized several *mata*s (literally, ideologies), acknowledging the existence of diversity.

Stylistic diversity in musical expression is virtually written into the script of Indian culture because of the large number of racial–ethnic–linguistic groups that inhabit the subcontinent. A degree of homogeneity was probably achieved during the Mogul era, when musician communities were concentrated in and around Delhi, and were supported by the patronage of the Imperial court. After the Mogul Empire disintegrated, musicians migrated to the smaller principalities under British protection in search of alternative patronage. Once art-music was allowed to intermingle with the local cultures under conditions of relative isolation, the essential diversity of Indian culture re-surfaced effortlessly and got crystallized in the form of *gharānā*s.

Considering the powerful forces working in favour of diversity, it is truly remarkable that the essential core of Hindustani music has remained uniform throughout non-peninsular India, and stable for centuries, with diversity manifested largely in the manner of rendition. The melodic and rhythmic content of Hindustani music originates in the *rāga*s and *tāl*s of the system, which are common to all *bānī*s of *dhrupad* and the *gharānā*s of post-*dhrupad* genres. The architecture of *rāga* presentation is determined by the genre that is performed. It is only in the manner and mode of rendition that the tradition exhibits considerable diversity. This diversity needed names for identification. The word *gharānā* emerged as the most appropriate for this purpose.

The word *gharānā* is derived from *ghar* (house/home, from the Sanskrit noun: *gr̥ha*). In Hindi and Urdu, *gharānā* is a collective noun denoting those who live under the same roof; therefore, a family, a lineage, a clan. The first significance of the term is thus derived from heredity, or ties of kinship.

The names of *gharānā*s are most commonly the names of places, such as Agra, Rampur, Gwalior, Jaipur, Atrauli, Kairana, Indore, etc. The second significance of the term, therefore, derives from the place of origin. Because the nomenclature implies the existence of distinguishing features, it recognizes that the distinctiveness of each *gharānā* is attributable, in considerable measure, to its place of origin.

Gharānās named after their places of origin almost always have the names of one, sometimes two, towering personalities treated either as their founders, or landmark personalities. The Kairana Gharānā of the *khyāl* is, for instance, associated with the name of Abdul Kareem Khan, considered the fountainhead of the distinctive style. Likewise, the Jaipur–Atrauli Gharānā of *khyāl* reveres Alladiya Khan as its founder, and the Etawah Gharānā of the *sitār* and *surbahār* treats Imdad Khan as its landmark personage.

Thus, we have three different, historical factors, converging to define a *gharānā* as a stylistic distinctiveness or an ideology of music-making, exhibiting signs of continuity over several generations. In plain language, once upon a time, there was a great musician, whose music was different from those who lived in other villages or cities. He groomed his sons as musicians and they sang a lot like him; and their music was also different from the music of those who lived in other places, and in the same respect as their father's was. And, this went on for several generations, as long as conditions were favourable.

Favourable Conditions

This caveat is important — "as long as conditions were favourable". Conditions do change, and often change radically enough to nullify the cultural meaning we attach to certain historical facts. This is why we need to examine the conditions that favoured the perpetuation of certain well-defined styles in the rendition of Hindustani music.

The scrutiny must relate to the basic notions defining *gharānās*. It is easy to appreciate the appearance of a great musician whose style influenced many other musicians of his own generation as well as the next. But, beyond this, the phenomenon requires some exploration. Why did the sons and nephews of musicians need, or want, to become musicians? And, why did the style of a musician from Gwalior, and his sons and nephews, need to be, or end up becoming, distinctly different from that of their corresponding generations from Agra or Jaipur?

Hereditary musicianship was a creation of genetic, familial, as well as economic factors. Genetic factors were conducive to the transmission of the musical sensibility, subject to the naturally determined pattern of probabilities. The risks associated with this mode of transmission were systematically reduced by a preference for marital alliances between the progeny of professional musicians. The concern for this risk was so great, especially amongst Muslims, that the community of professional musicians even permitted marriage between first cousins. The notion of the art as an asset, and the desire to keep it "in the family" encouraged in-breeding.

The children of musicians thus grew up in an environment dominated by the practice of music. Familial factors ensured that a great deal of learning of music took place involuntarily. The voluntary aspect of hereditary musicianship responded to the attractions of feudal patronage. The employment of *nawābs*, *mahārājās*, and *zamīndārs* under British protection, promised lifelong economic security, and constituted the most attractive market for musicians. Patrons were few and the supply of talent was unlimited, resulting in an intensely competitive situation for musicians.

The greatest amongst musicians were, of course, wooed by the most powerful amongst princes; but the rest struggled for survival. The "market" for art-music was too small to support its pursuance as an independent self-employed profession. Under these conditions, it was natural that patronage be regarded as an "asset" to be protected and, if possible, bequeathed to direct descendants. The incentive for doing so arose from the lack of widespread access to formal education, and the predominantly feudal-agrarian economy, which severely limited career options.

For musicians enjoying feudal patronage, the chances of bequeathing the patronage asset were perceived to be the greatest if they could turn their children into their own musical clones. The patron's heir, also chosen by heredity, and aesthetically nurtured on the senior musician's art, would — in all likelihood — also accept the heir to the musician's stylistic legacy. This likelihood made it attractive for the sons of musicians to be inducted early into the ownership of the art-asset and put through a rigorous process of aesthetic indoctrination. This process struck deep roots in the musical culture because the "market" — feudal patrons — rewarded its products. It often became a matter of "national" pride. A king could legitimately boast of his army, his elephants, his jewels, his palaces and even his *gharānā* of music.

Even without its cloning intentions, hereditary musicianship would have qualified as an eminently suitable vehicle for the Hindustani tradition, which requires the musician to perform the simultaneous roles of composer and performer. The demands of this duality have grown exponentially over the second millennium, as the role of the pre-composed element has shrunk, and that of the improvise elements has grown. As a corollary, the notion of a *rāga* has risen to progressively higher levels of abstraction. The combination of these tendencies has left the art with no effective mode of transmission other than the aural. Involuntary familial exposure to the art during the most formative years, accompanied or followed by a voluntary submission to the rigours of grooming, was therefore uniquely promising as a pedagogical culture.

Predictably, heredity could not retain exclusive control over the music world for long. Despite the painstaking "genetic engineering" practised by professional musicians — and perhaps also because of it — heredity turned out to be an unreliable guarantee of musicianship potential. In all probability, patronage also became progressively disenchanted with heredity, and more categorically committed to musicianship. Therefore, with the exhortation of patrons, and often under their orders, musicians began to groom promising talent beyond the orbit of kinship. But, since the nature of the art demanded intensive and involuntary exposure, and the "market" demanded stylistic continuity, the mentor–pupil relationship cast itself into the parent–child model of co-habitation, and total subordination verging on servility.

Although stylistic cloning was the explicit intent of this art transmission system, it could not possibly have been its result. In addition to the "generation gap", such as might have existed, three imperfections inherent to aural transmission took care of the element of change — imperfect perception, imperfect retention, and imperfect reproduction. Therefore, by and large, the system did not produce clones; but it did produce musicians who explicitly attempted continuity, while inevitably representing change. Depending on the quality of talent each *gharānā* produced, the strong bias towards continuity resulted in the progressive refinement and enrichment of the salient features of its style, in addition to giving the music a greater degree of aesthetic coherence. These processes yielded a variety of musical styles defined by a genealogy of tutelage, only partially coinciding with heredity.

Such an outcome was possible because, by and large, each lineage pursued its special interests relatively insulated from other lineages. Partial protection against dilution and disorientation came from the self-righteous and dogmatic attitudes that were cultivated during the period of grooming. These fortifications worked because of the appalling backwardness of the country in terms of transport and communications. Even early twentieth-century accounts of great musicians report that they took leave of their princely employers to go on concert tours, that could last several months, and even a couple of years.

The Golden Age of Hindustani Music

The *gharānās* thus came to be distinctive stylistic lineages of post-*dhrupad* art-music, shaped by feudal patronage, heredity, a rigorous pedagogical environment relying substantially on aesthetic indoctrination, and a backward economy starved of education, career options, transport and communications. The result they delivered was a variety of distinct musical styles within the same genre of music, with each style possessing an aesthetic coherence arising from a set of fundamentally held and assiduously cultivated musical values. The distinctive features of the *gharānās* have been the subject of considerable scholarly attention.

V.H. Deshpande (1987, 2nd edn.) offers a conceptual framework for the aesthetic classification of the *gharānās* of *khyāl* music. He classifies *gharānā* styles on a continuum defined by rhythmic orientation and melodic orientation as the two polarities. Amongst the *gharānās* considered by him, he places the Agra at the rhythmic orientation polarity, and Kairana at the melodic orientation polarity. At the exact mid-point of the continuum, he places Alladiya (Jaipur–Atrauli) as a complex fusion, and Gwalior as a simple fusion of the two orientations. Patiala is placed towards the melodic orientation pole, but considerably short of Kairana. The Indore/Bhindi Bazar Gharānā of Ameer Khan, falls between Patiala and Kairana, close to the melodic orientation pole.

This blossoming of the *khyāl* genre in various hues and fragrances, represented by towering musicianship in all the *gharānā*s, made it possible for the century preceding India's Independence (1947), to be described as the "Golden Age of Hindustani music". However, the *gharānā* system had exposed its limitations even before Independence.

Chinks in the Armour

Deshpande (1987) points out, with stunning validity, that the greatest vocalists of the Golden Age had been, almost without exception, disciples of multiple *gharānā*s. Evidently, the *gharānā* system was incapable of supporting the flowering of true genius, and forced it to seek a diversity of exposure in search of its own voice. This phenomenon suggested that stylistic loyalty to a single *gharānā* was no guarantee of quality musicianship and could, indeed, be an inhibitor of exceptional potential in so highly individualistic an art as Hindustani music.

Chinks in the *gharānā* armour expanded into gaping holes from the dawn of the twentieth century, when the print and electronic media weakened the hold of the personalized *guru–śiṣya* relationship over the art-transmission process.

In the first quarter of the century, V.N. Bhatkhande published his near-encyclopaedic re-interpretation and documentation of the Hindustani music tradition. From a pedagogical perspective, the most important aspects of his work were the development of an eminently usable notation system, the documentation of *rāga* grammar, and the publication of a large repertoire of *bandiś*es with notations. His contemporary, Vishnu Digambar Paluskar also published highly reliable documentation of *rāga* grammar and *bandiś*es. Paluskar, however, made a more immediate impact on the accessibility of musical knowledge and performing skills by setting up Gandharva Mahavidyalaya, India's first music university. In its early years, this university trained a virtual army of musical missionaries to run music schools all over the country.

Collectively, Bhatkhande and Paluskar provided a large part of the knowledge-base and the institutional framework to create an alternative pedagogical environment. They partially liberated the art transmission process from the one-to-one, personalized, *guru–śiṣya* relationship. But, even within the one-to-one relationship, they freed it partially from aural transmission. Their work enabled ample and unselective access to musical knowledge, made it less dependent on aural transmission, took some of the tyranny out of the teacher–taught relationship, and thus weakened the forces, which created the "cloning effect" characteristic of the *gharānā* phenomenon.

The momentum of homogenizing forces in the musical culture was greatly enhanced by the appearance of the radio and the gramophone record in the early years of the twentieth century. The electronic media ended the isolation of the different *gharānā*s from each other by making the music of every musician accessible to every other musician and aspirant to musicianship. These media also enlarged the market for art music. By the time the cost-effective audio-cassette made its appearance with concert-length recordings in the 1960s, pre-recorded music was emerging as a "virtual *guru*". Hereafter, technology and commerce worked in tandem to demolish traditional barriers to the acquisition of musical knowledge and skills, talent's entry into musicianship, and to the public's access to music.

However, even before this development, Independence and the launch of a parliamentary democracy has demolished the bulwark of the *gharānā* system — the feudal aristocracy. The demise of the feudal aristocracy was far more significant than is commonly recognized. In addition to the dispossession of a patron class, this transition took away an important quality control mechanism operating in Hindustani music. In the feudal era, only the finest musicians secured sine-cures of patronage. And, once they were appointed in the service of a court, they became models of musicianship for the laity, with the most promising talent within their territories gravitating to them for grooming. This process of automatic matching of talent to opportunity took a beating when the princely states were abolished.

Democratic India forced musicians to migrate from the smaller towns to the big cities. Economic development started offering musicians' children alternative career options. Heredity, already abandoned as the exclusive entry criterion, gave way to a talent-based selection system for grooming. But, the anonymity of urban life could not guarantee the automatic gravitation of the most promising talent towards the greatest musicianship. Even when such relationships did get forged, the stresses of managing self-employment left the greatest musicians depleted of energy and time for teaching. With the best of intentions, the rigorous institution of personalized tutoring, that had sustained the *gharānā* system in the feudal context, could not be supported in the urban context.

These factors, coupled with easier access to music through the electronic media, corroded the two most important features of the *gharānā* system — stylistic distinctiveness of the different *gharānā*s, and the aesthetic coherence in the music of each musician nurtured by a *gharānā*. These trends obliged Bonnie Wade (1984) to observe that the epitaph for the *gharānā* system was about to be written, if it had not been written already. This observation was valid not only for *khyāl* vocalism, for which it was intended, but also for the lineages of instrumental music, which have exhibited a comparatively lower level of stylistic diversity.

The Gharānā "Brands" Today

In the contemporary context, then, what does it mean, when a musician claims your attention as a stylistic descendant of Miya Tansen, or as the twentieth generation in an unbroken lineage of musicians?

First, what it does mean. It means that the musician has not drifted into music purely because of heredity, or by the absence of alternative careers, but chosen music as a voluntary pursuit. It also means that he has submitted himself to apprenticeship under an "authorized" teacher of a particular *gharānā*, and has been formally accepted into it. It implies that he accepts his accountability for adherence to the stylistic features for which his lineage is known.

Now, let us consider what his claim does not necessarily mean. It does not mean that his tutelage with his *guru* has been sufficiently long and intensive for him to internalize the aesthetic coherence and stylistic distinctiveness for which the lineage is respected. And, it can certainly not mean that his music is substantially free from all stylistic influences other than seniors of his own lineage.

A majority of musicians born in free India will be embarras-sed into silence by this interpretation of their *gharānā* claims. Amongst the leading *khyāl* vocalists of the younger generation, there is, admittedly, still a reasonable presence of *gharānā* linkages. In most cases, however, either the tutelage links are tenuous, or the lineages themselves are stylistically blurred, or the music flouts the hallmarks of the professed *gharānā*. These facts do not detract from their outstanding musicianship on dimensions of aesthetic coherence or stylistic distinctiveness. But they do demonstrate the marginalization of the *gharānā* as a determinant of style.

From the trends we observe, we are obliged to infer that, increasingly, the lineage of a musician can only be as relevant as that of a lawyer or a medical specialist, whom we, in India, trust in relation to his heredity, education, and apprenticeship. What do we need to know before we permit any of them to prove their worth to us? Whose son is he? What is his education? Whose student/apprentice is/was he? Did his father/mentor have a track record of producing illustrious protégés? What is/was his father's/mentor's specialization? And, what is his specialization?

Even if all these questions are answered satisfactorily for a musician, they do not, and cannot, establish a musician's talent, competence and integrity, any more than that of a lawyer or a surgeon. These, we can assess only by the manner in which they conduct themselves, and the competence with which they relate to our needs. This is, no doubt, bad news for music lovers who are looking for easy short-cuts to assessing musicianship, and imagined *gharānā* affiliations to be the key to it. Their only consolation is that misjudging musicianship is far less hazardous than misjudging the competence of a medical or a legal consultant.

Beyond two generations of probable relevance, *gharānā*s are now little more than misleading history for audiences, and an academic indulgence for critics. This truth calls for neither lament, nor rejoicing. Hindustani music is built on the foundations of continuity within change. This reality will remain operative as long as Hindustani music remains an improvisation-dominant tradition, impossible to transmit without a substantial dependence on the aural experience. The same is true of stylistic diversity. It existed before the *gharānā*s emerged, and will remain as long as India remains a multi-racial, multi-ethnic, multi-linguistic subcontinent.

With the fading away of the *gharānā*s, one model of continuity and diversity is being driven into history by political, social and economic changes. An alternative model, or perhaps a multiplicity of models is replacing the *gharānā* model, even if the emerging configuration of forces cannot yet be conceptualized. In the future, as in the past, the balance between continuity and change, and between homogeneity and diversity, will be decided by how audiences want art-music to relate to the world around them, and to their inner worlds.

PART II

Form, Idiom and Format

2.1

ARCHITECTURE IN MODERN HINDUSTANI MUSIC*

In Hindustani music, architecture would refer to the structural aspect of a performance that enables it to consummate its function — communicating the emotional content of a *rāga*, utilizing its melodic personality as the trigger for the emotional experience. Architectural values in classical music are more durable, and less culture-specific, than extra-architectural values because they are based on insights into the nature of the creative and auto-suggestive processes of the musician as well as the cognitive-responsive processes of audiences.

By the middle of the twentieth century, the vocal as well as instrumental manifestations of Hindustani music had cast themselves into a mature and sophisticated architectural model, which acknowledged its *dhrupad* legacy while also carving out a post-*dhrupad* evolutionary path. This model inspired the golden age of vocal music in the first half of the twentieth century, and instrumental music in the latter.

In the last few decades of the twentieth century, however, the music being rendered by a majority of the post-Independence generation of musicians has begun to suggest a

---

* Reproduced with the consent of Sangeet Natak Akademi, New Delhi, from *Sangeet Natak*, vol. XXXVI, no. 1, 2001.

considerable weakening of the structural model hitherto established. It appears almost as if "creator and spectator are locked in a conspiracy against history, geography, and specificity, which may be considered liberating or destructive . . . but which is entirely without precedent in the history of the arts" (Kenneth McLeish, 1993).

Theoretically, it can be argued that all art, and therefore all change in artistic expression, is automatically legitimate because it is a "natural" response to the socio-economic environment. In the same vein, it can also be argued, as long as it has an audience, contemporary artistic expression can be assumed, a priori, to have remained culturally relevant. Such assumptions may not, however, be entirely valid when the magnitude of discontinuities is abnormal enough to threaten the fundamental aspects of an artistic tradition. At such times, it could become important to acknowledge the breakdown of the mechanism that sustains the relationship between the arts and cultural meaning, and to aid its restoration.

An important part of this mechanism is a constant dialogue between the parallel traditions of scholarship and performance. In the interest of such a dialogue, it may be helpful to take another look at the modern architectural model of Hindustani music performance.

The Architectural Metaphor

Le Curbusier (towards a new architecture) describes a building as a machine to live in; nothing more, nothing less. To him, the plan, i.e. the functional organization of spaces, is everything; any element that does not derive inevitably from the plan is either sculpture or ornamentation, and therefore redundant to the essence of architecture. Drawing loosely on this conceptual framework, any artefact can be seen as having an architectural component, a sculptural component, and an ornamentational component. Here, architecture would refer to the manner in which the creation *functions*; the sculptural aspect would refer to the way it *looks*; and the ornamentational to the way it *pleases*.

In relation to music in general, one might say that all music has elements of architecture, sculpture and ornamentation, though their relative weightage would vary from one piece of music to another. The metaphor can provide a useful framework for understanding Hindustani music too. For instance, at a macro level, genres of Hindustani music can be classified as being architecture-dominant (*dhrupad*), sculpture-dominant (*khyāl*) or ornamentation-dominant (*ṭhumrī*). Then again, within the same genre, the musical temperaments of individual musicians can be described as architecture-oriented (Kesarbai Kerkar or Ameer Khan), sculpture-oriented (Omkarnath Thakur or Roshanara Begum), or ornamentation-oriented (Bade Ghulam Ali Khan).

By extending this analogy to the micro level, individual *rāga*-renditions can be broken down into architectural, sculptural and ornamentation facets. For the purpose of this discussion, we shall isolate the architectural, or structure-functional, aspect of *rāga*-rendition from its stylistic aspects.

Function and Structure

What is the "function" of a Hindustani music rendition? Its function is a comprehensive exploration of the chosen *rāga*. In this context, comprehensiveness encompasses the melodic as well as emotional character of the *rāga* rendered.

The melodic and emotional facets of a *rāga*'s personality are not distinct from each other, but intimately linked. The melodic facet of each *rāga*'s personality is pregnant with a well-defined emotional charge that does not require either a name or conscious awareness. To the Indian mind, this proposition is valid a priori. From this arises the proposition that the architecture of a rendition enables the effective exposition of the melodic facet of a *rāga*'s personality and thereby maximizes the probability of releasing the emotional charge inherent in it.

The primacy of architecture — rather than sculpture or ornamentation — as the repository of durable values has almost intuitive appeal because the functionality of any structure is based on principles that are either universal or reasonably stable in their validity. For instance, a residence in which the main entrance is through a bathroom or a kitchen, or a home with three bedrooms and twenty bathrooms, would be a piece of bewildering architecture in any era. Then again, in a society that respects privacy, a home with one bedroom leading into another, which leads into yet another, would be considered dysfunctional.

This analogy is valid with respect to classical music. But, there is a small difference. In Hindustani music, though not necessarily in architecture, the bewildering is automatically dysfunctional because the central vision of the creator needs to be intelligible before the creation can function as an object of aesthetic appreciation, or evoke an emotional response. Architecture in Hindustani music, then, refers to the manner in which a musician selects its elements or movements, and organizes them for exploration of the chosen *rāga* — explicitly for intelligibility, and implicitly for eliciting the desired emotional response.

In the post-*dhrupad* era, Hindustani music has acquired an overall linearity of progression, encompassing subordinate cyclicities within it. It is through this overall linearity that Hindustani music seeks to make itself comprehensible.

The Linearity of Progression

The primary linearity drives the music simultaneously through the following progressions, and arranges the different movements, sequentially, in progressive sequence:

1. from the melodically simple to the melodically complex.
2. from lower levels of svar-density towards higher levels of svar-density.
3. from the rhythmically simple towards the rhythmically complex.
4. from lower beat-densities (tempi) towards higher beat-densities.
5. from the relatively unstructured towards the more structured.

Anyone trained formally in the psychology or education will recognize these principles as being fundamental to learning, comprehension, and retention. As a demonstration of this principle in Hindustani music, consider the formal structure of *khyāl* presentation, consisting of a *baḍā khyāl* and a *chhoṭā khyāl*.

The *baḍā khyāl* commences with the *bandiś* and the *alāp*, which is very low in melodic density (*svar*s intoned per minute), is rendered at a very slow tempo (usually below 30 beats per minute-bpm), and is rhythmically unstructured. The next stage of development could be a *bol-bāṇṭ*, rendered at a slightly stepped-up tempo (perhaps up to 40 bpm); the melody is slightly more complex, denser in terms of *svar*s intoned per minute, and corresponds better to the beats of the rhythmic cycle. The third stage of the development could be *tān*s, which are even higher in melodic density and melodic complexity, are sung at a tempo stepped up even further, and involve melody corresponding more systematically to the beats of the rhythmic cycle. This linear progression of melodic and rhythmic density and complexity is elevated to a still higher level in the *chhoṭā khyāl*, which may commence at 160 bpm, and accelerate to 240 bpm before it closes.

The overall linearity of progression is important because it is consistent with the way the human mind works. If its unidirectional flow is not maintained, the comprehension of the music ceases to be effortless. To the extent that the listener is required, intermittently, to focus his cerebral faculties to comprehend the music, he becomes less responsive to its emotional charge.

This unidirectional flow is equally important for the musician himself because, in an improvisation-dominant art form, the musician is also his own audience. He is absorbing the music sequentially even as it is being created, and responding cumulatively to it much the same way as the audience is. The deliberateness of the structurally meticulous approach is, therefore, essential to the autosuggestive process by which the musician "works himself" into the realm of the *rāga*'s emotionality. A disciplined adherence to the linearity cannot, of course, guarantee either the musician's transportation into a different realm, or that of his audience; but it certainly maximizes the probability of such an event.

In the *baḍā khyāl*, for instance, once the rendition has progressed to the *tān* stage, the musician cannot retrogress into *bol-bāṇṭ*, or alternate between *bol-bāṇṭ* and *tān*s, except for an occasional breather, or to create an element of surprise. If he does so, he is not only disturbing the process of comprehension by the audience, but also upsetting the process by which he leads himself into the emotional content of the *rāga*'s personality from its melodic facet.

Such a musician is in poor control over his own cerebral, aesthetic, and emotional processes, and cannot therefore exercise any significant control over his music. This is why the connoisseur of music is unwilling, or perhaps unable, to distinguish between a musician who is steadfast in his adherence to the principle of linear progression and one whose music touches the heart.

The Cyclicity of Melodic Exploration

While the linearity of the structure addresses itself to the universal psychology of human comprehension, the cyclicity protocol governs the more culture-specific and *rāga*-specific aesthetic values. As a culture-specific feature, it confirms the cyclical notion of time common to all ancient civilizations (*Time: Rhythm & Response*, Marie-Louise von Franz, 1978). As a *rāga*-specific requirement, it ensures that the melodic personality of the *rāga* is fully explored, and the probability of eliciting the target emotional response is maximized.

Cutting across the central strand of linear progression, or superimposed upon it, *rāga* presentation involves two cyclicities — the cyclicity of melodic exploration within each movement, and that of the rhythmic cycle, wherever operative. From the architectural angle, the model for melodic exploration is more significant because it is relevant for the classical genres of Hindustani music, irrespective of the existence or absence of central linearity.

At least since Miya Tansen (*Sangeet Chintamani*: K.C.D. Brihaspati, 1989), Hindustani music has had a four-stage melodic development protocol. Tansen recommended a *pada* (from Sanskrit *padya*, or poetry) of four stanzas. There would be no sanctity to the number four unless the stanzas were intended also to be composed differently, with each having a specific melodic–aesthetic function. Collectively, just as the poetic verses in a *pada* are intended as a complete expression of an emotional statement, the four parts of the melody are intended as an aesthetically satisfying exposition of the *rāga*. Significantly enough, Tansen also prescribed that the *rasa* of the poetry and that of the *rāga* should be in perfect consonance.

Therefore, we have four melodic movements, with their distinctive melodic patterns: *sthāī, antarā, sañchārī, ābhoga*.

1. *Sthāī*: Melodically, this is understood as covering the lower half of the melodic canvas: from the lower octave up to the mid-point of the middle octave. By convention, the melodic development commences at base — *sa*, descends to the bottom of the lower octave, and then ascends upwards towards base — *sa* and beyond.
2. *Antarā*: Melodically, this is interpreted as covering the upper half of the melodic canvas: between the mid-point of the middle octave and the outer limit of the higher octave. Here, the higher octave *sa* receives special emphasis as a climactic point of ascent from the mid-octave region.
3. *Sañchārī*: *Sañchār* in Sanskrit means disseminating, or dispersing over distances. The term negates the idea of both, the ascending progression characteristic of the *sthāī-antarā* and the winding-up notion in the fourth part, the *ābhoga*. *Sañchārī* is necessarily a free flowing movement covering the entire melodic canvas, usually at a slightly accelerated pace.
4. *Ābhoga*: The word means satiation and completion. The connotation here is of winding up, wrapping up, and rolling up the canvas opened up systematically by the *sthāī* and *antarā*, and then painted in detail by the *sañchārī*. Here, there is disagreement over the proper melodic structure, but none about what the word means or the melodic intent.

There do exist some differences of opinion over the melodic form and sequencing of the *sañchārī* and *ābhoga*. These differences are insignificant in the face of the fact that contemporary musicians have all but dropped these concepts of melodic exposition from their treatment of a *rāga*. On a close scrutiny of *bandiś*-renditions in contemporary instrumental music, it is evident that, increasingly, the *antarā* too is falling into disuse. It is conceivable that, in the near future, even the *sthāī* will be truncated, and all that will remain of the *bandiś* is the *mukhḍā* (the opening phrase of the *sthāī*).

Music is a language. The rules of grammar, whether in a spoken language or in music, have the purpose of aiding communication without requiring great learning either on the part of the sender or the receiver of the communication. If the emotional statement inherent in every *rāga* is to be understood, the aid of grammar is required. The current grammar of each *rāga* prescribes rules to ensure that even an undistinguished musician can do a fair job of communicating its emotional content. The four-stage melodic development can be seen, therefore, as a similar risk-control device because it can also ensure that every *rāga*, no matter what its character, has an equal and adequate chance of being successfully rendered.

Particularly important in this respect is the directional and regional character of *rāgas* (*aṅga prādhānya* and *diśā-prādhānya*). Some *rāgas* are *āroha-pradhān*, while others are *avaroha-pradhān*. Then some *rāgas* are *pūrvāṅga-pradhān*, while others are *madhyāṅga-pradhān* or *uttarāṅga-pradhān*. These facets of a *rāga*'s personality risk being underemphasized if a musician sacrifices the *sañchārī* and *ābhoga* movements, which are spared from mandatory ascending–descending protocol. A recognizable melodic outline of a *rāga* can, of course, be presented without the *sañchārī* and *ābhoga*; and this is indeed being done most of the time in contemporary Hindustani music. The abbreviated form, however, cannot qualify as a *rāga*-exposition because a *rāga* is more than a melodic entity.

A *rāga* is an aid to the contemplation of a particular facet of the human mind, and carries within itself the "racial memory" of experiencing certain emotions. Our *rāgas* are archetypal entities, pregnant with not only deep cultural meaning, but also have a universal component of meaning. Thus, every *rāga* is an isolation of one aspect of man's mind for elaborate exploration. If this were not so, a *rāga* would be no different from a song — incapable of contemplation.

The Econometric Model

It is possible to visualize the superimposition of cyclical melodic expositions onto the central linearity of progression using the classic time-series graph in econometrics. As its central tendency, there is a secular trend-line of progressive enhancement of melodic density and complexity. Cutting across this trend-line are cyclical melodic expositions of each movement, which would also provide for random distortions of the cycles (see Graph 1).

In the "Hindu" notion of time, linearity is only a myopic view of the essential cyclicity of time. As a model of time, this graph, with a dominant linear tendency, and subordinate cyclical tendencies, suggests a "non-Hindu" socio-cultural

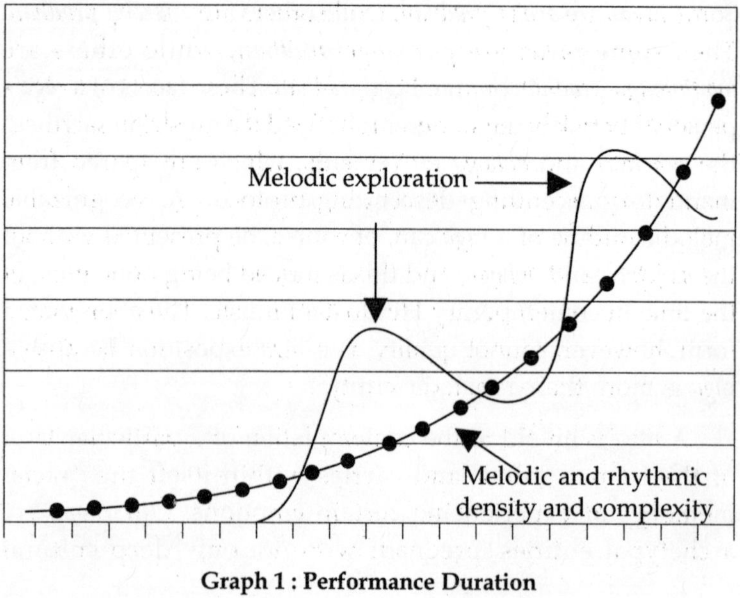

Graph 1 : Performance Duration

foundation. This suggestion has historical validation because modern Hindustani music is a fusion of "Hindu" musical ideas with Perso-Arabic (Islamic) influences. In this respect, it represents a departure from the architecture of the medieval *dhrupad* genre, which was closer to the Hindu roots of our musical tradition, and which isolated the dominant cyclicity of the *pada*-rendition from the predominant linearity of the preceding *alāp*. The econometric model is especially interesting because it finds an oblique echo in the cultural process.

A Case Study

In June 1991, Ustad Vilayat Khan recorded his creation, Rāga Sāñjh Sārāvalī, for India Archive Music Ltd., New York (IAM CD 1040). For its architecture, this recording will qualify amongst the classics of recorded Hindustani music. The music is a single-piece *vilambit* (*baḍā*) *khyāl*-style presentation in *tīntāl*, lasting seventy-four minutes. The rendition is in three phases: (a) *alāp*, (b) *laya-bānṭ*, and (c) *tāns*.

The recording was analysed manually for melodic progression and the progress of the tempo. For the purpose of the analysis, the performance was divided into 119 musical statements, separated from each other either by a *mukhḍā*, a *tihāī* substituting for a *mukhḍā*, *antarā*, or a *tihāī* substituting for an *antarā*. The notation of every melodic statement was done manually.

The melodic span of each musical statement was plotted graphically with a scaling of tonal frequencies to the *mandra-saptak sa* = 1. The melodic plot of the entire 74-minute *baḍā khyāl*-style presentation is shown in Graph 2. Graph 3 plots the tempo of the performance, measured from the beats of the *tablā* accompaniment throughout the performance, using a stopwatch.

In Graph 2, it is observed that Ustad Vilayat Khan takes

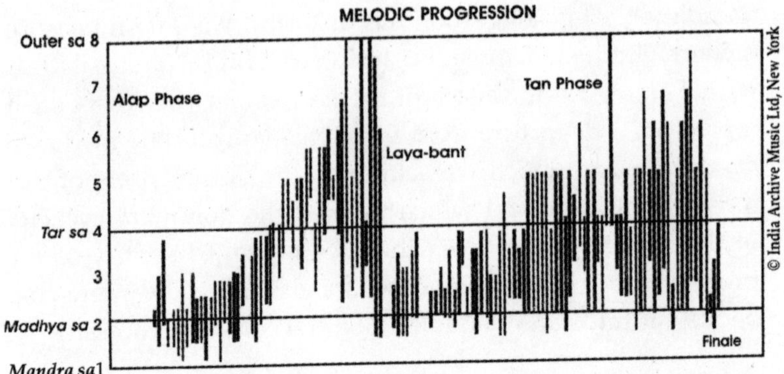

Graph 2

the *alāp* through his elaborate version of *sthāī, antarā, sañchārī* and *ābhoga*. He then re-establishes the *bandiś* with a *laya-bānṭ* movement, and then launches the *tān*s section. It is also worth noting that the melodic plot of the *tān*s section is almost a mirror image of the *alāp* section, suggesting that the same conceptual framework of *sthāī, antarā, sañchārī* and *ābhoga* also guides the melodic pattern of his *tān*s. A careful listening of the recording will reveal that the progression logic is not limited only to the melodic span of the *tān*s, but also covers the melodic density and complexity dimensions.

In Graph 3, we observe that the *alāp* is rendered at 36 bpm. There is a small *joḍa*-type section at 40 bpm, which steps up to 44 bpm in the *laya-bānṭ* movement. The *tān*s begin at 46 bpm, and step up gradually to 64 bpm, just prior to the anti-climactic finale.

This analysis establishes that the music of the living greats does follow the structural approach. On this basis, one can argue that the architecture of their presentation holds an important clue to the greatness of their music. This analysis also suggests that their approach to music-making is potentially decipherable, and that the econometric model presented above is a suitable representation of the architecture of modern Hindustani music.

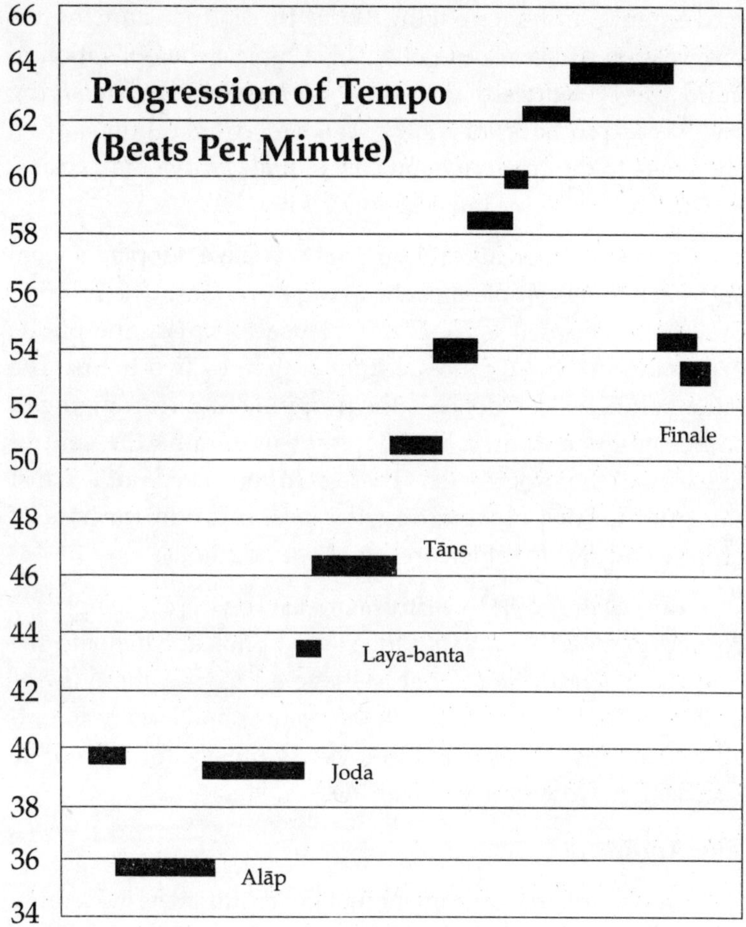

Graph 3

The Duration Factor

In defence of the short-cuts and disorder in vogue on the contemporary concert platform, it has been argued that concert durations no longer permit a leisurely and comprehensive exposition of a *rāga*. Under such conditions, a telescoping of the presentation protocol is unavoidable. There is some validity to this argument. It does not, however, discharge the musician of the responsibility of preserving the central linearity of the movements and sequencing them in distinct and logical progression. It also does not absolve him of the obligation to build the cyclicities that lead to the aesthetically satisfying melodic exploration of a *rāga*. The present conditions are a challenge to the creativity and conceptual clarity of musicians, and not a license for musical jaywalking.

The modern greats still amongst us have adopted a dual approach to the problem of shrinking durations. One solution they have adopted is to simply refuse to satisfy the public expectation of three pieces within a span of two hours. The other solution in evidence is the dropping and rearranging of some movements in a manner that maintains the central linearity of the progression. These solutions need not exhaust the possibilities of handling the presentation formats of Hindustani music under present-day conditions.

Some of the younger instrumentalists on the contemporary concert platform — notably the sitārist Shujaat Khan and the sarodist Tejendra Majumdar — have addressed these issues intelligently, and come up with interesting, and largely acceptable, solutions. This leaves other young musicians no credible excuses for structural waywardness.

The Argument

It cannot be anyone's argument that great musicians inexorably submit every rendition of every *rāga* to the cyclical discipline of melodic exploration and the linear sequencing of individual movements. If this were so, their music would be boring beyond description. The contention is that, like a great architect, the great musician never loses sight of the functionality of his artefact, and is a disciplined presenter of his art. He selects his elements in consonance with his central vision, arranges or sequences them meticulously for effortless comprehension, and allows the melodic treatment of every movement to release its emotional charge.

At the highest level of musicianship, the soundness of architecture is therefore a fundamental differentiator between durable and ephemeral music. Interestingly, however, the same quality can also serve as a discriminator between music and merely pleasant sounds at the lowest level of musicianship.

The issue of structure is worth reiterating at this stage in the history of Hindustani music because the current attack on structured music is an attack on the *rāga*. Without the systematic and elaborate exploration of *rāga*s by exceptional musicians, the Indian musical mind would have been unable to develop and sustain the *rāga* as an archetypal entity, and an inexhaustible reservoir of creative energy. The archetypal stature of the *rāga* cannot survive without the deliberateness and elaborateness of its expositional protocol. Structural wantonness in the presentation of Hindustani music will cause a *rāga* presentation to degenerate either into a random juxta-position of familiar phrases, or into an exercise in tonal kaleidoscopy.

Contemporary crusaders for innovation might be permitted to liberate their music from architecture as well as the archetypal *rāga*; but only after they have come up with an acceptable and intelligible alternative within the Hindustani tradition. Until then, their music will have to acknowledge that a concern for structure has neither exposed any internal contradictions, nor militated against change, nor proven the uselessness of form in Hindustani music.

2.2

INSTRUMENTAL IDIOMS
AṄGA OR APAṄGA?

AN important facet of post-Independence Hindustani music has been the eclipse of vocal music by instrumental music in terms of popularity. The boom in instrumental music has brought to the forefront many instruments, which were, until recently, not accepted on the mainstream concert platform. On the other hand, traditional instruments too have attempted, with varying degrees of success, to develop new musical languages and idioms in order to cater to a new generation of audiences.

The flute and *sāraṅgī* are now following the *sitār aṅga* (glimpse/facet/idiom). The *santūr* is playing a combination of *sitār* and *tablā* idioms. The *sitār* is moving towards the *gāyakī aṅga* (vocalism). Instrumental music is in a state of flux, and demands an assessment of its endeavours and the resultant tendencies.

These trends are neither new nor, in themselves, disturbing. Originally, Indian art-music regarded instruments capable only of accompaniment to vocal music. It pays to recall that even the venerable *rudra-vīṇā*, the grandmother of several Indian instruments, was once considered a *śuṣka vādya* and forbidden for solo performance. Since instrumental music developed as a significant solo art-form, musical ideas and practices have been freely exchanged between vocal and instrumental music, and even between the different instruments. The cause for anxiety lies in the experimental frenzy evident in recent years, which will impoverish, rather than enrich, instrumental music.

Instrumentalists are increasingly willing to deny the ergonomic and acoustic character inherent to their respective instruments. The result is a growing variety of instruments, and a shrinking variety of idioms; a growing range of sounds accompanied by a shrinking diversity of content.

When musicians deviate radically from the native or natural idioms of their instruments, they can easily create music which is at war with itself. This appears to be happening on a considerable scale now, and audiences are expected to hail such stylistic and idiomatic innovations as new *aṅgas*, even when their aesthetic value qualifies them as *apaṅga* (crippled). In such a confused environment, the music community needs to develop a well-considered perspective on the issues.

Source Material of the Hindustani Tradition

The source material of contemporary Hindustani music is traceable to three principal music-making models in art-music:

The gāyakī (vocal) model: This model is based on melodic continuity, and the dominance of the melodic element over the rhythmic element.

The rudra-vīṇā/tantakār model: In this model, plucking of the strings serves as the mode of sound activation. The act of plucking creates an element of melodic discontinuity as well as rhythm. Though within limits, the *tantakār* model offers a large range of stylistic and idiomatic options in terms of the balance between the melodic and rhythmic elements.

The pakhāwaj/tāl-vādya model: In this model, sound activation occurs via the striking of the surface of the instrument, and is intended to create rhythmic patterns. The melodic content of its music, if any, is incidental and limited.

The three main models, therefore, are: the music of melodic continuity, the music of melodic discontinuity, and the music of rhythm. Until recently, the wind and bow instruments did not have either a significant solo presence or stature in art-music. Hence, they cannot be said to have an independent music-making model that has evolved as a tradition.

A fourth, and hybrid, model developed as a combination of the second and third models. This model arose from the music of the *sarod*'s ancestor, the *rabāb*. The *rabāb* is a plucked instrument, but has a resonator covered with animal skin, which gives it an acoustic facet akin to a *tāl-vādya*. The Kabuli *rabāb* came to India with *paṭhān* soldiers, who played martial tunes on it. These features encouraged a percussive-melodic model of music-making in which the rhythmic element dominates the melodic element.

Adoption and Adaptation

As instrumental music developed into a solo art-form, the various modern instruments adopted the three basic models. Adoption was accompanied by adaptation, and further development designed to exploit their distinctive acoustic character. Through the first half of the twentieth century, wind and bow instruments followed the vocal model because the music of melodic continuity was their obvious territory.

The *sitār* adopted and adapted the *rudra-vīṇā/tantakār* model because this is where it logically belonged. The present-day sophistication of *sitār* music owes a great deal to the mature *rudra-vīṇā* legacy.

In the early stages of its hundred-year history, the *sarod* developed its idiom as a refined version of the *rabāb*. In the next phase, it took two different directions. Ustad Alauddin

Khan steered it towards the *rudra-vīṇā* model, while Amjad Ali Khan's father, Ustad Hafiz Ali Khan and Mohammad Ameer Khan (the *guru* of Pt. Radhika Mohan Maitra), reinforced and refined the percussive bias of its *rabāb* legacy. By its very nature, the *sarod* could not do away with the *tantakār* idiom altogether. But, under the influence of Ustad Ali Akbar Khan, it drifted away from the percussive-melodic model. Soon thereafter, the *santūr* took over the percussive-melodic model, and emerged as a significant instrument on the art-music scene.

The *tablā* has, from the very beginning, been a protégé of the *pakhāwaj*; hence its language has evolved as logically from its predecessor's as the *sitār*'s has from the *rudra-vīṇā*.

Until the 1970s, this pattern of appropriate and logical evolution of musical languages prevailed amongst modern instruments. Thereafter began the movement that poses issues of *auchitya*, and of the distinction between *aṅga* and *apaṅga*.

Deviations and Innovations

The most controversial trends are apparent in the music of the wind and the bow instruments, which have moved sharply towards the *tantakār* model. By virtue of their design and sound-activation technology, however, the wind and bow instruments are suited for the music of melodic continuity and the subordination of the rhythmic element to the melodic element. Wind instruments were designed as an acoustic enhancement of the human breath; and bow instruments were designed explicitly as the closest possible mechanical approximation to the musical capabilities of the human voice.

In the Indian tradition, the vocal musical expression has the highest ranking. There are good reasons for this. On purely technical considerations, no instrument can match the acoustic and melodic potential of the human voice. As a vehicle for musical ideas, too, the vocal expression ranks supreme as a unified and unfettered expression of the body, the mind, and the soul, being activated by *prāṇa*, the human breath or the life force. This also makes it the most potent device for spiritual pursuits, thus emphasizing the meditative-contemplative foundations of our art-music tradition. Hence, vocal music is regarded as the originator of all melodic ideas, and also their most authentic exponent. Against this yardstick, every other musical expression is considered a compromise.

Playing *sitār* music on the flute or *sāraṅgī* is an issue in *auchitya* because the instruments were not designed for it. The transgression is more significant because they have deserted a superior model in favour of music belonging to an inferior category of instruments. The much-touted *tantakār aṅga* on the flute or *sāraṅgī* is, by this yardstick, an *apaṅga*.

Against this backdrop, what can we say of the *gāyakī aṅga* (vocalized idiom) on the *sitār* popularized by Ustad Vilayat Khan? Melodic discontinuity is inherent in the *sitār*'s design. A rhythmic element is built into its character by the required frequency of sound priming. By extracting longer acoustic sustain from the instrument, and reducing the frequency of fretwork and strokes, the *gāyakī aṅga* sitārist executes melodic expressions strongly suggestive of singing. This is accompanied by a variety of other devices to magnify the illusion of a vocal performance.

Against the human voice as the yardstick, the *sitār* is an inferior vehicle for the musical idea. In the *gāyakī aṅga*, the musician enables the instrument to transcend its limitations, and to simulate the aural experience of a superior musical expression. This innovation adds something to the acoustic and musical potential of the *sitār*.

The *gāyakī aṅga* on the *sitār* deals in the aesthetics of illusion — illusion of a superior experience — whose purpose is to evoke a sense of marvel. As a response, marvel is distinct from laughter, which is the aim of mimicry and caricature.

Ustad Bismillah Khan has often given us glimpses of the *tantakār aṅga* on the *śehnāī* with plectrum stroke effects like *dir-dir-da,* and *da-dir-dir-dir*. His is not an idiomatic shift into an inferior melodic experience. He merely offers fleeting illusions evoking a sense of marvel; but they never become a caricature of the *sitār* or *sarod*, eliciting laughter. Bismillah Khan is never guilty of *auchitya-bhaṅga.*

The aesthetic of illusion does not raise issues of *auchitya* because, in this case, the protagonist does not deny his own identity.

Auchitya in Innovation

Contemporary music offers outstanding examples of *auchitya* as a perfect congruence between the ergonomic-acoustic character of the instrument and its idiom. The most outstanding examples are the *sarod* idiom of Ustad Ali Akbar Khan and the *santūr* idiom of Pt. Shivkumar Sharma. Both play percussive-melodic instruments, and have developed idioms that make brilliant use of melodic discontinuity as a musical element.

Towards the end of the last century, the *sarod* started its journey as an extension of the *rabāb*. In the 1930s, the legendary "Baba" Alauddin Khan, and his brother, Ayet Ali Khan, re-engineered the instrument into a sophisticated and versatile acoustic machine. Baba also introduced elements of *rudra-vīṇā* music into the language of the *sarod*. But, the development of an idiom that truly exploited the instrument's unique character had to wait until Ali Akbar Khan.

Khansaheb Ali Akbar retained the inevitable moorings of *sarod* music in the *tantakār* idiom, but revolutionized everything else. The Ustad's contribution to the evolution of the distinctive *sarod* idiom is encyclopaedic. But, one feature stands out. It is the dramatic use of geometric and kaleidoscopic tonal patterns, exploiting the semi-polychord facet of the *sarod*.

This feature not only enhances the melodic language of the plucked-lute family of instruments, but also exploits the multiple timbres available on the different strings. This development is uniquely appropriate to the *sarod*, and merits documentation as a classic example of *auchitya*. Ali Akbar Khan gave the *sarod* a language distinctive enough to place it beyond the magnetic fields of the vocal expression as well as other instruments.

In the same mould is the *santūr* idiom of Pt. Shivkumar Sharma. The *santūr* had a Persian idiom, an Afghan/Kashmiri idiom, but no idiom in Hindustani art music. Pt. Shivkumar saw in this staccato, percussive-melodic, polychord the potential for a scintillating musical language, with an emphasis on geometric and kaleidoscopic tonal patterns and an accentuated rhythmicality.

Pt. Shivkumar Sharma follows the *sitār/tantakār* protocol for *rāga* presentation. But, the content of his music is a *tablā* connoisseur's delight. While the average listener is enraptured by the acoustic charm of his *santūr*, cultivated listeners gape in awe at his melodic-rhythmic interpretation of the *tablā* idiom — *peśakār*s, *quaidā*s, *bandiś*es and *chakradār*s. Like Ustad Ali Akbar Khan, Pt. Shivkumar Sharma is the originator of an idiom uniquely suited to his instrument.

Some kind of perspective emerges from this discussion. The more recent percussive-melodic instruments, like the *sarod* and the *santūr*, have freed themselves substantially from the shadow of the mature traditional models, and developed their own musical languages. What the *sarod* and the *santūr* are doing today is an affirmation of their acoustic character.

The *sitār* continues to build on the foundations provided by the *rudra-vīṇā* idiom. It is attempting to enhance its acoustic capabilities, along with the shaping of a more sophisticated idiom. The *tablā*, likewise, continues to build upon its *pakhāwaj* legacy.

Amongst the major instruments of contemporary music, it is the wind and bow instruments, which seem to be groping for an evolutionary direction. The best they have come up with, so far, is a denial of their ergonomic-acoustic character, a stifling of their melodic potential, and an abandonment of the vocal ideal to which they traditionally belong.

Fortunately, the wind and bow categories can boast of one splendid exception. Consider how seamlessly N. Rajam has integrated ideas from the *tantakār* idiom into the traditional vocalism of the violin. Her *drut bandiśes* end with a *jhālā*. But it is a *jhālā* for the violin, and not a sitārist's *jhālā*. It is a *jhālā* in concept but not in technique. It conjures an aural experience of a *jhālā*; but, unlike the *sitār jhālā*, it does not involve 480 wrist-movements per minute.

Rajam's music demonstrates the possibility of enhancing the idiomatic richness of the music of wind and bow instruments without raising issues of *auchitya*. Her music, and that of Ustad Ali Akbar Khan and Pt. Shivkumar Sharma, have also established the viability of an instrumental idiom liberated from an a priori ideal in vocalism. But, as these precedents suggest, a worthwhile direction can emerge only from a discovery and exploitation of the distinctive character of each instrument.

The argument here is that, as a tendency, drifting towards an "inferior" idiom in search of novelty risks creating *apaṅga* music. An original solution to this problem must certainly be feasible. But, until it emerges, it might be in the interests of *auchitya* that the wind and bow instruments stay with their traditional, and logical, home in the vocal model.

Auchitya: The Idea

As an aesthetic yardstick, *auchitya* is, admittedly, a dynamic concept. What was *anuchit* a hundred years ago has probably become *uchit* today; and what we might consider *anuchit* today, could well be accepted as *uchit* a few decades from now. Our notion of *auchitya* must, therefore, allow for change. While accepting this caveat, we need to understand *auchitya* as an idea, which is much bigger, and far more fundamental, than our immediate concerns.

The *auchitya* yardstick is not satisfied by acceptability to the public. *Auchitya* is a sense of propriety, of balance and moderation. It demands a clear perception of a unique identity and destiny. It assumes a sense of history and attributes sanctity to the strand of continuity between the past, the present and the future. It implies a faith in the value of evolutionary rather than revolutionary transformations, and a sense of responsibility towards orderly change.

Auchitya is not the voice of status-quoism as much as it is of sanity. In its widest sense, *auchitya* is the yardstick by which oriental societies judge the conduct of their leaders in all fields of human endeavour, including the cultural. It is in this sense that many Hindustani instrumentalists, including some of the most successful ones, might be answerable for the results of their innovative zeal.

2.3

THE JUGALBANDĪ RACKET

NOT a season passes, nowadays, without the announcement of a "first time ever" *jugalbandī* concert between one big-name musician and another. Most of these turn out also to be the "last time ever" events involving the pair. The conclusion is obvious: Audiences are seduced by the promise, and cheated by the product. This does not appear to discourage either big-name musicians or their concert organizers. They seem surprisingly eager to risk their credibility repeatedly for the rewards of a one-night stand. For the organizers of such events, as well as audiences lured by them, a little background could be useful.

A duet, as a presentation format, is fundamentally inconsistent with the meditative-contemplative character of Hindustani music. Being a predominantly improvised form, it can assume only one musician. Any accompaniment, whether drone, melodic or rhythmic, must function under his/her control.

In contrast, Carnatic music can support the duet format on a larger scale, allow a larger orchestra, and also permit a freer interaction amongst the members of the ensemble. The difference arises from the role of the pre-composed element in the music. In contemporary Hindustani music, the pre-composed element has only a marginal role. Because of this, a soloist with a skeletal ensemble is the norm; a pair of collaborating performers is a rarity; and a successful and durable duo is a phenomenon.

Despite the hurdles, a number of extraordinary duet performers have, in recent years, trained our ears to the duet as an engaging presentation format. A quick survey reveals some patterns. A more authoritative and comprehensive survey is undoubtedly possible, but considering the burden of evidence, it is unlikely that it would reveal radically different patterns.

Jugalbandī Patterns

In all, sixteen significant partnerships, representing different degrees of acknowledged success, are considered. The sample is based on the significance and stature of the musicians involved. The list has some overlaps, with musicians like Ustad Ali Akbar Khan and Ustad Vilayat Khan having partnered several instrumentalists over the years.

The sixteen partnerships fall into four categories:

1. Traditional vocal, i.e. *dhrupad* and *khyāl*;
2. Traditional instrumental, combining instruments of the same basic organological classification (*sitār/sarod* and *sitār/surbahār*);
3. Modern instrumental, combining organologically dissimilar instruments (e.g., *sitār/śehnāī* or *santūr/*flute);
4. Experimental, which fall in none of the above categories and are still at an experimental stage of evolution.

The largest, the most successful, and the most durable category is the traditional vocal, with six duos. Without exception, these pairs are brothers not far removed from each other in age, and trained simultaneously by the same *guru*, in most cases their father.

The traditional instrumental category reports four winning partnerships. They have ties of shared tutelage, but not necessarily of kinship. In this category, one exception is significant — the brief but memorable collaboration of Ustad Vilayat Khan and Ustad Ali Akbar Khan in the 1950s.

The modern instrumental category has three partnerships. Amongst these, Bismillah Khan/Vilayat Khan and Shivkumar Sharma/Hariprasad Chaurasia have been sensational successes, while the Bismillah–V.G. Jog team did not get far. None of these pairs shares a bond of common *guru*s or even *gharānā* affiliations.

The fourth category, with four experimental partnerships, is a mixed bag. This could be a gross understatement of the numbers in this category. And, any number will become obsolete before any listing of this category is published. This category includes duets of the flautist, Hariprasad Chaurasia with Hindustani as well as Carnatic vocalists, and Dr. Balamuralikrishna's Carnatic/Hindustani dialogues. Their success and durability are still a question mark.

The Burden of Evidence

On historical evidence, the success rates of duet pairs can be attributed predominantly to the acoustic compatibility of the music of the duo, and also to stylistic affinity acquired from a common *guru*. Ties of kinship between them could be a conducive, though not critical, success factor. However, if the team-mates are individually of the highest calibre, and admire each other, acoustic compatibility becomes a non-issue, as does kinship or shared tutelage.

The majority of non-starters amongst duet concepts belong to the "experimental" category. On the other hand, the traditional vocal and the traditional instrumental categories continue to produce winning duos in every generation.

The modern instrumental category can perhaps withstand some experimentation because, provided other ingredients of success are in place, the chances of success are reasonable.

Significantly, in many cases, studio recordings of instrumental duets have been more consequential than live concerts. This is understandable. Once the essential ingredients of a satisfactory aural experience are in place, a successful duet is a product of a partial surrender of individual freedom, careful planning, and intuitive anticipation. The studio context is more conducive to such a process than a live concert. Considering the growing sophistication of audio engineering, the studio recording could become an even more powerful vehicle for duet-music in the future, and perhaps even redefine the ingredients of a successful duet product.

Consider this "duet" concept. There exists, in the archives of a recording company, an unpublished duet of Ustad Vilayat Khan on the *sitār* with himself on the *surbahār*. He first recorded the *sitār* track, put on the headphones, and recorded the parallel *surbahār* track. This could be an indication of duet products of the future. Similar "duets" of other leading instrumentalists are now conceivable.

Though the aesthetic acceptability of such electronically engineered duets remains untested in the market, their potential for acoustic compatibility and "teamwork" cannot be matched by the finest duet recorded in real time. However, audio engineering alone does not appear to provide a surefire route to success considering that even impressively coordinated and "processed" duet recordings by second-level musicians have failed. This suggests that, in a duet, Indian audiences are not content merely with a pleasant sound and the absence of confusion: they want to feel the simultaneous and distinctive presence of two great musicians for the cost of one concert in terms of time and money invested.

These factors make duet concerts a demanding proposition in Hindustani music, with only maestros having a decent chance of success. This also makes duet concerts prohibitively expensive and financially risky. Both musicians charge their full fees, sometimes insist on two percussionists, and could even demand a premium for playing a duet. No wonder, then, that the duets format invites so much experimentation, and the experimental events are backed by so much media hype.

Experimentation and Propriety

In itself, experimentation can hardly be questioned — all artistic endeavour thrives on it. Questions of propriety, however, arise when experimentation ignores the fundamental character of the art-form and the motives for pursuing it are apparently more commercial than artistic.

This conservative line of argument can be challenged on the grounds that it considers the durability of a duet concept or partnership the essential validation of its value and success. It might also be contended that dynamic audience profiles and changing audience tastes demand continuous experimentation, unfettered by pre-conceived, and probably invalid, notions about what is "proper", and what is not.

We do, however, need to interpret the evidence of the marketplace. The experimental *jugalbandī* product appears to fail consistently in delivering what it promises. Time and again, it fails to generate a repeat purchase demand on a credible scale. One may therefore ask whether the "experimental" product fulfils a genuine cultural need. If the marketeer is neither fulfilling a genuine consumer need, nor produces evidence of repeat purchase demand, he probably has no business to be in the business.

The market, which has seemingly encouraged the *jugalbandī* racket, is itself giving discouraging signals. Audiences are now disenchanted with the untested duet product and are becoming highly selective about concert attendance. As the competition intensifies between the concert platform and pre-recorded music for a share of the music lover's discretionary time, the experimental *jugalbandī* concert must inevitably lose out even faster to the superiority of concert alternatives, and to pre-recorded *jugalbandī*s. The writing is on the wall for the new breed of *jugalbandī* impresarios who believe that a sucker is born everyday.

2.4

TIHĀĪS . . . AND THE RAPE OF MELODY

IN recent years, the melodic *tihāī*, a triplet melodic device, has emerged as a significant musical expression, especially in instrumental music. As a melodic expression of rhythmic intent, it belongs to the same category as puns in literature. The pun is a form of humour, and has its own aesthetics. Increasingly, however, the melodic *tihāī* is either being used excessively, clumsily and mechanically, or is being deployed as a piece of titillation and entertainment.

Fortunately, the aesthetic deployment of the melodic *tihāī* is still alive in circulation to enable us to document its musical meaning and distinguish between different levels of musicianship.

A melodic *tihāī* takes shape when a melodic statement is rendered thrice in a row in such a manner as to convert the resulting pattern into a rhythmic statement. The melodic *tihāī* was probably inspired by the rhythmic *tihāī* form in percussion. Percussion itself is believed, by some, to have developed the *tihāī* in response to the needs of accompaniment to Kathaka dance.

An expanded form of the *tihāī* is the *chakradār*, which consists of melodic statements in multiples of three, with two or more *tihāī*s dovetailed into each other. There are several dovetailing patterns in vogue, the most common being the same *tihāī*, rendered thrice.

Interestingly, some orthodox *gharānā*s of music frown upon the *tihāī* and *chakradār* as melodic expressions. One of the objections is that the *tihāī* form belongs to the territory of dance, an "inferior" art-form. Others regard it as a childish display of arithmetical prowess, which, in their opinion, represents a mediocre level of musicianship. Though some of these reservations ring true even in the context of present-day instrumental music, we need to acknowledge that these are prejudices carried over from an era dominated by vocal music, especially the poetry-dominated vocal music of the *dhrupad* era. Where the poetic form is held sacred, one can plausibly regard the rhythmic use of melody as an intrusion upon the aesthetics of melody as well as poetry. This might, incidentally, explain why the melodic *tihāī* does not feature significantly in Carnatic music, which is dominated by pre-composed *kr̥ti*s.

In contemporary Hindustani music, the modern *khyāl* genre does not accord the same sanctity to the communication of literary meaning as the mediaeval *dhrupad* did, and Carnatic music still does. Moreover, the *sitār*, *santūr*, and the *sarod* dominate the contemporary Hindustani environment. These instruments have a built-in rhythmic element in their music because of the need for plucking or striking of the strings for sound activation. The melodic *tihāī* is predominantly and legitimately their territory. The dominance of these instruments of percussive-melodic tendency is now a reality. We must, therefore, accept the triplet melodic-rhythmic form as an integral part of contemporary music, and appreciate its use as a musical device.

The Logic of Tihāīs

In all ancient civilizations, great sanctity is attached to the number "Three". Hindu mythology treats the number as representing *trimūrti*, the holy trinity of Brahmā, Viṣṇu and Maheśa, respectively the Creator, Preserver, and the Destroyer of the Universe. Likewise, the Judaic–Christian tradition pays its obeisance to the Father, Son, and the Holy Ghost. But, for listeners of Hindustani music, it is unnecessary to get so esoteric about the *tihāī*.

According to musicologist Ashok Ranade (via a private interview with the author), the number of times a melodic line is repeated in a *tihāī* has a very specific significance. There is an aesthetic relevance to three, which cannot be replaced by two, or four, or eight or ten. The appeal of the *tihāī* (triplet) lies in its ability to create and release aesthetic tension within a short span of time, and thereby function as an interesting punctuation.

The first time any melodic statement is rendered, it merges with the melodic landscape. On the first repetition (second iteration), it evokes bewilderment. On the second repetition (third iteration), however, it reveals its intent by fulfilling its rhythmic function, and thus releases the aesthetic tension. From this logic, one can appreciate that if a *tihāī* culminates with any number of iterations, other than three, it performs no aesthetic function at all.

The melodic *tihāī* probably originated as a convenience. As Hindustani music emerged from its pre-composed origins to evolve as an improvisation-dominant art-form, such a device became necessary. Musicians often found themselves completing a round of improvisations a few beats before they could rejoin the pre-composed *bandiś*. In their search for an appropriate melodic device for filling this gap, they drew upon the resources of the percussion idiom. Over time, this joinery device acquired a sophistication of its own. And, along with sophistication came an attention-enhancing character appropriate for its place in the logic of *rāga*-presentation.

The propriety of its attention-enhancing character arises from its placement at the transition from one kind of progression/logic to another. The *tihāī* is used when the music is making a transition from the linear or unfettered logic of the improvisations to the cyclical framework of the *bandiś*.

Placement, Function and Aesthetics

As a piece of joinery, the *tihāī* is encountered in two placements: one, as a replacement for the *mukhḍā*, and the other, as a replacement for the *āmad*. The *mukhḍā* is the opening phrase of the *bandiś* which culminates at the *sama*. The *āmad* is the phrase which precedes the *mukhḍā*.

The *mukhḍā tihāī* can start from any beat of the rhythmic cycle but must, by definition, end on the *sama*. In its melodic structure, it will usually — though not always — end on the *svar* on which the *sama* of the composition's pre-composed *mukhḍā* falls. Only by fulfilling these requirements can it logically be followed by the pre-composed follow-through of the *mukhḍā* of the *bandiś*. *Chakradār*s are most frequently used in the same manner as *mukhḍā tihāī*s, although their use in *āmad* placement is not ruled out.

The *āmad tihāī* can, likewise, start on any beat of the cycle, but must, by definition, end on the beat before the commencement of the *mukhḍā*, and generally on a *svar*, from where a smooth transition to the pre-composed *mukhḍā* of the composition is possible.

There also exists a third *tihāī* placement, the *baḍhat tihāī* (the progressive *tihāī*), mainly found embedded in *behlava* improvisations in instrumental music. Rhythmically, this *tihāī* is structured like a *mukhḍā tihāī*, but does not link the improvisations to the composition. Instead, it is followed by further improvisations. Thus, the function of the *baḍhat tihāī* is merely to link a free-flowing improvisation with the rhythmic cycle, and not with the melodic-rhythmic frame of the composition. This *tihāī* is generally used when the musician takes up a prolonged improvisation, covering several rounds of the rhythmic cycle. Appropriately for its role and placement, the *baḍhat tihāī* is generally short, and melodically and rhythmically un-dramatic.

The placement of a *tihāī* determines its melodic–rhythmic structure, and its intrusiveness. Obviously, the *mukhḍā tihāī*, which replaces the single most important melodic phrase of the composition, and arrives at the *sama*, tends to be the most intrusive. By the same logic, the *āmad tihāī* is less intrusive than the *mukhḍā tihāī*, and the *baḍhat tihāī* is the least intrusive.

The *tihāī* appears to have no fixed rules for structuring. Several *gharānā*s have an inventory of pre-composed rhythmic *tihāī* patterns, which they adapt melodically to different *rāga*s and mathematically to different *tāl*s. The pre-composed *tihāī*, however, can fail to make the desired impact if handled only mathematically, without due consideration to the overall tenor of the presentation, and the melodic–rhythmic structure of the improvisations into which they are dovetailed.

The Aesthetic and the Grotesque

In the music of the great masters, we see the *tihāī* in its intended form — as a masterpiece of spontaneous melodic–rhythmic improvisation. In recent times, the most brilliant use of the *tihāī* is attributed to Ustad Ali Akbar Khan and Ustad Vilayat Khan. Elderly connoisseurs go into raptures recalling the *tihāī*s they have heard from these luminaries in the 1960s and early 1970s, their peak performing years.

Every one of their *tihāī*s was unique and spontaneous. Very often, even the most astute audiences failed to notice the appearance of *tihāī*s in their performances until the triplet formations were well into the third iteration — it was almost as if their *tihāīs* took shape in their minds unbeknownst even to themselves. Their culmination seemed as much of a surprise and a delight to the *ustāds* themselves as it was to the audiences. So intuitive, and formidable, was the command they displayed over melody and rhythm that, they could pick up any phrase from any *rāga* on any beat of the rhythmic cycle, and construct from it a *tihāī* or *chakradār* of unfailing rhythmic accuracy.

Recently, the present author had occasion to review a recording by a young sitārist which had a 14 minute presentation of a slow-tempo *bandiś* with 18 *tihāīs*, one every 45 seconds. The *tihāīs* had replaced the improvisations as the content of the music. Arithmetic had replaced music. And, such instances abound. Today, one sees a real danger that the appropriate and elegant use of the melodic *tihāī* or *chakradār* will depart from Hindustani music along with some of our living legends. This is a disturbing prospect.

It is fair to ask why we should concern ourselves so much with the *tihāī* form, which constitutes such a small part of a *rāga* presentation. Such a query will amount to asking why careful attention should be paid to the joinery in a piece of furniture. And, the answer is obvious. Functionally, it is the joinery that holds the piece together, and makes it stable. Aesthetically, if so designed and crafted, the joinery can also make it more beautiful.

Your carpenter will tell you that, in a piece of furniture, the joinery should ideally be invisible. An avant-garde designer might convert the joinery into a major design feature. But, neither your friendly neighbourhood carpenter, nor the award-winning designer, will allow the joinery to replace the substance of the artefact, or become dysfunctional.

The grotesque has a place in art. But, when art becomes grotesque, it gets derailed from its elevating ideals.

PART III

The World of Rāgas

3.1

THE RĀGA-NESS OF RĀGAS

EVEN a casual listener of Hindustani music is aware that the word *rāga* is used to describe the melodic facet of a piece of music. He also knows that a *rāga* is not a pre-composed melody. The same *rāga*, performed by different musicians, or by the same musician on different occasions, can sound entirely different while yet retaining a strong basis in familiarity. He also knows that there are hundreds, perhaps thousands, of *rāga*s in circulation, and that experienced listeners can distinguish one *rāga* from others. From this, most listeners can infer that a *rāga* is, broadly, a melodic structure, tight enough to remain distinct and identifiable, and yet loose enough to form the basis for considerable improvisational freedom.

This inference is not wrong. But, it jumps the first step in understanding the notion of a *rāga* — the word *rāga* itself. The word *rāga* does not have a musical or melodic meaning at all; it has only an emotional meaning. In Sanskrit, and in most Sanskrit-based Indian languages, the word *rāga* is normally encountered as a suffix: *anu-rāga* (attraction/affinity) or *vai-rāgya* (indifference/apathy/detachment). The meaning of the suffix becomes clearer by tracing the root of the noun *rāga* to the verb *rañjan*, to colour, or to tinge. When we colour, or tinge, something, we contribute to it a subjective element, which warrants a subjective response. In behaviourist terminology, therefore, the notion of the *rāga* deals with the totality of the communication process — generation of the stimulus as well as the elicitation of the response. In common usage, the word has come to describe a melodic structure, the stimulus, because the music world has accepted a correspondence between the stimulus and the response, and feels comfortable in using the word *rāga* to describe the former.

This leads to the proposition that *rāga*, as commonly understood, is a melodic representation of an emotional statement, and a vehicle for its communication. But, since music is capable of communicating a whole range of human emotions, we must reckon with a qualitative aspect of the emotional response that each melodic structure is associated with. The notion of a *rāga* is, therefore, inseparably linked with the concept of *rasa*, crudely translated as "the essence". The Indian aesthetic tradition bases its understanding of this aspect on the eight-way *rasa* classification of Bharata in the treatise on the performing arts (*Nāṭyaśāstra*: 200 BCE–CE 200). Different *rāga*s are associated with different categories of emotional states based on the accumulated experience of Indian society. These associations have yet to be either validated or rejected — even in a culture-specific context — by the application of modern psychometric tools. (For a discussion on *rasa*, see Chapter 3.5.)

The *rasa* issue is a little more complex than it appears at first. A *rāga* can be pregnant with more than one *rasa*; one of them can be dominant, while others are subordinate to it. Alternatively, one of the several possibilities may be more popular today, while others may have been more widely pursued in the past, or occupy the attention of the music community in the future. Another perspective on the same issue is that a *rāga* expresses different *rasa*s at different tempi, different levels of melodic density, and in the different regions of the melodic canvas. To this extent, a musician has a choice —

whether made consciously or otherwise — in terms of which of the *rasa*s should dominate his presentation, and this choice influences the manner in which he interprets or presents the *rāga*.

Even if you regard them as fanciful or arbitrary, these psycho-acoustic associations remain the basis on which the Hindustani musician undertakes his music-making endeavours. He assumes the *rasa*s of the *rāga* to be inherent or implicit in the melodic structure, determines which of them should dominate his rendition, designs every facet of the presentation accordingly, and "works himself" into the appropriate emotional state by auto-suggestion. The auto-suggestive process is aided by a host of related associations that *rāga*s have come to acquire in the Hindustani tradition. These include mythological, historical and environmental (time of the day, seasons, etc.) associations, which enable a *rāga* to be visualized, personified, and occasionally, even deified as an object of contemplation. To this extent, the *rāga–rasa* relationship is germane to our understanding of the notion of a *rāga*.

This leads to the proposition that a *rāga* is the melodic stimulus, believed to have a high probability of communicating a particular emotional idea to audiences. And, it is, of course, a melodic structure, tight enough to remain distinct and identifiable, and yet loose enough to form the basis for considerable improvisational freedom. But, why does Indian tradition require *rāga*s, when the art-music traditions of other mature civilizations have produced great music even without such a device?

The only answer to this question is that it is a choice the Indian musical culture has made. The phenomenon of the *rāga* reflects the special genius of Indian society for balancing continuity with change, conformity with individuality, and discipline with creativity. When manifested in a specific artistic expression, such as a music performance, this genius ensures that the aesthetic experience enjoys the benefits of familiarity along with novelty. But, accepting that the cultural process is an open-ended historical process with no pre-determined destination, the tradition accepts that, in time, everything changes. Each generation of musicians and audiences is free to choose the parameters of continuity / discipline / conformity / familiarity, and impose on them their own parameters of change / creativity / individuality / novelty. *Rāga*s have thus evolved as ever-growing and ever-changing repositories of aesthetically coherent melodic ideas. Since the advent of recording technology, *rāga*s have become even richer and more easily accessible reservoirs of aesthetically compatible melodic ideas, without losing their propensity for reflecting changing aesthetic values.

*Rāga*s can, and do, change even over time. For instance, only a couple of centuries ago, the scale that we recognize as Kāfī today, was called Bhairavī. When, why, and how the old Bhairavī dropped its *śuddha* (natural) *Re* (2nd) and *Dh* (6th) in favour of the *komal* (flat) *svar*s (tones), to acquire an entirely different melodic personality, is a subject for conjecture. And, Bhairavī's transformation, as everyone knows, continues unabated even in our times. The Bhairavī transition is rather gradual compared to that of many other *rāga*s, which may have changed substantially, over a much shorter period of time.

This brings us to the proposition that, for every generation of musicians and audiences, each *rāga* is defined by a set of features / attributes, which constitute its current "grammar" — features that make the *rāga* identifiable, and distinct from other *rāga*s. Considering that Hindustani music grants the musician the simultaneous roles of a performer and a composer, and every performer cannot be a great composer, the grammar of the *rāga* protects the performance against aesthetic incoherence, while also shielding audiences against possible bewilderment.

These rules of grammar have assumed greater importance as Hindustani music has moved towards presentation formats providing progressively greater improvisational freedom to the performing musician.

The present writer's understanding of these rules draws on three sources — authoritative modern and contemporary texts, the *guru*s who have taught him music, and his own analysis of over a hundred *rāga*s recorded by over fifty prominent musicians. For explaining *rāga* grammar, the present writer has found it efficient to segment the rules into two categories — melodic grammar, and aesthetic grammar. By melodic grammar is meant the selection, sequencing, and relative importance of *svar*s in a *rāga*, while aesthetic grammar refers to aspects of shaping a distinctive aural and emotional experience in performance. Aesthetic grammar may be considered prescriptive more than mandatory.

Admittedly, this distinction is unacceptable to the conceptual framework of linguistics because, if anything is called grammar, it can only be mandatory, and anything that is discretionary does not qualify as grammar. In the conceptual framework of musicology, too, the distinction is probably debatable because both facets of *rāga* grammar have aesthetic implications, and classifying only one of them as "aesthetic" is indefensible.

However, for those who are not performing Hindustani musicians, the distinction appears to aid comprehension for two reasons. First, a *rāga* can remain identifiable and distinct even by adherence only to the melodic grammar, while ignoring its aesthetic grammar. Second, aesthetic grammar is more susceptible to different levels of adherence, and different interpretations, by different members of the same generation of musicians, and is more likely to change over a period of time than melodic grammar. Aesthetic grammar may therefore be considered a facet of usage — a means of sharpening or fine-tuning the aesthetic intent of melodic grammar — and thus fall on the borderline between grammar and literature.

The Melodic Grammar of Rāgas

Melodic grammar begins with the permissible *svar*s of a *rāga*. The vast majority of *rāga*s utilize a minimum of five *svar*s. The few *rāga*s, which use four *svar*s, are performed only rarely — obviously due to their limited melodic potential. On this basis, *rāga*s are classified into *chatusvar* (quadratonic): *auḍav* (pentatonic), *ṣāḍav* (hexatonic), and *sampūrṇa* (heptatonic). *Rāga*s which use a different number of *svar*s in the ascent and the descent are described by a hyphenated description such as *auḍav-sampūrṇa* or *ṣāḍav-sampūrṇa*.

In this classification, Indian theory does not habitually double-count the *komal* (flat) and *tīvra* (sharp) *śruti*s (micro-*svar*s) of the same *svar* when both are used. For communicating this feature to readers cultivated in the Western traditions, I have found it useful to use terms like "hyper-hexatonic" or "hyper-heptatonic" for such *rāga*s.

Although the *svar*s permitted in a *rāga* constitute the basis of its melodic grammar, and are therefore mandatory, they are subject to an occasional influence of aesthetic grammar. This dimension arises from the practice, in some *rāgas*, of non-standard intonation, deploying pitches (relative to the fundamental/scale-base) other than the twelve standard pitches as defined by the Hindustani scale. In most cases, the microtonal values of these intonations would be a subset of the larger universe of twenty-two micro-*svar*s accepted in Carnatic music, though they may not be intoned quite the way the Carnatic tradition intones them.

Some musicians, however, claim that their idea of "non-standard" intonation goes beyond the generally accepted twenty-two *svar*s of Carnatic music. Many of these prescriptions are based on principles of acoustic correspondence between *svar*s even if musicians advocating the practice cannot always articulate them. But, some of them might well be purely aesthetic. In Rāga Pūriyā, for instance, some *gharānā*s (stylistic lineages) prescribe the intonation of *komal Re* (2nd) in the microtonal region below the standard frequency of *komal Re*. In a similar deviation, the *komal Ni* of Rāga Aḍāṇā is prescribed at a pitch between the standard *komal* and *śuddha Ni* (7th) frequencies. Interestingly, however, there are also *rāga*s like Śrī, where some musicians and even authorities recommend a suppressed frequency of *komal Re*, while others prescribe an enhanced frequency.

Such instances abound in Hindustani music. Non-standard intonation of *svar*s, though not rendered in notation, is not a figment of imagination. It is a very explicit part of the grammar of some *rāga*s. It is documented in several texts on *rāga*-grammar, and perpetuated by the personalized system of aesthetic indoctrination prevalent in Hindustani music. Its advocates also practise it with explicit intent. However, it is unclear whether this feature of *rāga*-ness, prescribed selectively, should be classified as melodic grammar, which is mandatory, or aesthetic grammar, which is prescriptive. Only a substantial survey of performances of relevant *rāga*s, using pitch measurement equipment, can resolve this issue.

The second dimension of melodic grammar of a *rāga* is its scale, consisting of the *āroha* (ascent) and the *avaroha* (descent). Although a simple sequential listing of the permissible *svar*s in ascending and descending order is often encountered, it is misleading because it fails to account for the sequence in which the *rāga* permits their deployment. On these grounds, there exists a strong and valid opposition to the very notion of *āroha–avaroha* representation of a *rāga*'s melodic personality. This objection is particularly potent because the same scale can deliver a multiplicity of *rāgas*, as in the case of Mārwā, Pūriyā, and Sohinī. It seems legitimate, therefore, to accept a *rāga's chalan* (skeletal phraseology) as a superior alternative. However, as an acceptable compromise between the two views, we also sometimes encounter grammatical documentation with a scale adjusted for the permitted sequencing of *svars*.

The *chalan* is a set of phrases, generally arranged in ascending and descending formation. Most *rāgas* can be adequately represented by a *chalan* of eight or fewer phrases. This device is indeed superior to the simple, sequential, scale because it provides the essential building blocks of the melody. It always includes the *pakaṛ* (signature/catch phrase), which identifies the *rāga* beyond reasonable doubt. Collectively, the *chalan* phrases represent the identifiable and distinctive melodic personality of the *rāga*. They achieve this status by also incorporating several elements fundamental to defining the *rāga's* melodic grammar.

The first such element is the sequence in which the permissible *svars* can be used for phrasing. The phrasing structure reflects the permissible *alpatva/bahutva* (abbreviated/elongated intonation) of the *svars* within a phrase and also the manner of their treatment or intonation. The second important element is the identification of the *nyāsa svars* of the *rāga* — *svars* permitted for use as terminal or resting points in the phrasing. The *nyāsa svars* can often be critical to the differentiation between *rāgas* using an identical set of *svars*. The distinctive aural experience of Mārwā, for instance, is considered safe with only two permissible resting/terminal points: *Dh* (6th) and *Re* (2nd). Any other terminal point in phrasing can cast an unintended shadow of either Pūriyā or Sohinī on the *rāga*.

Two of the *nyāsa svars* — though not always the most frequently used, and the second most frequently used — are the *vādī* (primary dominant) and the *saṁvādī* (secondary dominant) *svar*s of the *rāga* respectively. The *vādī* and the *saṁvādī* are generally located in different halves of the scale. The *vādī–saṁvādī* notions, memorized unquestioningly by students of music theory, are often a musicologist's nightmare. Far too often for comfort, the present writer has found even the most learned and authoritative of modern commentators on *rāga* grammar circumspect and tentative about the identity of the *vādī–saṁvādī svar*s of *rāga*s. In addition, authorities often differ on this subject. In many cases, authorities have identified *nyāsa svar*s, but shied away from naming either the *vādī* or *saṁvādī svar*s, sometimes both.

Approaching this problem from an empirical and analytical perspective is not always more helpful. The present author's attempt at verifying the melodic personality of the popular and seemingly non-controversial *rāga*, Ahīr Bhairav, was an eye-opener. He surveyed eight recordings of the *rāga* by the biggest names in contemporary Hindustani music. He found that only four of the eight maestros treated *Mā* (4th), the documented *vādī svar* of the *rāga*, as even a *nyāsa svar*. Of these, only two made a special effort to give it the status of a probable *vādī*. Only one musician had squarely, and explicitly, treated *Mā* as the *vādī* of the *rāga*.

This need not mean that the texts are wrong or confused. Nor need it imply that leading musicians perform the *rāga* incorrectly. It could merely suggest that the dialogue between theory and practice required of a vibrant art-music tradition has ceased to function, and that the *vādī–saṁvādī* notions may now require fresh thinking, probably along with several other notions of *rāga* grammar. If the *vādī* and the *saṁvādī* are indeterminate for some *rāga*s, it might be necessary to accept this reality. If this is found to occur on a large scale, we might even shift this facet of *rāga*-ness out of mandatory/melodic grammar, treating it as a facet of prescriptive/aesthetic grammar. The intuitive and conceptual appeal of the *vādī–saṁvādī* notions is, however, so strong, that music theory will probably persist with their mandatory status, and performance will continue to handle music as it has always done.

Most modern authorities on *rāga*s have documented the above aspects of *rāga*-grammar. Selectively, rather than systematically, some texts have ventured beyond them into what the present writer has described as the "aesthetic grammar".

The Aesthetic Grammar of Rāgas

The aesthetic grammar of a *rāga* is related partially to its melodic grammar, and partially to the *rasa* (emotional content) associated with the *rāga*. This is why the present writer has described it as lying on the borderline between grammar and literature.

The basic concept in aesthetic grammar is the location of the *rāga*'s centre of gravity or its epicentre. This is normally defined as a tetrachord (a set of four *svar*s), which ought to dominate the aural experience of the *rāga*. Unlike Western music, which divides the octave into two tetrachords, with the scale split into equal and mutually exclusive halves, the Hindustani system defines the *rāga*'s centre of gravity assuming three overlapping tetrachords — the *pūrvāṅga* (lower tetrachord: *Sā-Re-Gā-Mā*), the *madhyāṅga* (middle tetrachord: *Gā-Mā-Pā-Dh*), and the *uttarāṅga* (upper tetrachord: *Pā-Dh-Ni-Sā*).

The region defining a *rāga*'s centre of gravity is tangentially related to the *vādī svar* of the *rāga*. It is important to define such an epicentre as a region, in addition to its focal point (*vādī*), in order to avert the risk of its dilution by a disproportionate amount of improvisational energy being invested outside this region. If, for instance, a musician tarries substantially in the lower tetrachord in Sohinī, he exposes the *rāga* to a risk of confusion with Mārwā or Pūriyā. This risk remains significant even if his phraseology adheres strictly to Sohinī because, these *rāga*s are intended to act differently upon the neuro-acoustic triggers in the human mind.

Even for *rāga*s, which do not have so fragile a *rāga*-ness, the systematic and purposive crafting of a melodic centre of gravity is important. Marwā, for instance, is performed equally effectively with its centre of gravity in the *uttarāṅga* of the lower octave, and the *uttarāṅga* of the middle octave. But, a choice needs to be made. Likewise, Kedār is equally emotive with its epicentre in the *madhyāṅga* and the *uttarāṅga*. But, again, a choice is necessary to make. Making the choice is important because it often distinguishes a piece of effectively rendered music from barely competent music. It is interesting to observe how, on a bad day, unfocused or indecisive handling of a *rāga*'s primary region of the melodic canvas has marred the performances of even the greatest musicians.

A broader version of the epicentre/centre of gravity notion is the notional scale-base. Fundamentally, all *rāga*s make melodic sense only in relation to the scale-base at the *madhya saptak* (middle octave) *Sā* and a scale of *Sā* to *Sā*. Yet, some *rāga*s are most effectively rendered assuming a different scale base. The scale-base of *gara*, for instance, is explicitly defined as the lower-octave *Pā*. Mārwā, Pūriyā, and Sohinī are also good, though less dramatic, examples. The contemporary Mārwā is most effectively performed assuming the scale-base at the lower-octave *Dh* (scale: *Dh* to *Dh*). It is differentiated from Pūriyā with the scale-base at the lower-octave *Ni* (scale: *Ni* to *Ni*), and Sohinī with its scale-base at the middle-octave *Gā* (scale: *Gā* to *Gā*).

In this context, the present writer recalls a remarkable

recording of Sohinī by Shivkumar Sharma. Throughout the performance, he totally avoids melodic execution in the region below the middle-octave *Gā*, using the scale-base at *Sā* merely to provide the reference point of tonality for the *rāga* to make melodic sense. This is, of course, a rare instance of fastidiously sound music. But, it demonstrates the logic of a notional scale-base as an important operating principle for the aesthetic integrity of some *rāgas*.

Related to these prescriptions are biases in favour of specified melodic directions. Certain *rāga*s are described as *āroha-pradhān* (ascent-dominated) while others are described as *avaroha-pradhān* (descent-dominated). Learned texts frequently refer to the relationship between the melodic centre of gravity of a *rāga* and its directional bias. Bhatkhande, for instance, virtually equates *rāga*s with their epicentre in the *uttarāṅga* with those that are descent-dominant. An empirical survey of contemporary practice may not support so sweeping a generalization. But, there is ample justification for regarding the directional dominance of melodic movements as an independent, and additional, discriminator between *rāga*s.

The operation of this discriminator can be seen clearly, once again, in the treatment of Mārwā, Pūriyā, and Sohinī by great musicians. I have had an occasion to analyse a recording by Vilayat Khan featuring the three *rāga*s. On this recording, the maestro has demonstrated, in quantifiable terms, the creation of the desired directional biases by the use of ascents structured as strings of descending phrases, and descents structured as strings of ascending phrases.

This consecutive rendition of Mārwā, Pūriyā, and Sohinī by Vilayat Khan is significant also for its illustration of the other two aspects of aesthetic grammar discussed here. It demonstrates the use of different notional scale-bases, and different melodic centres of gravity/epicentres as differentiators between *rāgas* using the same set of permissible *svars*. The Vilayat Khan rendering suggests that the crafting of the desired aural image by the deployment of these devices is probabilistic in nature. No *rāga*-presentation can entirely forego any region of the melodic canvas, or entirely ignore the universal scale-base at *Sā*, or entirely neglect ascending or descending melodic phrasing. But, the great musician, because of the clarity of his musical vision, engineers an unequivocal aural image of the *rāga* in the listener's mind through a multi-dimensional reinforcement of the melodic idea which best expresses the emotional statement he wishes to make.

This brings us back to where we started — that a *rāga* is a melodic representation of an emotional idea; and a melodic vehicle for its communication. An understanding of its *rāga*-ness helps the musician to create a stimulus, which has a high probability of eliciting the desired emotional response from audiences. Admittedly, great music, like great literature, tends to transcend grammar, often liberating it from itself. When this happens, grammar gets re-written. But, for the less epochal moments in music, the grammar — as understood in each era — remains the stepping stone to literature.

Postscript

Since the writing of this chapter over a decade ago, my notion of *rāga*-ness has assimilated a few ideas, which have, by now, achieved sufficient clarity to be shared. I may introduce them briefly here. They are discussed in some detail in Chapters 3.5 and 3.6.

By defining the *rāga* as "a melodic representation of an emotional idea", we have stepped into the territory of linguistics. In this territory, the *rāga* can be understood as a specialist vehicle for communicating emotional ideas. There is a sizeable and influential segment of scholarly opinion which does not accept music as a language. I have argued that reservations on this subject are only partially valid with respect to *rāga*-based music, and that the concepts of linguistics can be immensely useful for understanding the manner in which the *rāga* functions as a cultural force, and as a driver of individual performances.

A conceptual framework conceived to handle the uniqueness of the *rāga* phenomenon will have to acknowledge three levels of *rāga*-ness. At the highest level, there is the "formless form" of a *rāga*, an unlimited source of aesthetically compatible melodic ideas. At the intermediate level, there is the "consensual form" of the *rāga*, incorporating all the known facets of its melodic personality, aggregated from all its performances in the past and present. At the immediate level, there is the "manifest form", which confronts the audience. The manifest form is shaped by the manner in which the performing musician draws upon the melodic–aesthetic resources of the formless form and the consensual form, and deploys them in performance. In shaping the manifest form, the formless form and the consensual form of the *rāga* operate through the agency of the genre in which the *rāga* is performed. An important part in this process is played by the *bandiś* (the pre-composed element) which hosts the *rāga* performance.

The three levels represent the same emotional idea, but are distinguished by their respective specificity. The manifest/ communicable form, being the most specific, inevitably shapes and reshapes the consensual and the formless, as much as it is itself governed by them.

Whether in the context of a specific performance, or as a cultural force, the *rāga* works through the notion of *rasa*, the supreme concept in Indian aesthetics, and a major concept in Indian philosophy. *Rasa* defines the primary aim of artistic activity, and links man's artistic endeavours and involvements to his emotional and spiritual life. Understanding these linkages is important in order to appreciate their relevance — or otherwise — to art music as a contemporary profession, and to the totality of the cultural process.

3.2

RĀGAS : RIGHT AND WRONG

MUSICIANS of stature are often found criticizing other musicians for incorrect renderings of *rāga*s. Likewise, critics and scholars frequently pull up musicians for performing a *rāga* improperly. Even the discerning listener is often bewildered by the crossfire. Every objection to a particular treatment of a *rāga* cannot be valid; nor can every objection be invalid. Some efforts at developing a rational viewpoint on the subject of *rāga* authenticity are, therefore, in order.

As a backdrop to this issue, we must appreciate the socio-economic context in which music practice evolved up to the nineteenth century. The major seats of musicianship were the courts of the feudal aristocracy, which patronized great musicians. These principalities were isolated from each other by primitive modes of transportation, and communication. This was an era without radio, without telephony, and without mass-distributed pre-recorded music. Very few musicians knew precisely what their neighbours, just a couple of hundred miles away, were singing.

Considering these features of the nineteenth-century environment, it is the similarities in the treatment of *rāga*s between different *gharānā*s and musicians that are more surprising than the dissimilarities between them. Although all *gharānā*s sang music derived from the same musical tradition, most musicians of that era had imbibed it through personalized oral transmission. The documentation of the tradition was not accessible to a majority of these musicians, partly because much of it was in an archaic language, and partly because scholarship was scarce amongst professional musicians.

The vast area of similarity in the presentation of music was evidently based on the very strong framework that Hindustani music inherited in the twentieth century. This framework probably belonged to *dhrupad*, or its predecessors, with their strong bias in favour of the pre-composed element. The differences probably began to surface as the post-*dhrupad* genres eclipsed the pre-composed element and expanded the role of improvisation.

The whole issue of grammar and or "right" or "wrong" interpretations of *rāga*s gathered momentum in the late nineteenth/early twentieth century when scholars started documenting the consensus between major musicians on the melodic features of the *rāga*s they heard. Bhatkhande provided, for the first time in recent history, a comprehensive conceptual framework for defining the essentials of *rāga*-ness. This was a priceless contribution, because any art form ensures orderly evolution for itself only by interacting with a parallel body of scholarship.

A rational viewpoint on *rāga* authenticity must, therefore, balance the demands of Hindustani classical music as a performing tradition with the demands of theoretical soundness. Such a perspective becomes easier to develop once we recognize the categories of issues that arise in the debate on *rāga* authenticity.

Nomenclature

Vocalists of the Jaipur–Atrauli Gharānā sing a *rāga* called Khambāvatī, which is identical to Rāgeśrī as understood in all other *gharānās*, and is also at variance with the grammar of Khambāvatī as documented by early twentieth-century authorities. Does this make the Khambāvatī of the Jaipur–Atrauli musicians "wrong"?

If the commonly understood Rāgeśrī and the recognizable or documented Khambāvatī were very similar *rāgas*, it would imply that the Jaipur–Atrauli musicians do not recognize the subtle distinction between the two *rāgas*. Since this happens not to be the case, a sane view would be to judge the Jaipur-Atrauli Khambāvatī on the yardstick of the commonly understood Rāgeśrī, and allow the *gharānā*'s musicians, if they so wish, to call it Khambāvatī. After all, you cannot lynch a musician for giving a different name to a well established and coherently rendered melodic entity!

Consider another similar, though not identical, example. The Chandrakauṅs sung by Agra Gharānā vocalists is very different from the *rāga* that is understood as Chandrakauṅs by other *gharānās*, and audiences in general. It is, in fact, a *rāga* unique to this *gharānā*, and performed only by its musicians. Does the Agra Gharānā's Chandrakauṅs become "wrong" merely because audiences, in general, do not associate it with their notion of Chandrakauṅs?

The same view here is to judge the *rāga* by the basic yardsticks of *rāga*-ness. First, is it distinctive enough from other *rāgas* to warrant independent status as a *rāga*? Second, is it an aesthetically coherent and pleasing melodic entity? If the *rāga* passes these two tests, it deserves to be evaluated by the yardstick of its own grammar, rather than by the grammar of Chandrakauṅs as sung by other *gharānās*.

Rare Rāgas and Their Compounds

Śuddha Chhāyā is the dominant component in the popular compound *rāga*, Chhāyānaṭ. Likewise, Bhīm is the dominant component of the compound *rāga*, Bhīmpalās. Similarly, Rāga Alhaiyā is a component of the popular *rāga*, Alhaiyā Bilāwal. In their original/pure form, Śuddha Chhāyā, Bhīm, and Alhaiyā, and other similar *rāga*s, are performed only rarely because they are almost indistinguishable from their more popular compounds.

The problem does not end here. In some *gharānā*s, many compositions in these *rāga*s are performed in both forms: the pure form and the compound form. Moreover, some compositions in the compound form can be easily mistaken for the pure form, and vice versa. As a result, one may find that Bhīm, or Alhaiyā, or Śuddha Chhāyā performed by one musician may sound different from the same *rāga*s performed by another musician. Alternatively, you could find two different names describing two pieces of music, which you find indistinguishable in terms of their *rāga*-ness!

In such cases, what is the rational view to adopt? This problem really has no solution. The only sensible stance is to ask the musician how his interpretation of what he has performed differs from its pure or compound twin, and accept the explanation as valid if his rendition is consistent with the melodic definition.

Creative Licence

There exists a concert recording of Bihāg by Omkarnath Thakur, in which he has used phrases treating *Re* as a full-bodied *svar*, rather than the subliminal accidental considered proper in the *rāga*. There also exists a recording of Bhīmpalās by Ameer Khan, in which his ascent into the *uttarāṅga* (upper tetrachord) follows the Gawoti pattern rather than the distinctive Bhīmpalās pattern. Are we to conclude from these recordings that these luminaries were not adept at these *rāga*s?

In such cases, the most reasonable response is to recall the tens of times these greats rendered these *rāga*s in perfect consonance with their grammar as commonly accepted. In a specific context, great musicians have a variety of "reasons" for deviating from the familiar, and they are not accountable to us for their exercise of creative licence. If, however, a particular creative licence becomes a habit with a musician, it may, or may not, raise fundamental theoretical issues.

Take the instance of Omkarnath's treatment of the *Re svar* in Bihāg. Let us suppose he habitually treated the *svar* in this idiosyncratic manner. What would be a reasonable view on this?

The yardstick, in this context should be twofold: Does the resultant melodic entity remain well within the recognizable boundaries of the *rāga*? Does the resultant melodic entity steer clear of the risk of confusion with another established *rāga*? As long as these two conditions are met, the apparent transgression should be acceptable either as a creative licence, or an individualistic interpretation adding to the richness of the *rāga*.

It is the acceptance of such passable transgressions by audiences and the community of musicians that contributes to the evolution of *rāga*s, and even the emergence of new ones.

Rāga Evolution

*Rāga*s do change and evolve. And, some of this evolution takes place because great musicians leave a stamp of their own personalities on the *rāga*s they perform. The Rrāga Mārwā, for instance, was performed largely as an *āroha-pradhān* (ascent-dominated) *rāga* with its centre of melodic gravity in the *uttarāṅga* (upper tetrachord) until its rendering by Ameer Khan on a long-playing record. Since then, Mārwā has acquired a strong *pūrvāṅga-pradhān* (lower-tetrachord dominant) melodic identity. On the melodic features of this *rāga*, Ameer Khan would appear to be at variance with early twentieth-century scholars like Bhatkhande. Can we, by this yardstick, pronounce Ameer Khan as being in error?

A more significant case of *rāga* evolution is Rāga Lalit, which, according to Bhatkhande, utilizes the *śuddha Dh svar*. This will come as a surprise to most contemporary listeners because Lalit no longer uses *śuddha Dh*. In fact, a lot of contemporary musicians consider the use of the *śuddha Dh* in Lalit-related phrasing as the signature for Ādi Basant/Śuddha Basant besides, of course, other aspects of *rāga*-grammar.

Consider also Kesarbai Kerkar's two available recordings of Tilak Kāmod. In one of them, she has performed the early twentieth century form of the *rāga* which deploys the *śuddha* (natural) as well as *komal* (flat) *Ni svar*s, while in the second, she performs the new form, with only *śuddha Ni*. Those, who have not been exposed to the old form, will conclude that Kesarbai did not know the distinction between Tilak Kāmod and Deś. Audiences are not expected to be familiar with the evolutionary paths of all *rāga*s over a century or more. But, such instances should alert us to the risks of rushing into judgement with respect to *rāga* authenticity.

Another facet of *rāga* evolution is the tendency amongst musicians to simplify the rendition of *rāga*s by introducing phrases which current grammar does not permit, but are contextually not disruptive of the *rāga*'s melodic personality.

Consider, for instance, the *uttarāṅga* ascent of Kedār. The theoretical position approves of *Mā^-Pā-Sā'*. Over the years, musicians have varied this ascent to include *Mā^-Pā-Dh-Ni-Sā'* as well as *Mā^-Pā-Ni-Sā'*. Taken in isolation, these phrases can be mistaken for phrases of other *rāga*s. However, in the context of a Kedār rendition, with appropriate phrases preceding or succeeding them, they do not create any dissonance amongst listeners.

The rational view here is to accept that *rāgas* are not static melodic entities. Their strength lies precisely in their ability to evolve in response to the creative visions of maestros, and the acceptance of them by changing audience tastes. Theory will, as always, be a couple of steps behind practice. In a performing tradition, theory can document practice, but it cannot expect to dictate it.

Grammatical Prudence

Some *gharānās* permit the use of phrases such as *Re-Pā-gā* and *Pā-Sā-dh* in Darbārī. Although this usage is increasingly rare, the users of these phrases would include musicians who are otherwise considered theoretically sound.

Several objections have been raised against such usage. *Re-Pā-gā* provides a strong suggestion of Malhār, while *Pā-Sā-dh* belongs to Āsāvarī. Because the two phrases are acoustically congruent in first–fourth correspondence, it is also argued that they compete with Darbārī's own congruent set of distinctive phrases: *gā-Mā-Re* and *dh-ni-Pā*, with oscillated treatment of *gā* and *dh*.

Here, the yardstick of distinctiveness comes into sharp focus. These two phrases provide strong suggestions of other, mature *rāgas*. In addition to this, they conflict with a similar, though distinctive pattern fundamental to the melodic character of Darbārī. The resultant melodic entity therefore appears to breach the recognizable boundaries of Darbārī as presently understood.

Let us consider another, though less dramatic, instance of probable imprudence in a seemingly non-controversial *rāga* like Yaman. In recent years, many musicians, including the most respected, have considered it permissible to use *Re* as a *nyāsa svar*, the terminal point of a phrase in this *rāga*. This has been questioned on the grounds that, *Re* being adjacent to *Gā*, such usage dilutes the dominance of the *vādī*, the pivotal *svar* of the *rāga*.

This argument has instant theoretical appeal because the idea of *rāga*-ness cannot be reduced to a mere scale, and every permitted *svar* cannot qualify as a *nyāsa svar*. On closer scrutiny, however, the objection might appear draconian. The treatment of *Re* as a melodic focus, as commonly practised, neither suggests another *rāga*, nor pushes the *rāga* beyond its recognizable boundaries. However, such usage creates the possibility of a grammatical issue. Whether it actually dilutes the prominence of the *vādī svar* will depend a lot more on specific treatment of melody by a musician than on the theoretical position on propriety.

The Bottom Line

Where does this discussion leave us? It must leave us with a great deal of caution, and even diffidence, about sitting in judgement over *rāga* authenticity. But, it does identify a handful of issues, which frequently place a question mark over a musician's interpretation of a *rāga*. The question to consider, then, is: Who applies the yardstick; and, with what motivation?

What novices perform is of no consequence to anyone; and undiscerning listeners do not have the knowledge to apply any yardstick to what they hear. The *rāga* authenticity issue is, therefore, between the leading musicians of each generation, and the corresponding generation of cognoscenti. The cognoscenti use the weapon of *rāga*-grammar to enforce upon their aural experience a comfortable degree of familiarity. The musician of stature, on the other hand, is driven by the urge to liberate literature from grammar and is under no obligation to dish out repackaged doses of the familiar.

If we accept that today's grammar is derived from yesterday's literature, and today's literature will rewrite grammar for tomorrow, the two parties to this issue must always be engaged in a state of debate. The debate, in fact, represents the dialectic that guides our musical tradition along its evolutionary path.

Considering the significance of this process, responsible participants in it need to raise the level of debate above the nuts and bolts of a *rāga*'s melodic identity. They must come to grips with the fundamentals of *rāga*-ness, while accepting that a *rāga* does not exist in isolation, but takes shape in performance, and its boundaries are redrawn — if ever so imperceptibly — by every rendition.

At the fruitful level of debate, the crucial issues are: Is the melodic identity — no matter by what name called — sufficiently distinctive? Does it steer sufficiently clear of the risk of confusion with other well-established melodic entities? Is it consistent in its painting of the melodic canvas? Is it aesthetically coherent? Does it make a discernible emotional statement? Once we raise the debate to such issues, words like "right" and "wrong" will either acquire their appropriate meaning, or become irrelevant.

3.3

RĀGA CHEMISTRY AND BEYOND

CLASSICAL music audiences often encounter *rāgas* in a deliberately modified, rather than pure, form. The transformations are created by systematically pushing the melodic features of familiar *rāgas* beyond their recognizable boundaries. When confronted with the unfamiliarity of these aural images, the listener seeks clues to their musical intent in their nomenclature. The names are not always helpful because naming conventions do not exist. Even when some convention appears to have been followed, the nature of the transformation that the major *rāga* has undergone in order to yield a derivative remains mostly opaque.

Some would frown upon a classification–codification approach in understanding *rāga* transformations on the grounds that it militates against the creative process. On the other hand, the need for audiences to understand and classify the departures from the familiar cannot be wished away. If they are likely to drift towards some metaphoric understanding anyway, they might welcome some help.

In the present writer's efforts at deciphering the melodic intent and content of *rāga* transformations, he has found the rudiments of chemistry useful. The chemical metaphor is not out of place because, while transgressing its recognizable boundaries, a *rāga* is exposed to an interaction with the entire universe of *rāgas*, each with its own melodic identity. A "chemical" reaction takes place between the base-*rāga* and the *rāga*-universe, and the base-*rāga* is transformed. The resultant melodic entity retains some "native" features of the base-*rāga*, while acquiring features "alien" to it. The new melodic entity lends itself to categorization in the language of chemistry on the basis of how the "native" and the "alien" are melodically reflected in the resultant melodic entity.

Rāga transformations appear, broadly, comparable to three types of derivative chemical entities — allotropes, compounds, and emulsions. This list is limited by the totality of the present writer's exposure to music, and by his ignorance of chemistry. As a useful starting point for an analyst of greater competence, let us consider the chemical metaphor through contemporary examples.

The Allotrope

In the mid-1980s, Vilayat Khan recorded a *rāga* called Vilayat Khani Kānhaṛā for HMV in India. In the early 1990s, he rechristened it Enayet Khani Kānhaṛā as a tribute to his father, the legendary Enayet Khan, and recorded it for India Archive Music, New York. Both recordings, considered independently and together, constitute the basis of this description.

This *rāga* is a melodically enhanced version of Darbārī Kānhaṛā. It uses the *śuddha Gā* (3rd) and *Ni* (7th) *svars*, in addition to the *komal gā* and *ni svars* "native" to Darbārī Kānhaṛā. The phraseology of the *rāga* is identical to that of Darbārī Kānhaṛā. Darbārī phrases using the "native" *Gā/Ni svars* alternate with the same phrases using the "alien" *śuddha svars*.

The dominant melodic idea or aural image of the *rāga* remains anchored firmly in Darbārī Kānhaṛā. In its totality, Vilayat Khani Kānhaṛā/Enayet Khani Kānhaṛā is an individualistic, special, or idiosyncratic version of Darbārī

Kānhaṛā; nothing more, nothing less. The closest approximation to this configuration in chemistry is that of an allotrope.

Allotropes are different physical forms of the same element. Coal and diamond are both, for instance, allotropes of carbon. They differ in the way the atoms bond with each other and arrange themselves. In addition to differential physical characteristics, allotropes are also supposed to exhibit different chemical properties. This would be true of Darbārī Kānhaṛā and Enayet Khani Kānhaṛā. In isolated passages, Enayet Khani Kānhaṛā does throw seductive glances at Guñjī-Kānhaṛā and/or Chandra Kānhaṛā. With a slight shift in handling, Enayet Khani Kānhaṛā could easily become a compound of two or three *rāgas*. Vilayat Khan, however, does not allow this to happen.

Before we consider melodic compounds, let us consider the contemporary Bhairavī, whose melodically enhanced form has driven the original (early twentieth century) form, called Śuddha Bhairavī, out of circulation.

Is the modern Bhairavī an allotrope of the Śuddha Bhairavī? This question probably points towards to the evolutionary path of the *rāga*. In the early twentieth century, when Śuddha Bhairavī of *komal Re-Gā-Dh-Ni svars* accepted the *śuddha Re* and *Dh svars* as a melodic enhancement, the modern Bhairavī with a minimum of nine *svars* would have been considered an allotrope of Śuddha Bhairavī. Today, with Bhairavī permitting the use of all twelve *svars*, and the Śuddha Bhairavī almost out of circulation, we do not need to think of the two *rāgas* as allotropes, even though such a description would be conceptually valid. In less than a century, Bhairavī has enlarged is *svar*-material by five *svars*, and we still call it Bhairavī.

As pure speculation, a similar path can plausibly be traced by Darbārī Kānhaṛā, if the Vilayat Khani Kānhaṛā/Enayet Khani Kānhaṛā transformation strikes deep roots in the musical soil, and displaces today's Darbārī Kānhaṛā. We cannot predict whether this will happen, nor can we be sure that it will not. If it happens, the surviving melodic entity might still be called by the same old name — Darbārī Kānhaṛā — even though it will not be Darbārī Kānhaṛā as we know it today.

The point to note here is that the evolution of a *rāga* may start with the emergence of an allotrope, with the allotrope ultimately driving the original out of circulation, but retaining the name of the original. To the extent that grammarians document *rāga*s periodically, the evolutionary path may be traceable. But, in the absence of an effective dialogue between scholarship and musicianship, nomenclatures of melodic entities may often remain at the mercy of musicians responding to the need of audiences for a basis in familiarity.

The Compound

A compound *rāga* comes into being when two *rāga*s are fused together in such a manner as to retain both their melodic personalities in the compound so created. In the compound *rāga*, there is no distinction between "native" and "alien" melodic features. Both are transparently present, though their relative presence in the aural experience may vary from musician to musician, and even from concert to concert for the same musician.

Some musicians and scholars have argued that the purpose of compound *rāga*s is to obliterate the individual identities of the component *rāga*s by merging them into a novel resultant entity. However, this view is not supported either by the practice of compound *rāga*s, or by the conventions pertaining to the fusion of *rāga*s for the purpose of creating compounds.

A compound is a substance formed from two or more elements chemically united in fixed proportions. In Hindustani music, the compounds, answering to this definition, are used for fusing two *rāga*s, and are the most commonly encountered *rāga* transformations.

In theory, the fusion is done by one of the two classical methods. The directional fusion results from the ascent (*āroha*) of one *rāga* being fused with the descent (*avaroha*) of the second *rāga*. The scalar fusion deploys one *rāga* in the lower tetrachord (*pūrvāṅga*) and the other *rāga* in the upper tetrachord (*uttarāṅga*). Theoretically, thus, the "fixed proportions" requirement of the molecular structure in a compound is met.

Amongst the popular compounds, the Kānhaṛā group *rāga*s, other than Darbārī Kānhaṛā (the primary Kānhaṛā), generally correspond to the directionally fused category. Kāfī Kānhaṛā, for instance, is a fusion of the Kāfī ascent with the Darbārī descent (*ni-Pā-gā-Mā-Re-Sā*). Likewise, Chandra Kānhaṛā is generally a fusion of Chandrakauṅs ascent with the Darbārī descent.

The compounds fused at the scalar midpoint belong mainly to the Bahār and Malhār group. This is because Bahār and Malhār are both ascent-oriented and upper tetrachord dominant *rāga*s. They are highly eligible for fusion with *rāga*s whose melodic soul resides in the lower tetrachord, or are descent oriented. Bageśrī-Bahār, Bhairav-Bahār, and Deś-Malhār are examples of this category.

The existence of fusing conventions should not convey the impression that compound *rāga*s, like the *rāga*s in their pure form, have a clearly defined grammar. First, any two compatible *rāga*s can be fused either directionally or at the mid-point of the scale, thus resulting in at least two feasible variants of the same compound. Second, considering that a compound *rāga* is the product of the creative urge to enlarge the melodic potential of one of the two component *rāga*s, musicians differ substantially from each other in the manner in which they treat the fusion.

The conventions pertaining to fusion have other limitations, too. A formalistic approach to the fusion would be inadequate for fusing two *rāga*s, like Aḍāṇā and Bahār (in the compound *rāga*, Aḍāṇā-Bahār), both of which have ascending phrases that constitute their respective signatures, and also have their melodic soul residing in the upper tetrachord. A strict directional fusion of the two would be insufficient for solving the aesthetic problem. The total solution, in such cases, has to allow both the *rāga*s to express their melodic signatures, even though this implies a substantial duplication of *rāga* identities in the upper tetrachord and in ascending motion.

In the real world, therefore, while the classical conventions for the formation of *rāga* compounds serve as important guidelines, the music, as performed, might often treat the phrases of the component *rāga*s as the building blocks of the fusion rather than conform to classical conventions. This brings us to the third type of *rāga* transformation, the emulsion, which explicitly configures phrases rather than scalar regions or directional motions.

The Emulsion

In chemistry, an emulsion is a fine dispersion of minute droplets of one liquid in another in which it is not soluble or miscible. The droplets are so small that they remain suspended indefinitely in the suspension medium, unaffected by gravity. If, however, the force of gravity is greatly increased in a high-speed centrifuge, the suspension can be broken down into its components.

In a *rāga* transformation of the emulsion type, the phrase, rather than the scalar canvas, determines the fusion of component *rāga*s. Typically, the melody is constructed fusing the distinctive phrases of the component *rāga*s as its building blocks. Because of this, the emulsion is clearly, and explicitly, decipherable as a tapestry of phraseologies borrowed from the component *rāgas*.

In rendition, the *rāga* emulsion is the most difficult form of transformation because of the constant *rāga* switching it demands. Because of this, it has emerged as a forte of the Jaipur–Atrauli Gharānā (stylistic lineage). Vocalists trained in this *gharānā* perform all *rāga* combinations in the emulsion format, almost totally shunning the compound form. This special penchant for the difficult and the challenging has made musicians from this *gharānā* the foremost exponents of combinations of three or more *rāgas*, for which the emulsion form is ideal, and unavoidable.

Amongst the most memorable achievements in this category, as performed by Jaipur–Atrauli singers, are Kesarbai Kerkar's renditions of Sampūrṇa Mālkauṅs, a blend of Mālkauṅs, Bāgeśrī and Kāfī, and of Khaṭ, claimed to be a blend of six different *rāgas*, of which the predominant are Deśī, Jaunpurī, and Sūhā Kānhaṛā. Concert recordings of Kesarbai Kerkar's renditions of these *rāgas* have been in grey-market circulation for several years now.

The Jaipur–Atrauli practice of adhering exclusively to the emulsion approach suggests that the conceptual framework of chemistry holds the clue to the various options for the melodic enhancement of the mature *rāgas*.

Chemistry Defines Options

To demonstrate this point, let us consider the ramifications of Sampūrṇa Mālkauṅs as a *rāga* enhancement concept.

Mālkauṅs is a pentatonic (*auḍav*) *rāga*, omitting *Re* (2nd) and *Pā* (5th) *svars*. When its transformation is intended to be a "Sampūrṇa Mālkauṅs", it must, by definition, be enhanced to include the two missing *svars*, *Re* and *Pā*. This enhancement can be effected by any of the three transformations listed here.

An allotrope of Mālkauṅs, which includes the use of *Re* and *Pā*, has been performed by several vocalists and instrumentalists. Their interpretations differ from each other. But the treatment, in all cases, ensures that the resultant melody remains rooted in the Mālkauṅs character, and avoids the risk of even momentary intrusion from other mature *rāgas*.

If a musician wishes to present a heptatonic (*sampūrṇa*) version of Mālkauṅs as a compound, he can perform Kauṅsī-Kānhaṛā, which is most commonly a blend of Mālkauṅs with Darbārī Kānhaṛā. Kauṅsī-Kānhaṛā is a Sampūrṇa Mālkauṅs in concept — though not by nomenclature — because it uses *Re* and *Pā* in addition to the Mālkauṅs *svar* material; but it also a compound because it fuses Mālkauṅs and Darbāṛī Kānhaṛā. In Kauṅsī-Kānhaṛā, the *rāgas* are more commonly fused directionally, in the form of a Mālkauṅs ascent and a Darbārī Kānhaṛā descent. Theoretically, however, Mālkauṅs in the lower tetrachord and Darbārī Kānhaṛā in the upper tetrachord, or the other way round, are feasible alternatives.

And, finally, we have Kesarbai's version of Sampūrṇa Mālkauṅs which is an emulsion of Mālkauṅs, Bāgeśrī, and Kāfī, constructed with alternating and interlocking phrases from all the three *rāgas*.

The Rāga-mālikā

In recent years, the subtlety and complexity of the *rāga* enhancement idiom have often been confused with the popular *rāga-mālikā* (literally, a link-chain of *rāgas*) form of presentation. This confusion requires to be cleared. In the *rāga-mālikā* form, a series of *rāgas* is presented, in sequence, without a break. The common practice is for the musician to commence with one *rāga*, and to take a detour into a series of different *rāgas* before returning to the original *rāga* before closing the rendition.

In this format, there is no attempt to forge a new melodic

entity. There are no conventions for linking the *rāgas*. The transition from one *rāga* to another can be made at any point, almost at will. The only link, a tenuous one at that, is forged by using one *svar*, or a phrase, which is important to both the sequentially linked *rāgas*. The critical feature of this form, therefore, is not the comprehensive skill and aesthetics of *rāga* chemistry, but the momentary delight of a near-imperceptible transition from one *rāga* to another.

In an interview with a leading American producer of Hindustani music in 1991, Vilayat Khan claimed that the origins of this form could be traced to a practice prevalent in the royal courts of early twentieth century. It was common, in that era, for princes to invite musicians from other courts for a few weeks at a time to perform at their courts. During these visits, visiting musicians performed at the host court over several evenings in a row.

During such visits, the visiting musician occasionally performed one *rāga* for an entire evening, drifted into a second *rāga* before ending the concert, and picked up where he had left off on the next evening. The same procedure was evidently repeated every evening until the last evening of his performing visit. On the final day, the musician would drift back, imperceptibly again, into the *rāga* with which he commenced his guest-appearance at the court.

Though further details about the traditional approach to *rāga-mālikā* presentation are not available, it would appear that it emerged as an attention-holding device for a concert that was intended to stretch over several evenings. By drifting into a second *rāga* before ending an evening's rendition, the musician probably wanted to ensure a return of the same audience to hear him the next evening.

On the modern concert platform, this elaborate procedure has been abbreviated to suit its compulsions, which generally permit only two hours even to the most distinguished musicians. In the contemporary context, therefore, the *rāga-mālikā* is no more than a convenient format for presenting glimpses of several *rāga*s within a single presentation merely because there is insufficient time for a relaxed and comprehensive display of musicianship.

The contemporary *rāga-mālikā* is, therefore, a mechanical device not to be confused with the products of *rāga* chemistry. Even if the name suggests something more ambitious, it is merely a link-chain of *rāga* fragments.

Beyond Chemistry

While chemistry is a useful aid to the understanding of *rāga* enhancement practices, they are a part of a creative process aimed at shaping a novel musical experience. It is worthwhile, therefore, to consider the cultural and aesthetic issues that lie beyond chemistry. Why is it that, despite over 1,000 mature *rāga*s being in existence, musicians appear to be attracted towards *rāga* enhancement devices? The question probably has two answers — one aesthetic, and the other practical.

The aesthetic answer lies in the individuality of the aesthetic product the musician creates with *rāga* enhancement devices. Conventions for this process do exist, but what is delivered in a transformed *rāga* presentation is an individualistic creation. To the musician's mind, the rendition of such a creation may not seem like an alternative to a *rāga* rendered within its recognizable melodic boundaries. It is simply his creative choice and individual statement, requiring no validation beyond the musical sense it makes to his audiences.

The practical answer probably lies in the fact that the range of *rāga*s in circulation at any given time is limited. Every generation of audiences, and indeed of musicians too, is familiar with only a limited number of *rāga*s. In the first quarter of the twentieth century, V.N. Bhatkhande presented compositions of 181 *rāgas*, of which he described only forty-five as being *prasiddha* (famous/popular). The remaining were classified as *aprasiddha* (rare). Since Bhatkhande's era, the cognoscenti amongst classical music audiences have been outnumbered by the "innocenti". A contemporary enumeration of popular and widely recognized *rāgas* may, therefore, be even smaller than that of Bhatkhande's. Because of this phenomenon, a musician is naturally more confident of sharing a novel aesthetic experience through an unfamiliar juxtaposition of familiar aural images than he would be with a rare *rāga*. By the same logic, *rāga* chemistry would probably be far too demanding for contemporary audiences. This may be why *rāga* allotropes, compounds, and emulsions are tending to get eclipsed by the *rāga-mālikā*, a mechanistic pretender which can provide only flashes of surprise, without the sustained aesthetic delight characteristic of true *rāga* chemistry.

Under conditions of diluted musicianship and audience profiles, it is tempting to suspect that the practical has overshadowed the aesthetic consideration. As a cultural phenomenon, then, the progressive shrinkage of the familiar, along with the growing popularity of populist formats like the *rāga-mālikā*, could be depleting the vastness and richness of the living *rāga* tradition.

3.4

KEDĀR AT SUNRISE?

KEDĀR being performed at sunrise is an outrageous idea for a majority of Indian connoisseurs. But, the time may have come for them to reconsider the Time Theory of *rāga*s, as dissenting voices have emerged, and not all of them deserve to be ignored.

In Hindustani music, every *rāga* is prescribed for performance during a specific three-hour time slot of the twenty-four hour daily cycle. Musicologists have, for long, challenged the validity of the convention, as well as the assumptions underlying the adherence to it. They are now joined by a substantial segment of music lovers, who ask why the timings of concerts — generally between sunset and midnight — should limit the variety of *rāga*s they hear on the concert platform.

It is interesting that Carnatic music, a product of the same tradition as Hindustani music, follows no such prescription. Even in the age-old tradition of Haveli Sangeet, the *dhrupad* of the Vaiṣṇava temples, compositions in Mālkauṅs — regarded as a late evening *rāga* — are sung routinely during the *śr̥ṅgār darśan*, around ten in the morning. Consider also the fact that, inside a modern auditorium, environmental conditions are identical at any time of the day and throughout the year. Also note that there is no way of controlling the time of the day or night, or part of the year, during which audiences will listen to pre-recorded music, which is now the primary vehicle for the delivery of music. Therefore, a debate over the validity of the conventions is legitimate.

Despite the unresolved issues surrounding the time theory, significant Hindustani musicians have not, so far, deviated blatantly from its prescriptions on Indian soil. With their livelihood increasingly dependent on foreign as well as uninitiated Indian audiences, the deviations could begin soon. We have, therefore, to prepare ourselves for resolving the imminent conflicts between our rationality and conventional notions of artistic propriety.

Tradition represents the accumulated experience of a society, even if its logic is opaque to us. Over a period, practice can deviate imperceptibly from the logic, and the deviations somehow get accepted. In its totality, our response to music is, therefore, a complex combination of culturally conditioned and universal aesthetic values and tendencies.

We can neither accept traditional notions merely because they represent the accumulated wisdom of society, nor reject them merely because their logic is not transparent to us. With this perspective, we need to consider the time theory of *rāgas*, and how it can fit into our understanding of music.

The fundamental concept in Indian aesthetics is *rasa*. *Rasa* refers to the specific state of mind that any artistic endeavour seeks to elicit, communicates, or reflects. Every *rāga* — loose and coherent at the same time — is a tool by which the musician maximizes the possibility of eliciting the target emotional response from his audiences.

On what basis has tradition assumed a correspondence between a *rāga* (a melodic structure) and its *rasa* (emotional content)? This assumption is validated by experience and general acceptance. The experience also leads the tradition to believe that each pattern of melodic stimuli has the highest probability of eliciting the target emotional response during certain hours of the day/night or during certain seasons of the year. Thus has evolved a performing tradition, which assumes, broadly, a three-way correspondence between melodic patterns (*rāga*s), emotional states (*rasa*s), and environmental and climatic variables.

Many non-musical factors do, of course, influence our receptivity and response to a musical presentation. But, a musician can only control musical variables; and this is what the performing tradition helps him to do. In doing so, the tradition attempts to harmonize musical variables with environmental variables, based on its understanding of the relationship between the two. At the root of these prescriptions is the oriental notion that man is most at peace with himself when he is at peace with nature. Arbitrary and even fanciful as these prescriptions may appear, they relate music to a reality whose relevance the latest researches in physiology are beginning to vindicate.

The proposition is that our bodily and emotional states respond constantly to changes in the quality of sunlight, and climatic factors such as humidity and temperature. If this proposition is acceptable, it is logical that there should be specific environmental conditions most conducive to each category of emotional experience. Our performing tradition has attempted to stabilize its understanding of these probabilities with the benefit of centuries of trial and error.

This configuration of ideas came closer to "scientific" respectability when V.N. Bhatkhande (*Bhatkhande Sangeet Shastra*, vol. IV, 2nd edn., 1970, pp. 21-23) observed a relationship between *rāga* forms and their time-specific prescriptions. Since then, other scholars and musicians have identified additional patterns, which provide some support for the Time Theory of *rāga*s as an evolved parameter in the *rāga* classification matrix.

The Theory

The Hindustani performing tradition divides the day into eight equal parts of three hours each. The musical clock is standardized with the notional interval between sunrise and sunset being assumed to be twelve hours, or consisting of four three-hour parts. Each *rāga* is assigned its most appropriate part of the day (after sunrise) or night (after sunset) for performance. Some *rāga*s are prescribed for performance in the twilight zone — around sunrise or sunset. And, there are some *rāga*s, though very few, which are permitted for performance at any time of the day or night.

Even for *rāga*s associated with seasons of the year, the time of the day is considered a binding prescription. The seasonal prescription dominates the selection. But, the time of the performance is not allowed to contravene the time-based principles of melodic classification.

For instance, Bahār, the *rāga* of spring, and Malhār, the *rāga* of the rainy season, both use the *komal svar*s of *Gā* (3rd) and *Ni* (7th). Therefore, unless they are performed as compounds of morning *rāga*s, they are performed after sunset, though only during the appropriate season. These seasonal *rāga*s, and their compounds, can be performed along with (before or after) non-seasonal *rāga*s of the appropriate time segment.

The tonal commonalties between *rāga*s prescribed for different times, and the pattern of transitions, are seen to track the movement of the sun along its geocentric path. Although a *rāga* is defined by a large number of rules designed for aesthetic coherence, the time theory is discussed primarily with respect to the basic aspect of *rāga* grammar — its *svar* material. As a basic classification based on *svar* material, *rāga*s are divided into three categories:

Rāgas that use the Flat Svars of (Re and Dh [2nd and 6th])

These *rāga*s are prescribed for performance either around sunrise or around sunset. The suppressed/debilitated micro-*svar*s of the *Re* and *Dh* are suggestive of the semi-awake condition, and are believed to have an aesthetic affinity with the quality of light in the twilight zones. Some senior vocalists also report that, during these periods, the throat muscles tend to become loose, and the accurate rendition of *śuddha Re* and *Dh svar*s becomes difficult. There could, therefore, also be a physiological basis for this pattern.

The twilight periods — sunrise and sunset — have a very deep cultural meaning. For instance, *rāga*s of the twilight zone are also called *rāga*s of the *godhūli belā* (*go* = cows + *dhūli* = dust + *belā* = time). This is the time when the cows raise a lot of dust on the village roads either on their way out to the grazing pastures at sunrise or on their way back home at sunset.

To the Indian mind, this is an emotionally charged description. The cow plays a pivotal role in India's primarily agrarian economy, and is held sacred. The sanctity of the cow, and of all the activities associated with dairying as an occupation in the rural context, has been reinforced in mythology by the depiction of Lord Kṛṣṇa as Gopāla (the Divine Cowherd).

There also exists a tradition, in many parts of the country, of lighting a lamp before the earthen water-pot in the household around sunset, as a mark of welcome and respect for the spirits of the ancestors, which are believed to visit the family home to quench their thirst. Sunrise and sunset are also times when the typical Hindu family congregates around the altar to offer its prayers.

Sunrise, noon, and sunset are the prescribed times for the chanting of the Gāyatrī Mantra, the most powerful psycholinguistic device — incidentally, an ode to the Sun God — for aspirants to worldly and other-worldly progress.

As a combination of economic forces, ancestor worship sentiments, religious sentiments, and spiritual aspirations, and of course, as a natural response to the quality of light, the Hindu mind has given this group of *rāga*s a strong bias in favour of the devotional aspect of life. In the Hindu mind, sunrise and sunset are appropriate times for acknowledging the glory of God.

Of the three major classifications, the time–*rāga*–*rasa* equation appears to hold most consistently for the Group 1 *rāga*s.

Rāgas that use the Śuddha Svars of Re and Dh (2nd and 6th)

These *rāga*s are prescribed for performance after the first group, that is, between 7 and 10 a.m. and between 7 and 10 p.m. This prescription sees the stepping up of the *Re* and *Dh* *svar*s from *komal* to *śuddha* as symbolizing the completion of the night-to-day or day-to-night transition that commences in the twilight. There could well be a physiological basis for this prescription, too.

Rāgas that use the Flat Svars of Gā and Ni (3rd and 7th)

These *rāga*s are prescribed for the remaining parts of the day/night: 10 a.m. to sunset and 10 p.m. to sunrise.

In addition to these three indicators of the time dimension in the performing tradition, the use of the *Mā* (4th) plays an important role. This, however, is a weaker and less consistent pattern than the first three.

The Indian scale works a notion of seven *svar*s or intervallic transitions from the scale-base to the scale-peak. The 4th (in a frequency ratio of 1:1.33 to the scale-base) is therefore, notionally, the mid-point of the Indian scale, with three *svar*s below it, and three above. The solfa symbol *Mā* is itself an abbreviation for *madhyam*, which means mid-point.

It has been observed that, largely, *rāga*s performed during the day (sunrise to sunset) use the *śuddha Mā* (4th) *svar*, either solely or as the dominant of the two *Mā svar*s when both are used. As the sun approaches dusk, the *tīvra* (sharp) *Mā* (4th) appears on the scene, and even dominates the melody until late into the evening.

It is important to note that these are not rigid rules. They cannot be so, simply because the primary classification of *rāga*s is based on *rasa*, and not on *svar*-material. And, the Indian aesthetic sensibility is far too mature to assume a mechanistic correspondence between *svar*-material and the emotional content of all its melodic potentialities.

Even the *rasa* classification of *rāga*s is merely indicative because the *rasa* of a *rāga* can be as much a matter of interpretation as of the intrinsic psycho-acoustic propensity of the *svar*-material. Different musicians, of comparable stature can, and do, interpret the same *rāga* in obviously different *rasa*s.

The Time Theory is, then, an effort by musicologists to identify the patterns of commonality between *rāga*s prescribed by tradition for performance during different parts of the day. They are pointers to the possibility that certain *svars*, or combinations of *svars*, might have a higher probability of communicating certain emotions appropriate to certain times of the day/night than others.

A Rational Perspective

The theory, as understood so far, falls short of being a comprehensive and fully organized system of relationships.

Some psychometric experiments have been conducted to verify the association of melodic patterns with time-slots in the audience mind. The results are, so far, tentative in their confirmation.

Quite irrespective of what any kind of scientific enquiry says about these psycho-acoustic notions, it will not change the way different categories of audiences relate to music. It might, therefore, be necessary for the "believers" to accept that, maybe, the Time Theory works for them because they have Indian bodies, and Indian minds, of a particular generation, responding under the sunlight quality and climatic conditions characteristic of the Indian subcontinent.

The generational issue might be more important than is easily appreciated. Generations brought up on pre-recorded music, and in acoustically and environmentally engineered auditoria, may be relatively insensitive to, and consequently unsympathetic, to the Time Theory.

Climatic conditions, too, cannot be an insignificant factor. If the Hindustani and Carnatic traditions are derived from a common source, the Time Theory was probably common to them until their bifurcation believed to have taken place in the twelfth/thirteenth centuries. Why did the Carnatic tradition abandon the theory, while the Hindustani tradition retained it? We could speculate that, by virtue of being closer to the equator, the southern states experience a far lower level of variation in climatic conditions within the day and between the different seasons than the northern, non-peninsular, states do. This could be the reason why the Rāga Hindolam/Mālkauṅs does not suggest, to Carnatic audiences, as radical a contrast with the Rāga Bhairavī/Hanumatoḍī in aesthetic value and emotional content, as it does to Hindustani audiences.

Once we appreciate this logic, it can be extended farther.

A Sunrise Sonata composed in Kedār by a Swedish composer need not raise eyebrows even with cultivated Hindustani audiences, because a Swede's relationship with sunlight is radically different from ours.

As Hindustani music addresses an increasingly diverse global audience, the musician becomes progressively incapable of controlling the time and environmental conditions attendant to the performance. Thus, as the context of the musical experience undergoes a fundamental transformation in terms of audience profiles and the environmental conditions, conservative connoisseurs may have to loosen their strictures further. Why should it be wrong for an Indian to perform Kedār at the Bhairav hour, but okay for a Swede to do so?

Postscript

Since the publication of this discussion, learned friends have raised two issues with me. The first is why I am in a hurry to write the epitaph for the Time Theory of *rāga*s. And, the second is why I am focusing so sharply on the cross-cultural relevance — or otherwise — of the Time Theory. The two issues are linked and, despite the risk of repeating myself, they need to be dealt with.

As a musician, I persist with my adherence to the time-related prescription for *rāga* performance. As a behavioural scientist, I consider the assumptions underlying the theory to be plausible, though perhaps verifiable only in a culture-specific context. As an observer of the cultural process, however, I am obliged to acknowledge the debilitation of the time-related prescription as a regulator of practice. In short, my espousal or dismissal of the Time Theory will make no difference to the speed with which it is relegating itself to the world of academic indulgences.

The Time Theory assumes the context of a stage concert held at a certain time exclusively addressing the audience in attendance. By its very nature, the theory also assumes an audience cultivated in the same musical culture as the musician. From the professional musician's perspective, both these contexts have now become marginal realities.

Indian audiences at stage concerts, who relate meaningfully to time-related prescriptions, are shrinking in numbers. Concerts within India are fast becoming insignificant contributors to a musician's professional income. Foreign concert audiences, which account for the major part of their concert income, cannot be expected to respond to the time-related aesthetic assumptions of the music because of a radically different relationship with sunlight, and other cultural factors. For them, the musician has the freedom to either perform audience-friendly repertoire independent of time-related prescriptions, or limit his choice to tradition-backed repertoire. Readers can guess which of these two options would be more prudent, more rewarding, and more likely.

Once issues of prudence and rewards come into play, an allied possibility also becomes worth considering. How long can it be before Indian concert audiences become culturally as "foreign" as foreign audiences? And, how long can it be before Indian musicians start treating Indian concert audiences also like foreign audiences?

The concert context itself has now become a miniscule part of the totality of the interaction between musicians and their audiences. The overwhelming majority of encounters between Hindustani music — like all other music — and its audiences are taking place through the electronic media with a global reach. There is no way in which anyone can control the time of the day or night at which, or the context in which, a particular piece of music is heard. In this respect, the prospect of irrelevance stares the Time Theory in its face.

Once you combine the effects of prudence, rewards, and irrelevance, the time-related prescriptions for the performance of *rāga*s expose their redundancy. All that is left of its value is the level of individual comfort. For the conservative musician, and for the orthodox music lover, it defines one level of emotional comfort with a *rāga*. Nothing more; nothing less.

3.5

RĀGA, RASA, MEANING

DURING one of his conversations, Ustad Vilayat Khan said to me — "the three most important things to understand about our music are . . . *rāga*, *rāga*, and *rāga*".

I once had a challenging recording to review, and felt the need for superior wisdom. I approached the eminent musicologist, Ashok Ranade for guidance. He heard the recording and said — "focus on the *rāga*-ness. Once you have a grip on that, everything else will fall into place." The *rāga* is, indeed, the fountainhead of musical energies, which makes everything else in Hindustani music fall into place.

Hindustani music is synonymous with *rāga* music. Every facet of the musical endeavour is designed to contribute towards the *rāga*'s flowering in performance. A command over the abstraction called *rāga* is the ultimate aim of music education. The *rāga* provides the melodic raw material for the performance, along with its latent emotional charges. And, fidelity to the *rāga* is the primary criterion by which discerning listeners judge individual performances, and the capabilities of a musician.

The Notion of a "Commanding Form"

The notion that every work of art is governed by a "commanding form" is prominent in the writings of Susanne

K. Langer, the modern American thinker on art. In the context of Western art-music, Langer accords the status of the "commanding form" to the composition, as it is this musical form which determines the whole subsequent process of invention and elaboration. The eminent aesthetician, S.K. Saxena in *Hindustani Sangeet and a Philosopher of Art*, argues that, in Hindustani music, the *rāga* rightfully occupies this status.

He argues that the composition (*bandiś*) is not the primary musical idea in Hindustani music. Even the composition has to be in conformity with the *rāga*. In terms of the musician's attentiveness, too, the *rāga* shapes the totality of performance more comprehensively than the specific detail of the *bandiś*. According to him, therefore, it is the *rāga* which is the hero of Hindustani music.

In commending the *rāga* as the commanding form, Saxena quotes the following passage from Susanne Langer with reference to the "commanding form":

> Perhaps the most striking thing about "musical form" is (its) objective character. Once the matrix of musical thought, the "Commanding Form", has been grasped by one's artistic imagination, it assumes a peculiarly impersonal status, like something "given". Great musicians have spoken of the musical idea with an unmistakable feeling of moral obligation and a sense of responsibility for its development and perfection.

Can the *rāga* be said to be a "form" at all? Saxena answers in the affirmative. A *rāga* may be credited with a shape. *Svar*s in a *rāga* are related to each other in a very specific manner, and because of their internal relatedness, a *rāga* is possessed of a distinct appearance which makes it identifiable, and distinguishable from others.

Saxena concludes that, as the constituting, overarching,

enabling, and regulatory principle of performance in Hindustani music, the *rāga* satisfies Langer's notion of the "commanding form".

This proposition has tremendous intuitive appeal. But, it could face some resistance from learned opinion in the Hindustani music world. The issues are discussed in the next chapter.

Psycho-acoustic Hypothesis

In an earlier chapter (Chapter 3.1), the *rāga* has been defined as "a melodic representation of an emotional idea". This definition is based on the fact that each *rāga* shapes a distinct pattern of melody by its unique selection, sequencing, and treatment of the *svar*s. Because of the distinct pattern, each *rāga* suggests a different emotional idea to the listener. But, the *svar*s of the scale have no musical meaning in isolation, though they have acoustic meaning and — according to the Indian view — also possess individual aesthetic value. So, when a *rāga* organizes them in a specific manner with the intention of communicating an emotional idea, there is a tacit assumption of a cause–effect relationship — something akin to a theory.

This possibility of an emotional response is known to exist, even if it cannot be quantified. And, because it is known to exist, the musician endeavours to deploy his musical imagination, training, and skills with the objective of maximizing the chances of eliciting the associated/expected/intended emotional response.

Since the *rāga* is a "formless form", its impact depends on the quality of the communicable form which interprets it for the audience, and the receptivity of the audience. In addition, the impact may depend on a host of non-musical factors associated with the performance, such as the venue, climatic conditions, and quality of the sound system. Considering the uncertainties surrounding the conceivable result, the cause–effect assumptions of the *rāga* do not justify the metaphorical status of a theory. But, because there is a known possibility of an emotional response, it may be metaphorically called a hypothesis. The crucial distinction is made between "known possibility" and "predictability".

This "known possibility" assumption has two important implications. First, that it is a culture-specific assumption, though it does not explicitly rule out cross-cultural appeal. Second, that it differentiates Hindustani music fundamentally from the aesthetic assumptions of pre-composed art-music traditions, such as the Western tradition.

The culture-specific character of this assumption has been dealt with by S.K. Saxena in his recent work, *Hindustani Music and Aesthetics Today*. He interprets classical definitions of *rāga*s to make the following point. To the innumerable melodic patterns that can be derived from the *svar*s of the scale, society has applied some yardstick of selectivity which enables a few of them to participate in the musical culture. This yardstick is expressed in the oft-cited classical definition: "That, which pleases, is a *rāga*." Better articulated definitions found in classical literature have clarified that the quality of pleasingness cannot be universal. The "known possibility" jurisdiction of a *rāga* is defined by those who are cultivated in its understanding.

The cliché that music is a universal language needs to be cited with extreme caution in the context of Hindustani music. Art music traditions — like languages — are intrinsically "parochial". Yet, any of them can have some features which are "catholic", making them accessible, and even appealing, to audiences beyond the culture that has cultivated them. However, appeal and comprehension of emotional meaning are different things. Trans-cultural appeal is possible without the delivery of the emotional meaning accorded to it by its native culture, because meaning is language/culture specific.

The oblique distinction between Hindustani and Western music arises from the degree to which the driving force of musical performance is pre-composed. Western art-music recognizes the greatness of specific works, specific manifestations of the composer's art and craft, because they have acquired a degree of predictability in eliciting a specific range of emotional responses when performed. Such works could answer to the metaphorical description of "theories" of emotional potency.

In Hindustani music, the performance is largely a "real time" creation of the musician, who deploys pre-composed as well as improvised elements in a seamless integration under the overarching control of the *rāga*. An attribution of "greatness" to a *rāga* is inconceivable, because it is only a repository of aesthetically compatible melodic ideas. The tradition does, indeed, recognize the greatness of some compositions for their intrinsic beauty. But, the composition is hardly ever performed by itself. This is why Hindustani music acknowledges the greatness of musicians and individual performances, but not of the controlling principle of music-making — the *rāga*.

Each time a *rāga* is performed anywhere by anyone, it is a unique event in terms of the musical product created, the receptivity of the audience, and non-musical factors that may help or hinder the success of a performance. Isolated consummation of a performance in a rich emotional experience will occur. But, their probability does not belong to the *rāga*. The *rāga* will forever remain a hypothesis, and its performance will remain a process of testing it. It will be tested ad infinitum, uniquely manifested each time, with neither the possibility nor the intention of ever becoming a theory of predictable emotional responses. On its open-ended path, guided by the objective of obtaining an emotional response, it can keep changing imperceptibly and, over time, perhaps even change radically enough to warrant a change of name. It is the absence of oracular finality in any individual manifestation of a *rāga* that keeps the Hindustani music-scape perennially fresh, without ever losing its basis in familiarity. This is fundamental to the character of *rāga*-based music.

Is the Rāga a Language?

By referring metaphorically to the *rāga* as a hypothesis, we are not stating an arbitrary proposition. Even in the exact sciences, a hypothesis has a piori plausibility based on astute observation or theoretical speculation. Through an observation of its aesthetic impact in countless performances over a long period, every *rāga* acquires an association with a distinct emotional meaning, or a limited range of meanings. *Rāga*s acquire their meaning in much the same way that words and phrases in a language acquire their meaning — by the association of sound patterns with events or ideas or feelings. And, as in any spoken or written language, so also in *rāga*-based music: only those who know the language — those who relate to the associations by prior familiarity — are expected to understand the meanings.

The *rāga* behaves like a language in some other ways, too. Even amongst Indian aspirants, the learning of *rāga*s is considered to be as complex and inadequately understood a process as the learning of languages. This might explain why the *rāga* has proven to be the most bewildering barrier for foreign musicians seeking credible performing competence in Hindustani music. It is accepted that languages function similarly as cultural bulwarks for different ethnic–linguistic groups.

Interestingly, musical potential and competence appear to be closely connected with linguistic versatility. Musicians from the bi-lingual region on the Maharashtra–Karnataka border have virtually ruled the twentieth-century Hindustani concert platform — Savai Gandharva, Bhimsen Joshi, Kumar Gandharva, Gangubai Hangal, to name a few.

Scholars have reservations about accepting music as a language because it does not support the notion of lexical meaning — meaning you can look up in a dictionary and understand what the speaker/writer is trying to say. With specific reference to *rāga*-based music, this objection seems feeble.

Music in general may be said to allow a sound pattern to be interpreted more variously than a spoken or written word or statement by members of the same ethnic–linguistic–cultural group. This may only justify seeing music as a language with different (lower) probability of comprehension for the intended meaning. But, *rāga*-based music may not require a major concession on this account. And, here is why. In addition to the existence of a reasonable approximation to lexical meaning (for those who know the language), *rāga*-based music also deploys sequencing and contextual placement of its sounds in order to deliver the intended meaning. This feature (syntax) is as relevant to *rāga*-based music as it is to English or German or Sanskrit.

Like any spoken or written language, the *rāga* has well-defined grammatical coordinates, which control the delivery of meaning in each individual *rāga*. Its grammatical structure provides as much scope for individuality and creativity of expression as the grammar of languages provides for literature.

The linguistic analogy is reflected in a well-articulated ideology of performance in several segments of the Hindustani tradition. Musicians actively involved with teaching are frequently found to indoctrinate their students into treating performance as a process of telling a story. This stance has the effect of focusing the musician's efforts sharply on holding the listener's interest, enticing him to flow with the tide of the "narrative", and ensuring his comprehension of the emotional idea being delivered to him. The psychological distance between the musician and his listener, which is intrinsic to the abstract quality of art music, is also reduced by this stance. It works within the architecture of the genre in which the *rāga* is performed, and imbues every movement with a "conversational" manner of structuring and executing the melody. On attentive scrutiny by a cultivated listener, the music of many eminent Hindustani musicians will reveal evidence of such a stance in operation.

It therefore appears that *rāga*-based music is amenable to the conceptual framework of linguistics. But, as we can appreciate, the idea of compiling a dictionary of *rāga* meanings — no matter how well researched — would be futile in addition to being inimical to the very concept of *rāga*. The musician explores the latency of meaning in the formless form, and the listener discovers the meaning by contemplating upon its manifest form. When such a process is encountered in literature, we call it philosophy. The simultaneous process of exploration and discovery of meaning relates the *rāga* ultimately to wisdom. The *rāga* is the acoustic/melodic and emotional path to this ultimate destination — one of the several identified by Hindu thought.

The assumptions underlying this proposition can be inferred from the traditional framework of meaning, which governs the practice and appreciation of the art form.

The Rasa Theory

The principal concern of the performing arts is — how does a performance work upon the spectator's mind, heart and soul, and what are the qualities of an artistic endeavour that makes it work better? A theoretical framework, commonly referred to as the theory of *rasa*, is the Indian answer to these questions. The framework identifies the innate dispositions and emotional propensities of all humans (audiences) which can be activated by artistic endeavours, the qualities of the artistic endeavour which enhance the chances of evoking an emotional response, and the qualifications of audiences capable of responding emotionally to a performance. A brief introduction will suffice here.

The earliest systematic articulation of this framework is available from Bharata's *Nāṭyaśāstra* traced to the early years of the Christian era, and from commentaries written in the tenth century CE by Abhinavagupta. It was a mature framework by Bharata's time, suggesting that it predates him. Manifestly, the framework deals with the aesthetics of Sanskrit drama which, in that era, included theatrical, musical as well as choreographic presentations, with the notion of *rasa* as the integrator of the various art forms. Conceptually, the framework is applicable to any of the performing arts individually, and has had a profound influence on theory and practice in each of them as also, indeed, of the literary and the visual arts.

What Is Rasa?

The literal meaning of the word *rasa* is juice/extract/essence. The full scope of the connotations can be understood from its lexicographic interpretation. The *Sanskrit Dictionary* (Monier-Williams) has the following entry:

> Sap or juice of — plant; juice of fruit; any liquid or fluid; the best or finest part of anything; essence; marrow; elixir; potion; seminal fluid of Shiva; charm, pleasure or delight; the taste or character of a work, the feeling or sentiment prevailing in it.

All these connotations are relevant for understanding the connection between *rāga* and *rasa*.

In the context of theatre, *Nāṭyaśāstra* explains *rasa* through a metaphor from cookery. Just as a gourmet is able to savour food made from various spices and obtain pleasure from it, the cultivated spectator can savour the primary emotions suggested by the acting out of the various emotions through the appropriate technique of histrionic presentation, and derive pleasure. Significant in this metaphor is the immediacy and effortless quality of the experience, and the implication that *rasa* is not a single discrete flavour, but a synergistic effect of the various spices used in the preparation of a dish. Hence also, the reference to the cultivated spectator as the qualified recipient of the aesthetic values inherent in the performance.

Lewis Rowell in *Music and Musical Thought in Early India* (1992: 328) articulates the aesthetic meaning of *rasa* thus:

> By *rasa*, we mean a transcendent mode of emotional awareness by which all aspects of a performance are integrated, an awareness that rises above the circumstances that awakened it (the poetical content, the stage spectacle and the musical clues) and generalizes the individual emotional states of the spectator into a single emotional "field".

The Aim of Artistic Endeavour

According to the *rasa* theory, the aim of any artistic presentation is to induce, in the spectator's mind, a heightened awareness of one of the *sthāī bhāva*s or innate dispositions and latent energies common to all humans. The simultaneous activation of any of the *sthāī bhāva*s in the work of art and in the spectator's mind constitutes the experience of *rasa*. The clear implication here is that the performance is purposefully structured, deploying a variety of devices, to manipulate the emotional states of the audience.

Nāṭyaśāstra listed the first eight *sthāī bhāva*s. Abhinavagupta added the ninth. They are collectively known as the *navarasas* (the nine *rasas*). Each *sthāī bhāva* is associated with its corresponding *rasa*.

1. *rati bhāva* (love) corresponding to Śṛṅgār Rasa (erotic),
2. *hāsa bhāva* (mirth) corresponding to Hāsya Rasa (comic),
3. *śoka bhāva* (sorrow) corresponding to Karuṇa Rasa (pathetic),
4. *krodha bhāva* (anger) corresponding to Raudra Rasa (furious),
5. *utsāha bhāva* (energy) corresponding to Vīra Rasa (heroic),
6. *bhaya bhāva* (fear) corresponding to Bhayānaka Rasa (terrible),
7. *jugupsā bhāva* (disgust) corresponding to Bībhatsa Rasa (odious),
8. *vismaya bhāva* (wonder) corresponding to Adbhuta Rasa (wonderous), and
9. *sama bhāva* (equanimity) corresponding to Śānta Rasa (tranquil).

What the performance activates is the *sthāī bhāvas*, which are stable and permanent facets of human nature. What the audiences experiences is *rasa*, which lasts only as long as the performance lasts. Ephemeral as it is, *rasa* is a heightened awareness of one of the *sthāī bhāvas*, as it is the distilled expression of various minor emotional ideas that may have been activated in order to address the major dispositions of the human psyche (the *sthāī bhāvas*). It is experienced with knowledge of its unreality — as a general idea of a feeling, rather than a personal emotional experience. This is what can make the aesthetic experience of even normally unpleasant *sthāī bhāvas*, such as disgust or fear, pleasant. The pleasure arises from the cleverness with which the emotional idea is communicated, and the awareness of being able to feel without being affected.

The inventory of *sthāī bhāva*s and *rasa*s in circulation exploded after Bharata and Abhinavagupta, with every critic proposing additions without considering the fundamentals of the theory. Amongst the later additions, the major *rasa* to gain acceptability was *bhakti rasa*, man's devotion to his chosen deity. Another addition, relatively minor, was *vātsalya rasa*, the emotion that binds parents to their children.

Against this backdrop of the *rasa* theory, the musical culture has accepted the notion of a *rāga* as a melodic representation of an emotional idea. And, indeed, some *rasa*s — such as Hāsya (comic), Raudra (furious), Bhayānaka (terrible), and Bībhatsa (odious) — are recognized as being beyond the representational reach of music as an art form. By implication, *rasa*s that constitute the special territory of music are also identified. Performances are valued for the clarity of aesthetic intent, and its translation into experience for the audience.

Towards Mystical Aesthetics

The writings of Abhinavagupta tilt the *rasa* theory firmly towards the philosophical dimension of human nature. Having accepted that the aim of performance is to reach out to the *sthāī bhāva*s in the human psyche, he raises the ideal of aesthetic experience to a level of a near-mystical experience.

His major contribution was the addition of ninth *rasa* — Śānta — the state of peace, tranquillity, and the absence of emotional turbulence. He argued that all the earlier *rasa*s identified by *Nāṭyaśāstra* related to worldly goals, and missed out on man's highest aspiration, *mokṣa* (enlightenment/liberation from the cycle of death and rebirth). Śānta Rasa, according to him, must enjoy the highest place in the hierarchy of *rasa*s.

He reminds us that the *sthāī bhāva*s are the product of the *vāsanā*s (passions) and *saṁskāra*s (influences) accumulated by the soul through thousands, perhaps millions, of lives lived in human or sub-human forms. These tendencies inhibit man's experience of beauty as an awareness of his divine nature. For Abhinavagupta, it would appear, the purpose of addressing the *sthāī bhāva*s is not giving pleasure, but neutralizing their qualitative facet for inducing a higher state — bliss.

According to him, the eligible recipient of the *rasa* experience is a person of high intellect, and emotional receptivity. When exposed to an artistic endeavour of the desirable quality, he is able to disconnect himself from the mundane reality, lose all consciousness of the here and now, and identify himself completely with the performance by allowing the artistic endeavour to penetrate the *sthāī bhāva*s, and to give the spectator access to bliss, which is a cognizance of his divine self.

Transcendentalism

While modern aestheticians appear to favour the emotion-specific view of the *rasa* experience, Abhinavagupta's view also has a following. The passage from Rowell quoted above suggests that the *rasa* experience transcends its qualitative aspect, and tends to create an emotional state that is beyond classification. According to this view, the *rasa* experience, at this level, is not the activation of any particular *sthāī bhāva* (e.g. sorrow, compassion, disgust), but a general state of enhanced emotionality, or pure unqualified delight.

This view would broadly echo the Hindu view of theistic devotion. By complete immersion in the *saguṇ/sākār* (the One with attributes/the One who has a form) — man may attain union with the *nirguṇ/nirākār* (the One beyond attributes/the One who is Formless).

In the explanatory notes (glossary) to my book *Khayāl Vocalism : Continuity within Change* I had published the following entry for the term *rasa*.

Rasa

The Indian aesthetic tradition views the sensory experience as a pathway to the emotional, and the emotional as a pathway to the spiritual. This reflects the fundamental transcendentalism of Hindu thought. All art is, therefore, validated by a single dominant criterion — its ability to elicit an emotional response. This criterion acknowledges that, at its most intense, the experience of beauty evokes a response that transcends its qualitative aspect, and acquires a mystical quality. This defines the potential of the artistic endeavour, and its reception, for personality transformation and spiritual evolution. At the intermediate aesthetic level, however, the tradition allows for the classification of works of art on the basis of the quality of the emotional response. The name given to these qualities is *rasa*, a metaphorical expression derived from the Sanskrit *rasa* (extract/essence/juice).

In his review of my book published in the *Journal of Sangeet Natak Akademi*, the pioneering philosopher of Hindustani music, Dr S.K. Saxena, gave this entry a nod of approval. This encourages me to suggest a more ambitious hypothesis.

If the *rasa* experience is an awareness-altering experience, the pursuit of *rasa*, as life's work, can be a personality-transforming avocation. Its aim and result would be the attainment of bliss as a permanent state of Being.

Admittedly, the personality-transforming potential of *rasa* (the aesthetic experience) cannot compare with that of real-life experience of emotions as a personalized response to personal realities. But, Immanuel Kant could be right when he says — "We dwell on the contemplation of the beautiful because this contemplation strengthens and reproduces itself" (*The Critique of Judgement*). This description recalls the dictionary meaning of "addiction", signifying a craving for progressively larger doses of an awareness-altering substance. If this is the inherent quality of aesthetic contemplation, high frequency, high intensity, experience of *rasa* spread over a long period of time could be totally distinct from the transient inebriation of *rasa* as an occasional aesthetic encounter — and infinitely more durable.

This hypothesis is plausible because the enfeebling of the *sthāī bhāva*s is explicitly considered by the Indian philosophical tradition as a mark of wisdom and enlightenment. Such a person would answer to the ideal of the *triguṇātīt* in *Bhagavad-Gītā*, or the Superior Man in Taoist literature:

> equal in happiness and suffering, regards gold and mud and stone alike, is equal before the pleasant and the unpleasant, equal before praise and blame, equal before honor and dishonor.
>
> — *Bhagavad-Gītā*, text, translation, and commentary by Maharshi Aurobindo, 3rd edn., 2006, chapter 14, pp. 24-25

Spirituality in Hindustani Music

The "spirituality" of Hindustani music has been rather cynically marketed as its distinguishing quality to the international music community. This claim can be considered with two prefatory observations.

First, though Hindustani music may have features conducive to the semblance of "spirituality", it is not clear if it is uniquely equipped to capture the supra-aesthetic potency of music. Second, as S.K. Saxena points out, the spiritual significance of a work of art "depends also, and importantly, on what kind of a person the individual contemplator is, and not only on what the work itself may be said to contain"

(*Hindustani Sangeet: Some Perspectives, Some Performers*).

We may identify the two dimensions of spirituality, as outlined by Saxena (ibid.) — the secular and the non-secular. The secular manifestation of spirituality can surface in the exploration of the "formless" *rāga*-form with the objective of its embodiment in communicable form. This is an inward looking, meditative process, demanding immense grammatical alertness, independent thinking, recall, organization, integration, and imagining. At its best, the process is intellectually demanding, and emotionally exhausting. In this process, as it progresses and shapes the exposition of the *rāga* through the agency of the genre in which it is performed, audiences may become aware of a profundity. The necessity of this process to performance may, therefore, be conducive to a semblance of spirituality.

The non-secular connotation of spirituality refers to the life of the spirit, or feelings that are religious, sacred, holy or divine. According to Saxena, such aesthetic perceptions are possible in the rendition of explicitly devotional song-text, the melodic charm of the rendition, a visible serenity in the rendition, and a contagious immersion of the musician (*tādātmya*/one-ness) in the act of contemplation.

There appears to be a third dimension to this notion of spirituality associated with Hindustani music, though not entirely unrelated to the two discussed above. The eminent musicologist, Ashok Ranade, had once said to me — "there is a uniquely Indian relationship between the musician and his art, and we should never lose sight of it when we write about Hindustani music". He was evidently alluding to something more abstruse than the universal anxiety of artists relating to the effective delivery of aesthetic value to their audiences.

The influential German composer, Reinhardt Stockhausen probably refers to this feature of Indian music in his book

Towards a Cosmic Music, when he says:

> When a musician walks on stage, he should give that fabulous impression of a person who is doing a sacred service. In India . . . , when a group of musicians are performing, you don't feel they do it to entertain you. They do it as holy service. They feel a need to make sounds, and these sounds are waves on which you ride to the eternal.
>
> — 1st edition 1989: 6

The phenomenon Stockhausen describes arises possibly from the sense of diffidence — and even awe — with which the Indian musician approaches the task of performing a *rāga*. To quote Ustad Vilayat Khan (private conversation), "A *rāga* is bigger than the collective imagination of all the musicians who have ever lived, or will ever be born". Faced with so daunting an object of contemplation, the only possible stance for a musician is total surrender. Being a "formless form", and a source of inspiration, the *rāga* is easily viewed as a divinity to whom the musician prays, entreating it to descend into its melodic form. This idea is verbalized in the *Rāgavibodha* of Somnātha (CE 1609):

> That is called Rupa (form) which by being embellished with sweet flourishes of *svar*s brings a Rāga vividly before one's mind. It is of two kinds — Nadatma (one whose soul or essence is sound), and Devamaya, one whose soul or essence is an image incarnating the deity), of which the former has many shapes, and the latter has only one. — 5.11

William James (*The Varieties of Religious Experience*) is apparently on the same wavelength:

> The 'divine' mean(s) . . . such a primal reality as the individual feels impelled to respond to solemnly and gravely. . . . The personal attitude which the individual finds himself impelled to take up towards the divine . . . shall

> have to confess to at least some amount of dependence on sheer mercy. — Collies Books, 3rd printing, pp. 48, 57

In a general sense, then, the "holy service" stance can be seen as an expression of the sanctity of a musician's relationship with his art. This idea is consistent with the Hindu doctrine of *karma*. According to this doctrine, every human thought, word, and deed has consequences, for which the individual is accountable in eternity. Even those activities man pursues for pleasure are not "*karma*-neutral", and equally subject to the doctrine. But, because man is limited in his ability to control, or even anticipate, these consequences, every aspect of life deserves a reverential deliberateness of conduct. In a man of wisdom, this becomes a habitual pattern of behaviour, and can suggest — as it does to Stockhausen — the stance "of a person who is doing a sacred service".

The obvious beneficiary of such a stance is *rasa* because the process of musical creation is driven by the musician's self-actualization aspirations, with the need to please audiences becoming incidental. Such a stance will also deliver music of higher moral value because it will address the nobler — rather than the baser — emotional propensities and dispositions latent in human nature.

To assess the probability (or otherwise) of encountering such reflections of "spirituality" in the present context, Saxena defines spirituality thus:

> What exactly is meant by spirituality? It is an invasive orientation of one's whole being and attitudes . . . (which) could take the form of an intense yearning for the divine . . . a pervasive coloring of one's whole being . . . (which) calls for *tadatmya* (intense oneness) with the act in question . . . (which is the result of) lifelong practice of the art of melody and rhythm (resulting in) the spiritualization of one's conduct and attitudes in daily life . . . (reflected in) their lives

> and personalities (being) blessed with what the Bible speaks of as "riches of the spirit" and the *Bhagvadgita* as "Daivi Sampada" (Divine Wealth).
>
> — *Hindustani Sangeet: Some Perspectives, Some Performers*, 2010: 136

He asks, with considerable justification, whether such attainments, or even aspirations, can reasonably be expected from musicians pursuing art music as a profession.

Art-Music as a Profession

Hindustani art-music is a self-employed profession addressing a global audience (market). What does this imply for the goals of artistic endeavour in Hindustani music?

In the recent past, the pursuit of *rasa* does not appear to have posed any conflict for professionals in art-music. In fact, in each generation of twentieth century art-music professionals, the ardent devotees of *rasa* have achieved the highest stature (and indeed, market rating). Though the musical culture may also have rewarded the pursuit of less lofty ideals, it has not left the pursuit of *rasa* unrewarded. But, the twenty-first century has begun. And, it could be different.

Because the art music professional's livelihood needs to be supported by audiences, the devotee of *rasa* needs to find eligible audiences in sufficient numbers who subscribe or respond to his artistic values. To recall Abhinavagupta's description of the eligible audience — one who is able to disconnect himself from the daily reality, lose all consciousness of the here and now, and identify himself completely with the performance in search of bliss, which is an awareness of his divine self.

Stated thus, the scenario may justify pessimism rather than its opposite. Today, art music addresses a faceless global audience primarily through the electronic media. Addressing a cultivated audience in a face-to-face concert encounter is now a rarity in the life of a professional musician, and also perhaps dispensable to the economics of his existence. Under these conditions, addressing the lowest common denominator in human nature would hold the promise of a comfortable life.

Such are the indications available from an observation of the emerging scenario. Having become unviable as an objective for professional musicians, the pursuit of *rasa* could disappear as a quality of music available in the public domain. The ideal of *rasa* may then remain the restricted pursuit of a sub-culture, motivated by its potential for the cultivation of the human personality.

In the present, this sub-culture shows signs of being defined by a generational and socio-economic divide. But, this is not its intrinsic quality. Outgrowing the seductions of frivolous music may well be a necessary qualification. But, the lure of an emotionally rich and intellectually absorbing musical experience is not an outcome only of having experienced a lot more of life. Nor need it be defined by economic well-being enjoyed independently of art-music. It may also be acquired through the osmosis of familial values, or carried forward from earlier lives by the more evolved souls. This sub-culture will almost certainly remain a microscopic minority in the art-music world. Numerically, it could shrink faster in the future than it has so far done.

A successful musician of the post-Independence generation (who wants to remain anonymous) remarked to me recently that one becomes a great musician only when starvation is the alternative. By implication, if starvation is not an acceptable alternative, greatness is not a viable aspiration. Those who are equipped for both must then live in lifelong torment of a choice they could not make, or did make but can neither live with, nor reverse.

3.6

THE RĀGA-NESS OF COMPOSITIONS

IN THE earlier chapter, I have outlined Saxena's proposition that Langer's notion of the "commanding form" is appropriate for the *rāga* in Hindustani music. His advocacy of the *rāga* argues against the claim of the composition (*bandiś*) for this status. The "commanding form" is a unitary and indivisible idea. The either/or connotation of the Langer–Saxena proposition can cause some dissonance amongst learned members of the music community.

They could legitimately ask why the tradition acknowledges the greatness of some compositions and even composers; why some compositions have remained in circulation for centuries. They may also ask why some *rāga*s have many compositions in circulation, and others have very few; why *rāga*s with solitary compositions are almost extinct. They could ask why the teaching of multiple compositions in each *rāga* has long been considered a valuable vehicle for imparting the knowledge of *rāga*s. They may also ask why some musicians insist that they have been trained to handle each composition in a *rāga* differently — almost as if it was a different *rāga* — rather than treat all as the same *rāga*.

The Composition in Hindustani Music

The pre-composed element in Hindustani music is called *bandiś*.

The word derives from the Sanskrit verb — *bandhan* (to bind). And, this is precisely what the *bandiś* does. The *bandiś* binds together melodic, rhythmic and the poetic elements (where relevant), into a self-sufficient, pre-composed piece of music. The *bandiś* conforms to the rules of the *rāga* in which it is composed, and the rhythmic pattern of the *tāl* to which it is set. It is assessed for its intrinsic aesthetic value, independently of its use as the frame for the improvisational movements characteristic of the genre in which it is composed.

The art and craft of composition has been treated with great respect in the Indian tradition. The landmark musicological text, *Saṅgīta Ratnākara* of Śārṅgadeva (thirteenth century CE), lays down elaborate qualifications for composers. The eight verses constituting these qualifications are paraphrased here: (from *Sangeet Visharad*, 21st edition, 1997, Sangeet Karyalaya, Hathras, pp. 219-20)

> One who is a master of the literary art as well as the vocal art; one who is a master of grammar, lexicography, and metre in literature; one who is conversant with the various human emotional states and also with the languages and musical practices of the various regions of the country; one who has achieved effortless command over vocal and instrumental music as well as dance; one who is endowed with a fertile imagination, and command the attention of an audience as a performer; one who has evolved a transparent personality free from strong likes and dislikes and has a sound assessment of propriety in the exercise of his creative freedom; one who is well versed in the rules governing composition in the various genres, and is also an effortless poet; one who is an adept at executing melody across three octaves with, or without, poetic articulation; such a person is qualified for creating compositions or merit.

In the sixteenth century CE, Miya Tansen prescribed four criteria for an acceptable *dhrupad* composition. A composition, according to him (a) should have four rhyming stanzas of verse, (b) should have been composed by a learned *guru,* (c) can represent any of the *rasas*, and (d) the dominant *rasa* in the poetic element should be consistent with that of the *rāga* in which the *dhrupad* is composed (K.C.D. Brihaspati, *Sangeet Chintamani*).

By making the composer accountable for the totality of the aesthetic experience, these medieval postulates appear to subordinate the role of the performer to that of the composer. This implication — even if intended at the relevant time — is no longer sustainable because of the significantly enhanced role of improvisation in the performance of music. The import of these prescriptions is, however, clear. A composition is not intended to merely represent the *rāga* in communicable form. It is an enhancer of its emotional charge, and a concentrator of its aesthetic energies, supported by the rhythmic and poetic elements. The articulation of these concerns by the tradition warrants a closer look at the relationship between the *rāga* and the *bandiś*. In this context, we need to look at the *rāga* once again.

Rāga Reconsidered

The *rāga* needs to be viewed from two angles — as the driving force of a particular performance, and as a cultural phenomenon. While the "commanding form" proposition might have intuitive appeal with respect to the former aspect, it appears less persuasive when viewed in the latter perspective. The dissonant aspect of the proposition is that the two perspectives cannot be separated from each other. The *rāga* may have unlimited melodic potential; but it has no known attributes other than those it has acquired from its performance. At the same time, every performance needs to be compliant with the attributes that the *rāga* is understood to have by the community it addresses. And, the community understands the *rāga* through certain attributes because they have been, and continue to be, evident in performance.

Once again, we may turn to the linguistic analogy for clarity on this argument. A language has no known attributes independently of its usage in communication. At the same time, each event of the language being used needs to conform to the attributes of the language — as in place at any given time — in order to achieve its communicative purpose. But, each use of the language contributes, even if imperceptibly, to what the language is, and what it is becoming. Like a language, the *rāga* permits a substantial diversity of expression, allowing this freedom to alter its own attributes. Admittedly, the *rāga* is a definitive form; but it is a formless form inaccessible except through its consensual form. And, the consensual form is changing, all the time in response to the demands that the process of communicating emotional ideas makes on it. Its accessible/consensual form has a weak claim to being definitive, if its attributes are subject to a self-revising pattern of behaviour and, therefore, transient.

I recall a conversation with Ustad Vilayat Khan (19 October 2002) during which the maestro outlined how a *rāga* should be handled in performance. He said, the musician should be mindful of the *reet*, *rivāj*, *rasm*, *rasa*, and *raṅg*. I requested him to explain the ideas he had articulated. I paraphrase here his explanation:

> By *reet*, I mean the rules that everyone accepts. If you don't respect them, the *rāga* cannot make sense, and your performance is rejected. By *rivāj*, I mean the conventions that might not be strictly "legal", but are largely acceptable to the community. The *rasm* is a ritual or minority practice — even an eccentricity — which makes your rendition distinctive and memorable.
>
> The *rasm* is an interesting feature. If a certain fringe element or eccentricity becomes popular, and is adopted by a large number of musicians, it becomes a part of the *rivāj*, and may lose its memorable quality. Likewise, if a certain *rivāj* becomes

> universal practice, it will be accepted as legal and get documented by scholars as the *reet* of the *rāga*.
>
> The *rasa* is obvious — a *rāga* gives you a choice — several shades of meaning. It is good to have a clear idea of what kind of response you want from the audience. For the last feature — *raṅg* — there is no definition. It is beyond your control and beyond everything you can say about music. If God is smiling on you that day, you will drench your audience in the *raṅg* (colour) of your rendition.

In this conversation, the Ustad defines three levels of acceptability for *rāga* attributes as represented in performance, the possibility of new attributes being introduced, and of some attributes rising in the hierarchy to finally become a part of the governing principle of performance. He is describing the democratic cultural process by which a musician submits his art to regulation by the authority he himself helps to shape. By implication, every performance draws on the collective musical wisdom of the community, while also contributing to it.

Several years ago, a Western scholar, intrigued by the *rāga* phenomenon, had asked me a question, which has remained unanswered. I attempt to answer it here. The question was: "Does the *rāga* exist? And, if so, where?"

Having lived and worked with *rāga*s for almost six decades, I am attracted to the idea that a *rāga* is an archetypal entity in the Jungian sense. Though this direction of speculation continues to engage my mind, I prefer, for now, to use more familiar analogies.

The linguistic analogy can affirm that a *rāga*, indeed, exists as definitely as a language. By the same analogy, the *rāga* does not reside either in treatises on *rāga* grammar or in any document that claims to be a lexicon of *rāga*s. Like a language, the *rāga* exists in the collective memory of the community, as a set of associations related to specific sound patterns. As a cultural force — and like a language — it is shaped by usage, and in turn, governs usage. We may say that the *rāga* resides in its performance, which, in turn, shapes the *rāga*.

Since each performance is shaped by the interaction between the musician and his audience, the depository of *rāga*-ness in the collective memory is constantly shuffling and reshuffling its inventory of melodic images to keep the aesthetic resources of the *rāga* perennially relevant.

In this sense, the *rāga* is similar to a market for financial instruments. It is sustained by the auto-reflexive behaviour of the active members of the concerned community. Such behaviour arises, as George Soros points out (*The Alchemy of Finance*), when individual intelligence is locked in interaction with collective intelligence for self-serving purposes. The individual intelligence (investor or musician) and the collective intelligence (the market or the *rāga*) constantly anticipate, interpret, and influence each other's behaviour. The processes of the collective entity (the market or the *rāga*) are caused and sustained by the beneficial effects they have for the self-serving objective of all participants. This analogy can travel much farther, but need not do so here.

For investors in a financial market, the motivation is profit. In the case of musicians, the self-serving objective lies in the preservation and ideally, the enhancement, of the aesthetic relevance of their music to the community. Just as the aggregate behaviour of a financial market can be attributed to macro-economic forces, the trends in the melodic personalities of *rāga*s can be attributed to socio-economic and larger cultural forces.

The Composition and Performance

A performance of Hindustani music is a seamless integration of two components: the pre-composed element called the *bandiś* or *chīz* (*pada* in the medieval *dhrupad* genre), and the improvisational movements dovetailed into the frame of the *bandiś* in accordance with the protocol of the particular genre (*dhrupad/khyāl/ṭappā/ṭhumrī,* etc.). While this suffices as a functional description of the role of the *bandiś* in an improvisation-dominant tradition, it does not articulate its aesthetic implications.

The obvious implication is that the *bandiś* integrates the entire rendition into a coherent and satisfying wholeness. In a sense, then, the *bandiś* merges the improvisatory movements with itself. Effectively, the *bandiś* becomes a moderator of the *rāga*'s manifestation in the performance.

The frequent description of the *bandiś* as "a melodic map of a *rāga*" is overly simplistic. Any *rāga* is a virtually infinite source of melodic ideas, impossible to map with one *bandiś*. In most cases, even the known facets of a *rāga*'s melodic personality would be too numerous to be captured in a single *bandiś*. So, while every *bandiś* will tend to capture the minimum identifying attributes of a *rāga,* it can only focus selectively on the other potentialities of the *rāga*'s personality. Feasibility is one aspect. The other is intentionality.

A *bandiś* is an assertion of the composer's musical personality. The very urge to compose a *bandiś* in a *rāga* tends to arise from dissatisfaction with *bandiś*es available in the public domain, or an individualistic interpretation of the *rāga*'s melodic personality. In some cases, the facet may have remained hitherto unexplored, or just be an eccentricity that the composer wishes to introduce as his signature. Interestingly, some of the celebrated *bandiś*es have been considered grammatically eccentric in their time. And, some of them have redefined grammar.

We have to accept that any *bandiś* can only be a partial manifestation of the *rāga*'s personality, and will also bear the imprint of the composer's musical personality. The *bandiś* thus offers a distinctive perspective on the *rāga*, which the improvisatory movements will tend to support in order to achieve the aesthetic integration of the pre-composed and improvised elements. It is in this sense that the *bandiś* can be seen to moderate the *rāga*'s command over its performance. But, being a manifestation of *rāga*-ness — even if partial or idiosyncratic — the *bandiś* shapes the *rāga* by the manner in which it shapes its performance.

This is admittedly a circular argument. But, it is faithful to the reality, and therefore unexceptionable. The abstract and the consensual personalities of the *rāga* may together command the background and even the middle ground of its performance. But, the foreground of the musical experience, as encountered by audiences, is shaped in large part by the *bandiś*.

With these observations, we may express our reservations about the proposition that the *rāga* is the "commanding form" in Hindustani music, with its status comparable to that of a composition in Western art music. Whether in the context of an individual performance or as a cultural force, the *rāga* does not have an autonomous status. The *rāga* acts largely through the agency of the *bandiś* which holds the rendition together. And, the *bandiś*, along with the improvisations that it hosts, tends to shape and reshape the *rāga*'s personality each time it is performed.

A Postscript

The above discussion might suggest the universality of the *bandiś* as the bedrock of *rāga* performance in Hindustani music. Such an implication would not be entirely valid. It is fair to acknowledge the significant segment of the music world which has treated the *bandiś* as "a mere peg to hang the *rāga* on" (B.C. Deva, *Introduction to Hindustani Music*).

Until the 1950s, *khyāl* vocalism was dominated by three

gharānās, which performed music securely anchored to the *bandiśes* — Gwalior, Agra, and Jaipur–Atrauli. Until then, the medieval *dhrupad* genre, strongly rooted in *bandiśes*, also enjoyed a reasonable presence. Instrumental music — led by the *sitār* and *sarod* — was also highly *bandiś*-oriented.

By the 1960s, however, Kairana vocalism, which substantially loosened the grip of the *bandiś* over performance, gained ascendancy. Under the influence of this vocal style, instrumental music began to drift towards a weaker — often no more than notional — presence for the *bandiś*. This trend was accelerated by the *khyāl*-inspired music of Ustad Vilayat Khan in the 1970s, followed on a large scale by younger sitarists and sarodists.

The wheel turned full circle in the 1980s, with the emergence of Kishori Amonkar, a Jaipur–Atrauli musician, as the most influential female vocalist. She restored the *bandiś* to its bedrock status, without sacrificing the richness of the improvisation that Kairana musicians had introduced to vocalism. Under her influence, Jaipur–Atrauli vocalism regained its following, with the rest of the music world — vocal as well as instrumental — aiming for a similar balance between pre-composed and improvised elements.

The cycle of decline and revival of the *bandiś* in Hindustani music is interestingly reflected in the musical journey of Shujaat Khan, the heir to the Vilayat Khan legacy, who has risen to the peak of the profession through the 1980s and 1990s. I quote here an extract from an interview he gave me on 16 January 2004.

> The early days were of playing the true Vilayat Khan music. Then came the stage of Western influences. Both these faded away. Then I was on a simplification and relief trip. . . . I started simplifying *bandiśes*. That effort also went so far that the *bandiś* virtually lost its contours, and almost became a

> scale rendering to percussion accompaniment. Both these fads passed. Then, at one stage, I started working on introducing the unexpected in my phrasing strategy — the kaleidoscopic juxtaposition of notes and phrases, Ustad Ameer Khan's gift to Hindustani music. Even in this direction, I went so far that, sometimes, I lost a grip over the expected. This too passed. . . . And, finally, my current fad. *Bandiś*es — vocal and instrumental — have traditionally been composed to begin on certain beats of the rhythmic cycle. I am now working on composing and playing *bandiś*es, which commence on unconventional beats of the rhythmic cycle. Their beauty is highlighted when I take an amad tan and dovetail it smoothly into the *mukhḍā*. The subtle interplay of melody and rhythm in such dovetailing fascinates me. . . .

In these observations, the young maestro describes his rediscovery of the *bandiś* as a valuable piece of music by itself, and as an aesthetic driver of performance. These indications would reinforce the line of reasoning that the *rāga*'s independence from the *bandiś* is difficult to establish in performance. An overdependence on the improvisatory element, at the cost of the *bandiś*, does not appear to work. The delivery of a *rāga*'s aesthetic value appears to require the agency of a hospitable pre-composed element, the *bandiś*. However, there is something more fundamental happening to the *rāga*, and to the *bandiś*, which warrants attention.

The traditional model of a performance being a unique integration of pre-composed and improvised elements could be heading for irrelevance. In pre-recorded music, the musician now has access to a fully integrated and pre-composed piece of music of proven aesthetic value. In effect, pre-recorded music has converted a creative process meant for interactive contemplation into an aesthetic product ready for consumption. Reverting to the analogy of the earlier chapter, the musician now has easy access to a proven "theory of emotional potency" comparable to a composition in Western art-music, far more valuable to him professionally than a psycho-acoustic hypothesis.

He no longer needs to immerse himself in the *rāga* or the *bandiś*. He merely has to master the reproduction of a recording he can memorize. He can now completely surrender the role of composer to a recording he admires, and restrict himself to being a mere performer. This option is being increasingly exercised by professional musicians, and enjoys the tacit approval of audiences. Here we are describing a situation close to that of Western art-music. In this situation, *rāga*-ness begins to look like a subject for study by archaeologists rather than musicologists. The implications of this phenomenon for Hindustani music have yet to be conceptualized. But, the region of possibilities can be identified.

Ashok Ranade has argued that the Hindustani tradition has, for long, featured the parallel evolution of substantially pre-composed and improvised genres of mainstream music. Parallel to the medieval *dhrupad*, the dominant genre with a strong pre-composed tendency, *khyāl* evolved as a genre which gave substantial freedom for improvisation. As *dhrupad* receded from the mainstream, the *khyāl* evolved into a structured and architecturally disciplined genre. While this was happening, the *ṭhumrī* evolved as the less formalistic and libertarian genre as a counterpoint to the *khyāl* (*Journal of the Indian Musicological Society*, 1999).

Now, under the influence of recording technology, the *khyāl* and the post-*dhrupad*/*khyāl*-inspired instrumental genres are drifting towards becoming pre-composed genres. Interestingly, the *ṭhumrī*, which saw a lean period in the last quarter of the twentieth century, is showing signs of revival — perhaps to fill the vacancy for an improvisation-dominant genre. Under the impact of recording technology, the *ṭhumrī* too could drift towards becoming a pre-composed genre.

If pre-recorded music has the effect of discouraging the dual role of the musician as composer and performer, the *rāga* and improvisation both become redundant to Hindustani music. The Indian musical culture could then be substantially impoverished, and one of the finest achievements of human civilization could be lost.

It is, of course, possible to take a less alarmist view of this, or any other, cultural phenomenon. Some commentaries on the music scene written in the eighteenth and nineteenth centuries have been found to lament, in effect, that Hindustani music was going down the drain. Interestingly, the future they feared is the period we regard as the golden age of Hindustani music. Perhaps, then, every generation of observers finds it difficult to come to terms with the change it witnesses and underestimates the resilience of the *rāga*-based tradition. In this respect, our generation could be no less myopic than earlier ones.

PART IV

The Major Genres

4.1

AN INTRODUCTION TO DHRUPAD

THE term *dhrupad* (*dhruva* = immutable/fixed + *pada* = Hymn/verse) refers to a genre of *rāga*-based music which dominated Hindustani music between the fifteenth and the eighteenth centuries. Its distinguishing features are (a) a deliberate, unhurried style of presentation involving graceful, rounded — rather than angular — melodic contours, (b) an austere, rather than ornate, approach to melodic phrasing and *rāga* elaboration, (c) the sanctity attached to the literary component and the melodic structure of the verses, and (d) a highly-structured method of melodic development, tending towards a pre-composed art-form. Because of the poetic bias of the genre, the conceptual aspect of *dhrupad* music has its moorings in vocal music. However, instrumental music, mainly the *rudra-vīṇā* [popularly known as the *bīn*, a fretted stick-zither), dance, and even theatrical performances, have also been associated with the *dhrupad* tradition.

Contemporary authorities consider *dhrupad* the successor of the *prabandha gān* genre (eleventh century CE). *Prabandha gān* (*prabandha* = organization/structure, *gān* = song/singing)

Note: Adapted from sleeve-notes for recordings written by the author for India Archive Music Ltd., New York, and a paper titled "Dhrupad: An Introduction", published by the author in the *Journal of the Indian Musicological Society*, Issue of 1999.

enjoyed great popularity between the eleventh and thirteenth centuries. From the fourteenth century onwards, *dhrupad* replaced *prabandha gān*, reaching peak status and popularity between the fifteenth and eighteenth centuries. *Dhrupad* is, therefore, described as a medieval genre.

Raja Man Singh Tomar (ascended 1483) of Gwalior, who patronized excellence in the performing art as well as scholarship, is considered a landmark figure in *dhrupad* history. Gwalior and the neighbouring principality of Rewa, which the legendary Miya Tansen (1491–1583) once served, were the original centres of *dhrupad* music. The Golden Age of *dhrupad* commenced when Emperor Akbar (r. 1542–1605), invited Tansen to the Imperial Court. Later, Vrindavan and Mathura established their own *dhrupad* schools. In the south, the patronage of Sultan Ibrahim Adil Shah II, a contemporary of Emperor Akbar, made Bijapur a major centre of the *dhrupad* genre. At its zenith, *dhrupad* held sway over the whole of non-peninsular India.

According to Parjnananda, while *dhrupad* was still at its peak, Perso-Arabic religious music was influencing some lesser-known streams of *prabandha gān*, to shape the modern, *khyāl* genre. Thakur Jayadev Singh, another distinguished scholar, traces the origins of the *khyāl* to the *rūpakālapti* genre, known to have been in practice from the eighth/ninth centuries. In knowledgeable contemporary circles, it is widely believed that the *khyāl* emerged as a fusion between *dhrupad* itself and *qawwālī*/Kaul music, a devotional genre associated with Islamic Sufi sects. Quite irrespective of which of these theories is accepted, there is little doubt that *dhrupad* and *khyāl* have been contemporaries and rivals for a substantial part of *dhrupad*'s dominance over Hindustani music.

Dhrupad was debilitated by the decline of its strongest patron, the Mogul Empire, in the early nineteenth century. At that stage, leading musicians — so far concentrated in Delhi and its neighbourhood — began migrating to smaller principalities in search of alternative patronage. This process created new centres of *dhrupad* music, mainly in the fertile Indo-Gangetic plains of eastern India, but also exposed *dhrupad* to a diverse musical environment. In their new environments, many lineages of *dhrupad* musicians diverted their energies to the *khyāl* genre, and virtually spearheaded its ascendancy over the receding *dhrupad* genre.

In the early years after Independence, the *dhrupad* genre was frequently described as "a museum piece". This description was probably more appropriate to the art of the *rudra-vīṇā* (*bīn*), than to the vocal art. The vocal art still boasted of a reasonable presence on the concert platform along with quality musicianship. Even amongst *khyāl* singers, *dhrupad* had remained relevant as an essential part of training — the repository of the sciences of breath control and intonation.

The *dhrupad* revival, such as is evident, was fuelled primarily by the following the genre acquired in Europe and other Western societies. It began when the Indologist, Alain Daneilou, and the UNESCO, introduced the pre-eminent *dhrupad* vocalists, Nasir Aminuddin and Nasir Moinuddin Dagar, to Europe. The success of this effort made *dhrupad* a unique phenomenon in art-music — losing ground in its home and acquiring an enthusiastic following amongst alien audiences.

The West's recent enthusiasm for *dhrupad* was repeating *dhrupad*'s history of 500 years ago, when its adoption by another foreign race, the Moguls from Central Asia, gave it a long lease of life in the face of a challenge from the rival *khyāl* genre. Although the two contexts are not strictly comparable, this recurrence could suggest features that give *dhrupad* a greater universality of appeal than its rivals and successors.

In the 1970s and 1980s, as the Indian currency depreciated speedily against the major international currencies, *dhrupad*'s growing international constituency stimulated a great deal of activity in India. An important part of the action was a substantial inflow of fresh talent, especially into the vocal art, which was the more vibrant of the two streams of. By the end of the twentieth century, the art of the *bīn* had become a "museum piece", while the vocal art of *dhrupad* could boast of a small group of credible musicians at home, who were dependent largely on the Western market for their livelihood.

An Aesthetic Perspective

Dhrupad, the performing art, evidently developed from the migration of an older tradition of devotional songs performed in the Vaiṣṇava temples to the secular environment presided over by the feudal aristocracy in medieval north India. (Selina Thielemann, *Journal of the Indian Musicological Society*, 1999, ed. Deepak Raja & Suvarnalata Rao) Because of this background, it retained its bias in favour of the poetic form. The *dhrupad* genre is therefore anchored to the melodic–poetic axis, in contrast to the *khyāl* genre, which revolves around the melodic–rhythmic axis giving the literary component only a subordinate role.

The poetic bias also explains the tendency of *dhrupad* towards being a pre-composed genre of music. This tendency is significantly manifested in its principles of melodic organization and the correspondence between the melodic structure and the poetic form. For melodic organization, the *dhrupad* tradition prescribes a four-stage development. In contemporary terminology, they are called (a) *sthāī*, (b) *antarā*, (c) *sañchārī* and (d) *ābhoga*. Although compositional formats vary, each step is conceived with a well defined aesthetic function. The *sthāī* and the *antarā* unfold the melodic canvas in progressive sequence from the lower octave to the upper, while the *sañchārī* summarizes the *rāga*'s melodic profile, and the *ābhoga* "winds up" the *rāga* exposition, folding back the melodic canvas. Although this protocol pertained initially to the composition of the melodic–rhythmic shell of the poetic form, it has been accepted as a general principle, valid also for the elaborate *alāp* that precedes the presentation of the composition in contemporary *dhrupad*. This protocol continues to be treated with great respect in the post-*dhrupad* genres, and is conspicuous in the performances of the greatest musicians of our times.

Corresponding to this principle of melodic development, Miya Tansen laid down that a *pada* should have four rhyming stanzas. The majority opinion amongst fifteenth- and sixteenth-century scholars favoured a three-stanza *pada*. In more recent times, the *pada*, as performed, has shrunk to just two stanzas — the *sthāī*, and the *antarā*. The literary component of the *pada*s has been predominantly in praise of Hindu gods and goddesses. Many *pada*s were written on musicological themes. As *dhrupad* became a resident of the princely courts, *pada*s also came to be composed in praise of emperors and princes.

In recent times, several lineages of *dhrupad* practitioners have veered away from the melody–poetry axis towards the melody–rhythm axis, forsaking the primacy of the literary element. But, the derailment was probably less widespread than was made out to be. For, the *dhrupad* mainstream did, indeed, incorporate different sub-streams called *bānī*s (lit. languages/dialects) with their respective stylistic biases.

Stylistic Diversity

Raja Man Singh Tomar's treatise (*Māna-Kūtūhala*) mentions the four *bānī*s. In his time, these classifications were based on the language/dialect in which the *pada* was written: "Gauhar" from Gwalior, "Dagar" from the Dangar region near Delhi, "Khandar" from the Khandar region, and "Nauhar" from the dialect spoken by the Nauhar community. In later years, the four *bānīs* came to signify stylistic distinctions.

Dhrupad musicians of the Gauhar Bānī concentrate their musical energies on the Śānta Rasa (the tranquil emotional state). Dagar Bānī emphasizes the Mādhurya (tenderness) and Karuṇa (pathos) Rasa. The Khandhar Bānī expresses the Vīra Rasa (the sentiment of valour). And, finally, Nauhar Bānī specializes in the music of Adbhut Rasa (the sentiment of surprise/marvel). Up to the time of Tansen (sixteenth century), practitioners of each of the *bānīs* chose *rāgas* and poetry in accordance with their emotional/stylistic biases. In later years, however, this integrity of approach lapsed, and musicians began to adopt multiple *bānīs* in their musical demonstrations.

In terms of musical expressions, a differentiation between the *bānī*'s is indicated from an observation by Ustad Vilayat Hussain Khan, the scholarly vocalist of the Agra Gharānā. According to him, the Khandar is replete with heavy *gamaks* (a magnified *vibrato*); Nauhar combines *gamaks* with brisk passages; Dagar presents its music with aplomb; Gauhar, patronized by Miya Tansen, is devoid of *gamaks*, and moves primarily with graceful *mīṇḍ* (smooth intervallic transitions using grace notes).

The different *bānīs* of *dhrupad* ceased to retain their formal identities in the sixteenth century after the death of Miya Tansen, and merged into the new Senīya Gharānā, with Tansen himself as the titular fountainhead. This was merely a "political" alignment, and even Tansen's immediate descendants could not entirely ignore the stylistic variety they had inherited. The lineage of his son, Bilas Khan specialized in the Gauhar Bānī, and partially patronized Dagar Bānī. The lineage of his son-in-law, Misri Singh (Naubat Khan) were specialists of the Khandhar and Dagar Bānī.

Although contemporary *dhrupad* musicians profess allegiance to *bānīs* through their stylistic lineages, the stylistic distinctions between them are, by and large, no longer discernible. This could be because, due to the shrinkage in the number of *dhrupad* practitioners over the last century, aspirants to the art have had to draw on a multiplicity of sources for their musical ideas and melodic technique, including the modern *khyāl* idiom. As a result, the only viable classification in contemporary *dhrupad* vocalism is between aggressive styles revolving around the poetic–rhythmic axis, and relatively softer styles anchored to the poetic–melodic axis.

Gharānās of Dhrupad

The diversity of approach and style in *dhrupad* is now represented by five major *gharānās* practising the genre (Selina Thielemann, "Classical Dhrupada: The Principal Gharānās", *Journal of the Indian Musicological Society*, 1999, ed. Deepak Raja & Suvarnalata Rao).

1. ***The Dagar Gharānā***: This is the oldest *gharānā* of classical *dhrupad*, having been founded by Nayak Haridas Dagar in the sixteenth century. Its descendants converted to Islam during the eighteenth century. In recent times, its most eminent representatives have been vocalists, Nasir Moinuddin Dagar (1919-66) and Nasir Aminuddin Dagar (1923-2002) and the *bīn* maestro, Zia Mohiuddin Dagar (1929-90).

2. ***The Darbhanga Gharānā***: This *gharānā* was founded in the eighteenth century by two brothers, Radhakrishna and Karttaram, whose descendants have carried the "Mallik" surname. In the post-Independence era, the most distinguished musicians of this lineage have been Ramchatur Mallik (1906-90) and Vidur Mallik (1936–2002).

3. ***The Bettiah Gharānā***: Though founded in the seventeenth century, this *gharānā* flourished during the nineteenth century, and wielded tremendous influence over *dhrupad* in the entire eastern region. Musicians of Bettiah are believed to have taught the founders of the once influential Bishnupur Gharānā in Bengal. Bettiah is represented, on the contemporary concert platform, by Indrakishore Mishra (b. 1957).

3. ***The Talwandi Gharānā***: This *gharāṇā* originated in north-west India, now in Pakistan, and is currently based in Lahore. Although its music is entirely based on *dhrupad*, it has "Islamized" its poetic content. Very little is known about its contemporary musicianship.

4. ***The Mathura Gharānā***: This is the oldest *gharānā* of Haveli Sangeet, the *dhrupad* tradition of the Vaiṣṇavite temples. Though its members have stepped out of the ecclesiastical environment for a nominal presence on the concert platform, their art has not made a complete transition to the elaborate format of contemporary *dhrupad*.

It may be noted that only three of these *gharānā*s — Dagar, Darbhanga, and Bettiah — have a significant presence on the contemporary concert platform.

Melodic Expressions in Dhrupad

The *alāp* in the *dhrupad* genre, considered the soul of the genre, has often been described as a "journey into pure sound". This is a poetic description of the genre's substantial reliance on the individual *svar*, rather than a phrase, as the basic building block of melody. The *dhrupad alāp* displays a preference for single intervallic transitions, and relationships between two *svar*s. Individual transitions may, however, touch several tonal and micro-tonal bases on their path. In contrast, post-*dhrupad* genres favour greater melodic agility, and rely more on phrasing involving two or more intervallic transitions, and relationships between three or more *svar*s at a time. In its vocal manifestation, this philosophy of the *dhrupad alāp* converts the yogic practice of *prāṇāyāma* (breath control/mastery over the life force) into a science of intonation. As an approach to musical expression, the practice of this science is associated with each intonation being backed by the controlled power of exhalation, resulting in a sense of introspection, serenity and repose.

The inventory of expressions in *dhrupad* manifest this technique of breath control along with the resultant melodic continuity, and the austerity of expression consistent with a meditative art form. *Dhrupad* thus rules out the more agile and ornate melodic expressions typical of the vocal genres that succeeded it. An important manifestation of this distinction is its elephantine gait. The pedagogy of *dhrupad* contains a large inventory of melodic expressions. However, four basic techniques may be mentioned here.

For convenience of comprehension, these expressions may be classified into: (a) melodic continuity, and (b) melodic discontinuity. The melodic continuity expressions consist of the *mīṇḍ*, *sūta*, and *gamak*, while the discontinuous expression is limited primarily to the *khaṭakā* (jerky motion).

The *mīṇḍ* is a continuous intervallic transition from one *svar* to another. Its melodic contour can be concave or convex; but never angular. This is the primary melodic expression in *dhrupad*, and emphasizes the near-absence of disjunct or staccato expressions. Generally, the word *mīṇḍ* is used for a short-to-medium span intervallic transition.

The broad-span continuous intervallic transition, generally devoid of obvious concavity or convexity, and corresponding to a complete exhalation, is called a *sūta*. The *sūta* may be unidirectional or bi-directional within the same exhalation. The *sūta* generally traverses tonal distances more briskly than a *mīṇḍ* does. This vocal expression is believed to have been borrowed from the *ghasīṭ* (dragging) technique of the *bīn*, which is executed with a glide of the fingers across the fretboard under a single stroke of the plectrum. The aural experience of the *sūta/ghasīṭ* is that of a *svar* being dragged from tonal point to another point at a considerable distance.

The *gamak* creates a pulsating or quivering effect — a magnified *vibrato* — by repeatedly attacking a *svar* from a lower *svar*. The melodic contour of a *gamak* is concave. The *gamak* is generally used for distances of up to two, and occasionally three *svar*s. The *gamak* is ideally suited for medium-to-high density melodic execution. In high-density execution, it approaches staccato intonation.

Perceptible melodic discontinuity in *dhrupad* is handled primarily with the *khaṭakā* expression. It is deployed for short-span intervallic transitions, most commonly in descending melodic motion. A *khaṭakā* represents a sudden, jerky drop of intonation from one *svar*, to a lower *svar*, with a momentary break in exhalation.

The Tāls of Dhrupad

In response to a query, Selina Thielemann, the eminent *dhrupad* scholar, wrote (e-mail of 18 October 2002):

> *Dhrupad* compositions are set basically to six *tāls*: *Chautāl* (12 beats), *dhamār* (14 beats), *rūpak* (7 beats), *tīvra* (7 beats), *jhaptāl* (10 beats), and *sulatāl* (10 beats). Ustad Fahimuddin Dagar would accept these as the only six *tāls* employed in *dhrupad*. Compositions in *matta tāl* (18 beats) are of recent origin. I only know of a few such compositions composed by the Gundecha Brothers. This is the information for classical *dhrupad*. However, devotional *dhrupad* (*dhrupad*

performed in the temples of the Vaiṣṇava sects) is performed strictly in *chautāl.*

Despite the variety of *tāl*s reported by Ms. Thielemann, contemporary *dhrupad* restricts itself almost entirely to *chautāl*, *dhamār*, and *sulatāl*.

Rāga Presentation Structure

In the *dhrupad* genre, the established model for *rāga* presentation prescribes two phases. Phase I is solo, and without percussion accompaniment. Phase II is performed to accompaniment by the *pakhāwaj*, the double-conical barrel drum. The solo Phase I has three stages of development:

1. ***The vilambit* [*slow tempo*] *alāp***: This is a free-flowing, anarhythmic exposition of the *rāga*'s melodic personality, structured in consonance with well-established rules of melodic progression. Its character in vocal and *bīn* renditions is identical, except that the vocal rendition uses meaningless consonants such as *tā, nā, rī* as articulation. The *vilambit alāp* has two movements — the *sthāī*, rendered in the lower half of the melodic canvas, and the *antarā*, rendered in the upper half. The *sthāī* begins with improvisations around the tonic accompanied by a few phrases identifying the *rāga* beyond reasonable doubt. It then descends into the lower octave, thereafter ascending step-by-step up to the mid-octave region. The *antarā* begins in the mid-octave region, ascends into the higher octave with a restful pause *en route* at the upper *sā* (tonic), and descends finally to the tonic. In rare cases, a musician may decide to append a *sañchārī* and/or *ābhoga* movement to the *vilambit alāp* as a "winding up" movement, deploying broad-span melodic phrasing, bypassing the discipline of step-by-step melodic

progression typical of the *sthāī* and the *antarā*.

The melodic progression in the *dhrupad alāp* often appears less methodical than that of the modern *khyāl* genre. This is because it habitually progresses in broader melodic spans. This feature arises from the notion of the *rāga*'s melodic personality in *dhrupad*, shaped by the melodic lines of the *padas* the musician has learnt, which in turn are shaped by the poetic lines of the verse. This feature of *dhrupad* relates to the "narrative" experience of melody in *dhrupad*, contrasted with the "symmetric" and "geometric" experience enabled by the shorter-span phrasing and progression typical of the *khyāl* genre (Refer: The Experience of Melody: From Dhrupad to Santūr, Chapter 3.5).

2. ***The madhya laya* [*medium tempo*] *alāp***: With this stage in the *alāp*, a pulsation enters the melody. This corresponds to the nomenclature and melodic–rhythmic character of *joḍ* on the *bīn*. In the vocal manifestation, the *madhya laya alāp* utilizes meaningless consonants such *nom, tom, ta, nā, rī,* etc., to heighten the rhythmicality of the aural experience, and to mimic the regular frequency of strokes on the *bīn*, its traditional accompaniment. For this reason, this stage onwards, the unaccompanied solo rendition is often described as the *nom tom alāp*. This *nom tom* phonetic is a remnant of what was once a rhythmic chanting of the name of Lord Viṣṇu — *oṁ hari ananta nārāyaṇa*. The distortion probably took place either due to the aversion of Muslim musicians to chanting the name of Hindu gods, or purely because of phonetic convenience in rendition. The *madhya laya alāp/joḍ* is structured to a simple pulse at the rate of one to two beats per second, and typically uses broader-span phrasing strategies

than the *vilambit alāp*. The *madhya laya alāp* also generally conforms to the principles of melodic progression in two movements — the *sthāī* and the *antarā*. The valedictory *sañchārī/ābhoga* movements are rare in the *madhya laya alāp*, though an approximation to them may be found in the third phase, the *drut alāp*.

3. ***The drut [fast tempo] alāp***: This corresponds to the nomenclature and melodic–rhythmic structure of the *jhālā* on the *bīn*. The vocal rendition of the *drut alāp* retains the use of meaningless consonants for convenience of high-density melodic–rhythmic articulation. The *drut alāp* is performed at a stepped-up tempo relative to the *madhya laya alāp* — at a pulsation rate of four beats per second or higher. In the vocal rendition, this requires the articulation to shift from a two-beat pulse to four-beat and eight-beat patterning of the meaningless consonants. The *drut alāp* also conforms to melodic patterning on the basis of *sthāī* and *antarā* movements, but tends to deploy broader spans of phrasing than the earlier two movements of the *alāp*. In rare cases, it may be stepped up a notch to form a fourth tier of the unaccompanied solo presentation. The fourth tier, when present, approximates the free-flowing *tān*s of the post-*dhrupad* genres.

In mid-twentieth-century recordings, and in contemporary *dhrupad* concerts, the *drut alāp* is occasionally found to have been rendered to *pakhāwaj* accompaniment, with distinctly titillating results. This practice would appear to militate against the austerity of the genre, and could represent an attempt by recent and contemporary musicians to revive audience interest in a dying art form.

A durational analysis of *dhrupad* performances (Selina

Thielemann, *The Darbhanga Tradition*, 1st edn. 1997, Indica Books, Varanasi) establishes the three/four-tiered *alāp* as consuming over 60 per cent of the duration of a *rāga* presentation. Presentations in *dhamār* and the minor rhythmic cycles may, however, frequently devote a lower share of duration to the *alāp*.

The *alāp* is followed by a Phase II, consisting of a pre-composed *pada*, along with improvisations thereon. The *pada* may be set to any of *tāl*s accepted in the *dhrupad* tradition. The percussion-accompanied Phase II has two stages of development:

1. ***Complete rendition of the pada, in both its parts*** — The *sthāī* and the *antarā*, and *sañchārī-ābhoga*, if present. In case of *pada*s in *dhamār* and the minor *tāl*s, contemporary practice permits some improvisatory movements to be inserted between the *sthāī* and the *antarā*.

2. ***Improvisatory movements***: In *pada* rendition, orthodox *dhrupad* permits only such forms of melodic improvisation, as would protect the integrity of the poetic element.

   Improvisations in *dhrupad* consist of a sequence of rhythmic variations [*layakaaree*] within the metric cycle based on either the division of beats [*laya-bāṇṭa*] or divisions of the words [*bola-bāṇṭa*] . . . the use of solfa syllables or embellishments on the vowel "aa", as characteristic of the *Khyāl*, are prohibited. *Layakaaree*s in slow tempo consist of stretched notes; the syllables are extended to note values longer than or equal to those of the basic composition. In medium tempo, the syllables are grouped into two or three per beat, and the *layakaaree*s are sung [at] approximately double the speed of the composition,

> suggesting a speed approximately four times faster than the composition. Some singers may further speed up, to the eighth degree, in which case the comprehensibility of the syllables may be disturbed. . . . In some *dhrupad* traditions, it is common practice to repeat the basic composition at various levels of speed ranging from double speed to the sixth or eighth degree but never slower than the composition itself. — Thielemann, 1997, ibid.

Variants on the Rāga Presentation Structure

For vocal music, as well as the *bīn*, the above model for *rāga* presentation is generally followed for the first/main *rāga* in a concert, which will have a *pada* set to *chautāl* of 12 beats. With this as the basic format, several variants have been common in recent/contemporary *dhrupad* practice. The choice of the format depends greatly on the time available for the performance, and the inclination of the performer (Thielemann, 1997, ibid.).

1. Three-tier *alāp*, followed by a *pada* in *chautāl* — the primary *dhrupad* format.
2. Three-tier *alāp*, followed by a *pada* in *chautāl*, and then by a *dhamār* composition in the same *rāga*.
3. Three-tier, or even single-tier *alāp*, followed by a *dhamār* composition.
4. Three-tier or single-tier *alāp*, followed by a *dhamār* composition and a *sulatāl* composition.
5. A three-tier *alāp*, followed by a *chautāl* composition, and a *sultāl* composition.

The Ensemble for Dhrupad Performance

In vocal as well as *bīn* presentations, the ensemble for contemporary *dhrupad* performance is austere. It consists of a pair of *tānpūrā* for drones, and *pakhāwaj* as percussion accompaniment. *Bīn* accompaniment for vocal performances, once the norm, is now rare. Up to the middle of the twentieth century, *dhrupad* vocalists, like contemporary *khyāl* singers, occasionally performed with a *sāraṅgī* as melodic accompaniment. However, with the growing shortage of *sāraṅgī* players, especially those trained in *dhrupad*, this practice has fallen into disuse.

A special note has to be taken of the role of *pakhāwaj* accompaniment in a *dhrupad* recital, which varies considerably from the role of the *tablā* in post-*dhrupad* music. While, the basic composition is being performed, the *pakhāwaj* behaves very much like *tablā* accompaniment for *khyāl*, providing the metric structure (*ṭhekā*) of the *tāl*. But, once the *pada* rendition is over, and the improvisations begin, each of them takes off on his independent improvisatory trip, often competing with the other in the invention of increasingly complex rhythmic variations.

This feature of *dhrupad*, coupled with the excessive rhythmic bias in the improvisatory movements of *pada* rendition, obliged late nineteenth/early twentieth-century musicologists like V.N. Bhatkhande and D.L. Roy (Ranade, *JIMS*, 1999) to compare *pada* rendition to a wrestling bout between the musician and his percussionist. They pronounced it an unpleasant aural experience that could only doom the genre to an untimely demise. It is now believed that *dhrupad* succumbed to this obsession in an attempt to resist the challenge posed by the *khyāl* genre. Although some contemporary *dhrupad* musicians have tried to resist a drift in this direction, they do not seem to be unanimous about this being a problem waiting to be solved.

A Structural Analysis

This structure of a *dhrupad* performance can be interpreted in two different ways:

First, the *dhrupad* format represents a sequential separation of the strictly melodic from the poetic–rhythmic. The *alāp* is pure melody. It has *laya* (pulsation) but no *tāl* (cyclical rhythmicality). The *pada*, on the other hand, is dominated by poetry. The manipulation of the melodic and the rhythmic elements, beyond the confines of the basic frame of the composition, is severely restricted. In comparison, the *khyāl* requires the simultaneous manipulation of the melodic, the rhythmic, and the poetic elements right from the beginning.

Second, the *dhrupad* format represents a sequential separation of the linear progression of music from the cyclical flows. The progression of the *alāp*, from the lower octave to the higher, from a subtle *laya* to the explicit, and from a slow tempo towards the higher, is a predominantly linear structure. The *sañchārī* and *ābhoga* sections of the *alāp*, as originally conceived, had an element of cyclicity. However, with these two movements having fallen into disuse, the *dhrupad alāp* has become a linear melodic entity. While the *alāp* is linear, *pada* rendition is cyclical in its structure. The poetic–melodic–rhythmic shell of the presentation is cyclical. Improvisations, whether melodic or rhythmic, remain within a restricted periphery of the melodic–rhythmic–poetic frame of the composition, and are therefore largely cyclical.

In *dhrupad*, therefore, the *alāp* moves in a well-defined direction, while the *pada* goes nowhere. *Khyāl*, in comparison, plunges simultaneously into the linear and cyclical flows of the musical idea. It progresses simultaneously on the melodic and the rhythmic dimensions in terms of density and complexity. The *khyāl* is therefore continuously going somewhere. *Khyāl* progresses towards a destination that appears to justify the musical endeavour more categorically than *dhrupad*.

The notion of "going nowhere", or "going somewhere", and the implications of this notion for the build-up and release of anticipatory tension, defines an important structural divide between the medieval *dhrupad* and the modern *khyāl* forms.

The Nature of Appeal

Dhrupad is frequently considered more "intellectual", while the *khyāl* is considered more "emotional" in its appeal. This view needs to be reconsidered.

A significant justification for *dhrupad*'s "intellectual" label might rest on the richness and sanctity of its poetic element, relative to the *khyāl*. Most scholars are agreed that the richness of *dhrupad*'s literary content is now history, and its significance too has shrunk substantially over the centuries.

The *dhrupad* genre has been described as *svarāśrit* and *padāśrit*. By this description, its soul lies in its melodic and poetic elements, and the relationship between the two. Since a *rāga* is a melodic vehicle for an emotional statement, and the poetic element of the *pada* imparts explicit meaning to the emotional communication of the melody — refer to Tansen's tenets enumerated above — the elicitation of an emotional response would appear to be the predominant aesthetic intention of *dhrupad* as a genre.

Another way of looking at this issue is the level of freedom *dhrupad* allows the musician in the different departments of musicianship. The constraints on improvisational freedom — melodic, rhythmic or poetic — are so great that the only real freedom musicians enjoy is in the soul-power and the emotional intensity with which they imbue their music. Whatever a genre permits, it encourages. By shutting the doors to freedom in most departments, *dhrupad* focuses the musical energies upon the most fundamental dimension of musicality: helping the aesthetic impact of *svar*-delivery to transcend its known psycho-acoustic parameters.

The aesthetic ideal of *dhrupad* would appear to be the experience of the *svar* as *svara* (*sva*=the self + *ra* = illumination). For achieving this result, medieval musicological texts have defined ideal *svar*-delivery as a product of two qualities: *anuraṇan* and *dīpti*. Neither of these terms is satisfactorily translated. Their intent is, however, to relate voice production and *svar*-delivery to the auto-suggestive and personality-transforming potential of the act of music-making. This deduction again appears to support an "emotional" label for *dhrupad* more than an "intellectual" one.

As a genre, *dhrupad* invests an extraordinary proportion of musical energy into the acoustic and aesthetic cultivation of voice production and *svar*-delivery. Consequently, the individual *svar* becomes as basic a unit of the musical expression as the phrase that it constructs.

The phrase, as a unit of music, has an element of design in it, which defines the relationship of the expression to a *rāga*. Pattern recognition is largely a cerebral process. When, as in *dhrupad*, the individual *svar* receives focused attention, it enables its aesthetic enjoyment, independently of the phrase and the *rāga*. A *svar* in isolation, by virtue of its momentary, and even illusory, isolation from the phraseological context, is a more probable stimulus for an emotional response than an intellectual one.

The comparison with *khyāl* points towards another aesthetic dimension of *dhrupad*. *Khyāl* requires the simultaneous manipulation of the melodic with the poetic and the rhythmic, and of the linear with the cyclical. A genre requiring the simultaneous manipulation of two or more variables is intellectually more absorbing and demanding than a genre that isolates them for sequential handling. By this logic, again, the structure of the *khyāl* can be considered more "intellectual" than that of *dhrupad*.

Considering the totality of these factors, a contemporary view would justify an "emotional" label for the *dhrupad* genre, and an "intellectual" label for *khyāl*. The caveat to any such labelling temptation is, of course, that it identifies biases and tendencies without necessarily providing the basis for a mutually exclusive classification.

Dhrupad Today

The epilogue to a global survey of *dhrupad* (*Journal of the Indian Musicological Society*, Annual Issue of 1999, ed. Deepak Raja and Suvarnalata Rao), assessed *dhrupad* with the following observations:

> The decline of *dhrupad*, and its surrender to the *khyāl* wave, is a socio-cultural phenomenon, reflecting changing audience profiles, and aesthetic values. *Dhrupad* probably declined in popularity because of its resistance to change, restrictions on individual creativity, and its failure to accommodate changing audience tastes. Comprehensive *rāga* presentation in Hindustani music needed to do something to avert extinction. It did so by loosening the rigid *dhrupad* format, and found a ready solution in the already mature rival, the *khyāl* form.
>
> Some *dhrupad gharānā*s, however, resisted the *khyāl* wave, and persisted with the *dhrupad* format. Their tenacity was rewarded with the opening up of the European market for Hindustani music in the 1960s, and subsequent revivalist attempts at home. Thanks to these efforts, young vocalists with respectable performing standards have partially restored the genre to the mainstream concert platform. These musicians are attempting to impart to *dhrupad* a greater acceptability amongst contemporary audiences. In creating an audience for their music, their focus seems to include Indian audiences nurtured in the Carnatic tradition, and receptive audiences in Europe and the US.

Their efforts appear to be winning back mature Hindustani audiences who had either rejected *dhrupad* as an unpleasant experience or who had not heard quality *dhrupad* for a long time. For the newer audiences, especially the younger and uninitiated audiences, *dhrupad* is a novel experience, but more accessible than *khyāl*. In south India, *dhrupad* claims acceptance because of two factors: a general opening up of the Carnatic-oriented market to Hindustani music, and the similarity of the *dhrupad* format to the *rāgam-thānam-pallavī* format in Carnatic music.

In the domestic music market, with an ample availability of other genres of classical and semi-classical music, audience preferences or loyalties are not shaped by the genre as much as by individual musicianship. In Europe and the US, on the other hand, there appears to be a genre-based following for *dhrupad*. Driven by economics, *dhrupad* is now evolving primarily within an orbit defined by Indian musicians, and trans-culturally receptive Western audiences, enthusiasts, musicians, and scholars. Today, European and American audiences and students largely sustain the livelihood of Indian *dhrupad* performers. *Dhrupad* is moving towards becoming a European and American genre of Indian origin, performed largely by Indians, but increasingly also by Western musicians. The larger implications of this reality have yet to be ascertained.

This configuration of tendencies is unique in the history of Hindustani music. Never before has a genre been pronounced dead in India, experienced so shaky a revival with hard-core home audiences, and become popular enough with alien audiences to become so totally dependent on them. This makes *dhrupad* one of the enigmas of cultural anthropology.

4.2

AN INTRODUCTION TO KHYĀL

THE *khyāl* is the dominant genre of mainstream vocal music today, and has been so for over two centuries. Because of the primacy of vocal music in the Hindustani tradition, it has also had a considerable influence on the evolution of instrumental music. The word *khyāl* is of Perso-Arabic origin, and has been variously translated as idea, imagination, subjectivity, individuality, and impression. All these connotations are consistent with the character of the genre. Bhatkhande suggests that the term may have originally denoted licentiousness (*Bhatkhande Sangeet Shastra*, vol. I, 5th edn., 1981). This suggestion has some merit considering the vast creative freedom accorded to the musician by the *khyāl*, compared to the highly disciplined formalism of its medieval predecessor, *dhrupad / dhamār*.

> Among all Hindustani vocal genres, the *khyāl* provides its performers the greatest opportunity and challenge to display the depth and breadth of musical knowledge and skills. Its essence lies in the manner in which artists take the characteristics that distinguish *khyāl* as a genre, make those choices that lie within their group traditions, summon their own creative individuality, and create a unique *khyāl* at each performance. — Bonnie C. Wade, 1st edn., 1984

Note: Adapted from a backgrounder for incorporation in commentaries on *khyāl* music produced by India Archive Music Ltd., New York.

The *khyāl* genre is distinguished from other major genres of Hindustani vocal music — *dhrupad* and *ṭhumrī* — by a linear (progressive) intensification of melodic and rhythmic densities and complexities, and a cyclical treatment of melodic and rhythmic elements within the central linearity of rendition.

The Plastic Arts Metaphor Applied to Khyāl Music

Every artefact can be seen to have an architectural element, a sculptural element, and an ornamentational element. The architectural element relates to the structural and functional relationship between the parts. The sculptural element deals with the contours it defines from a reasonable distance. The ornamentational element concerns itself with features that endear the artefact to the viewer from close quarters. Architecture deals with the manner in which an artefact *functions,* sculpture, with the way it *looks,* and ornamentation, with the way it *pleases.*

In general, one might say that all music has elements of architecture, sculpture and ornamentation, with their relative weight varying between the different genres, and even between the different styles/*gharānā*s within the same genre. Using this framework for understanding the principal genres in Hindustani music, *dhrupad* can be described as architecture-dominant; *khyāl* can be described as sculpture-dominant; and *ṭhumrī* can be described as ornamentation-dominant (refer Chapter 2.1).

Interestingly, however, what differentiates the *khyāl* genre from *dhrupad* and *ṭhumrī* most conclusively is its architecture. The architecture of *khyāl* vocalism is characterized by an end-to-end linearity, shaped by a progressive intensification of tonal and beat densities and complexities in its rendition. It is probably this unidirectional flow of musical energies that enables the artistic effort to focus itself sharply on the melodic effort, and thus to define *khyāl* as a sculpture-dominant genre.

This linearity of architecture distinguishes *khyāl* from both *dhrupad* and *ṭhumrī*. But, the difference between sculpture and ornamentation being one only of perspective, the sculpture-dominant character of *khyāl* still needed protection from a drift towards the ornamentation characteristic of the *ṭhumrī* genre. It is by this logic of differentiation between the genres that *khyāl* evolved as a genre unidirectional in its architecture, elaborate in its approach to sculpture, and judicious in its deployment of ornamentation.

History and Evolution

The legendary thirteenth-century poet-musician Amir Khusro is popularly credited with the invention of the *khyāl* form. This belief is conceptually fallacious because no individual can be credited with the creation of a genre. This attribution of even an initiating role to Amir Khusro is contentious. The architecture and stylistics of the *khyāl* form apparently pre-date Khusro by several centuries. Thakur Jaydev Singh traces the *khyāl* form to the *rūpakālapti* form within the *sādhāraṇī śailī* of vocal music in practice in the eighth/ninth century. He credits Amir Khusro, however, with giving it a Perso-Arabic name, introducing it to the patronage of Muslim rulers, and encouraging its practice amongst singers of *qawwālī*, a form of Sufi religious music (*Nibandha Sangeet*, ed. L.N. Garg, 2nd edn., 1989).

The *khyāl* represents a fusion of older Indian musical traditions with Perso-Arabic influences starting from the twelfth/thirteenth century. The genre acquired some stature under the patronage of the Sharqui *sultāns* of Jaunpur (fifteenth century), and attained maturity and sophistication under the patronage of Emperor Mohammad Shah of Delhi (eighteenth century). Since then, the *khyāl* has eclipsed the medieval *dhrupad/dhamār* genre, and replaced it as the predominant genre of mainstream vocal music.

Sultan Hussain Sharqui (r. 1458-99) of Jaunpur encouraged

the evolution of a *kalāvantī khyāl* based on musical forms prevalent in his region as distinct from the *khyāl* inspired by the *qawwālī* encouraged by Amir Khusro (1253–1325). The immortal composer Niamat Khan "Sadarang" in the employ of Emperor Muhammad Shah, reportedly composed *khyāls* as a challenge to the supremacy of *dhrupad/dhamār*, by recasting poetic and melodic material drawn from the medieval genre.

The medieval *dhrupad/dhamār*, which dominated the mainstream between the thirteenth and the eighteenth centuries, and the modern *khyāl* genre, which overtook it in later years, have thus been contemporary rivals for almost the entire period of *dhrupad/dhamār* dominance. Ashok Ranade, the eminent musicologist, has argued that, neither of the two can be described as having been derived from the other, though both would have influenced each other to some degree. *Dhrupad/dhamār* evolved as a highly formal and disciplined art-form with a tendency towards being a predominantly pre-composed genre of music. In a parallel development, the *khyāl* evolved as a predominantly improvise form, and a vehicle for individual creativity (*Journal of the Indian Musicological Society*, 1999).

The Gharānās of Khyāl Music

The century preceding India's Independence, which witnessed the flowering of the *khyāl* genre in various hues and fragrances, is often described as the Golden Age of Hindustani music (V.H. Deshpande, *Indian Musical Traditions*, 2nd edn., 1987). Its foundations were laid in the sunset years of the Mogul Empire (mid-eighteenth century), when a vast resource of musicianship emigrated from Delhi and its environs towards smaller principalities in search of patronage. Several of these feudal principalities, protected by India's new British rulers, became patrons to lineages of musicians (*gharānās*), which cultivated distinctive musical styles within the broad framework of the *khyāl* genre.

For a variety of reasons, *gharānās* of *khyāl* music have come to acquire their names either from the principalities where they were cultivated, or from the name of a towering vocalist, who is recognized as the founder of the distinctive style of *khyāl* music.

Vamanrao Deshpande recognizes six distinct *gharānās* as stylistic lineages: Agra, Gwalior, Jaipur–Atrauli, Patiala, Indore, and Kairana (V.H. Deshpande, ibid.). Bonnie Wade recognizes six significant *gharānās* of *khyāl* music. They are Gwalior, Agra, Sahaswan/Rampur, Alladiya Khan (also known as Jaipur–Atrauli), Kairana, and Patiala. She considers the Indore/Bhindi Bazar Gharānā too close to Kairana to qualify as an independent *gharānā*. She, however, acknowledges its principal exponent, Ustad Ameer Khan, as being amongst the towering individuals whose music she does not identify with any of the major *gharānās* (Bonnie C. Wade, 1984).

Deshpande (op. cit.) cautions enlightened opinion against glorifying the *gharānā* system and placing an undue premium on stylistic conformity amongst its followers. He reminds us that the greatest vocalists in recent memory, almost without exception, acquired their art from more than one *gharānā* or *guru*, and openly credited their accomplishments to the multiplicity of influences.

Deshpande (op. cit.) offers a conceptual framework for the aesthetic classification of the *gharānās* of *khyāl* music. He classifies *gharānā* styles on a continuum defined by rhythmic orientation and melodic orientation as the two polarities. Amongst the *gharānās* considered by him, he places Agra at the rhythmic orientation polarity, and Kairana at the melodic orientation polarity. Placing them at the exact mid-point of the continuum, he regards Alladiya (Jaipur–Atrauli) as a complex fusion, and Gwalior as a simple fusion of the two orientations. Patiala is placed towards the melodic orientation pole, but considerably short of Kairana. The Indore/Bhindi Bazar Gharānā of Ameer Khan falls between Patiala and Kairana, close to the melodic orientation pole.

With specific reference to the two polarities, Agra at the rhythm-oriented end, and Kairana at the melody-oriented end, Deshpande (op. cit.) observes that rhythm is the principle of motion, while melody is the principle of repose. The bias towards the rhythm end indicates animation, playfulness, and dynamism, while a bias towards the melody end is soothing, tranquillizing, and even depressing.

Wade (1984) adopts a more elaborate framework for comparing *gharānā* stylistics. The dimensions she lists are:

1. Voice- vocal technique, voice quality, range, ornamentation.
2. Preferences with respect to *rāga*s.
3. Preferences with respect to *tāl*s.
4. Preferences with respect to compositions.
5. Preferences with respect to performance tempo, and its acceleration.
6. Balance between rhythmic and melodic elements.
7. Structure of slow-tempo *khyāl* presentation.
8. Preferences with respect to improvisatory movements and types of articulation.
9. Strategies with respect to slow-tempo and medium/fast tempo *khyāl* presentations.

Although these dimensions have been proposed as a differentiator between the musical styles of the different *gharānā*s, they are equally applicable as a framework for analysing *khyāl* music at an individual level.

The Ensemble for Khyāl Performance

The minimum ensemble for a *khyāl* performance consists of a drone (*tānpūrā*) and a percussion accompaniment (*tablā*). A majority of concert performers today use two *tānpūrā*s, along with a melodic accompaniment provided either by a *sāraṅgī* or a harmonium player. In addition to this standard ensemble, some vocalists accompany themselves on a *svarmaṇḍala,* a harp belonging to the box-polychord family. Ustad Bade Ghulam Ali Khan was the first significant vocalist to use the *svarmaṇḍala*. Several eminent vocalists, notably, Smt. Kishori Amonkar and Pt. Jasraj, have followed his example.

The *tānpūrā, svarmaṇḍala,* and the melodic accompaniment — *sāraṅgī* or harmonium — perform a very significant and complex role in *khyāl* music. Their role relates as much to aiding the music-making processes of the vocalist, as to enriching the totality of the musical experience for audiences.

The Format of Khyāl Presentation

The *khyāl* genre subsumes three categories of compositional format: the slow-tempo *baḍā khyāl* (major *khyāl*) and the medium-to-fast tempo *chhoṭā khyāl* (minor *khyāl*), both based on a piece of poetry, and *tarānā*, a medium-to-fast tempo compositional form structured around meaningless sound syllables borrowed mainly from the stroke patterns of the plucked instruments (e.g., *da, ra, dir*) and beat patterns of percussion (e.g., *dha, tirkit, dhin*).

The *khyāl* genre permits the musician considerable freedom in structuring his presentation. Different *gharānā*s, and even individual musicians, have their own predilections in terms of the presentation format. Contemporary *khyāl* presentation does, however, tend to follow one of the two principal presentation formats:

The most common format in *khyāl* presentation is a *baḍā*

khyāl in *ektāl* (12 beats), or *jhūmarā* (14 beats) or *tilwāḍā* (16 beats) or *tīntāl* (16 beats) followed by a *chhoṭā khyāl* in *tīntāl* (16 beats) or *ektāl* (12 beats). In such a presentation, the rendition almost always begins with either an *auchar*, a brief free-flowing introduction of the *rāga*'s melodic personality, or merely a *rāga-vākya*, a couple of phrases seeking to achieve no more than identification of the *rāga*. An *auchar–baḍā khyāl–chhoṭā khyāl* presentation can last 35-45 minutes. In rare cases, the vocalist might add a third composition, a *tarānā* in the same *rāga*. This extension could consume an additional ten to fifteen minutes, bringing the total duration to about an hour.

In a less common format, deployed mainly by Agra and Gwalior vocalists, the slow-tempo *baḍā khyāl* is omitted. In its place, the vocalist presents an elaborate, three/four-tiered, *dhrupad*-style *alāp* without percussion accompaniment, followed by a *chhoṭā khyāl*. In such cases, the *khyāl* rendition generally begins at a medium tempo, and accelerates gradually to reach the normal, brisk, *chhoṭā khyāl* tempo. It is rare for such presentations to end with a *tarānā*.

An even less common format in contemporary *khyāl* presentation is a single medium-tempo composition, normally without an elaborate *alāp*. The composition is generally in *rūpak tāl* (7 beats) or *jhaptāl* (10 beats), and sometimes *tīntāl* (16 beats). The rendition is generally maintained at the same tempo throughout, with only marginal acceleration, if at all. This format is generally avoided for the first or main *khyāl* rendition in a concert. This type of medium-tempo *khyāl* presentation rarely lasts more than 20 minutes.

Melodic Expressions in the Khyāl Genre

Melodic execution in Hindustani music, essentially, avoids abruptness in intervallic transitions. This feature has been described as "conjunct" melody, as distinct from the "disjunct" melody found in Western music. In medium and high *svar-*

density expressions, as also for the expression of explicit rhythmicality, staccato expressions are, however, frequently encountered.

The theory of music performance describes at least ten forms of melodic execution/intervallic transitions (*Sangeet Kaladhar*, Dahyalal Shivram, 2nd edn., 1938). Other texts have larger inventories. The definitions from the texts are imprecise, and vary from text to text. The categories of melodic contours encountered in contemporary *khyāl* rendition would, however, outnumber all inventories considered together.

The principle categories of intervallic transition/phrasing/melodic expressions are:

1. ***Mīṇḍ***: The *mīṇḍ* is the basic form of intervallic transition in *khyāl* music. It involves a melodically continuous dragging of one *svar* to another, touching all the microtones along the path without allowing any of them to be perceived as having been explicitly intoned.
2. ***Kaṇ***: The word means "fraction". When an intervallic transition between *svar*s involves a fractional use of the first *svar*, it is called a *kaṇ*. A generous use of the *kaṇ* is considered more proper in the semi-classical *ṭhumrī* renditions than in *khyāl*.
3. ***Murkī***: Like the *kaṇ*, the *murkī*, too, is used more generously in the *ṭhumrī* genre. The *murkī* involves the execution of a phrase normally using at least three *svar*s in brisk, wrap-around, jerky expression, as in *pā-mā^-dhā-pā*. The *khyāl* generally deploys single-loop *murkī*s. Multiple-loop *murkī*s are used in the *ṭhumrī* genre.
4. ***Gītakīrī***: The brisk and explicit intonation of three or more adjacent *svar*s, whether in ascent or descent, without a jerk or wrap-around melodic motion, is called a *gītakīrī*.

5. ***Khaṭakā***: The word means "a jerk". This melodic expression is generally used for a transition between *svar*s at least two/three *svar*s apart, and in descending transition. The expression drops from the higher *svar* to the lower *svar*, with a jerk. This is specially useful in *rāga*s such as Gauḍ Sāraṅg (Descent: *sā'-pā-mā-gā/re-gā-re-mā-gā-pā-re-sā*). The *sā-pā* and *pā-re* transitions in Gauḍ Sāraṅg require the *khaṭakā* expression almost as mandatory for *rāga* identification.
6. ***Gamak***: The *gamak* expression arises from a repetition of the same *svar* at a medium-to-high *svar*-density. Taking the support of the lower *svar* without its explicit intonation, the musician repeatedly hammers the target *svar* to create the *gamak* expression.
7. ***Jamjam***: This expression also uses two adjacent *svar*s with one being emphasized by repetition, and differs from the *gamak* in that the *jamjam* explicitly intones both the adjacent *svars*, as in *gā-mā-mā/gā-mā-mā/gā-pā-pā/mā-pā-pā*.

These categories of melodic expression define the sculptural and ornamentational facets of a vocal recital. *Gharānās*, and individual musicians, differ in their preferences in this regard. These preferences, collectively, constitute a major part of the "stylistics" of *khyāl* music.

The Poetic Element in Khyāl Vocalism

The role of the poetic element in *khyāl* has been a subject of some bewilderment as well as debate. The song texts of *khyāl bandiś*es are primarily in Braj Bhāṣā, a dialect of Hindi spoken in and around Mathura. *Khyāl*s are, however, sung by musicians and heard by audiences from all parts of the country, most of whom do not understand the literal meaning of the poetry. Despite this, *khyāl*s lyrics in other languages have not been as popular, and Braj Bhāṣā verses have not been translated into either mainstream or regional languages. Moreover, a large number of vocalists, including the greatest, have been casual about the articulation of the poetic element, treating it almost on par with the meaningless consonants of a *tarānā*. And, yet, there is no general revolt in the music world against the apparent assault on the integrity of the *bandiś*, or on the listener's rights. These facts do not reflect a blind adherence to tradition as much as they acknowledge the role of the poetic element in *khyāl* vocalism.

Deshpande (1987) has argued, persuasively, that the art of singing could achieve its highest level of perfection in *khyāl* because, in this genre, the poetic element surrendered its literary function to its musical function. This musical function has several dimensions. The phonetic and syntactical structure of the poetry imparts concrete form to the *bandiś*, independently of its semantic significance. It enhances the musical value of the *bandiś* by adding a psycho-phonetic dimension to the psychoacoustics of the melodic–rhythmic shell. The semantic significance of the poetry activates the auto-suggestive process of the musician, helping the music to explore the emotional content of the *rāga*.

Deshpande's argument is supported by the fact that the twentieth century has witnessed equally great *khyāl* music from vocalists who treated *khyāl* verses rather casually, and those who systematically exploited its semantic significance. *Khyāl* gives the individual musician the choice. No wonder *khyāl* lyrics are written by musicians rather than poets, and rarely command respect as poetry.

Articulation in Khyāl Music

The *khyāl* genre deploys three categories of articulation:

1. ***Bol***: The poetic form, representing a vast range of

themes, which holds together the melodic and rhythmic elements in the composition (*bandiś/chīẓ*).

2. ***Sargam***: The use of solfa symbols as textural consonants in the improvisatory movements.
3. ***Ākāṛ***: The vowel *ā*, used in the improvisatory movements.

The *tarānā* does not use the poetic form in the main body of the *bandiś/chīẓ*. However, there exists a tradition of inserting Persian and Urdu *rubāīs* (verses) into the *tarānā* as a relief from the otherwise meaningless consonants constituting the phonetic element of the form. In the improvisatory movements, the *tarānā* form is permitted the use of *sargams* as well as *ākār*.

These three forms of articulation have collective, as well as individual, roles in the rendition of *khyāl* compositions. At the purely phonetic level, they provide the musician with three distinct textural devices. The poetic form is a balanced and unpredictable mix of vowel and consonant articulations, generally with a bias towards the softer consonants. The *sargam* device uses only consonants, and the range is limited to seven. The *ākār* has only one vowel, though individual styles can occasionally vary the articulation slightly. Collectively, the three devices contribute to the textural richness of the phonetic component of *khyāl* music.

The three forms of articulation also represent three different levels of abstraction in terms of meaning. The poetic form represents explicit meaning, which interacts, potentially, with the melodic element of the phrasing in the expression of its emotional content. The *sargam* represents musical meaning, by virtue of direct correspondence between the intonation and the articulation. The *ākār*, being a vowel phonetic, is totally abstract, with the meaning being provided only by the melodic contours of the intonation.

The deployment of the three forms of articulation is guided by aesthetic considerations, and by the stylistic predilections of individual *gharānā*s and vocalists. The poetic form is, for instance, used predominantly in slow and medium *svar* density movements. This is because high-density melodic expressions can jeopardize the integrity of the poetic form and the intelligibility of explicit meaning.

The *sargam* is used predominantly in medium-density movements. In such movements, it provides a textural option for the poetic form, and greater freedom for melodic–rhythmic improvisation than the poetic form will permit. It tends not to be used in very high-density melodic movements because consonants militate against high-frequency articulation, in addition to being less pleasing than vowels.

The *ākār* articulation is the most versatile, but is also the most demanding in terms of lung-power, and is therefore used selectively. Being a vowel form, it is most useful in movements where the melody is not required to express an explicit rhythmicality. Such movements are the low *svar*-density *alāp,* which is free from explicit rhythmicality, and the high-density *tān*s where the rhythmicality is built into the fixed ratio between the *svar*-density of the melody and the tempo (beat-density) of the rhythmic cycle at the particular stage of rendition.

The Structure of Compositions

Baḍā and *chhoṭā khyāl* compositions, and also *tarānā* compositions, have two stanzas, represented by two melodic sections: the *sthāī*, and the *antarā*. The *sthāī* is, as a rule, centred in the lower half of the melodic canvas, except when the melodic centre of gravity of the *rāga* falls in the *uttarāṅga*. The *antarā* is identifiable by a deliberate ascent to the upper tonic, with its follow-through centred in the upper half of the melodic canvas. The *antarā,* however, ends with a descent to base-*sā*. The two parts together represent a comprehensive map of the *rāga*'s melodic personality. The *sthāī* also functions as the nucleus of the *khyāl* presentation — the basic theme or refrain to which the rendition returns, repeatedly, after each round of improvisations.

Khyāl Presentation Protocol

The *baḍā khyāl* rendition begins with the presentation of the *sthāī* and *antarā* of the *bandiś*, and is followed by improvisatory movements, woven around the *sthāī*. It is not uncommon, however, for the *antarā* to be introduced after the first improvisatory movement.

The *baḍā khyāl* uses three improvisatory movements, each distinct in the melodic–rhythmic structure. The sequencing of these movements is in consonance with the convention of progressive enhancement of melodic and rhythmic density and complexity. In recent times, it has become customary to match this progression, at each transition, with a perceptible stepping-up of the basic tempo of the *tāl* performed by the percussionist.

1. ***Alāp***: The *alāp* is a free-flowing, rhythmically unstructured improvisation of low melodic density, in which the melodic lines attempt no correspondence with the beats of the *tāl*. The *alāp* acknowledges the rhythmic cycle only at the end of each round of improvisations, when it has to rejoin the *sthāī*. For the purposes of articulation, an *alāp* can either use the poetic element of the song (*bol-alāp*), or the abstract *ākār* (the vowel form *ā*), or a combination of the two. In rare cases, solfa symbols (*sargam*) are also found in the *alāp*.

2. ***Bol-laya* [*articulation in correspondence with rhythm*]**: The *bol-laya* movement is also referred to as *bol-bāṇṭ* (emphasis shifts on the poetic element). *Bol-laya*/*bol-bāṇṭ* is a pulse-driven movement of medium melodic

density, which introduces a moderate degree of correspondence, and even playful interaction, between the articulation, the melodic contours, and the beats of the rhythmic cycle. For articulation, a vocalist can use either the poetic form, or *sargam*, or a combination of the two. Only in rare cases is the *ākār* articulation encountered in the *bol-laya* movement.

3. ***Tāns***: *Tāns* are highly structured melodic runs of medium-to-wide melodic span, and high *svar*-density. They achieve a strong correspondence between their melodic contours and beats of the rhythmic cycle, and can exhibit a lively interaction with them. The melodic structure of *tāns* is derived from a typology that has matured over centuries of evolution. For articulation of *tāns*, a vocalist can use either the poetic element of the *bandiś*, *sargam*, or *ākār*, or a combination of the three.

For those familiar with the medieval *dhrupad* genre, it is easy to see that the improvisatory movements of the *baḍā khyāl* correspond to the *vilambit*, *mahālaya*, and *drut alāp* of a *dhrupad* presentation. Structurally, though not historically, the *baḍā khyāl* inserts the *alāp* of a *dhrupad* rendition into the rendition of the pre-composed *bandiś* as a chain of improvisatory movements. With this structural departure from the *dhrupad* format, the *baḍā khyāl* permits the simultaneous manipulation of the melodic and rhythmic elements, and creates a presentation format with an end-to-end linearity of melodic–rhythmic progression. This structural alignment is accompanied by a substantial enlargement of freedom in the choice of textural, sculptural as well as ornamentational devices to establish the *khyāl* as a distinctive genre of vocal music.

The *bandiś ṭhumrī*, a lively vocal form, originally evolved as an accompaniment to footwork-dominant sub-forms of Kathaka dance, inspires the second *bandiś*, the *chhoṭā khyāl*.

The *bandiś ṭhumrī* is characterized by a one-to-one correspondence between the poetic, the melodic, and the rhythmic elements. This makes the form ideal for rendition in the faster tempi.

A *chhoṭā khyāl* presentation begins with the rendition of the *sthāī* and the *antarā* and is followed by the improvisatory movements. Here again, it is common for the *antarā* to be introduced after a few rounds of improvisation rather than immediately after the *sthāī*. In rare cases, one may encounter elements of *alāp* and *bol-laya* in the *chhoṭā khyāl* too. However, in consonance with the tempo and the aural flavour of the *chhoṭā khyāl*, the improvisations are dominated by *tāns*, generally rendered at a *svar*-density at least twice the beat-density of the rhythmic cycle. In the *tāns*, the vocalist has the same choice of articulation as in the *baḍā khyāl*. *Tarānā* renditions follow the same format as the *chhoṭa khyāl*, except that the absence of poetry, and the availability of meaningless consonants for articulation might encourage a greater display of rhythmic dexterity and virtuosity.

The Typology of Tāns

The melodic patterns in *tāns* are constructed from five basic patterns: (i) *baḍhat*, (ii) *laḍīguthāva*, (iii) *sapāṭ*, (iv) *chhūt*, (v) *hopping tāns*.

Baḍhat* (*progressive*) *Tāns: There are two concepts of *baḍhat* (progression) in *tān* construction. The first is to construct them in progressively ascending melodic waves, each wave ascending further upwards than the previous one. The first wave ascends from a certain base, mostly base *sā*, ascends upwards up to a point, returns to base, ascends again, this time a little farther, returns again to base, and so on. The second approach to *baḍhat tāns* is patterned as a series of short *tāns* woven around one melodic focus after another in ascending order, without returning to base *sā* after each ascent, but instead reverting to the *sthāī*. The phraseology of *baḍhat tān*s can either be flat-out or zigzag. Their identifying feature is the progressive unfurling of the melodic canvas. *Baḍhat tān*s are, by their nature, appropriate for the ascent.

***Laḍīguthāva* (*chain-knitting*) *Tān*s**: *Laḍīguthāva* is a special category of *baḍhat tān* in which the melodic development moves progressively upwards, but continuously without returning to a base, using a very complex web of inter-locked patterns woven around each *svar* along the path. Their identifying feature is the complexity of the melodic web in progressive ascending or descending motion. *Laḍīguthāva* is perhaps the most demanding *tān* pattern because of short spans of improvisations and their seamless knitting into an ascending chain. This requires a total mastery over the melodic features of the *rāga*.

***Sapāṭ* (*flat-out*) *Tān*s**: *Sapāṭ tān*s ascend or descend in a cascading motion, with straightforward runs on the *rāga* scale without any twists and turns, with a single intonation supporting the execution of every *svar* on the intended melodic path. They have the desired impact when their melodic span covers at least one full octave. *Sapāṭ*s are rendered in ascending as well as descending movements.

***Chhūt* (*leaping*) *Tān*s**: *Chhūt tān*s are constructed by establishing a geometric (generally first-fifth or first-fourth) tonal relationship between phrases of short melodic spans, delivered in different regions of the melodic canvas. Their structure appears to leap from *svar* to distant *svar* in the process of generating waves of corresponding phrases. The *chhūt* pattern can be descending or ascending; but a set of *chhūt-tān* waves will generally be rounded off by a descending *sapāṭ*.

***Hopping Tān*s**: These *tān*s, generally found in ascending formation, hop across alternate *svar*s, often repetitively. For example, *sā-gā-sā-gā, re-mā-re-mā, gā-pā-gā-pā, mā-dhā-mā-dhā,*

Depending on the grammar of the *rāga*, these *tān*s may skip more than one *svar* in each hop. For obvious reasons, they are sometimes referred to as two-by-two *tān*s. The hopping/two-by-two *tān* is also inspired by one of the *alaṁkār*s. It acquired the status of a *tān* variety primarily as a speciality of the Jaipur–Atrauli Gharānā vocalists, particularly, Kesarbai Kerkar.

Amongst other *tān* structures, a significant, but simplistic in construction, is the *alaṁkār tān*. *Alaṁkār*s (lit: ornamentation) are a large group of practice exercises of varying complexity given to students with the dual purpose of training them in the precise delivery of *svar*s irrespective of the order in which they are arranged, and preparing them for the techniques of improvisation fundamental to Hindustani music. *Alaṁkār tān*s are recognizable by their symmetric progression such as: *sā-re-gā-gā, re-gā-mā-mā, gā-mā-pā-pā, mā-pā-dhā-dhā.*

The Aesthetics of Tāns

In the architecture of the *khyāl* genre, the *tān*s represent a culmination of melodic density and complexity. The advanced level of melodic density automatically makes the *tān*s a display of virtuosity, and in the advanced level of complexity, the musician has the opportunity of demonstrating his virtuosity, imagination, as well as aesthetic sensibility. But, the issue of aesthetics in *tān*s is much larger than complexity.

At every level, melodic density has a different psycho-acoustic implication. Pt. Omkarnath Thakur (1897–1967), for instance, refused to sing *tān*s in Nīlāmbarī, because they would militate against the *rasa* of the *rāga*. Swimming against the tide of generalized expectations of *khyāl* presentation protocol, he established Nīlāmbarī as one of his most memorable and popular *rāga*s.

The character of the *rāga* is also an issue in the selection of *tān* patterns. The melodic personality of every *rāga*, and also its emotional charge, are residents of its *chalan*. The *chalan* of each *rāga* limits the musician's options in terms of patterning strategies for *tāns*. *Rāgas* with a zigzag *chalan* cannot, for instance, support the *alaṁkār* or *sapāṭ tān* patterns. Such *rāgas* could, on the other hand, be ideally suited for the hopping or *laḍīguthāva* pattern.

Another major issue of aesthetics in *tāns* is the level of melodic density (intonations per second). Above a certain level of *svar*-density, some *tān* patterns will tend towards an unmusical aural experience. And, there is a threshold of *svar*-density beyond which all *tān* patterns will sound unmusical. The frontiers of musicality are, of course, fluid. But, they demand respect from each generation of musicians.

The issue of aesthetics in *tāns* stands at the borderline between art and entertainment. If taken seriously by musicians, it can often restrain the demonstration of virtuosity. The greatest of musicians have been guilty of opting for virtuosity at the cost of aesthetics, and the most highly cultivated amongst connoisseurs have been guilty of forgiving them.

Trends in Khyāl Vocalism

The *khyāl* genre has been defined by its "formal aloofness". However, the history of the genre in the twentieth century is replete with vocalists — all of formidable stature — who have deviated either from its formalism or its aloofness, or both. Of the two deviationist tendencies, the revolt against aloofness shows a greater resemblance to a movement. Deshpande (1987) describes it as a romanticist movement, comparable to a similar movement in Western classical music. The movement argues in favour of explicit emotional stimuli in art music, in addition to the architectural and sculptural variables of the aural experience. The phenomenon is particularly relevant to *khyāl* vocalism because of the freedom it gives the musician, and the premium it accords to his role as a composer over that of a performer.

Stylistically, the recent history of the *khyāl* can be viewed in three phases. The first phase covers the pre-Independence era, dominated by Ustad Faiyyaz Khan. The second phase covers the quarter of a century thereafter, with several giants straddling the *khyāl* platform, approximately ending with the demise of Ustad Ameer Khan in 1974. The third phase begins with the trailblazing emergence of Pt. Kumar Gandharva and Smt. Kishori Amonkar.

At the dawn of the last century, Ustad Abdul Kareem Khan (1872–1937). had already paved the way for a combination of classicism with romanticism. In the next generation, Ustad Faiyyaz Khan (1886–1950) took the process farther, though with an entirely different style. On a partial review of his radio broadcasts, it appears that he adopted a mildly informal approach to *khyāl* architecture, in addition to introducing elements, which were explicitly solicitous of an emotional response. Expressions typical of the *ṭappā* genre, derived from the songs of camel drivers in north-west India, entered *khyāl* music for the first time in Faiyyaz Khan's renditions. On the evidence of 78-RPM records, the same appears to be broadly true of Pt. Ramkrishna Vaze (1871–1945), Pt. Omkarnath Thakur (1897–1967), partially their contemporary, was a fastidious formalist, but a die-hard romanticist.

In the second phase, Pt. D.V. Paluskar (1921-55), Kesarbai Kerkar (1890–1977), and Ustad Ameer Khan (1912-74) were exemplary models of formalism as well as aloofness. This phase witnessed a solitary deviant, Ustad Bade Ghulam Ali Khan (1903-68). He was, broadly, in the Faiyyaz Khan mould, with an informal approach to architecture, and an inclination towards seductive ornamentation, and emotionally potent musical communication.

Amongst significant vocalists of the third phase, Pt. Bhimsen Joshi (b. 1922) stands alone as the bulwark of the *khyāl*'s formalism and aloofness. In this phase, Pt. Kumar Gandharva (1925-92) rebelled against both, aloofness as well as formalism. His junior by a few years, Smt. Kishori Amonkar (b. 1931) has remained steadfast in her respect for *khyāl* architecture, while rebelling against its aloofness. Their approximate contemporary, Pt. Jasraj started as a follower of the fastidious classicist, Ustad Ameer Khan, but has drifted steadily away from the formalism as well as aloofness of *khyāl* vocalism.

The significant aspect of romanticism in the third phase was the consolidation of the infusion of melodic expressions characteristic of the semi-classical, folk, regional, and popular genres of music into *khyāl* vocalism. As a result, *khyāl* was faced with a blurring of the stylistic divide between genres of vocal music.

In all probability, these tendencies had their socio-cultural logic. By this time, several leading performers of the semi-classical and romantic *ṭhumrī* and allied genres — Siddheshwari Devi, Rasoolan Bai, Begum Akhtar, Bade Ghulam Ali Khan, Barkat Ali Khan — had departed from the scene, leaving the genres starved of quality musicianship. Simultaneously, *khyāl* singers with *ṭhumrī* training had also faded away. Emotionally satisfying genres were beginning to disappear from the art-music platform. Around the same time, Jagjit Singh, an outstanding singer of the *ghazal*, a poetry-dominated genre, was enhancing its melodic content to corner a part of this vacant space. The *khyāl*, at that stage, attempted to fill the vacuum with a dual strategy — allowing *khyāl* itself to drift towards a more explicit and ornate emotionalism, and adopting the highly stylized *bhajan* as a tail-piece replacement for the *ṭhumrī*. Little wonder, then, that by the dawn of the twenty-first century, the *ṭhumrī* is all but extinct, and the distinctiveness of the *khyāl* is sustained almost entirely by its architecture.

The resilience of *khyāl* architecture cannot be taken for granted considering that it has been breached by some of the most formidable vocalists of the twentieth century. For the moment, the opinion-makers of the art-music world are committed to its structuralism. However, a more permissive music establishment is likely to emerge soon out of the cultural discontinuities imposed by Independence. As a result, a more complete expression of post-modern tendencies can now be considered imminent in *khyāl* music.

4.3

AN INTRODUCTION TO ṬHUMRĪ

THE *ṭhumrī* is a modern genre of semi-classical music, which originated as an accompaniment to the Kathaka genre of north Indian dance, and evolved later as an independent art form. Its name is traced to *ṭhumkā* in Hindi and its dialects, an onomatopoeic expression representing the sound of the graceful steps of a dancer with ankle bells.

The genre subsumes two sub-genres — a brisk and lively form called the *bandiś ṭhumrī* and a leisurely, sentimental form called *bol-banāo ṭhumrī*. The latter is allied closely to *dādarā*, *chaitī*, *kajrī* and other semi-classical forms, which are highly stylized versions of the folk music of the Benares region. Though the *bol-banāo ṭhumrī* is a later development, the two sub-genres evolved probably in response also to different choreographic formats — the *bandiś ṭhumrī*, to footwork dominant formats, and the *bol-banāo ṭhumrī*, to mime dominant formats. The *bandiś ṭhumrī* started moving towards the mainstream in the eighteenth century, reached its zenith in mid-nineteenth-century Lucknow, and was near extinct by the

Acknowledgement: This essay draws generously on the authoritative work of Peter Manuel of the City University of New York. *Ṭhumarī : In Historical and Stylistic Perspectives*, 1st edn., 1989, Motilal Banarsidass, New Delhi. The present author also acknowledges with gratitude Manuel's consent for this reliance, and his suggestions on the coverage of the subject.

early twentieth century. The *bol-banāo ṭhumrī* flowered in nineteenth-century Benares, acquired the stature of a mainstream genre in the early twentieth century, and is now seemingly heading for extinction.

Kathaka dance as well as the *ṭhumrī*, evolved in the neighbourhood of Mathura, the birthplace of Lord Kr̥ṣṇa. Thematically, both genres are immersed in the Bhakti movement, and the amorous joys of Rādhā, a cowherd's daughter, and her divine paramour, Kr̥ṣṇa. Their legendary romance, defining the ambiguous zone between the accessible and the unattainable, became a metaphor for man's spiritual quest. The cultural expressions of the metaphor thus came to have a female protagonist, anguished by separation from her beloved, and yearning for union with him.

The *ṭhumrī* genre represents the refinement and stylization of folk sources from the Brij (Mathura/Vrindavan) region by courtesans in response to the entertainment needs of a cultivated aristocracy. Until the end of the nineteenth century, courtesans were the predominant performers of both, the Kathaka genre of dance, and the *ṭhumrī* genre of vocal music. To this extent, the alluring qualities of the genre also reflect the manipulative intent fundamental to the relationship between courtesans and their clients.

Along their evolutionary path, the two *ṭhumrī* sub-genres (*bandiś ṭhumrī* and *bol-banāo ṭhumrī*) have interacted intimately with the art-music mainstream, and may be seen as informal and romanticist manifestations of the very aesthetic forces that were driving classical music into the modern period. Superficially, the *bandiś ṭhumrī* corresponds to the *chhoṭā* (*drut*) *khyāl*, and the *bol-banāo ṭhumrī* to the *baḍā* (*vilambit*) *khyāl*. Unlike, *khyāl*, however, the *ṭhumrī* genre is dominated by its poetic element. The *bandiś ṭhumrī* revolves around the poetic-rhythmic axis with a subordinated role for melody, and is thus closer to the music-making philosophy of the medieval *dhrupad* genre. The *bol-banāo ṭhumrī*, on the other hand, revolves around the poetic-melodic axis, with a subordinated role for rhythm. To this extent, it is unlike *khyāl* as well as *dhrupad*.

Using the architectural metaphor, *ṭhumrī* may be classified as an ornamentation-dominant genre, differentiated from *dhrupad*, which may be considered architecture-dominant, and the *khyāl*, which qualifies as a sculpture-dominant genre.

Sources of the Ṭhumrī Tradition

As a genre performed in accompaniment to interpretative dance, the *ṭhumrī* tradition is traceable to Bharata's *Nāṭyaśāstra*, the ancient text on dramaturgy, and its description of a dance-form called *lāsya*. It was a solo female dance, accompanied by female singers and an orchestra. The dancer interprets accompanying songs describing the lover, and complaining about him. The dancer's technique was primarily *abhinaya* (mime), and portrayed Śṛṅgār (amorous) and Karuṇa (pathos) Rasa. A similar dance and music form, called *paṇik*, appears in the ninth-century work, *Dattilam*. In eleventh-century texts, there are references to a dance of folk origin, called "Dombika", deriving its name from the Domb gypsies, who made a living as singers and dancers, and whose art was adopted by the courtesans of that era. On this evidence, scholars suggest that the *ṭhumrī*, as an artistic tradition, could be as ancient and continuous as *khyāl* and *dhrupad*.

The precursors of the *ṭhumrī* genre were associated with the pre-modern stage in the evolution of Kathaka dance. The word Kathaka derives from a community of professional storytellers of the same name, going back to the pre-Christian era. This community specialized in narrating stories from the Hindu myths with the help of mime and accompaniment. The Kathakas were Kṛṣṇa devotees, and deeply absorbed in the cult of Rādhā and Kṛṣṇa.

The folk-material for Kathaka dance and the *ṭhumrī* came from three medieval dance-and-music traditions — Charcharī, Rāsak and Horī. Charcharī was an erotic dance, accompanied by music sung to songs in the present-day Kāfī scale and the *chañchār tāl*, which is, to this day, amongst the mainstays of the *ṭhumrī* genre. The Rāsak was an erotic fertility dance performed to the accompaniment of music in *rasa tāl*, which coincides with *kehervā*, a major *tāl* of the *bol-banāo ṭhumrī* genre. This form apparently evolved into the *rāsa-līlā* of the Kr̥ṣṇa cult, whose exponents shaped Kathaka dance and *ṭhumrī* genres. Horī as a dance-and-song form was also called Horī–*dīpchaṇḍī*, *dīpchaṇḍī* being another name for *chañchār tāl*.

It would appear that these folk genres had considerable acceptance amongst the nobility — Hindu and Muslim — in medieval India. The patronage of genteel society induced their adoption and refinement by courtesans. In this process they absorbed the influence of the *khyāl* tradition without losing their moorings in the folk traditions.

The folk anchorages are evident in the choice of *tāl*s as well as the melodic framework within which the genre functions. Even in the deployment of *tāl*s, which are considered "classical," the *ṭhumrī* has retained an accentual pattern that is distinctively folk in its spirit. Despite the *khyāl* influence, both *ṭhumrī* forms have remained within the melodic orbit of amorphous folk-derived modal entities, which dominated its precursors. The differing melodic biases of the two sub-genres may reflect the difference between the aesthetic values of eighteenth- and nineteenth-century Lucknow and nineteenth- and twentieth-century Benares, the dance forms each related to, and their respective patronage profiles.

Stylistic Evolution

By the eighteenth century, the *bandiś ṭhumrī* had achieved a mature form, was performed primarily as accompaniment to

Kathaka dance, but increasingly also as an independent genre of music. At its zenith during the reign of Wajid Ali Shah (1822-87) in Awadh, the *ṭhumrī* was a medium or fast tempo *tīntāl* composition, but occasionally in *rūpak* or *ektāl*, rendered with *bol-bāṇṭ*, *tān*s and *layakārī*. However, by this time, the genre was no longer rendered exclusively in the fast tempo.

Throughout the nineteenth-century, the Kathaka–*ṭhumrī* form was performed primarily by courtesans. The presentation format consisted of two sub-forms. One was the sitting format in which the courtesan sat on the floor, sang a verse, and then enacted it, deploying mime and the language of the torso. Following such a presentation, she would stand up and then render a footwork oriented dance item.

The sitting format of Kathaka–*ṭhumrī* rendition achieved a totality of involvement in direct interface with her audience. It also enabled exceptional vocalists, who no longer had the figure for dancing, to continue longer in the profession. The intimate context of the sitting format, conducive to the delivery of the emotional experience, could have encouraged the slowing down of the tempo of rendition, and thus paved the way for the *bol-banāo ṭhumrī*.

With growing sophistication in dance as well as *ṭhumrī*, there emerged different categories of courtesans — those who only sang and those who only danced. The role for a specialist singer opened the door for male vocalists as accompanists, and stimulated the evolution of its independent idiom.

In the early twelfth-century, the Lucknow-style *bandiś ṭhumrī*, which already had an affinity with the *chhoṭā khyāl*, virtually merged with the classicist genre. Its place was taken by the slow-tempo *bol-banāo ṭhumrī*, which bore a superficial resemblance to the *baḍā khyāl*. This development took place primarily in Benares, and also partially in nearby Gayā. Both these cities had an ample patronage base amongst the local aristocracy. By the late nineteenth century, conditions were conducive for Benares, already an important Kathaka–*ṭhumrī* centre, to spearhead the fructification of emerging tendencies.

The *bol-banāo ṭhumrī* of Benares is, in fact, performed as a part of a cluster of sub-genres derived from the folk music of the region. In its allied forms like *chaitī, kajrī, fāgun*, etc., the melody is so simple and predictable that its *rāga*-ness is questionable. And yet the presentation is stylized and sophisticated enough to make even its folk origins immaterial. While the *bandiś ṭhumrī* relied primarily on the formal *tīntāl*, the *bol-banāo* adopted the informal and folksy *kehervā, dādarā* and *dīpchaṇḍī* as the primary *tāl*s. It dropped the rhythmic cleverness of the *bol-bāṇṭ* and the virtuosity of *tān*s typical of *bandiś ṭhumrī*s, and stuck to the poetry–melody axis for its delivery of musical value. For rhythmic excitement, it borrowed the *laggī* practice from folk music, which permits the percussionist to demonstrate his musicianship in brief interludes, and as the finale of a *bol-banāo ṭhumrī* rendition.

The most significant aspects of Benares *ṭhumrī*'s stylistic tendencies in the early twentieth century were the steady deceleration of the tempo of rendition, a sharper focus on the emotive and melodic treatment of the song-text to the practical exclusion of virtuoso vocalism, and a heightened emphasis on the folk melodic and rhythmic elements in the *ṭhumrī*, along with its allied sub-genres.

The period from 1920 to 1960, regarded as the Golden Age of Hindustani music, was a significant period for the *ṭhumrī* genre. The entry of the gramophone record and the radio in the early twentieth century, and the growth of the urban middle class created a larger and qualitatively different market for Hindustani music. The *ṭhumrī* came out of the courtesan districts, and entered the concert hall and people's homes. While the erotic and the aesthetic were both important to the courtesan's salons, the erotic became inappropriate in the new context, and the aesthetic gained ascendancy. The *ṭhumrī* shed its stigma as leading *khyāl* singers added it to their repertoire, and enriched it immensely.

As a result, a full concert of semi-classical music typical of the Benares tradition disappeared from the scene. With the virtual cannibalization of the *ṭhumrī* tradition by the *khyāl* platform, the specialist *ṭhumrī* singer, as a distinctive class of musicians, started becoming extinct. This represented a considerable depletion of the musical culture, considering that the great Benares courtesans could hold an audience for two hours with a feast of semi-classical music. Such a concert would begin with a 30-minute *bol-banāo ṭhumrī,* followed by a *ṭappā,* and then by a *dādarā,* a *bandiś ṭhumrī,* a *chaitī,* a *kajrī,* and end with another *bol-banāo ṭhumrī.*

Another significant consequence of the *ṭhumrī*'s migration to the concert hall was the disappearance of the sitting format of Kaṭhaka-*ṭhumrī* presentation. The format was unsustainable because a sitting performer suffers poor visibility beyond a few rows in an auditorium. This loss of intimacy and immediacy of artistic communication impoverished the choreographic as well as musical arts.

The *ṭhumrī* genre evolved almost hand-in-hand with the *khyāl* genre, to wean away audiences from the medieval *dhrupad* genre. It emerged as a significant romanticist genre, and undertook a steady deceleration in the tempo of rendition in order to become a more effective vehicle for sentimental musical ideas. Its trajectory has been synchronous with the decline of feudalism and the rise of bourgeois capitalism. In these developments, Peter Manuel sees a parallel with the socio-economic conditions that led to the rise of the romanticist movement (*Parlando Rubato*) in Western classical music. He equates *dhrupad* with the feudal values of heroism, and the *khyāl* and *ṭhumrī* as reflecting the relaxed mores of bourgeois society.

Ashok Ranade, sees the evolution of the *ṭhumrī* within the framework of a dialectic process in the musical culture. He argues that, at each milestone in its recent history, the Indian musical tradition has tended to create parallel genres, one with a formalistic tendency, and the other giving the musician a wider scope for individual creativity. According to him, *khyāl* and *ṭhumrī* were both reactions against the rigidity of the medieval *dhrupad* genre. The evolution of the *ṭhumrī* gathered momentum when the *khyāl* began to crystallize as a formalistic genre. In the most recent stage, while the *ṭhumrī* was defining unprecedented degrees of individual creative freedom, it was challenged by its own antithesis in the *ghazal*, a relatively *rāga*-neutral genre, but with a substantial role for the pre-composed element (Ashok D. Ranade, "Perspectives on Dhrupad", *Journal of the Indian Musicological Society*, Issue of 1999, ed. Deepak Raja and Suvarnalata Rao).

Landmark Personalities

Men, who have been patrons, composers, and teachers of the Kathaka–*ṭhumrī* arts, ironically, dominate the roster of landmark personages. The primary reason for this is the culture of anonymity that characterizes the world of courtesans. Though many courtesans belonged to eminent lineages of artists, matrilineal pedigree did not have sufficient respectability to give them a place in history. Only with the advent of recording industry in the early twentieth century did their art achieve recognition.

The *ṭhumrī* attained its zenith in eighteenth-nineteenth-century Awadh (Lucknow). The Lucknow tradition is traced back to one Prakashji, an exponent of the *rāsa* form, who migrated from Allahabad and secured the patronage of Nawab Asafuddaula (r. 1775-97). Prakashji's sons, Durga Prasad and

Thakur Prasad became tutors to the next *nawab*, Wajid Ali Shah and ushered in the flowering of the *ṭhumrī* and Kathaka dance as state-supported arts. Durga Prasad had two sons, Kalkaji Maharaj and Binda Din Maharaj (1836–1917). The latter is credited with having introduced *ṭhumrī* to Kathaka dance by composing *ṭhumrī*s specifically as support for interpretative dance, and making it the pre-eminent song form accompanying Kathaka performance.

Wajid Ali Shah was undoubtedly a pivotal patron of the Kathaka–*ṭhumrī* renaissance. Under the tutelage of Durga Prasad and Thakur Prasad, he became a formidable dancer. He trained with Sadiq Ali Khan to become a fine vocalist. He penned three volumes of song-texts for the *ṭhumrī*, *dādarā*, *khyāl* and *sadra* genres of vocal music. He scripted a Vaiṣṇavite dance drama called "Indra Sabhā" in Urdu, with songs in Braja Bhāṣā. His *ṭhumrī* composition *bābul morā naihar chhūṭo jāye* is amongst the immortal classics of modern music. In 1856, an entourage of 160 musicians accompanied Wajid Ali Shah to Calcutta, when British mercenaries exiled him with a privy purse worthy of his status. This exodus took the *ṭhumrī* to eastern India, and contributed greatly to its popularity.

Wajid Ali Shah's artistic passions were ably supported by Sadiq Ali Khan (1800–1910), a vocalist in his employ, descended from a lineage of *qawwālī* singers, associated with the early days of the *khyāl* genre. He devoted his energies to refining the *bandiś ṭhumrī*. He reportedly also initiated the deceleration of the tempo, thus laying the foundations of the *bol-banāo ṭhumrī*. His genius attracted some of the most talented musicians of his era as disciples. In addition to *ṭhumrī* exponents and composers, the list includes *khyāl* singers like Inayet Hussain Khan (1849–1919) of the Sahaswan Gharānā, Ramakrishna Vaze (1871–1945) of the Gwalior Gharānā, and the legendary harmonium exponent, Bhaiyya Ganpat Rao (1852–1920).

In this flowering, a pivotal role is attributed to Bhaiyya Ganpat Rao of Gwalior. He was trained in *dhrupad, khyāl* and the *rudra-vīṇā*, but fell in love with the newly-arrived harmonium and the *ṭhumrī* genre. He studied the *ṭhumrī* with Sadiq Ali Khan and Khurshid Ali Khan of Lucknow. Remarkably enough, he helped shape the incipient *bol-banāo ṭhumrī* by performing it on the eminently unsuitable harmonium, overcoming its technical limitations. Under his influence, the harmonium fast replaced the traditional *sāraṅgī* as the standard melodic accompaniment for *ṭhumrī*. Under the pseudonym "Sughar Piya", he composed a large number of *ṭhumrī*s, which became immensely popular. Some of the greatest *ṭhumrī* singers of his times were his students. Amongst them were great courtesans — Gauhar Jan, Jaddanbai, Malka Jan — and male vocalists — Mauzuddin Khan (1840–1926), Mir Irshad Ali, and Babu Shyam Lal.

Though independently of Ganpat Rao, his contemporary, Jagdeep Mishra of Benares performed a similar pioneering role in the evolution of the *bol-banāo ṭhumrī*. Mishra belonged to a family of hereditary Kathaka exponents, and is considered a co-founder of the Benares *bol-banāo* tradition.

In the Benares tradition of specialist singers, the last few greats in the twentieth century were Girija Shankar Chakravarty (1878–1948) in Bengal, a disciple of Bhaiyya Ganpat Rao, and the Benares courtesans, Rasoolan Bai (d. 1974), Siddheshwari Devi (1908-77), and Badi Motibai. While Girija Shankar trained some outstanding *ṭhumrī* singers like Naina Devi (d. 2002), the courtesans created an enviable niche for themselves on the concert platform.

Siddheshwari Devi was, by far, the most outstanding semi-classical vocalist of her times. She had studied *khyāl* and *ṭhumrī* with her aunt Rajeshwari Bai, Siyaji Mishra (a *sāraṅgī* player), Bade Ramdasji of Benares, Inayet Hussain Khan of

Lahore, and Rajab Ali Khan of Gwalior (1875–1959). The leisurely classicism of her *ṭhumrī* renditions brought them almost on par with the *baḍā khyāl*. In stature and popularity, Rasoolan Bai came next to Siddheshwari Devi. She had studied primarily with *khyāl* vocalists, *sāraṅgī* players and Kathaka exponents. She was famous for her *ṭhumrī*s, *dādarā*s, and *ṭappā*s. Her melodic range and imagination were limited, but achieved tremendous depth of expression. Badi Motibai, was a disciple of Siyaji Mishra, Mithailal Beenkaar and Mauzuddin Khan. Her singing bespoke her solid classical training, but lacked the leisurely appeal of Siddheshwari Devi.

Another significant vocalist from the courtesan tradition of the *ṭhumrī* was Begum Akhtar (1914-74) of Faizabad. She had studied *khyāl* with Wahid Khan and Ata Khan of Kairana Gharānā, and also from some Patiala maestros. She performed *ṭhumrī, ghazal, dādarā,* and the allied folk genres. Her *ṭhumrī*s were said to have been a combination of the Benares and Punjab styles. In contrast to the *baḍā khyāl*-like expansiveness of Siddheshwari Devi's *ṭhumrī*s, her *ṭhumrī*s were short, up to about ten minutes each. She devoted her energies primarily to the melodic development of the *ghazal*, a more poetry dominant form than the *ṭhumrī*, and enriched its melodic content enough to bring it almost on par with the *bol-banāo ṭhumrī*. She was a trendsetter in the evolution of the *ghazal* genre, which later cornered part of the aesthetic space of the *ṭhumrī*.

In the early twentieth century, the *bol-banāo ṭhumrī* entered the mainstream through the musicianship of *khyāl* singers, primarily as a tailpiece. Abdul Kareem Khan (1872–1936), the founder of the Kairana Gharānā of the *khyāl*, spearheaded this trajectory. He virtually redefined the *ṭhumrī* by taking the erotic, and partially the folk, out of the Benares *bol-banāo ṭhumrī*, and replacing it with an intense poignancy and devotional fervor. He made the *ṭhumrī* respectable in the *khyāl* world. The second and third generations of his lineage continued the dissemination of his style of *ṭhumrī*.

In the generation after him, the Agra Gharānā titan, Faiyyaz Khan (1886–1950) became immensely popular by adopting the erotic manner of the courtesan's salons in *bol-banāo ṭhumrī* rendition. He also revived the Lucknow style of *bandiś ṭhumrī*, and gave it an additional lease of life by training his foster-son, Sharafat Hussain (1930-85), as a brilliant exponent of the genre. In the succeeding generation, the brothers from Patiala, Bade Ghulam Ali Khan (1903-68) and Barkat Ali Khan, revolutionized the *bol-banāo* genre with their "Punjab *aṅga*" *ṭhumrī*. Because of greater visibility, Bade Ghulam Ali was the more important of the two.

Like Abdul Kareem Khan, Bade Ghulam Ali came from a *sāraṅgī* background, and exemplified formidable musicianship. His *ṭhumrī*s were rich in ethnic flavours from his native Punjab and the neighbouring Rajasthan, Sindh, Kashmir and the North-West Frontier. He is also credited with popularizing *ṭhumrī*s in *tāl*s other than the traditional *dīpchaṇḍī* (14 beats), by adding *dādarā* (6 beats), *keharvā* (8 beats), and *mughlai* (7 beats) *tāl*s.

Other than Kairana vocalists who adopted the *bol-banāo ṭhumrī* in a big way, the other eminent *khyāl* singers who performed the *ṭhumrī* with great élan around the middle of the century were Vilayat Hussain Khan of Agra (1885–1962), Mushtaq Hussain (1878–1964) of Rampur–Sahaswan, Rehmat Khan of Gwalior (d. 1922), and Kesarbai Kerkar of Jaipur–Atrauli (1892–1977). However, none of them contributed significantly to preserving or enhancing the distinctive identity of the genre. In fact, after Bade Ghulam Ali Khan, the *ṭhumrī* renditions of *khyāl* singers were increasingly criticized for not being sentimental enough. Soon thereafter, the *khyāl* itself started drifting towards a more explicit communication of sentimental values, thus depriving the *ṭhumrī* of its *raison d'être*.

Poetry in Ṭhumrī

The role of the poetic element in *ṭhumrī* is much greater than its role in the *khyāl* genre, but considerably smaller than its role in the *ghazal* genre. The *khyāl* genre can treat the poetic element as a mere textural articulatory element, while the *ghazal* genre demands respect for the autonomous literary quality of the poetry.

Although the *ṭhumrī* revolves around the poetic-melodic axis, the poet-composers have been primarily musicians and only secondarily poets. Except in rare cases, the verse is of mediocre literary value, but an excellent vehicle for musical expression. *Bandiś ṭhumrī*s of considerable poetic merit are attributed to Lallan Piya (d. 1925) and Sanad Piya, two composers from Lucknow. Their compositions are still heard occasionally, but as *khyāl*s.

The great majority of *ṭhumrī* verse is written in Braja Bhāṣā, the dialect of Hindi spoken in the region around Mathura. Between the fifteenth and nineteenth centuries, this dialect was the primary literary vehicle of the Hindi-speaking region of the country. Braja Bhāṣā was also the primary language of the medieval Bhakti movement, which dominates the literature of the *ṭhumrī* genre. This movement was a rebellion against the stranglehold of the priestly class over the ecclesiastical affairs of the laity. It emphasized a personal God with whom a devotee could establish an emotionally intense relationship without the need for intermediaries. The movement found its most potent vehicle in the legendary romance between Rādhā and her divine paramour, Kr̥ṣṇa. At an abstract level, this movement came to represent man's spiritual yearnings, with God symbolizing the active principle and therefore the male principle, and man the passive and female principle.

Early *bhakti* poetry of saints such as Sūrdās, Mīrābaī, Kabīr, Nānak, Jāyasī, and Tulsīdās (fourteenth to seventeenth centuries) had great depth and vitality. In later years (seventeenth to nineteenth centuries) the poetry gave way to artificiality and shallow sensuality. The *ṭhumrī* grew primarily out of the devotional/romantic songs of the Bhakti cult of this latter period.

Predominantly, *ṭhumrī* poetry belongs to the Śṛṅgār Rasa — the romantic/erotic sentiment, in the eight-way classification of *rasa* (emotional/sentimental states) in Indian aesthetics. Even within this broad theme, the emphasis is on *viraha*, the pangs of separation from the beloved, and the longing for union. The explicit focus on the man–woman relationship with a female protagonist brings *ṭhumrī* poetry under the purview of the theory of *nāyikā bhed* (Sanskrit for: classification of heroines) in Indian dramaturgy. *Nāyikā bhed* identifies eight different situations in the amorous relationship (ten according to some authorities). These are not merely academic concepts for the thematic classification of verses, but an active part of the performing tradition. They aid contextual visualization and guide the auto-suggestive and communicative process of the performer, especially when the rendition is accompanied by an element of mime or dance.

The eight basic situational classifications (*aṣṭa-nāyikā*) are:

- *Vāsakasajjā*: One dressed up for union with the beloved.
- *Virahotkaṇṭhitā*: One distressed by separation from the beloved.
- *Svādhīnabhartṛkā*: One who dominates her lover/holds him subservient.
- *Kalahāntaritā*: One separated consequent to a quarrel.
- *Khaṇḍitā*: One enraged by her lover.
- *Vipralabdhā*: One deceived by her lover.
- *Proṣitabhartṛkā*: One with a sojourning lover.

- *Abhisārikā*: One on her way to a rendezvous with her lover.

Texts belonging to the above classifications have been identified in major anthologies of *ṭhumrī* verse. Of the last two categories, instances are rare:

- *Pravatsyātpatikā*: One distressed by news of her lover's departure.
- *Āgatapatikā*: One returning joyfully from her lover's abode.

There are, indeed, *ṭhumrī*s that are not classifiable under any of the above situational categories. The romantic aspects get de-emphasized more frequently in *bandiś ṭhumrī*s in order to accommodate physical imagery required to support choreographic portrayal. Legendary amongst composers of such *ṭhumrī*s was Binda Din Maharaj of Benares (d. 1917).

Rāgas in Ṭhumrī

The melodic framework of the genre derives from a group of relatively undifferentiated modal entities, almost certainly of folk origin. There is, indeed, a group of *rāga*s in Hindustani music which are typically *ṭhumrī rāga*s, although the genre does occasionally deploy a few *rāga*s found in the classical genres. The major *ṭhumrī rāga*s are: Dhānī, Tilaṅg, Śivarañjanī, Bhairavī, Khamāja, Pīlū, Gārā (including its transposed variants, Madhyamse Gārā and Pañcamse Gārā), Zillā, Kāfī, Pahāṛī, Mañja Khamāja, Māṇḍ, Kauśi-Dhānī, Sindhūra, Jaṅgula and Bihārī. However, two significant *rāga*s of the *ṭhumrī* and allied semi-classical genres — Deś and Tilaka Kāmod — are also found in the mainstream classical genres. We may add Jhiṅjhotī and Bhairavī to this group, though they still remain minor in the mainstream vocal genres.

There is a substantial relationship of tonal geometry and phrasing congruence between several of these *rāga*s, especially

Khamāja, Bhairavī and Kāfī, three immensely popular *rāga*s of the genre. This relationship makes it possible for a phrase from one *rāga* to be sung in the other *rāga*s, though with reference to a different scale-base. This creates a recurrence of the same melodic contours / motifs through the genre, makes the genre more accessible, and contributes to its stylistic distinctiveness.

The treatment of the melody in *ṭhumrī* renditions reflects their coherence within well-defined melodic settings many of which have fluid boundaries within their group. Despite the relative informality of grammar, the crossing of boundaries is judicious and tasteful. *Ṭhumrī* rendition is not permitted to degenerate into a *rāga-mālikā*.

Tāl in Ṭhumrī

The nineteenth-century *bandiś ṭhumrī* relied almost entirely on the formal *tīntāl*. Some *bandiś ṭhumrī*s were rendered in "Punjābī *tīntāl*", a dented version with a pronounced swing to it. This version, almost certainly of folk origin, was to later play a bigger role in the *bol-banāo ṭhumrī*. The *bandiś ṭhumrī* was a genre for the medium to fast tempo, with an explicit rhythmicality. In rendition, it also involved a lively interaction between the poetic–melodic and rhythmic elements. This equation between the different elements changed dramatically as the tempo of the *bandiś ṭhumrī* decelerated. The *bol-banāo ṭhumrī* took over and drifted closer to folk genres, and the genre itself became a vehicle for overt sentimentalism. Rhythm was now relegated to the back seat.

Cutting through the maze of multiple nomenclatures and multiple versions, and in contemporary language, the *bol-banāo ṭhumrī* primarily uses *chañchār* or *dīpchaṇḍī* of 14 beats in 3+4+3+4 subdivision, *keharvā* of eight beats in 4+4 subdivision, *dādarā* of six beats in 3+3 subdivision, and *tīntāl* of 16 beats, rendered in a stylized, or probably folk, manner. This version of *tīntāl* is, even today, known by several names — *sitārakhanī, addhā, punjābī*, and *qawwālī*. This idiom is an asymmetrical and dented interpretation of the symmetrical [4+4+4+4] subdivision of the *tāl*. The *sitārakhanī/addhā/punjābī/qawwālī*, generally played in medium tempo, interprets the 4-beat subdivision in the *tāl* as an 8-beat subdivision, and renders it with percussion strokes falling on the 1st, 4th and 7th markers of the notionally 8-beat subdivisions. Peter Manuel observes that this interpretation of the *tīntāl* brings its rhythmic experience remarkably close to the 14-beat *dīpchaṇḍī*.

Amongst the *tāl*s used in the *ṭhumrī* genre, *dādarā* of six beats poses a special problem because this happens also to be the name of a genre of vocal music belonging to the *ṭhumrī* family.

Dādarā: the Genre

Dādarā is currently the only genre in Hindustani music, other than *dhamār*, which bears the name of the *tāl* in which it is performed. This suggests the primacy of the rhythmic element to its character and aesthetics. Though this is helpful, it does not differentiate it clearly from the *bol-banāo ṭhumrī*. For, the *dādarā* genre itself is not performed exclusively in the *dādarā tāl*, but also in others, all of which are used in *bola-banāo ṭhumrī* — *kehervā* of eight beats, *mughlai* and *rūpak* both of 7 beats, and a fast *chañchār/dīpchaṇḍī* of 14 beats.

According to its enthusiasts, the *dādarā* genre does have some distinguishing features. It is performed at a faster tempo than the *bol-banāo ṭhumrī*, and has an explicit rhythmicality in rendition. Both these features are in contrast to the *bol-banāo ṭhumrī*, which is rendered at a leisurely pace and revels in the sentimentality of a subdued rhythmicality. Other clues have been suggested. But, none of them is more categorical. This situation probably leaves the *dādarā* substantially, though not entirely, at the mercy of arbitrary classification.

Ensemble for Ṭhumrī Performances

As a genre of vocal music, divorced from its function as accompaniment for Kathaka dance, the ensemble for the *ṭhumrī* in the latter half of the twentieth century has been similar to the modern *khyāl* genre. One *tānpūrā*, but occasionally two, as the drone, accompanies the vocalist. Melodic accompaniment is provided either by a *sāraṅgī* or a harmonium player, and percussion accompaniment is the *tablā*. A supporting vocalist has been encountered less frequently in the *ṭhumrī* than in the *khyāl*.

In the choreographic context, the orchestra is known to include a plucked instrument (*sitār* or *sarod*), and sometimes also the bamboo flute.

Bandiś Ṭhumrī: Structure and Rendition

The word *bandiś*, in this context, denotes a poetic–melodic–rhythmic composition. The name *bandiś ṭhumrī* suggests two important features — first, that it is a tightly composed piece of music, and second, that the pre-composed element dominates its rendition. As it evolved independently of the choreographic context, it acquired a substantial improvisatory component, which makes it indistinguishable from a *chhoṭā khyāl*. By the early twentieth century, when gramophone records arrived in India, the *bol-banāo ṭhumrī* had overshadowed the *bandiś ṭhumrī* and had also begun to influence its performance. Even the earliest 78-RPM recordings of the genre, therefore, bear no resemblance to the original. The description here relies substantially on secondary sources.

Despite being dominated by the pre-composed element, *bandiś ṭhumrī*s do not consistently exhibit a high level of originality in their melodic–rhythmic structure, although their poetry is generally of superior literary value than on *bol-banāo ṭhumrī*s. One famous Lucknow composer, Lallan Piya, is known to have set at least fourteen different lyrics to the same melody in Rāga Kāfī. However, several *bandiś ṭhumrīs* do exhibit rhythmic cleverness, a feature particularly useful in the choreographic context.

The *bandiś ṭhumrī* is generally composed in *madhya-laya tīntāl*. However, compositions in *rūpak, jhaptāl* and *ektāl* have also been in practice. The composition is generally in two parts, *sthāī* and *antarā*. The *sthāī*, usually of two poetic–melodic lines, is occasionally of three lines. In the shorter *tāls*, such as *rūpak* and *jhaptāl*, the *sthāī* can be longer. The *antarā* is generally at least as long as the *sthāī*, in most cases two or three poetic–melodic lines. There are also *bandiś ṭhumrīs* with several *antarās*, all performed to identical melodic contours.

In the austere format of rendition, the vocalist merely renders each part of the composition several times in sequence and repeatedly, without any improvisations whatsoever, but occasionally at a progressively higher tempo in each successive iteration. In such a rendition, each line may undergo some melodic variations without damaging the integrity of the poetic form, and without straying too far from the melodic contours of the pre-composed form.

In the more elaborate form, the vocalist follows up the rendition of the complete pre-composed form with melodic–rhythmic improvisations upon it in a manner that would challenge the dancer's interpretative skills. This form of *bol-bāṇṭ* or *layakārī* is almost certainly derived from the *dhrupad* genre. An enhancement over this level of improvisations is a duet between the vocalist and the percussionist (or, theoretically, the dancer too) in which the percussionist and/or the dancer attempt to accompany, anticipate, and even outwit the rhythmic intentions of the vocalist's *bol-bāṇṭ*.

Contemporary Kathaka maestros, like Birju Maharaj, have performed *bandiś ṭhumrīs* using *bol-bāṇṭ* as well as *bol-banāo* improvisations. This innovation is still consistent with the text-dominant character of the *ṭhumrī*, and with its original function as accompaniment to interpretative dance.

Bol-banāo Ṭhumrī: Structure and Rendition

The name of this sub-genre suggests its basic features — that the poetic element (*bol*) is the driver of the rendition, and that the rendition concentrates on the emotive and alluring embellishment (*banāo*) of the text. For this reason, the *bol-banāo ṭhumrī* has also been called the *artha-bhāva* (*artha* = meaning + *bhāva* = emotions) *ṭhumrī*. By implication, and by contrast with the *bandiś ṭhumrī*, the pre-composed element is de-emphasized in the *bol-banāo* sub-genre. The *bol-banāo ṭhumrī* is performed at a much slower tempo than the *bandiś ṭhumrī*. In the choreographic context, this form was appropriate for dance formats devoid of fast or intricate footwork. By the early twentieth century, it stabilized at a rendition tempo approximately twice the beat-density of the contemporary *baḍā khyāl*.

The *bol-banāo ṭhumrī* is not a pre-composed entity in the sense of having a stable poetic–melodic–rhythmic shell constituting the nucleus of the rendition. The song-text is stable, though the musician has the freedom to insert exclamatory expressions (e.g., *ho rāma*/O my Lord or *sāvariyā*/ beloved) during rendition, almost at will. The same song-text has been found set to different *rāga*s, and the same poetic–melodic shell has been found sung in different *tāl*s and at different tempi. Even an established poetic–melodic entity is not predictably recognizable beyond the *mukhḍā*. The rendition of the *mukhḍā*, generally a four-beat phrase, is syllabic, and sustains a degree of correspondence with the beats of the rhythmic cycle. Other than this, the entire rendition is a free-flowing interaction between poetic, melodic, and rhythmic elements.

The *bol-banāo* song-texts are generally more compact than those of the *bandiś ṭhumrī*. The song-text is in two parts, described as *sthāī* and *antarā*, more by convention than melodic logic. Unlike a *bandiś ṭhumrī* or a *khyāl* composition, the two parts of a *bol-banāo ṭhumrī* are not necessarily anchored in different regions of the melodic canvas. In a majority of the cases, the *sthāī* and *antarā* are both located in the same region of the canvas, with one of them having a slightly broader span than the other. This feature exploits the psycho-acoustics of relative pitch for sharpening the emotional communication of the song-text. Such concentration of poetic, and acoustic energies is appropriate in a genre that is explicitly sentimental in its character.

The format of rendition in *bol-banāo ṭhumrī* follows broadly the following order. The rendition is preceded by a solo (unaccompanied by percussion) free-flowing *alāp* of up to 2 minutes outlining the melodic features of the *rāga*. Thereafter, the *sthāī* begins with percussion accompaniment. After the *sthāī* has been rendered a couple of times, the *bol-banāo* improvisations begin. The progress of the improvisations is systematic, though informal. They begin with the lower octave, and progress gradually upwards. When they have reached an appropriate point in the *uttarāṅga*, the *antarā* is rendered. After the *antarā*, there is a *tablā* solo interlude, called a *laggī*, which is always in the 8-beat *kehervā* or the 16-beat *tīntāl*, irrespective of the *tāl* in which the *ṭhumrī* is rendered. After the *laggī*, the rendition may either come to a close, or return to the *ṭhumrī* for further *bol-banāo*, and further rounds of *laggī* interludes. Generally, all *bol-banāo* renditions end with a *laggī*.

The stylistic nuances of the *bol-banāo* process owe their character to the salons of the courtesans where the art evolved. In that context, the rendition was erotic allurement with the aim of obtaining the patronage of the wealthiest, handsomest, or otherwise most desirable members of genteel society.

Vocalism of such explicitly manipulative intent, when accompanied by the enticement of mime and gesture, corresponded uniquely to the "counterfeit" nature of aesthetic emotion, the artifice that is central to all art.

As described by Peter Manuel, the *bol-banāo* process uses segments of the song-text as a platform for a luxuriant and leisurely melodic ornamentation, with the purpose of making the words come to life. The *ṭhumrī* genre tends to rely heavily on the *kaṇ*, *khaṭakā* and *murkī* type of ornamentations, including strings of *murkī*s resembling the melodic mischief of the *ṭappā*, a genre inspired by the songs of camel drivers from India's north-western regions. Another typically *ṭhumrī* style idiom is the *pukār* (lit: a cry), which generally leaps from the mid-octave region to the upper tonic, and descends summarily to its starting point. These modes of melodic execution are so intimately associated with the *ṭhumrī* genre, that their use in the *khyāl* genre has been considered inappropriate.

Ṭhumrī in Instrumental Music

Considering the primacy of the poetic element as one of the defining features of the *ṭhumrī* genre, a *ṭhumrī* rendition on the instruments is an apparent contradiction. This is not entirely so because the *ṭhumrī* also represents a distinctive musical style. By adopting its musical elements — *rāga*s, *tāl*s, tempi of rendition, modes of melodic ornamentation, composition formats, and improvisational conventions — instrumental music has developed a "*ṭhumrī* style", which is sufficiently distinct from the *dhrupad* and *khyāl* inspired idioms in instrumental music. As a result, there has emerged a distinctive *ṭhumrī* style in instrumental music, which may possess greater vitality today than the *ṭhumrī* as a vocal genre.

The *ṭhumrī* genre has had the most profound influence on the idiom of the *sitār* and the *sarod*, the two instruments that rose to prominence in eighteenth- and nineteenth-century

Lucknow, the home of the Kathaka–*ṭhumrī* renaissance. The *sitār* inherited its original idiom from the *rudra-vīṇā*, the primary instrument of the medieval *dhrupad* genre. However, while the *rudra-vīṇā* could support only unidirectional strokes, the *sitār* enables bi-directional strokes. In the early stages of developing its own idiom, the *sitār* developed the slow-tempo Masit Khani composition format, named after Masit Khan, a Delhi-based sitārist. However, being ergonomically superior to the *rudra-vīṇā*, the *sitār* was in search of an agile idiom. Ghulam Raza Khan, a late eighteenth-century Lucknow sitārist, developed such an idiom by a direct and immensely successful transposition of the *bandiś ṭhumrī* composition format onto the stroke pattern of the *sitār*.

The nascent *sarod*, an important part of the Lucknow court under Nawab Wajid Ali Shah, had already inherited a bi-directional stroke pattern from its ancestor, the *rabāb*. Thus, along with the slow tempo Masit Khani format, the *sitār* and the *sarod* came to adopt the medium-to-fast tempo Raza Khani format as standard repertoire. Although both instruments have considerably diversified their repertoire in the twentieth century, the Masit Khani and Raza Khani formats remain, to this day, the mainstays of *sitār* and *sarod* music.

The flowering of the *ṭhumrī* style in the music of the plucked instruments is attributed to the lineage of Ustad Sahebdad Khan, the great grandfather of the contemporary sitārist, Ustad Vilayat Khan (b. 1928). Sahebdad Khan was a *sāraṅgī* exponent and a *khyāl* singer, who commenced the family's mastery over the plucked instruments — the *sitār* and the *surbahār*. The earliest recordings of Raza Khani format *ṭhumrī* on the *sitār* are those of his son, Ustad Imdad Khan (1848–1920), followed in later years by his grandson, Ustad Enayet Khan (1894–1938).

The execution of the vocal idiom on the *sitār* reached its highest level of sophistication in the hands of Ustad Enayet Khan's son, Ustad Vilayat Khan, who has not only adopted and adapted compositions from both the *ṭhumrī* sub-genres, but also successfully captured their musical experience in entirety, across all movements. The totality of his "*ṭhumrī* experience" also gains a lot from his brilliant vocalization of *bol-banāo* along with its rendition on the *sitār*. Ustad Vilayat Khan's *ṭhumrī*-inspired idiom has been imitated by a host of *sitār* and *sarod* players not only of his own stylistic lineage but also of the rival lineages.

The other major instrument to be influenced by the *ṭhumrī* genre was the *sāraṅgī*, which had become the standard accompaniment to the *ṭhumrī* as well as the *khyāl* by the nineteenth century. The *sāraṅgī* player has been an important link between the worlds of *ṭhumrī* and *khyāl* which, in any event, have never been totally isolated from each other. However, economic considerations probably drove the *sāraṅgī* player much closer to the world of courtesans, and consequently towards a stylistic bias towards the *ṭhumrī*. As a result, the austere *dhrupad* genre almost ignored the *sāraṅgī*, while many a competent *sāraṅgī* player has been disqualified from accompanying even *khyāl* singers. These reservations are, however, immaterial in the context of a *sāraṅgī* solo. As a soloist, a *sāraṅgī* player can do greater justice to a *ṭhumrī* rendition than any other instrumentalist, and is acceptable if his *khyāl* renderings admit an ornate sense of melodic design resembling the *ṭhumrī*.

The *ṭhumrī* genre has also partially inspired the content and style of *śehnāī* music, largely because of the towering influence of Ustad Bismillah Khan, who hails from Benares, the home of the *bol-banāo ṭhumrī*. Being a ceremonial instrument which addresses an involuntary audience of indeterminable profile, the *śehnāī* came to acquire a repertoire dominated by folk and regional music. When Bismillah Khan raised the *śehnāī* to the status of a concert instrument, he also made the *dādarā, kajrī, chaitī,* and *fāgun* songs of the Benares region an integral part of *śehnāī* repertoire. Appropriate to the concert hall, he developed an improvisational idiom inspired by the *bol-banāo* family of songs. *Śehnāī* players all over the country adopted this style until the regional and folk music of other parts of India began to compete with Bismillah's Benares for a place in *śehnāī* repertoire.

Like the *śehnāī*, though to a far lesser degree, the *bāṅsurī* (the bamboo flute), has conceded a significant place to the *ṭhumrī* and other semi-classical genres in its repertoire. This pattern is attributed to the phenomenal musicianship of two maestros, Pannalal Ghosh (1911-62) and Hariprasad Chaurasia (b. 1938). Ghosh tended to perform *bol-banāo ṭhumrī*s more frequently in the traditional *dīpchaṇḍī* (*chañchār*), while Chaurasia has an affinity for *kehervā, rūpak* and *dādarā*.

The Ṭhumrī Today

Although the *ṭhumrī* remains an integral part of Kathaka dance, the limits of the present author's competence oblige him to restrict this contemporary appraisal to its status as an independent genre of vocal music.

At the time of this writing (July 2003), the genre can claim only two vocalists of stature — Girija Devi (b. 1929) and Shobha Gurtu (1925–2004) — who are exclusively devoted to the practice of the Benares tradition of *ṭhumrī* and its allied genres, such as *dādarā, chaitī, kajrī,* etc. No heirs to their mantle are yet visible on the horizon.

Amongst the leading *khyāl* exponents, the notables amongst fine performers of the *bol-banāo ṭhumrī*, are Pt. Bhimsen Joshi (b. 1922), Ustad Niyaz Ahmed Khan (1928–2002), Parveen Sultana (b. 1948) and Prabha Atre (b. 1932). The *bandiś ṭhumrī*, interestingly, appears to be experiencing a minor revival. The younger male vocalists, like Rashid Khan, Ulhas Kashalkar, and Ajoy Chakravarty perform *bandiś ṭhumrī*s with great competence, distinguishing them astutely from the *chhoṭā khyāl*. Female vocalists of the younger generation have virtually abandoned the *ṭhumrī* genre altogether. This is important because, on the *khyāl* platform, women now outnumber men several times over.

On probabilistic reckoning, no more than one in twenty vocal music concerts in contemporary Hindustani music ends with either a *bandiś ṭhumrī* or a *bol-banāo ṭhumrī*. Around the middle of the twentieth century, the *ṭhumrī*'s share of the tailpiece position was at least five times greater than it is today. With the complete concert of semi-classical music revolving around the *ṭhumrī* having disappeared long ago, and its presence on the *khyāl* platform having shrunk dramatically, the *ṭhumrī* appears to be faced with extinction.

When we encounter such a situation, it is appropriate to look at the genre from two angles — as an occupant of a specific niche in the concert repertoire, and as an occupant of a well-defined aesthetic space. Both these issues are relevant to considering *ṭhumrī* in the present-day context.

Two factors have predominantly influenced the emergence of *ṭhumrī* substitutes in the tailpiece position — the de-emphasis of the romantic/erotic element in the concert hall context, and emergence of western state of Maharashtra as the home of *khyāl* vocalism. The state has a rich regional tradition of literature and music, with which classical musicians have, traditionally, maintained a strong link. Maharashtrian musicians have a relatively lower level of empathy with the language and stylistic values of the *ṭhumrī*, both of which are inseparably linked with the ethnicity of a small part of Hindi-speaking India. It is therefore natural that a poetry-driven musical genre like the *ṭhumrī* would appear less attractive to Maharashtrian vocalists than viable alternatives.

Interestingly, the younger male vocalists who are reviving the *bandiś ṭhumrī*, are all based in Kolkata, which has a long-standing relationship with the *ṭhumrī* because of Wajid Ali Shah's exile in that city a century and a half ago.

Because of Maharashtra's dominance over the *khyāl* platform, the tailpiece position has increasingly been taken up by classicist renderings of *bhajan*s (devotional songs) composed by the major poets of the Bhakti movement, by folk devotional genres from Maharashtra such as *abhaṅga*s and *kīrtan*s, and semi-classical songs from the Marāṭhī theatre, called *nāṭya-saṅgīta*. Most of these *ṭhumrī*-substitutes possess some features of either the *bol-banāo* or the *bandiś ṭhumrī*s, and fill a part of the aesthetic space earlier occupied by the *ṭhumrī*. None of them, however, occupies the entire aesthetic space of the *ṭhumrī*. This is to be expected, because the *ṭhumrī* was a unique product of a unique environment in a bygone era, and is probably unsustainable, in its original form, in the present-day context.

However, the aesthetic space the *ṭhumrī* occupied cannot disappear with the eclipse of the genre. The space exists, but can apparently not be occupied by a single genre. The encroachment into this space began around the middle of the last century when the Benares *bol-banāo* tradition was in full bloom, and originated from the classical as well as the light music ends. Starting with Bade Ghulam Ali Khan, *khyāl* vocalism moved towards a libertarian approach to architecture, an ornate sense of sculpture and ornamentation. In a sense, he was the forerunner of the romantic brigade — Kumar Gandharva, Kishori Amonkar, and Pt. Jasraj — who rebelled against either the formalism of the *khyāl*, or its aloofness, or both, thus driving the classicist genre closer to the emotional expressiveness of the *ṭhumrī*.

The other significant encroachment of the *ṭhumrī*'s aesthetic space came from the *ghazal* end, with Begum Akhtar as its high priestess. Inspired by her music, Jagjit Singh, Mehdi Hassan, along with several others, substantially widened the scope of melodic improvisation in *ghazal* rendition and raised it to a level of sophistication comparable to a *ṭhumrī*. However, the subsequent generations of *ghazal* singers have impoverished the genre in terms of melody as well as the poetry. The implications of this vacation of the *ṭhumrī* space by the *ghazal* are too early to ascertain.

The instrumental manifestations of *ṭhumrī* aesthetics appear to be in good health. However, they cannot substantially alter our assessment of the health of a text-dominant romanticist genre. Without the benefit of a crystal ball, the *ṭhumrī* today appears as nearly extinct as *dhrupad* did half a century ago. This may precisely be the issue. As *dhrupad* itself proved, genres of music do not simply vanish. They merely go underground, transform themselves, and surface again to reclaim audiences. When conditions are favourable, the *ṭhumrī* might have a good chance of doing so.

4.4

INTRODUCTION TO THE ṬAPPĀ*

LIKE the *ṭhumrī*, the *ṭappā* is a modern semi-classical genre of folk derivation, which flowered in Lucknow and Benares. However, while the *ṭhumrī* evolved from the cultural manifestations of the Bhakti movement around Mathura–Vrindavan, the *ṭappā* owes its inspiration to the songs of camel drivers in Punjab and India's North-Western Frontiers. The acceptance of the genre in genteel society by the late seventeenth century appears to have been synchronous with that of the *ṭhumrī*. Although the genre was practised by lineages of Kathakas, and by courtesans, it gained early acceptance amongst *dhrupad* and *khyāl* vocalists. As a result, the genre has escaped the social stigma that the *ṭhumrī* and its allied genres had to endure before semi-classical music entered the concert platform.

The pioneering role in the refinement of the folk idiom into a stylized genre is attributed to one Shorie Miya, whose signature appears at the end of many popular *ṭappā* compositions. "Shorie" was, apparently, the name of the wife of the *ṭappā* innovator, Ghulam Nabi, the son of Ghulam Rasool, an eminent *khyāl* vocalist in the employ of Nawab Asafuddaula (r. 1775-97) of Awadh (Lucknow). Ghulam Nabi was trained in *khyāl* vocalism, but did not have a voice suitable for the genre. He apparently travelled extensively in Punjab, mastered the *ṭappā* idiom, and matured it enough to return to Lucknow, and achieve distinction at the Awadh court. The genre continued to enjoy the patronage of the Awadh rulers during the reign of the Kathaka–*ṭhumrī* enthusiast, Wajid Ali Shah (1822-87).

Thereafter, it has had a trajectory similar to the *ṭhumrī*. It struck roots in Lucknow and Benares, acquired a significant following in eastern India probably through Wajid Ali's entourage in exile, and established itself as a companion to *khyāl* vocalism. In present times, though performances of the *ṭappā* are none too frequent, the genre appears to have withstood the pressures of the *khyāl*-dominated environment better than the *ṭhumrī*.

Historical Outline

This outline relies on the biographical sketches included in the epic work *Indian Music*, by Thakur Jaydev Singh (1st edn., Premlata Sharma, ed.), and a paper presented by Prof. Rohit Desai, archivist of Nadiad (Gujarat) at the Faculty of Performing Arts, Baroda University, in January 2003. The clues and links are far from categorical. However, some patterns can be discerned.

Shorie Miya (Ghulam Nabi) had four significant disciples: Prasiddhu Maharaj, Miya Gammu or Gammu Khan, Tarachand, and Mir Ali Saheb. Gammu Khan's son, Sadi Khan (Sadiq Khan?), and Babu Ramsahay (d. 1850), another eminent *ṭappā* singer, taught one Prasiddhu Maharaj, a member of the Kathaka community — unlikely to be the same Prasiddhu tutored by Shorie Miya — who together with his brother Manohar Maharaj, founded the Prasiddhu–Manohar lineage. Like several lineages of *ṭappā* singers, this lineage claimed significant musicianship in the mainstream genres of vocal music but, as an exception, also instrumental music. Prasiddhu's great-grandson, Ramkrishna Mishra taught and performed in Calcutta till 1955.

Gammu Khan's son, Sadi Khan/Sadiq Khan left Lucknow to settle in Benares, thus making the city an early partner in the evolution of the genre. His presence encouraged the leading courtesans of the era to master the art. The Prasiddhu–Manohar lineage also originated in the city, and made a significant contribution to the propagation of the *ṭappā*. Throughout the nineteenth and twentieth centuries, the courtesans of Benares remained important repositories of the *ṭappā* art. Of great importance to the surviving *ṭappā* tradition of Benares are the names of Bade Ramdasji (b. 1896), a *khyāl* singer, who trained several famous twentieth-century vocalists in the *ṭappā*.

The *ṭappā* entered the Gwalior *khyāl* lineage fairly early in its history. Natthan Peer Baksh (early nineteenth century), the founder of the Gwalior lineage, apparently studied the *ṭappā* with Shakkar Khan and Makkhan Khan, two famous disciples of Shorie Miya's father, Ghulam Rasool. Natthan Peer Baksh' grandsons, Haddu Khan and Hassu Khan (d. 1859), apparently adopted the *ṭappā* into the *gharānā*'s repertoire. Haddu Khan's son, Rehmat Khan (d. 1922), was a formidable *ṭappā* singer. Haddu Khan's son-in-law, Inayet Hussain Khan, founder of the Sahaswan–Rampur Gharānā of the *khyāl*, and his heirs, Mushtaq Hussain and Nissar Hussain, were also eminent *ṭappā* performers.

Hassu Khan's disciples, Devji Buwa, and Raoji Buwa perpetuated the *ṭappā* tradition in the Gwalior lineage. In the succeeding generation, Balkrishna Buwa Ichalkaranjikar brought the *ṭappā* into the *khyāl* mainstream in Maharashtra, while Narayan Buwa Phaltankar introduced the *ṭappā* style to the performance of *abhaṅgas* (Marāṭhī devotional songs). With their contribution, the *ṭappā* genre struck deep roots in the cultural soil of Maharashtra. The Gwalior *khyāl* lineage values its *ṭappā* repertoire as a means of cultivating exceptional vocal agility. Gwalior vocalists worked closely with musicologist, V.N. Bhatkhande, to document *ṭappā* songs, thus contributing to the stature of the genre as also its survival.

Through the nineteenth century, Lucknow remained active in the *ṭappā* genre, with Nawab Hussain Khan (d. early nineteenth century), and Chhajju Khan (d. 1870) on record as great practitioners of the art. In the late nineteenth century, eastern India exhibited great enthusiasm for the genre, with the performing and scholarly contributions of Gopeshwar Bannerji of Vishnupur (b. 1878), Raja Sourendra Mohan Tagore of Jorasanko (1840–1914), and Bholanath Bhatt of Darbhanga (1891–1971). Gwalior also remained an important centre of the *ṭappā* well into the twentieth century, with Balasaheb Guruji (d. 1919) and his disciple Nanu Bhaiyya Telang (d. 1948) distinguishing themselves.

According to Rohit Desai, approximately 100 *ṭappā* recordings have been published in the twentieth century. A limited discography identifies some of the most significant *ṭappā* singers of recent times (Rohit Desai and Sharadchandra Mehta: *Ṭhumrī, Dādarā, Horī, Chaitī & Kajrī: A Selective Discography*, Indian Musicological Society, Baroda, 1990). Though the document does not claim to be comprehensive, it gives a reasonable picture of the *ṭappā* scene. The overwhelming majority of the named *ṭappā* singers are specialist singers of the semi-classical genres: Badi Motibai, Doanni Jaan, Girija Devi, Hiradevi Mishra, Rasoolan Bai, Savita Devi, Siddheshwari Devi, Vidyadhari Bai, and Shobha Gurtu. The few *khyāl* singers named in the discography are Yunus Husain Khan (Agra), Mushtaq Hussain Khan (Rampur–Sahaswan), and Sharafat Hussain Khan (Agra).

Salient Stylistic Features

The identifying feature of the *ṭappā* is a vivacious, and even mischievous, treatment of melody. The melody is not only naughty within itself, but also in relation to the beats of the rhythmic cycle, and occasionally even rhythmically clever. The bouncy ethnicity of *ṭappā* melody has often been compared to a ride on the back of a camel. This interpretation of the camel-driver's song has intuitive appeal, even if its oblique attempt at explaining the melodic features of the genre is not convincing.

The primary devices for achieving the melodic effervescence of the *ṭappā* are strings of intricate symmetric phrases creating brisk *tān*-like passages, and *gītakīrī*, coupled with dramatic twists and turns, and frequent shifts in *svar*-density between melodic lines and sets of phrases. A *ṭappā* is so distinct a musical experience that it is easy to identify it with minimal familiarity, though difficult to describe. As a starting point for the entirely unfamiliar, a *ṭappā* may be described as an impish rendition of a *chhoṭā* (*drut*) *khyāl*, but considerably more puckish than a *bandiś ṭhumrī*.

*Ṭappā*s are composed mainly in *ṭhumrī rāgas*, such as Bhairavī, Khamāja, Deś, Kāfī, Jhiṅjhotī, Pīlū, Barwā. They are generally set to 16-beat variants of the *tīntāl*, such as *addhā*, *qawwālī* and *sitārakhanī*. A few *ṭappās* have also been composed in *ektāl*. In *ektāl*, as well as *tīntāl*, *ṭappā*s are sung in medium tempo. This tempo is mandated by the need for the genre's simultaneous indulgence in melodic and melodic–rhythmic playfulness. The lyrics are mostly in Punjābī or Sindhī, the languages of the north-west, and centred around the tragic romance of Hīra and Rāñjhā, an important part of the folklore of the Punjab region. Shorie Miya, however, enlarged the thematic content of *ṭappā* lyrics, and included general romantic themes, as also philosophical themes in his *ṭappās*. Compositions sporting the signature of "Shorie" Miya are still the most popular, though the genre has benefited from the contributions of several composers thereafter.

Because of its accent on complex melody, the *ṭappā* cannot accord any significance to its poetic element. *Ṭappā* lyrics are short — either two lines or two stanzas with two short lines each — and simple. As in *khyāl bandiś*es, the two sections are anchored in different regions of the melodic canvas, and function as *sthāī* and *antarā*. Many *ṭappā* songs also have a melodically distinct *mañjh* section between the *sthāī* and the *antarā*. A *ṭappā* is generally rendered relying only on the poetic–melodic form as the basic material. *Ākār tān*s and *bol-bāṇṭ*/*layakārī* of the *khyāl* variety, occasionally also found in *bandiś ṭhumrī*s, are not found in the *ṭappā*. Its *bol-tān*s have no identity independent of the lyrics. They are dominated by symmetry, and eschew other melodic patterns typical of *khyāl*.

The symmetry of *ṭappā tāns* is typically expressed in overlapping ascending or descending waves of phrases. Examples in Bhairavī:

> Descending: *ni-sā-re-sā-ni-dhā, dhā-ni-sā-ni-dhā-pā, pā-dhā-ni-dhā-pā-mā, mā-pā-dhā-pā-mā-gā.*
>
> Ascending: *gā-re-re-sā-re, mā-gā, gā-re-gā, pā-mā-mā-gā-mā, dhā-pā-pā-mā-pā.*

This symmetrical pattern may sometimes include shifts of *svar*-density. A consistent feature enhancing the knotted character of *ṭappā* passages is the looped or bi-directional phrases used to build the melody. This feature is best exploited in highly malleable *rāga*s like Bhairavī, and Kāfī, where intricate phrasing within short melodic spans can help create bewildering and even stunning effects. The demands of lithe melodic execution may explain why, only one *khyāl gharānā* has taken to the *ṭappā* in a significant way, and, other than this, the genre has been the preserve of female singers.

As a challenge to musicianship, the *ṭappā* tests the agility of the vocalization mechanism, and the fertility of the melodic imagination. Less obviously, though more meaningfully, the *ṭappā* also tests the vocalist's command over *rāga* grammar and the rhythmic element. A *ṭappā* singer is required to use the laxity of grammar in *ṭhumrī rāgas* and the melodic freedom granted by the genre to establish the character of the genre. But, this has to be achieved without letting the basic *rāga*-ness of the *rāga* recede out of focus. The demands on the rhythmic skill arise from the pattern of melodic structuring typical of the genre. Once a *tān* pattern has been commenced, it has to be carried through at least two more symmetric iterations in different regions of the melodic canvas before the improvisation can return to the pre-composed shell of the rendition. The dovetailing of intricate *tān* clusters with the *bandiś* requires consummate rhythmic skill.

Although the *ṭappā* apparently relied on the *bandiś ṭhumrī* and the *chhoṭā khyāl* for its format, it has, in turn, influenced the *khyāl* genre by giving birth to a hybrid form, the *ṭap-khyāl*. This form is normally rendered in the "classical" *rāgas*, but has the distinct vivacity of the *ṭappā* in its treatment of melody. *Ṭap-khyāls* enjoy considerable stature because of their demanding aesthetics, and are performed in several *gharānās* of *khyāl* vocalism.

The Ṭappā Today

The presence of the *ṭappā* on the contemporary concert platform is slightly better than that of the *ṭhumrī*. While their relative relegation to the background may have some common features and causes, the *ṭappā* can be viewed individually.

The major repository of *ṭappā* musicianship was the courtesan tradition of Benares, which specialized in the semi-classical genres such as the *ṭhumrī, dādarā, chaitī* and *kajrī,* along with the allied folk-based genres of the region. This tradition was a unique product of its environment and its times, and has been speeding towards extinction, taking the *ṭappā* along with it.

The other significant repository of *ṭappā* musicianship is the Gwalior *khyāl gharānā*. From the second quarter of the twentieth century — after Omkarnath Thakur — this *gharānā* was unable to produce front-ranking musicians. In an effort to re-invent itself, it drifted towards the aggressive, rhythm-oriented, vocalism of the Agra Gharānā. One of the results of the Gwalior–Agra confluence was the gradual disappearance of the *ṭappā* from Gwalior repertoire. Traditional Gwalior vocalism is all but extinct. The *khyāl gharānās*, which gained ascendancy in the post-Independence era — primarily Kairana and Jaipur–Atrauli — ignored the *ṭappā* in favour of either the *ṭhumrī* or *bhajans*. Bengal, once an important *ṭappā* centre, is yet to produce front-ranking vocalists with any interest in the *ṭappā*.

On the contemporary platform, the *ṭappā* qualifies primarily as a tailpiece to a *khyāl* rendition, as an alternative to a *ṭhumrī*. The dominance of the *khyāl* platform by vocalists from Maharashtra has caused this role to be handed over to *bhajans* and *nāṭya-saṅgīta*. One of the keys to this phenomenon, though not a major key, may be that *ṭappā* lyrics are written in Punjābī or Sindhī, languages understood by even fewer people than Braja Bhāṣā, the language of the *ṭhumrī*.

Despite its limitations, several features suggest a better chance for the *ṭappā*'s survival than that of the *ṭhumrī*. The poetic element plays a far smaller role in the aesthetics of the *ṭappā* compared to the *ṭhumrī*, or even the *khyāl*. In addition, the *ṭappā* is not sentimental in its treatment of the melody. *Ṭappā* melody relies on vocal technique and melodic imagination, and not the communication of cultural meaning through poetry. To this extent, the *ṭappā* is probably less "parochial" than the *ṭhumrī*. Because of *ṭappā*'s excessively ornate treatment of melody, *khyāl*, the dominant mainstream genre, cannot encroach upon the *ṭappā*'s territory as easily as it could upon the *ṭhumrī*. Nor can the poetry-dominant genres like the *ghazal* compete for its aesthetic space from the other end. The revival of the genre, therefore, depends more on the interest of musicians and the acceptance of the genre by contemporary audiences. Indicators of these factors deserve attention.

The current scene can claim the towering presence of Girija Devi (b. 1929), and Shobha Gurtu (1925–2004) as specialists of the semi-classical genres who have excelled at *ṭappā* rendition. Amongst established *khyāl* vocalists, the significant *ṭappā* exponents are Laxman Krishnarao Pandit (b. 1932) and Malini Rajurkar (b. 1941). This picture looks dismal. But if we look for a ray of hope, Manjiri Asnare-Kelkar (b. 1971), a successful *khyāl* vocalist, is reviving a constituency for the *ṭappā*.

Her induction into the genre is interesting. Manjiri belongs to a thoroughbred Maharashtrian family, and had her initial training in the Gwalior tradition. Early in her grooming, she became a fan of Malini Rajurkar, especially of her *ṭappā* renderings. She acquired all available *ṭappā* recordings of Malini, painstaking took down notations, verified lyrics with published sources, and started performing them with great success (interview with the author on 5 May 2003). She later became a disciple of Madhusudan Kanetkar, the Jaipur–Atrauli Gharānā stalwart, who studied the *ṭappā* specially to be able to help her organize and polish her renditions.

These may be unorthodox conditions for the continuity of a genre, and this individual case might be no more than a straw in the wind. But, Manjiri's success with the *ṭappā* confirms several promising features of the genre. Most of all, it establishes its "non-parochial" character, the possibility of acquiring respectable proficiency without expert supervision, and the genre's continued appeal amongst audiences. These factors justify greater optimism for the *ṭappā* than for the *ṭhumrī*.

PART V

The Major Instruments

5.1

THE RUDRA-VĪṆĀ*

RUDRA-VĪṆĀ (commonly called the *bīn*) is an instrument of entirely Indian origin and considerable antiquity. It is revered because of its association with Rudra (Lord Śiva), the Originator of the performing arts. According to legend Śiva created the instrument inspired by the reclining image of Pārvatī, his Divine Consort. A categorical description of Lord Śiva's craftsmanship is not available from mythological texts. Nevertheless, the instrument now called the *rudra-vīṇā*, has inherited the legend, and its magical beliefs have been acceptable to several mystical cults — Hindu as well as Muslim. This feature of the *bīn* may be attributed partly to Śiva as an archetype, but largely to the *bīn*'s design and ergonomics.

The neuro-acoustics of *bīn* playing are well documented in the Indian mystical tradition. Such phenomena arise from the experience of intimate physical contact between the instrument and the musician during the act of playing. In the traditional posture, the *bīn* has a larger part of its body in contact with the musician's body than any other Indian instrument — touching the temple above the left shoulder, across the torso, and under the right armpit. And, each instrument is tailor-made to achieve a perfect fit to the musician's dimensions. As a result of this intimacy of contact, the vibrations generated in the act of playing on the *bīn* are magnified by the instrument, and transmitted back to the musician's body at critical neurological centres. The musician is thus a recipient of the physical vibrations of the *bīn*, along with its acoustic output. At its best, *bīn* music enables the musician to enter a trance-like state, which falls broadly within the category of mystical/religious experiences.

By organological classification, the *bīn* belongs to the fretted stick zither family of chordophones, fast heading for extinction on the Indian subcontinent. It is the progenitor of the idiom of the plucked lutes — fretless as well as fretted — which succeeded it as vehicles of the Indian art-music tradition. From the point of view of Indian organology, therefore, the distinction between the stick zithers and the plucked lutes is insignificant.

Organology

According to the organologist, Deva (B.C. Deva), India has a long tradition of stick zithers in art, as well as folk music. The tradition goes back to the *ghoṣak* and the *ektantrī-vīṇā*, both single-string, single-gourd, fretless instruments documented from the fifth century CE. Like the modern *bīn*, the *ektantrī*, first named in eleventh-century texts, was a revered instrument, being often called *bramha-vīṇā* — associated with Brahmā, the Creator. The *ektantrī* required the sound to be activated by right-hand plucking, and the melody to be executed by the left hand stopping of the string at different points along the bamboo stem with a small piece of bamboo. This instrument is considered the forerunner of contemporary fretless zithers such as the *vichitra-vīṇā* (*batta bīn*) in Hindustani music, and the *goṭṭu vādyam* in Carnatic music.

The addition of frets to fretless zithers is believed to have taken place around the eleventh century CE. This development gave rise to the *kinnarī-vīṇā* with multiple gourds as chamber resonators. The *kinnarī-vīṇā* came in two forms — the *bṛhat* (major) *kinnarī* with three gourds, and the *laghu* (minor) *kinnarī* with two gourds. The fretted, twin-gourd, *laghu kinnarī* is now considered the direct parent of the *bīn*. Having evolved in the twelfth or thirteenth centuries, the *bīn* is a creation of the middle ages, whose art has evolved over less than a millennium.

History

The art of the *bīn* is associated with the *dhrupad* genre of art music. The *bīn* originally accompanied vocal *dhrupad* recitals. The content of their music thus came to be identical in melodic and rhythmic respects, as also in the philosophy of music-making. It was common, amongst families of musicians, for the children to be groomed in the vocal as well *bīn* arts, the choice of profession being left to their individual predispositions. But the two arts also evolved their independent performing domains, which allowed both to express their respective endowments. By virtue of being companion arts, they influenced each other in a meaningful way.

The *bīn*'s most glorious period was the reign of the Mogul Emperor, Akbar (sixteenth century). Historian, Abul Fazal, mentions Shihab Khan and Purbin Khan as the pre-eminent *bīnkārs* (exponents of the *bīn*) in Akbar's court. Other prominent *bīnkārs* of the era were Bilas Khan and Imrat Sen, both sons of the legendary Tansen, his daughter Sarasvati, and Misri Singh, his son-in-law. Of these four, Imrat Sen and Misri Singh perpetuated the art of the *bīn*, while the others developed the art of the *rabāb*, forerunner of the modern *sarod*. In later years, thus, the legacy of the *bīn* emerged as the foundation of the arts of all plucked lutes.

Dhrupad and the *bīn* started losing ground in the late eighteenth century when the decaying Mogul Empire prompted leading musicians to drift away from Delhi and its neighbourhood in search of alternative patronage. This exposed them to diverse stylistic environments, many of which were already being swept by the achievements of the rival *khyāl* genre.

Vocal music having been the traditional reference point for instrumental music, the *khyāl* wave began to make a different set of stylistic demands on the art of the plucked instruments. The *bīn* was unsuited for the melodic agility of post-*dhrupad* music. By this time, the *sitār* was beginning to fill the vacuum, but was not yet acoustically sophisticated enough to challenge the *bīn*, especially in the leisurely rendition of the low-density melody, principally the *alāp*. To compete effectively with the *bīn*, sitārists devised the *surbahār* (around 1825), an instrument which combined the acoustic richness of the *bīn* with the ergonomic features of the *sitār*. This instrument could handle the *dhrupad*-style *alāp*, and also enable a transition from *dhrupad* to post-*dhrupad* stylistics. This led to the emergence of a multiple-instrument presentation format in the music of the fretted lutes — an elaborate *alāp* on the *surbahār* followed by post-*dhrupad* compositions on the *sitār*. As a solo instrument, the *bīn* ultimately succumbed to this challenge. Simultaneously, the decline of *dhrupad* vocalism was shrinking the *bīn*'s presence as an accompanist.

Around the same time, and responding to an urge similar to the development of the *surbahār* by sitāraists, *rabāb* players developed the *surśr̥ṅgār*, a cumbersome hybrid between the *rabāb* and the *bīn*. In terms of physical construction, several variants are reported (Allyn Miner, 1997). The most prominent amongst them was an instrument that had a lower gourd similar to the *surbahār*, a finger-board like the *rabāb*, and an upper gourd similar to the *bīn*. But, unlike the *rabāb*, the *surśr̥ṅgār* had a metallic finger board, and used metallic strings (Miner, ibid.). By the early twentieth century, the *surśr̥ṅgār* had acquired an enviable following in terms of stature, though small in numbers. *Surśṛṅgār* recordings of Alauddin Khan, Radhika Mohan Maitra, and B.K. Roy-chaudhury demonstrate the technical success at transferring the *bīn*'s acoustic richness and melodic potential to the *rabāb* family of instruments. But, once again, the ergonomic demands of post-*dhrupad* music triumphed. The *rabāb* quickly adopted the most promising features of the *surśṛṅgār* — the metallic fingerboard and metal strings — and re-engineered itself acoustically to transform itself into the *sarod*, driving the *surśṛṅgār* into history. The *bīn* thus became the grandfather of the *sarod*, yet another plucked lute to fill the vacuum it created.

Starting from the mid-nineteenth century, a majority of the lineages of *dhrupad* music diverted their energies to the *khyāl* genre. Simultaneously, there was a decline in the art of the *bīn*, as its practitioners bequeathed it to the emerging arts of the modern plucked lutes — the *sitār*, the *surbahār*, *surśṛṅgār*, and the *sarod*. The decline of the *bīn* was dramatic after Independence (1947) which dispossessed the feudal aristocracy, a part of which had continued to support *dhrupad* and the *bīn* in their sunset years.

In the early years after Independence, the *dhrupad* genre was frequently described as "a museum piece". This description was more appropriate to the *bīn*, than to the vocal art. For the *bīn* art, however, the transition from *dhrupad* to post-*dhrupad* music was unachievable, and *bīnkār*s were forced to make a living as vocalists or as performers and teachers of *sitār*, *sarod* and *surbahār*. This changed once Western Europe warmed up to *dhrupad* in the mid-1960s.

In the 1980s, after the vocal *dhrupad* genre had acquired an enthusiastic following abroad, the market for the *bīn* was cultivated by Asad Ali Khan, and Zia Mohiuddin Dagar, both scions of distinguished *dhrupad* lineages. Both performed extensively in the Europe and the US, and broke the traditional barrier to teaching the art beyond ties of kinship. Their acceptance of European and American students also laid the foundation of a self-propagating constituency for the *bīn* in the west. *Dhrupad* thus became a unique phenomenon in art music — losing ground in its home and flourishing amongst alien audiences.

At the moment of this writing, the vocal art of *dhrupad* boasts of a small group of vocalists who are credible musicians at home, but dependent largely on the Western market for their livelihood. Compared to *dhrupad* vocalists, the number of practitioners of the *bīn* is negligible. Asad Ali Khan, the seniormost contemporary *bīnkār*, foresees extinction for the *bīn* art unless job opportunities are created in India for its practitioners (Interview with Utpal Bannerjee, *Sruti*, Issue 217, October 2002).

Design

The *bīn* is an instrument of simple construction with a tubular stem acting as the column resonator, and two large dried gourds attached towards its two ends functioning as chamber resonators.

Traditionally, the stem was made of bamboo. Asad Ali Khan reports that fastening the gourds to the bamboo stem was a highly-skilled task because the two gourds had to bear the entire weight of the instrument, and withstand the tension of the musician virtually wrestling with it. The bamboo stem was originally polished with wax, and decorated with painted or inlay work in gold. Bamboo stems, however, had a limited life because they tended to split in a couple of years, thus weakening the acoustic output (Interview with the author on 11 January 2000). Bamboo was later replaced with *śīśam* wood, which was light enough, but lasted only six to eight years. With stems currently made from teak wood, the instrument has a useful life of about twenty years (Interview with Sunira

Kasliwal, *Kala Varta*, Journal of the Madhya Pradesh Kala Parishad, Bhopal, vol. 102, Year 19). Asad Ali Khan credits Zia Mohiuddin Dagar with design improvements, which made the instrument acoustically superior though heavier. He himself claims to have introduced changes, which have elongated the stem by about two inches, with similar objectives and results. The precise nature of these changes is not clear. However, the contemporary *bīn* certainly delivers a more pleasing acoustic output in the upper half of the melodic canvas than *bīn*s of the earlier generation did.

With a more durable stem, the gourds could be fixed to the stem. The contemporary design with detachable gourds is believed to have been developed by Z.M. Dagar, probably in response to transportation needs arising from frequent foreign tours. This belief is implicitly questioned by Hindaraj Diwekar, another contemporary *bīn* player (Hindaraj Diwekar and Robin Tribhuvan *Rudra-vīṇā: An Ancient Musical Instrument*) who claims to possess a 100-year old *bīn* with these features, purchased by his father in the 1930s.

The frets are made of wood, but have a metal cladding on top — either steel, copper, or brass. They were once attached to the stem with wax. However, over the last century, the frets are increasingly tied to the stem with cotton/nylon twines as on the *sitār*, or affixed with screws, or kept partially moveable by mounting them on an aluminium channel. The instrument has seven strings. Four are used for executing the melody, the remaining three functioning as *chikarī*s (drones). The twin-drone set on the inner side is tuned to the tonic of the middle and higher octaves, while the isolated drone on the outer side is tuned to the tonic of the lower octave. Z.M. Dagar, however, enlarged the drone set on the inner side to a triple-drone set, thus bringing the total number of strings to eight.

In the sunset years of *dhrupad* and the art of the *bīn*, its major centres were the Northern Provinces, Rajasthan, Bengal (including the present nation state of Bangladesh), and Maharashtra in western India. Consistent with this geographical concentration, Varanasi, Kolkata, and Miraj emerged as the major manufacturing centres of quality instruments. Thanks to this legacy, the instrument makers of Kolkata and Miraj emerged, in later years, also as prime suppliers of the modern plucked lutes — *sitār*, *sarod* and *tānpūrā*.

Ergonomics

The sound activation (plucking) of the *bīn* was traditionally done with the bare fingers, with the first three fingers deployed on the melodic strings, and the little finger being used for activating the *chikarī*. In recent years, the *mizrāb* (wire plectrum) of the *sitār* type has replaced the bare fingers for powering the strokes.

Bīn is unique amongst the major plucked instruments for the arrangement of its strings. The ultra-lower octave melody is played on the first/lowest/outermost string, rather than on the last/highest/innermost string, as on the *sitār*, *surbahār* and the *sarod*. This is efficient because the first string is strung at the lowest level of tension, and used almost entirely in the *mīṇḍ*-based (string-deflection) execution of melody, which requires the maximum fret-space. The low-tension mounting in the fret-space available for the first string enables almost a complete octave to be covered by string-deflection from a single fret.

According to Asad Ali Khan (ibid.), the *bīn* is the only Indian instrument, which is tailor-made for the musician — like an upper garment. This is so because it is held across the breast, and must be mechanically efficient for the music-making actions of both the hands, while also providing for the expansion and contraction of the rib cage in the process of breathing. For an instrument that is almost a millennium old, it is not surprising that a great deal of thought has gone into the ergonomics of music-making.

The traditional posture for performing was *vajrāsana* (a demanding yogic posture), with the top gourd resting on the left shoulder, and right gourd tucked under the right arm-pit. The thumb of the right hand is used as the fulcrum, affixed at an appropriate distance from the bridge carrying the strings from the bottom end of the stem. Amongst contemporary *bīn* players, Asad Ali Khan and Shamsuddin Faridi still perform in the traditional posture, while Bahauddin Dagar, following his father, Z.M. Dagar, has adopted a posture akin to the *sarasvatī* (Carnatic) *vīṇā*, with both knees folded inwards, and the top gourd resting on the left knee, while the lower gourd rests on the ground in front of the right knee. According to Bahauddin Dagar (Interview with the author on 9 November 2002), the ergonomics of the two postures are distinct, and either may be adopted depending on the musical style/bias of the *bīnkār*. He argues that the traditional posture is more suitable for latter half of *dhrupad* presentation, requiring melodic agility and higher stroke density, while the lap-top posture is more suitable for *alāp* rendition, without compromising the efficacy of stroke-craft.

The ergonomics of music making on the *bīn* were a major factor contributing its decline, and replacement by the *sitār*. In the right-hand (stroke-craft) department, the *bīn* could achieve neither the stroke density, the stroke complexity, nor the degree of control over the manipulation of acoustic output, which the *sitār* achieved in shaping post-*dhrupad* music. In the left-hand (melodic execution) department, the *bīn* fell short of the melodic agility and complexity demanded by post-*dhrupad* music. However, the *bīn*'s weakness in relation to the *sitār*, was an integral part of its design and function as accompaniment for *dhrupad* vocal music. Even during the Mogul period:

> a solo performance on the *vīṇā* (*bīn*) was frowned upon by the musicians — so much so, that it was called *śuṣka vādya* [dry instrument]. It is generally believed that the great *Vīṇā* player, Naubat Khan [Misri Singh] was seldom asked to give solo recitals in the court of Akbar. He usually accompanied Tansen on the *vīṇā*.
>
> — Sharmistha Sen, *String Instruments of North India*, vol. II

The *bīn* could develop an extremely sophisticated solo idiom because *bīnkār*s tested the limits of the instrument's capabilities in their endeavour to liberate their art-from its subordinate position relative to vocal music. With hindsight, we might argue that the role of an accompanist to vocal music was more inappropriate for a bowed and fretless instrument like the *sāraṅgī*. However, in the cultural and acoustic environment of the era in which their respective roles emerged, each was probably an appropriate choice.

Acoustics

Another anachronistic feature of the *bīn* is its acoustic output. The instrument was designed for an environment that relied on architecturally determined delivery of musical values. In the modern electronically engineered acoustic environment, the instrument requires extremely sensitive audio engineering. Musicologist, Ashok Ranade discusses these risks with respect to the ensemble for vocal *dhrupad* performance.

> The *bīn*'s acoustics are rich in sustain and the harmonics they deliver. Every time the string is struck, the resulting sound has a long shadow, which tends to drown out melodic subtleties in the vocal rendition. . . . The issue of accompanying instruments becomes even more critical in the contemporary environment of amplification electronics.

> Unless this is very astutely controlled, the rhythmic contours of the *pakhāwaj* (the barrel drum) and melodic contours of the *rudra-vīṇā* can create a blurred, and even confusing aural experience.
>
> — "Perspectives on Dhrupad",
> *Journal of the Indian Musicological Society*,
> Annual issue of 1999,
> ed. Deepak Raja & Suvarnalata Rao

This issue now stands partly resolved by the lapse of the *bīn*'s role as an accompanying instrument, and its re-engineering to suit the requirements of amplification electronics. However, the music of some contemporary *bīn* players does occasionally appear insensitive to electronic amplification.

Stroke Craft

The inventory of *bīn* strokes is built on three basic components:

1. *Da*: Downward/inward stroke of the index finger on the melodic string.
2. *Gā*: Downward/inward stroke of the middle finger on the melodic string.
3. *Rā*: Upward/outward stroke of the last finger on the *chikarī* drone

Based on these three building blocks, the *bīn* developed a complex stroke-craft, consisting of a large number of compound stroke-patterns corresponding to the patterns in the percussion idiom. Organologist, Sharamistha Ghosh lists twenty-four such patterns in her book on Hindustani string instruments. These patterns acquired special significance in the rendition of *tar-paraṇas*.

Techniques of Melodic Execution

The techniques deployed on the *bīn* are constrained by its

ergonomics, but perhaps more by the melodic austerity of the *dhrupad* genre, thus ruling out the more agile and ornate techniques used on the plucked lutes that succeeded it. An important aspect of this distinction is the strong bias *dhrupad* has in favour of single intervallic transitions as the building blocks of melody characterized by its elephantine gait. This defines a more deliberate and leisurely approach to melody making, compared to the *sitār* and the *sarod*, which habitually use a phrase consisting of two intervallic transitions as the basic unit of melody. The inventory of *bīn* techniques is large; however, four basic techniques may be mentioned here.

The left hand executes the melody on the *bīn* using two categories of techniques — (a) fretwork, which involves the movement of the fingers between the frets, and (b) string deflection, which involves the pulling of the string with one or more fingers static on a single fret.

Fretwork techniques: In addition to the straightforward melodic execution by movement of the fingers between frets, the *bīn* uses two types of fretwork technique: *ghasīṭ* (also called *sunṭa*), and *khaṭakā*.

Ghasīṭ (lit. dragging) does precisely that. It executes a phrase, usually flat-out and unidirectional, by dragging the left hand finger along the fret-board under the impact of a single stroke. This is accompanied by a light left-hand pressure over the string, so that the resultant glide delivers an aural impression of a fretless instrument. The *ghasīṭ* is deployed mainly for medium to long-span intervallic transitions.

Khaṭakā (lit. jerky motion) is also self-explanatory. It is deployed for short-span intervallic transitions, normally in descending melodic motion. It is also executed under a single stroke. The right-hand stroke is activated with the left-hand finger resting on one fret, while its follow-through in jerky motion implements the intervallic transition along the frets, using the residual power of the stroke, along with that of the jerky motion of the left-hand finger.

There are two principal deflection techniques (a) *mīṇḍ* and (b) *gamak*.

The *mīṇḍ* is a simple execution of a phrase by pulling the string from a single fret, and executing a phrase under the impact of a single stroke. Three-*svar mīṇḍ*s were common in *bīn* music. Advanced musicianship can usually stretch this to four.

The *gamak* creates a pulsating or quivering effect — a magnified *vibrato* — by repeatedly attacking a *svar* from a fret at a lower pitch. The *gamak* is generally used for distances of upto two, and occasionally three *svar*s.

Recent Bīn Music

A brief survey of mid, and late twentieth century *bīn* music may serve as a useful backdrop to understanding its contemporary manifestation. For this purpose, I draw gratefully upon a small sample of recordings made available by the English *dhrupad* archivist, Vincent Naughton. The recordings are of Dabeer Khan (1902-72), Sadiq Ali Khan (1893–1964), and Abid Hussain Khan (early twentieth century). In addition, I draw upon a few commercially available recordings of Zia Mohiuddin Dagar (d. 1990). This sample reflects merely the immediate availability of recordings.

Dabeer Khan was the grandson of Wazir Khan, a formidable *bīnkār* employed by the Rampur court, and a descendant of the legendary Tansen (by some accounts, a descendant of Faiyyaz Khan "Adarang", the nephew of Sadarang). Dabeer Khan was, for many years, in the employ of the sarodist, Radhika Mohan Maitra, who was the feudal chieftain of Rajshahi in present-day Bangladesh, and was also Maitra's tutor.

Available Dabeer Khan recordings are: Śuddha Sāraṅga (*ālāp-joḍa-jhālā*), Śuddha Toḍī (*ālāp-joḍa*), Lakṣmī Toḍī (*ālāp-joḍa-jhālā*), and Bilaskhani Ṭoḍi (*ālāp-joḍa-jhālā*). None of the available recordings has a *pada* rendered to percussion accompaniment. It cannot be determined whether this is a peculiarity of the sample recordings, or integral to Dabeer Khan's concert strategy.

In the Dabeer Khan *ālāp*, I find a considerable use of fretwork techniques, and a lesser use of the *mīṇḍ* and *khaṭakā* techniques than we would expect in the *dhrupad* genre. Compared to contemporary *sitār ālāps*, the stroke-craft as well as the fretwork sound coarse. The fretwork is agile, and appears to mimic the *sitār* style of rendition, with an effort to introduce tonal geometry into the phrasing. The steady and leisurely flow of improvisations typical of *dhrupad* is absent. Instead, we find frequent breaks of pace, with brisk passages punctuating the flow. The melodic approach of the Dabeer Khan *ālāp* was flexible. One of the *ālāp*s in the sample has no *antarā* at all, while another *ālāp* is elaborate, with a *sthāī*, *antarā*, and a brisk *sañchārī* movement.

In the Dabeer Khan *joḍa*, there were typically four levels of tempo. At the fourth level, there is a negligible use of the *chikarī*. In the *joḍa*, we come across a very demanding pattern of simultaneous striking on the melodic and *chikarī* strings — a feature later revived on the *sitār* by Ustad Vilayat Khan. In an unorthodox departure from *dhrupad* tradition, the fourth level of the *joḍa*, and the *jhālā* are performed to *pakhāwaj* accompaniment. The Dabeer Khan *jhālā* deploys both patterns of interaction between the melodic strings and the *chikarī* currently played on the *sitār* and the *sarod* — the first stroke on the melodic string followed by the *chikarī*, and its reverse. The reverse pattern was revived by Ustad Vilayat Khan on the *sitār*, and is played only in his lineage.

Sadiq Ali Khan belonged to a formidable lineage of *bīnkār*s known as the Jaipur *bīnkār*s. This lineage had, for a while, migrated to Golconda–Bijapur in the south, and also studied the art of the *vīṇā* from Carnatic musicians. The lineage later also adopted the *sitār* as a vehicle for their art. Sadiq Ali studied the *bīn* with his father, Musharraf Khan, a formidable *bīnkār*, in the lineage of the legendary Rajab Ali Khan of Jaipur. Despite the Jaipur background, anchored in the melodious Dagar Bānī style of *dhrupad*, Sadiq Ali had spent many years in Rampur, a centre of the aggressive Khandar Bānī style.

The available recordings of Sadiq Ali Khan are: Darbārī with *alāp* and a *dhrupad* composition in *chautāl*, *alāp-joḍa-jhālā* in Jhiṅjhoṭī, and *alāp* with *dhrupad* composition in Bihāga.

The Sadiq Ali *alāp* is steady-paced, with a highly refined left-hand technique sporting an adequate measure of *mīṇḍ*, fretwork, and *ghasīṭ* types of melodic execution. However, the pace of the *alāp* is less leisurely than the habitual pace of *dhrupad*. In some cases, the *alāp* is indistinguishable from an irregular *joḍa*. The use of the *chikarī* is irregular. The approach to phrasing, with attempts at symmetric and geometric phrasing suggests a melodic sophistication approaching that of the contemporary *sitār* idiom. In the *joḍa* section, we observe the use of heavy *gamak*s, and even *tān*s approaching the agility achievable on the *surbahār*. The *jhālā* incorporates complex stroke craft, in direct as well as reverse patterns. The stroke density in the *jhālā* compares favourably with that of contemporary *sitār* music.

In the *pada* rendition, the relationship between the *bīnkār* and his percussion accompanist corresponds to the "wrestling bout" description, with each of them taking off on his own trip immediately after the first iteration of the rhythmic cycle. In the improvisations around the *pada*, we observe the deployment of the *duguṇā*/*tiguṇā*/*chauguṇa* conventions of performing the *pada* at multiples of the base-tempo, as well as a generous use of *tar-paraṇas*. Interestingly, the *pada* rendition often ends with a *sitār*-style *jhālā*.

Abid Hussain *bīnkār* of Indore was the son of Jamaluddin *bīnkār*, both descended from the same lineage of *bīn/sitār* exponents from Jaipur, to which Sadiq Ali Khan belonged. This lineage also had a fruitful stylistic interaction with Senīya sitārists (descendants of the legendary Miya Tansen) who also served the Jaipur court. Abid Hussain's principal disciple, sitārist Bimal Mukherjee, described his *guru* as a versatile musician — a *bīn* player, sitārist, an accomplished *dhrupad* vocalist, and a veritable storehouse of compositions in the *dhrupad, khyāl, ṭhumrī*, Rajasthani folk, and *sitār* styles. (Proceedings of the Seminar on Sitār, ITC Sangeet Research Academy, 1992).

The only available recording of Abid Hussain's *bīn* performance is an *alāp-joḍa* and *chautāl* composition in Darabārī. The rendition is a thoroughbred *rāga* presentation in *dhrupad* style, albeit with a few post-*dhrupad* features. The solidity of his moorings in the *dhrupad* idiom might be attributed to his mastery over *khyāl, ṭhumrī* and folk genres, which would, expectedly, sharpen his faithfulness to the distinctive features of each genre.

The Darabārī *alāp* is an exquisite piece of leisurely *rāga* exposition, rendered at a steady pace, with graceful rounded melodic phrasing. The *alāp* has a *sthāī, antarā* and a *sañchārī*. The *joḍa* is equally steady, with regular *chikarī* perforation. At a higher tempo, the *joḍa* escalates to *chikarī*-punctuated *tāns*, akin to the enhanced-*joḍa* movement of Ustad Vilayat Khan's *sitār* idiom.

In the *chautāl pada* presentation, Abid Hussain uses *gat-toḍas* similar to the modern *sitār* idiom, coupled with complex stroke craft, as well as *tar-paraṇas* typical of the *bīn* idiom.

Rather unusually for the *bīn* of his era, we observe the use of clever *tihāī*s to round off the improvisatory forays — a prominent feature of *dhrupad* vocalism of his time, and of later *sitār/sarod* music. Like Sadiq Ali Khan, Abid Hussain also performed the *chautāl pada* in a progressive tempo, and ended it with a *sitār*-style *jhālā* movement.

In a conversation with B.R. Deodhar (1995), V.N. Bhatkhande (d. 1936) disapproved of Murad Khan, who had started performing on the *bīn* with *tablā* accompaniment, and had also adopted melodic ornamentations more suited to the *sitār* idiom, but inappropriate for the *dhrupad* genre. Mid-twentieth-century recordings, surveyed above, confirm that the *bīn* was fast becoming unsure of its moorings in the *dhrupad* genre. The ideation process of *bīnkār*s had substantially delinked itself from *dhrupad* vocalism, and linked itself to that of the *sitār*, while their ability to translate it into the content and technique battled against the limitations of the instrument. Under these conditions, it is hardly surprising, that the *bīn* revival should have benefited from a *bīnkār* who was sufficiently rooted in the *dhrupad* tradition, but free from the historical baggage of hereditary *bīnkār*s.

Zia Mohiuddin Dagar was a member of the Dagar family, deeply entrenched in *dhrupad* vocalism for several generations. He was an accomplished *dhrupad* vocalist and sitārist when he came to Bombay from his ancestral home in Udaipur in search of a career. As is to be expected of all *dhrupad* lineages, the Dagar clan had preserved the *bīn* as a part of a musician's training, although no one from it had yet chosen the *bīn* as a profession. Z.M. Dagar's father Ziauddin Dagar had studied the *bīn*, and played it in private. This background was evidently conducive for Z.M. Dagar's reinterpretation of the *bīn* art in the contemporary context.

According to his son, Bahauddin, Zia Mohiuddin hoped,

initially, to make a living as a sitārist in Bombay. The *bīn* inspired style of the *sitār*, however, failed to enthuse music lovers in the city. This obliged him to forsake the *sitār* and switch to the *bīn*. Bahauddin reports that early *bīn* recordings of Z.M. Dagar demonstrate his excellent technical command over all departments of *bīn* music, including the percussion-accompanied *pada* presentation. In later years, however, he abandoned dazzling artistry in favour of the more soulful and serene facets of *bīn* music. This stage in his evolution coincides with his growth in stature and influence, thus providing clues to his success.

Z.M. Dagar developed the *alāp-joḍa-jhālā* as the primary vehicle of his performing presence, only rarely extending *rāga* presentation into the percussion-accompanied phase. This bias of later years turned out also to be strategically sound. It placed the *bīn* beyond the bounds of comparison with the *sitār*, which had superior stroke-craft and melodic agility for percussion-accompanied music. Masit Khani and Raza Khani and other *gat*s composed for the *sitār*, along with their compatible improvisatory patterns, had converted the rhythmic action of plucking into a sophisticated art of interaction with percussion. The *bīn*, on the other hand, had to perform *pada*s composed for vocal rendition, and was relatively handicapped by the *dhrupad* tradition and by its own ergonomics, in the handling of percussion-accompanied music. In an interview with the present author (9 November 2002), Bahauddin Dagar admitted these limitations of the *bīn* in the percussion-accompanied segment of *bīn* music.

Published recordings of Z.M. Dagar's *alāp-joḍa-jhālā* in Yaman and Śuddha Toḍī are representative of his music. His *alāp* has the leisurely, graceful, rounded melodic contours typical of *dhrupad* vocalism, totally devoid of angularities in the expression. It relies heavily on *mīṇḍ*, with very sparing use of fretwork techniques. The melodic movements are disciplined, though within the broad-span *alāp* strategy of the *dhrupad* genre. The movements consist of a *sthāī, antarā* and a *sañchārī*. The *joḍa* — rendered at a steady tempo, without significant escalation — also relies heavily on *mīṇḍ*. It makes no demands of melodic agility on the instrument beyond what it can comfortably deliver. The *jhālā*, too, is delivered with the traditional *bīn* stroke patterns, with no attempt to compete with the artistry of the modern *sitār* idiom. Throughout his presentation, there is virtually no trace of the *sitār* idiom, of which he was an accomplished exponent.

In effect, Z.M. Dagar positioned the *bīn* in the small niche which his contemporary, Imrat Khan (Ustad Vilayat Khan's younger brother) had created for the *surbahār* as a specialist instrument for the *alāp-joḍa-jhālā* movements. While Imrat Khan's *surbahār* drifted towards the modern *khyāl*-inspired idiom, Z.M. Dagar provided an alternative, rooted in the medieval *dhrupad* genre. Like Imrat Khan, Z.M. Dagar exploited the acoustic richness of his instrument, and the special appeal of the *alāp-joḍa-jhālā* movements to give the *bīn* another lease of life.

The Disappearing Breed

The present author attempted a listing of significant *bīnkār*s in recent history from authoritative published sources. In such a compilation, it is inevitable that the issue of significance be blurred. A listed musician can either be a significant *bīnkār*, or a significant musician who is also a *bīnkār*. This distinction may not always be relevant because, in the *dhrupad* tradition, the art of the *bīn* was an important accomplishment of a musician, whether or not he performed on it professionally.

Paradoxically, after the progeny of the legendary Tansen (sixteenth century), the next significant *bīnkār* recorded in medieval history is the most luminous personage in the evolution of the *khyāl* genre of vocal music — Niamat Khan

"Sadarang". Apparently, Sadarang, a distinguished *bīn* player at the Delhi court, was dismissed from the service of Emperor Mohammad Shah (r. 1719-48) for refusing to accompany a vocalist, considering it a "menial" task for so eminent a soloist. He decided to settle his score with his employer and all contemporary vocalists by creating a more charming style of singing that would replace *dhrupad*. The rest, as they say, is history.

The survey delivers only twenty-four significant *bīnkār*s in the nineteenth century. This is more likely to reflect the poverty of documentation, than of the profession. The recorded history of the *bīn* in the twentieth century is probably more reliable. The first half of the century deprived the country of twenty-one significant *bīnkār*s. In the latter half of the twentieth century, ten significant *bīnkār*s departed from the scene. The survey reveals an amazing variety. For one, it includes Hindus and Muslims, each in substantial numbers. Secondly, it covers almost all parts of non-peninsular India. Thirdly, it includes professional musicians, priests, monks, aristocrats, royalty, and even courtesans. And, finally, it includes *bīnkār*s who founded great lineages of *khyāl* vocalism, as also those who taught great *sitār*, *surbahār* and *sarod* players. This variety reflects the all-pervasive presence of the *bīn* in Hindustani music before it relinquished it in favour of instruments of superior ergonomics. In a sense, the decline of the *bīn* also paved the way for the divorce of instrumental music from vocal music, setting each on an independent, though partially interactive, path of evolution.

At the time of writing, and on reasonable reckoning, there are only six living *bīnkār*s with training in a well-established lineage of *bīn* music — Asad Ali Khan, the son of Sadiq Ali Khan; Shamsuddin Faridi, the son of Mohammad Khan Faridi Desai; Pandharinath Kolhapure, the son of Krishnarao Kolhapure; Bindumadhav Pathak, the son of Dattopant Pathak;

Hindaraj Diwekar, the son of Shivrambuwa Diwekar; and Bahauddin Dagar, the son of Zia Mohiuddin Dagar. Only the last two named here belong the post-Independence generation. In the last quarter of the twentieth century, a few European students of the *bīn* have achieved a respectable level of competence. Amongst them is Philippe Bruguiere.

With respect to contemporary *bīnkār*s, the issue of significance is trickier than for those of earlier generations, though for different reasons. An important reason is that they constitute a trans-cultural mix, with some of them having remained either largely, or wholly, aloof from a performing presence. Any attempt to impose a yardstick of musicianship on so small and mismatched a population can easily deliver absurd results.

5.2

THE SITĀR*

THE *sitār*, the most popular representative of Hindustani classical music, belongs to the long-necked, fretted lute family of instruments. Over just three centuries of evolution, the instrument has evolved from very limited melodic capability to a level of great sophistication. Most of this evolution has taken place during the twentieth century.

Initially, it is believed, the *sitār* was used like a banjo, as a rhythmic accompaniment to *qawwālī* performances, filling the pauses between verses. In due course, musicians of exceptional talent became aware of the *sitār*'s melodic potential and developed it into a concert instrument.

The *sitār* acquired its independent status on the concert platform towards the end of the eighteenth century. *Dhrupad* was the dominant mainstream genre at that time. The ancient *rudra-vīṇā*, which had originally accompanied vocal *dhrupad* had by then laid the foundations of the *tantakār aṅga* (literally, the style of plucked instruments). In the early *tantakār aṅga* phase, the *sitār* adopted the *dhrupad*-based composition formats and instrumental techniques of the *rudra-vīṇā*. Under *dhrupad* influence, *sitār* music responded to the rhythmic patterns of the *pakhāwaj*.

By the end of the eighteenth century, musicians began to compose *gats* (compositions) of different structures especially for the *sitār*. The most significant amongst them were Masit Khan and Ghulam Raza Khan, both related by kinship to Niamat Khan Sadarang, the father of the modern *khyāl* style of singing, who served at the court of Emperor Mohammed Shah (1719-48).

Masit Khan's *gat* structure for *vilambit* (slow tempo) *tīntāl*, and the Raza Khani *gat* structure for *drut* (fast tempo) *tīntāl*, began the process of giving *sitār* music an identity distinct from the *dhrupad*-based music of the *rudra-vīṇā*.

The *sitār* technique uses four basic strokes of the plectrum:

Da: The inward stroke.

Ra: The outward stroke.

DiR: The inward followed by outward in quick succession.

Rda: The outward followed by inward in quick succession.

The Masit Khani and Raza Khani *gats* used this raw material for building a distinctive pattern, with each stroke falling on a beat of the rhythmic cycle. Thus, in essence, these *gats* constitute an interpretation of the rhythmic cycle which, naturally, influences the structure of melodic execution also. Their significance lies in freeing the language of the *sitār* from the vocabulary of *dhrupad*. During the nineteenth century, the Masit Khani and Raza Khani *gats*, together, became the basic framework of *rāga* presentation on the *sitār*.

The Masit Khani Gat

The 4-beat subdivision of the 16-beat cycle of *tīntāl* corresponds to the pattern of: *Da DiR Da Ra*, using only the first three strokes.

The Masit Khani *gat* format

Beat	12	13	14	15	16	1	2	3	4	5	6	7	8	9	10	11
Stroke	*Dir*	*Da*	*Dir*	*Da*	*Ra*	*Da*	*Da*	*Ra*	*Dir*	*Da*	*Dir*	*Da*	*Ra*	*Da*	*Da*	*Ra*

This 16-beat structure consists of one 8-beat structure rendered twice: *DiR Da DiR Da Ra Da Da Ra/DiR Da DiR Da Ra Da Da Ra.* When performed, this 8-beat element acquires a lilt which breaks down into a 5-3 subdivision as so: *DiR Da DiR Da Ra /Da Da Ra.* Thus, the Masit Khani *gat* superimposes a 5-3-5-3 asymmetry on the 4-4-4-4 symmetry of the cycle. This imposition of asymmetry over symmetry builds the tension; the tension creates the anticipation of its release; and the release creates the cathartic effect. Notice that every alternate 4-beat division contains the corresponding pattern *Da DiR Da Ra* strokes. And, yet, the totality of the stroke pattern creates a momentum quite distinct from that of the rhythmic cycle.

This partial liberation of melody from rhythm was a reflection of the same process that vocal music was undergoing with the ascendancy of the *khyāl* style over *dhrupad* music, and the emergence of the *ṭhumrī* style. Technically, of course, the *sitār* was, at that time, a couple of centuries away from being able to execute a melodic mimesis of either the *khyāl* or the *ṭhumrī.*

The Raza Khani Gat

At about the same time, Ghulam Raza Khan, a sitāraist from Lucknow, the home of the *ṭhumrī*, developed *drut tīntāl* composition patterns. Of the several structures developed by him, the most popular structure used all the four strokes of the *sitār* for his crisp composition:

The Raza Khani *gat* format simplified

Beat	5	6	7	8	9	10	11	12	13	14	15	16	1	2	3	4
Stroke	*Da*	*Ra*	*Dir*	*Dir*	*Da*	*Rda*	*Ra*	*Dir*	*Da*	*Dir*	*Da*	*Ra*	*Da*	-	*Da*	*Ra*

The Raza Khani *gat* distanced *sitār* music further from its *rudra-vīṇā* and *dhrupad* ancestry. For one, it was meant to be played at a pace faster than *dhrupad* music. And, secondly, these patterns drew their inspiration explicitly from post-*dhrupad* forms of vocalism. Because of the predominant *ṭhumrī* influence, many of the Raza Khani *gat*s were originally composed in the lighter *rāga*s such as Pīlū, Kāfī, Khamāja, Zillā, Deśa, Bhairavī.

In the early twentieth century, the *khyāl* influence on the *sitār* idiom became more pronounced as the instrument itself was modified to facilitate the stylistic drift towards vocalism. The pace of performing Masit Khani *gat*s slowed down to come closer to *khyāl* singing, and *rāga* elaboration techniques shifted away from the emphasis on rhythmic (right hand) dexterity, and towards melodic (left hand) refinement.

A further liberation of melody from rhythm followed, as a rich source of compositions from the various vocal styles (*dhrupad, khyāl, ṭhumrī* and *tarānā*) became accessible for adaptation to the *sitār*.

Sitār Styles

Today, it is possible to identify six distinct *gharānā*s of *sitār* music. The best known amongst them are the Etawah/Imdad Khan Gharānā represented by Ustad Vilayat Khan and the Maihar Gharānā represented by Pt. Ravi Shankar. The influence of vocalism is evident in both the major *gharānā*s, though in very different ways. But, neither of these *gharānā*s has altogether abandoned either the Masit Khani and Raza Khani format of compositions or the distinctive techniques that exploit the character of the *sitār* as an instrument of the fretted lute family. What they have, indeed, done is to re-invent *sitār* music by transcending the instrument's technical limitations. As a result, contemporary *sitār* music represents a blend of *tantakār* and *gāyakī* elements in terms of the choice of compositions, as well as the style and technique of *rāga* elaboration.

Techniques of Melodic Execution

The techniques of melodic execution on the *sitār* can be divided into two categories: (a) fretwork in which the fingers of the left hand move from fret to fret and (b) deflection, where the fingers are static on one fret, and tonal transition is achieved by pulling the string without movement between the frets.

Fretwork techniques belong to the traditional *sitār* idiom, developed before the *sitār* acquired sufficient strength to audibly deliver an array of *svar*s executed under a single stroke. The deflection techniques developed along with structural improvements in the *sitār*, and their maturation enabled the evolution of the vocalized idiom.

Fretwork techniques: In addition to the straightforward execution, there are mainly two types of fretwork technique: *krintan* and *ghasīṭ*.

Krintan requires the dexterous movement of two fingers over the frets. The first *svar* executed with a right-hand stroke supporting one left-hand finger resting on the fret-board. The subsequent *svar*s of the phrase are executed with the second finger hitting the appropriate fret in a hammering motion, but without further right-hand stroke support. With this technique, a phrase of up to four *svar*s can be executed. This technique is unique to the *sitār*, and originated even before the *sitār* acquired sympathetic strings, and has remained an essential feature of *tantakār aṅga* of the *sitār*.

Ghasīṭ (lit. dragging) does precisely that. It executes a phrase, usually flat-out and unidirectional, by dragging the left-hand finger along the fret-board over at least half an octave under the impact of a single stroke. This is accompanied by feather-touch left-hand pressure over the string, so that the resultant glide delivers an aural impression of a fretless instrument. It is not uncommon for the *ghasīṭ* to span a full octave unidirectionally, as it can do on the *rudra-vīṇā*. The *ghasīṭ* on the *sitār* is inspired by the *sūta* technique practised on the *rudra-vīṇā* which, in turn, is inspired by the vocal idiom of *dhrupad* music.

There are three principal deflection techniques (a) *mīṇḍ* (b) *murkī* and (c) *gamak*.

The *mīṇḍ* is a simple execution of a phrase by pulling the string from a single fret, and executing a phrase under the impact of a single stroke. Three-*svar mīṇḍ*s were common in *sitār* music up to the 1930s. The contemporary *sitār*, because of enhanced sustaining ability, can deliver a five-*svar mīṇḍ*.

The *murkī* is a special type of *mīṇḍ*, where the phrase involves a wrap-around execution with a jerky motion. The contemporary *sitār* can support a *murkī* of up to eight *svar*s under a single stroke.

The *gamak* creates a pulsating or quivering effect — a magnified *vibrato* — by repeatedly attacking a *svar* from a fret at a lower pitch. The *gamak* is generally used for distances of upto two, occasionally three, *svar*s.

The Singing Sitār

The supreme status of vocal music in the Indian performing arts tradition has made the lure of vocalism compelling for musicians performing on the various instruments. For the *sitār*, the principal obstacle to vocalism arises from the technical limitation of the plucking technique of sound activation, and low acoustic sustain. Hence, the need to move the left hand from fret to fret in order to execute the melody, and the need for the intermittent priming of the sound by strokes of the plectrum worn on the right index finger. Both these actions are perceptible, and therefore militate against the melodic continuity required of vocalism.

In order to bring the *sitār* close to vocal music, the design and construction of the instrument had to be modified, and the technique of playing the *sitār* — the right hand as well as the left hand — had to be developed to exploit the melodic potential thus released. Although technical changes were evolutionary, it is twentieth-century musicians and craftsmen who made the *sitār* capable of singing.

By the late nineteenth century, the commonly used wooden chamber-resonators of the early *sitār*s had been replaced by two dried pumpkins. In the early twentieth century, the basic seven-string *sitār* acquired an additional thirteen sympathetic strings tuned to the scale of the *rāga*. These changes gave a boost to amplification and sustenance.

In the 1950s, contemporary legends, Ustad Vilayat Khan, and Pt. Ravi Shankar worked closely with expert craftsmen to redesign the *sitār* for delivering their own distinctive styles of music. Of the two, the Vilayat Khan design was more revolutionary in terms of sound production.

Vilayat Khan's solution to the sustenance problem was a more powerful right hand stroke. He designed a thicker *tablī* (cover of the impact-receiving resonator), increased the height of the bridge that received the impact of the stroke, and introduced a metallic reinforcement of the joint between the chamber-resonator and the stem (column-resonator) to enable the instrument to withstand the power of his strokes.

By the late nineteenth century, the technique of producing melodic phrases by pulling the melodic string (called a *mīṇḍ*) from the same fret rather than moving the left palm between frets, had already been developed. But, up to the 1920s, the *sitār* was technically unable to deliver more than three *svar*s from one fret.

Ustad Vilayat Khan made a five-*svar mīṇḍ* possible by reinforcing the two bridges across which the wires are strung, altering the curvature of the frets and the stem, replacing the brass frets with frets from an alloy of superior malleability and acoustic quality, and introducing strings of a lower (thicker) gauge.

Because amplification electronics had, by now, reached a high level of sophistication, Vilayat Khan developed a method of directing the impact of his strokes towards achieving greater sustenance, rather than permit its dissipation on amplification. This was aided by a technique of fine-tuning the bridge that receives the impact of the stroke.

With these modifications and refinements, Ustad Vilayat Khan made it possible for both hands to move less frequently. Melodic expression could now be executed with a smoothness of flow approximating that of wind or bow instruments.

In order to simulate singing even more faithfully, Ustad Vilayat Khan introduced a method of tuning and strumming the strings to create an illusion of a continuous *tānpūrā* (a four/six-stringed drone instrument) accompaniment. This obviated the need for *tānpūrā* support, and brought the melody and its harmonic ambience, both, under the sitārist's own control.

5.3

THE SURBAHĀR*

THE *surbahār* is to the *sitār*, what the cello is to the violin. It is a large-size bass *sitār*, with a flat rather than rounded gourd at the base, and a rounded *sitār*-type, gourd-resonator at the top. In its contemporary form, the *surbahār* has a string-count identical to the present-day *sitār*, the difference being in the thickness of the strings, the pitch at which the instrument is tuned, and the tuning system covering four octaves.

Its construction gives the *surbahār* a deep, sonorous, long-lasting sound. The extra width of its stem enables the execution of *mīṇḍ*s of up to a full octave. These features facilitate the parsimony of strokes as well as left-hand movement between frets, both these being fundamental to achieving a higher degree of melodic continuity.

The invention of the *surbahār*, around CE 1825, is attributed, variously, to Ustad Vilayat Khan's great-grandfather, Ustad Sahebdad Khan, and to a lesser-known, Lucknow-based early nineteenth-century sitārist, Ustad Ghulam Mohammed. The latest research favours the latter attribution.

The purpose of developing the instrument was to enable *sitār*-players to present the elaborate *dhrupad*-style *alāp*

---

traditionally performed on the *rudra-vīṇā*. They designed the *surbahār* to combine the ergonomic facility of the *sitār* with the melodic potential and acoustic richness of the *rudra-vīṇā*. This combination looked attractive in an era in which the *sitār* idiom was, by and large, a prisoner of the medieval *dhrupad* style, and struggling to match the *bīn* in terms of acoustic richness and melodic content. With *alāp* presentations on the *surbahār*, *sitār* players succeeded in overtaking *bīn* players in terms of popularity and stature.

The idiom of the *surbahār* speedily achieved great sophistication. Initially, it was plucked, like the *bīn*, with bare fingers, but has been played, at different stages and by different musicians with one, two, and even three *mizrāb*s (plectrums).

Until well into the twentieth century, sitārists presented the *dhrupad* style *alāp* on the *surbahār*, followed by post-*dhrupad* styles of compositions on the *sitār*. As the *sitār* itself evolved technically and stylistically, it took over the elaborate *dhrupad*-format *alāp*, and added further sophistication to it. As a result, during the latter half of the twentieth century, the *surbahār* suffered a steady depletion in the number of competent performers, although not in the size of audiences.

The contemporary *sitār* of enhanced musical capability is now threatening the *surbahār* with extinction. This is ironic considering that the *surbahār* was originally developed by sitārists for their own musical needs. But, this is also inevitable because, the *surbahār* remained relevant only as long as it could motivate sitārists to master two different instruments. Against this prospect, understandably, design improvements aimed at enhancing the acoustic capabilities of the *sitār* looked like a more attractive proposition. Considering the success of these efforts, the *surbahār* risks drifting into history, unless the community of musicians develops an independent role or idiom for the instrument.

The *surbahār* remains, however, a major link of continuity between the *dhrupad* and post-*dhrupad* styles of instrumental music. Despite being rare, it remains an important part of the instrumental tradition of *dhrupad* music, and in the major *gharānās* of *sitār* music, which have helped the instrument make a transition into post-*dhrupad* stylistics. These traditions have not only preserved the art of the *surbahār*, but are also searching for a legitimate, and hopefully unique, role for the *surbahār* in the contemporary scenario of music on the long-necked fretted-lute family of instruments.

In the *dhrupad* stream, itself a greatly depleted segment of the music world, the *surbahār* has started replacing the *bīn* as a presenter of comprehensive *dhrupad* performances, including the *alāp*, as well as *dhrupad* compositions. However, the *dhrupad* side of *surbahār* music is still bereft of significant musicianship.

Surbahār and the Imdad Khan Lineage

Amongst musicians of the post-*dhrupad* genres, the Etawah/ Imdad Khan lineage has contributed most significantly to the development of the *surbahār*. The *surbahār* has hitherto been an essential part of the training of its members, irrespective of whether they performed on the *sitār* or the *surbahār*.

Ustad Sahebdad Khan, Vilayat Khan's great grandfather, was evidently competent enough on the *surbahār* for him to have been considered, by some, to be its inventor. His son, Ustad Imdad Khan was a formidable *surbahār* and *sitār* player, as were his two sons, Ustad Enayet Khan (Ustad Vilayat Khan's father) and Ustad Waheed Khan (Ustad Vilayat Khan's uncle). Starting from Ustad Imdad Khan, there exist 78-RPM recordings by way of evidence of the contribution of this lineage to the art of the *surbahār*.

Ustad Vilayat Khan, and his brother, Ustad Imrat Khan, both received training on the *surbahār* from their uncle, Ustad

Waheed Khan. At some stage, Vilayat Khan ceded the *surbahār* territory to Imrat Khan, and decided to concentrate on the *sitār*. The results of this bifurcation of territories have been most rewarding for the two brothers, and for the world of music in general.

In the hands of Ustad Vilayat Khan and his brother, Ustad Imrat Khan, the *surbahār* technique has achieved a melodic continuity far beyond that of the *bīn* or the *sitār*, and conceivable only on a fretless instrument. The three-tiered *alāp-joḍa-jhālā* format has remained the basic idiom of the *surbahār*; but stylistically, the *dhrupad* idiom has receded, giving way to a marked influence of *khyāl*-oriented treatment of melody.

In the mid-1960s, came their first attempt at enlarging the canvas of *surbahār* music, with the recording of a duet (A Night at the Taj: EMI:EALP:1323) with Ustad Vilayat Khan playing the *sitār* and Ustad Imrat Khan, the *surbahār*. On this landmark recording, they presented an *alāp* as well as a Masit Khani composition in Rāga Cāndanī Kedāra with percussion accompaniment.

This recording encouraged the notion of the *surbahār* as a male voice and the *sitār* as a female voice. It also brought the *surbahār*, for the first time in post-*dhrupad* music, out of its *alāp-joḍa-jhālā* territory, and into percussion-accompanied presentation of post-*dhrupad* compositions, including medium-paced *tāns* utilizing the *gamak* and *ghasīṭ* modes of execution.

This was followed by more duets of Ustad Vilayat Khan, not merely with Imrat Khan (Miyā kī Malhār: EMI: ASD:498:0), but also his son, Shujaat Khan on the *surbahār* (Navras:NRCC:0533). Shujaat Khan took the *surbahār* deeper into *sitār* territory by executing fast-paced *ekhar* (one *svar* per stroke) *tāns*, almost matching his father's *tāns* on the *sitār*.

The success of this supporting, though enlarged, role for the *surbahār* cannot be considered a final verdict on the unique potential of the instrument, because it merely represents the technical achievement of moving the *surbahār* into *sitār* territory. The present situation is not very different from that of the cello, whose musical value could not be unleashed by an intrusion into violin territory, but had to wait until composers like Bach and Boccherini started writing music specially for the cello.

5.4

THE SAROD*

IN TERMS of popularity and sophistication of its idiom, the *sarod* comes next only to the *sitār*. Its present stature as a mainstream instrument conceals the fact that until the end of the nineteenth century, it was a fairly crude acoustic machine. Its transformation into a scintillating instrument has taken place entirely in the twentieth century.

History

The contemporary *sarod* is about 100 years old. It has three identifiable ancestors. Two of these were *rabāb*s, short-necked fretless lutes with wooden bodies, cat-gut strings, and a skin-covered chamber resonator. The Persian *rabāb*, later came to be known as the Indian *rabāb*/*dhrupad rabāb*/*senīya rabāb*. The Afghan or Kābulī *rabāb*, which came much later, provided a direct impetus for its own transformation into the *sarod*. The third ancestor was the *surṣṛṅgār*, an indigenous adaptation of the Persian/*dhrupad rabāb*.

The Persian *rabāb* entered India in the eleventh century along with the Gazhnavid occupation of the Punjab. It became an important part of music in the early Mogul courts. During the mid-Mogul period, the legendary Miya Tansen at Emperor Akbar's court contributed substantially to performance on the *rabāb*. The Tansen lineage, through his son Bilas Khan, perpetuated the *dhrupad rabāb* tradition. The *dhrupad rabāb* remained, along with the *rudra-vīṇā*, a pervasive presence in the Hindustani mainstream for over 200 years after Tansen (Miner, 1997).

The Afghan *rabāb*, different in design from the Persian *rabāb*, entered India from Afghanistan with *paṭhān* soldiers in the employ of the early-Moguls. Soldier-musicians played martial tunes on it, and prized it for the fervor and beat it created. This instrument retained its Afghan music and identity until the mid-eighteenth century, when a line of *rabābīya*s established a link with Hindustani musicians, and diverted its music towards the mainstream (ibid.).

There is no evidence about when the Afghan *rabāb* was renamed the *sarod*. The earliest significant *sarodīya* on record is Ghulam Ali Khan (early nineteenth century), who was the grandson of Ghulam Bandegi Khan Bangash, a *rabābīya* from Afghanistan, and lived in Rewa and Lucknow to finally settle down in Gwalior (ibid.).

Despite its considerable status as a mainstream instrument, the *sarod* was, until the late nineteenth century, an acoustically unstable instrument with gut strings, and a wooden finger-board. It adopted the metallic fingerboard and metal strings probably from the *surśr̥ṅgār*.

After surrendering its most promising features to the *sarod*, the *surśr̥ṅgār* faded into history. Further re-engineering of the *sarod* took place during the 1930s to make it the sophisticated and versatile instrument we hear today. Most of this is credited to Ustad Alauddin Khan, and his brother, Ayet Ali Khan, who was also an expert craftsman.

After the short-lived *surśr̥ṅgār* experiment, the *rabāb/sarod gharānā*s have not been too enthusiastic about imposing melodic fluidity on the capabilities of the *sarod*, or to dilute the percussive element. Within limits, the instrument is being re-engineered to progressively offer a wider choice of idioms in terms of stroke-density relative to *svar*-density. The martial history of the *rabāb*, and the robust aural experience have begun to recede as dominant influences on contemporary *sarod* music. But, they remain firmly entrenched in the *sarod*'s musical personality.

Although the world of *sarod* recognizes several streams, its idiom is currently represented by three main lineages. The *rabāb*-inspired idiom of Ustad Hafiz Ali Khan, an early twentieth century maestro, was diverted towards a *khyāl* style vocalism by his son, Ustad Amjad Ali Khan. The Mohammed Ameer Khan/Radhika Mohan Maitra stream has reinforced its *rabāb*-oriented idiom in the music of its contemporary exponents, Buddhadev Dasgupta and Kalyan Mukherjea. The *rabāb* and *rudra-vīṇā* based style of Ustad Alauddin Khan inspired the genius of his son, Ustad Ali Akbar Khan, to launch the most comprehensive exploitation yet of the distinctive acoustic features of the re-engineered *sarod*.

Organology

By modern organological classification, the *sarod* is a short-necked lute of the plucked variety. However, it also straddles the membranophone category by virtue of having a leather-bound cover for the chamber-resonator.

Although a monochord, the *sarod* has some features of a polychord. The melody is executed on four strings. The melodic execution also exposes the melodic strings to raw or unaided participation. In addition, the modern *sarod* has a three-string set mounted and tuned explicitly for harp-like strumming to deliver either a chord or a melodic phrase compatible with the *rāga*.

Because of the uniqueness of this instrument, the Indian organological classification is also relevant. Bharata's

Nāṭyaśāstra (200 BCE – CE 200) classifies instruments into (a) *ghan* or solids, (b) *avanaddha* or covered with skin, (c) *suṣīr* or hollow and (d) *tata* or having strings. Using this classification as the basis, a seventeenth-century musicological text (*Sangītapārijāta* of Ahobala) mentions the *rabāb*, the ancestor of the *sarod*, below the drums, as a separate category called *tatāvanaddha* (*tat* + *avanaddha*) or a string instrument with a skin-cover. The creation of a special category, and its placement below the drums, recognizes not only its physical construction, but also acoustic character.

When the *sarod* discarded the wooden finger-board of its ancestor, the *rabāb* in the late nineteenth/early twentieth century, and adopted the metallic finger-board, it became the only lute still in the Indian mainstream to have a shell made of wood, and the upper made of skin and metal, thus defining its unique acoustics.

Design and Tuning

The shell of the *sarod* is carved, ideally, from a single block of teak (*Tectona grandis*) wood. The carved shell is about 32 inches, end-to-end. At the bottom, is a skin-covered elliptical or spheroid chamber-resonator, which extends into a tapering stem (column resonator) covered with a stainless steel finger-board. A second, but smaller, chamber-resonator mounted at the end of the finger-board, on the rear side, is optional. The finger-board extends into a bar, 10/14 inches in length, which holds eight pegs for the primary strings, for which two different tuning systems are in vogue.

The traditional tuning system, practised by the lineage of Pt. Radhika Mohan Maitra, uses five strings for melodic execution. They are tuned to Middle-octave *mā*, the tonic (*sā*), lower-octave *pā*, lower-octave *sā*, and ultra-lower *pā*, thus providing a melodic canvas of virtually four octaves. The last three constitute a *chikarī* (drone) set, with the innermost tuned to the tonic, and the outermost two tuned to the higher-octave *Sa*. In the modern system, practised by Ustad Ali Akbar Khan, and his disciples, the first four strings are tuned exactly as in the traditional system, thus limiting the melodic canvas to three-and-half octaves. In addition to the conventional *chikarī* set, this system, however, includes a set of three strings, mounted at a lower level, and tuned either to a chord or a melodic phrase compatible with the scale of the *rāga*. The contemporary *sarod* has fifteen sympathetic strings (sometimes fewer) mounted below the primary strings. They are tuned to the scale of the *rāga*.

Acoustics

The acoustics of an instrument depend on the materials from which it is made, as also its shape. In the *sarod*, the skin-cladding over the chamber-resonator primarily enhances percussive sustain. The metallic finger-board, devoid of a fibre-structure, deprives it of melodic sustain, even though it contributes to the instrument's timbre. Thus, despite substantial acoustic re-engineering over the last fifty years and its enhanced sustain, the *sarod* remains inferior on sustain, and superior on percussive potential, compared to the *sitār*, the other prominent lute in the Indian mainstream.

These features demand, from the *sarod*, a higher frequency of sound-priming than a *sitār* and impose, on the musical idiom of the *sarod*, a high stroke-density relative to the *svar*-density. A rhythmic bias is thus inherent in the design of the instrument. The enhanced melodic potential of the contemporary *sarod*, still inferior to that of the *sitār* or *surbahār*, has enabled it to shape a satisfying slow *alāp* of reasonable *svar*-density relative to stroke-density.

Ergonomics

The performer normally sits with his right knee folded over

his left knee. The left foot, folded to the right, supports the bulbous chamber-resonator. The centre of the stem is supported on the right thigh at an incline of 15/20°. The instrument is stable in this posture, leaving the left hand free to move at will for melodic execution. The instrument is plucked with a triangular plectrum cut out of coconut shell and laminated with shellac. Most sarodists hold the plectrum between the thumb and first and second fingers of the right hand. Sarodists of Pt. Radhika Mohan's *gharānā* use a two-finger grip. They believe that this produces a better percussive punch, and provides superior bi-directional mechanical efficiency.

The right arm wraps around the base of the chamber-resonator, the fore-arm rests at the root of the base, and uses wrist-movements for stroke-play, almost equally in both directions. The posture and the manner of handling the instrument results in the strokes being near-vertical. The downward is aided by gravity, while the upward is weakened by having to work against it. Because of multiple-string melodic execution, the span of movement in each direction is about 3.5 inches, the maximum rotation the wrist can manage with the fore-arm firm at the base.

The ergonomics of music-making on the *sarod* militate against strokes requiring the simultaneous execution of string-shifts and direction-reversal. Hence, the traditional idiom of the *sarod* has come to be dominated by multiple strokes supporting each *svar*, especially at medium-to-higher tempi. Although the more demanding *ekhar* treatment (one stroke per *svar*) is in greater evidence over the last three decades, a higher stroke density remains the distinguishing feature of the *sarod* idiom. In totality, the design of the instrument, and the ergonomics of music making together make the *sarod* a percussive-melodic instrument, and bias its musical idiom towards the rhythmic exploitation of its percussive character.

The Sarod Idiom

The contemporary *sarod* idiom is a blend of three principal stylistic influences, broadly represented by the three leading exponents of the instrument. The traditional *rabāb*-influenced idiom dominates the music of the *rabābīya* tradition of Pt. Radhika Mohan Maitra. The *rudra-vīṇā*-influenced idiom, following the medieval *dhrupad-dhamār* genre of music, dominates the music of the Maihar-Senīya Gharānā of Ustad Alauddin Khan. The influence of the post-*dhrupad* genres, mainly *khyāl* vocalism and contemporary *sitār* music of the Imdad Khan/Etawah Gharānā, dominates the music of the next generation of maestros, especially Ustad Amjad Ali Khan.

Running through all the contemporary manifestations of the *sarod* idiom lies an undercurrent that the *sarod* shares with the *sitār* idiom. Like the *sarod*, the *sitār* is a plucked lute, which developed its independent idiom as a solo concert instrument almost a century before the *sarod* did. This made a certain degree of borrowing inevitable. The sharing of idioms was facilitated by the sharing of a common home — pre-Partition Bengal of the nineteenth and early twentieth centuries.

Techniques of Melodic Execution

Melodic execution techniques on the *sarod* can be divided into three different types: (a) sliding of the finger along the finger board without lifting the fingers from the melodic string, (b) execution by the alternative/successive use of two fingers on the same melodic string, (c) multiple-string execution inevitably requiring the alternative/successive use of two fingers.

Type (a) techniques: The design and the ergonomics of manipulation of the instrument make this the basic technique of executing any melodic phrase in the slow-to-medium tempi, unless it requires the use of more than one melodic string. Thus, the fundamental melodic character of the instrument is conjunct rather than disjunct. It is the limited sustain of the instrument and the necessity for higher stroke frequency, which tilts the bias of the aural experience in favour of the rhythmic element and melodic discontinuity.

Mīṇḍ: The *mīṇḍ* is a unidirectional glissando of short-melodic span executed under a single stroke.

Murkī: The *murkī* is phrase executed by a bi-directional glissando under the power of a single stroke, and involving a wrap-around movement around one *svar* with jerky motion mostly at the point of direction-reversal.

Gamak: A *gamak* is a magnified *vibrato* created by repeatedly attacking a target *svar* from an adjacent *svar*, under multiple stroke activation.

Ghasīṭ: A *ghasīṭ* is a *mīṇḍ* of broad melodic span, generally a full octave or more. The technique is borrowed from the *sūta* technique of the *rudra-vīṇā*.

Type (b) techniques: Being a fretless instrument, finger-work belongs to the special effects department of the *sarod* idiom.

Sparśa: The *sparśa* involves the lifting of one finger from the string almost immediately after the stroke, and allowing the other finger to execute the adjacent *svar*. The two near-simultaneous *svar*s can be activated either under a single stroke or even two or more strokes.

Krintan: This technique, a specialty of the *sitār*, involves the execution of a phrase of four or more *svar*s under the power of a single stroke. The first *svar* of the phrase receives stroke power, while the subsequent *svar*s are powered by the action of the middle finger being lifted from one *svar*, and the index finger attacking an adjacent *svar* in hammer-like vertical impact.

Type (c) techniques: This facet of the *sarod* technique, possessing elements of the polychord, dominates the aural experience in the medium-to-faster tempi, especially in broad-span melodic phrasing. This facet is emphasized by regarding the multiplicity of melodic strings as a distinctive musical element rather than unavoidable. *Sarod* players revel in opportunities for a harp-like activation of the melodic strings, and compose symmetric, geometric, and kaleidoscopic patterns to maximise such exposure.

Since multiple-string execution requires lifting of at least one finger from any particular melodic string, the Type (c) special effects are a subset of the type (b) technique. Multiple-string execution of both, *sparśa* and *krintan*, is possible.

New Path to Sculpting of Melody

The search of the *sarod* for an idiom uniquely suited to its ergonomic and acoustic character, has contributed significantly to the melodic richness of Hindustani instrumental music. Because of its short stem, the *sarod* became the first plucked instrument in classical music to require multiple-string melodic execution for even a single full octave. It is therefore described as a semi-polychord. Because of its design, it delivers distinctively different timbres on each string. Thus, the instrument became not only a canvas of pitch-frequencies, but also a canvas rich in multiple timbres. This combination inspired the development of a new approach to the melodic interpretation of *rāga*s.

Conventional wisdom regarding Hindustani music says that the basic building-block of its melody is a phrase of two or more *svar*s, characterized by at least two melodic transitions to define three points in conjunct — rather than disjunct — intervallic transition.

This description, arising from the vocal music model, implicitly recognizes three kinds of melodic path:

1. the melodic or *rāga* driven, which composes and arranges phrases with the purpose of exploring the melodic character of the *rāga*,
2. the symmetric, which composes and arranges phrases in order to exploit the symmetry of the *rāga*'s permissible phraseology without the existence of any correspondence between the *svar*s and the transitions, and
3. the geometric, which composes and arranges phrases in order to emphasize the congruence between permissible phrases as defined by the first-fourth or first-fifth correspondence between the *svar*s and the transitions within each phrase.

In the latter half of the twentieth century, the *sarod*, and later the *santūr*, a classic polychord, obliged us to recognize a fourth path to melodic development, arising from their highly evolved contemporary idioms.

The technique of sound-activation on these instruments (plucking or striking) imposes a discontinuity on the melodic flow. This has encouraged musicians to develop a path of disjunct rather than conjunct melodic development. This path dispenses with the phrase as the basic building-block of melodic development, and utilises permissible *svar*s either in isolation, or in groups of two, in interesting juxtaposition.

The tonal patterns so developed — if they can be called patterns — can often be non-descript in terms of its *rāga* connotation, though not inimical to the *rāga* being performed. By suppressing the listener's consciousness of the specific *rāga*, these patterns divert the attention of the listener from the melodic component, towards the manipulation of timbres, volume, and rhythmic patterns, these being the primary territory of the sound-priming action (strokes).

This path to melodic development enables the *sarod* to fully exploit its distinctive acoustic character — by highlighting the manipulation of timbres and time-intervals through high-frequency, variable-frequency, and multiple-string stroke craft. The primary musical purpose of this path is non-melodic. Yet, these expressions have to be described as melodic because they are not harmonic. But, to the extent that they do not have a well-defined melodic contour, they can be described as kaleidoscopic.

5.5

THE SANTŪR

THE *santūr* is a unique instrument in Hindustani music. It has risen from virtual oblivion to the peak of popularity in an unusually short time — less than three decades. It is the only string instrument subjected to percussive sound activation. All others are either plucked or bowed. The *santūr* is also the sole survivor in its organological classification of struck polychords. Three instruments in this grouping have vanished in recent times — the *jala-taraṅga,* a set of china clay cups of different sizes tuned to scale by filling them with water, the *kāṣṭha-taraṅga,* an Indian version of the xylophone, and the *tablā-taraṅga,* a set of treble drums tuned to different pitches to produce melody. The acceptance of the *santūr,* after the failure of the other three, is explained by its ergonomic and acoustic superiority, and the contribution of Pt. Shivkumar Sharma.

Sharma started performing classical music on the *santūr* in 1952, but attracted national attention only after his concert at the Sur Singara Samsad festival at Bombay in 1955. The instrument's acceptance on the art-music platform took years of struggle. But, Shivkumar and his instrument became an instant rage with composers of music for the movies. The *santūr* soon penetrated the public mind as the musical signature of the Kashmir Valley where many of India's films were shot in the 1960s. That phase of the *santūr*'s glory receded in the 1980s when Kashmir became unsafe as a location, and film music started going electronic. By this time, Sharma and the *santūr* were firmly entrenched on the classical platform.

Sharma's ascendancy on the art-music horizon attracted a large number of musicians to take to the *santūr*. As a result, the instrument and its idiom are now in a state of flux, with every *santūr* player attempting to explore new musical directions, and redesigning the instrument to suit his own musical vision.

Organology

The *santūr* belongs to the box polychord variety of struck instruments. Until recently, it was virtually unknown to Indians outside the Kashmir Valley, where it was common as an accompaniment for vocal renditions of *sūfīānā mauṣiqī* (chants of the Sufi sects). Shivkumar Sharma (in a private interview on 2 December 2003) questions the popular notion of *sūfīānā mauṣiqī* as folk music. He prefers to describe it as Kashmiri classical music. It uses melodic structures (called *maqāms*, as in Persian classical music), and rhythmic cycles (*tāls*) of four or eight beats derived from Hindustani as well Persian traditions, requires considerable training, and acknowledges different levels of musicianship. It is performed at a slow, deliberate tempo, and is accompanied by the *tablā*.

The instrument is related to similar instruments in the neighbouring regions of the Middle East and Central Asia. According to Shivkumar Sharma, similar instruments (the hammered dulcimer/cimbalom family) exist in Persia, Iraq, China, Tibet, Hungary, Kazakhstan, Uzbekistan, Greece, Ireland, Italy, and even in the foothills of the Alps. There exists one platform-mounted variant in central Europe, which is played in a standing position, and has foot-pedals for acoustic manipulation. That is probably the father of the piano. Some authors have linked the name to the *Psantir*, a similar instrument known to Mesopotamians since the pre-Christian era. The name is, however, in all likelihood of Sanskrit, or Persian origin. The original Sanskrit name for it is *śatatantrī* (*śata* = 100 + *tantrī* = stringed instrument), and the Persian name, now popular, is *santūr* (*sad* or *san* = 100 + *tūr* = strings).

The Persians believe that the instrument originated in their land, and travelled from there to other parts of the world. The theory of Indian origin is also plausible considering that polychords of various types have been a part of the Indian musical tradition from ancient times. This family faded away after the tenth century CE, leaving only two significant survivors, both of the box polychord variety — the *svarmaṇḍala* and the *santūr*. The descriptions of *śatatantrī-vīṇā* and the *vāna-vīṇā* in ancient Indian literature closely approximate the *santūr*. However, organologists have been unable to establish the evolutionary connection between them and the present-day instrument (B.C. Deva, *Musical Instruments of India*, 2nd edn., Munshiram Manoharlal, New Delhi, 2000).

After studying this dulcimer/cimbalom family of instruments in several parts of the world, Sharma (ibid.) discovered that the Indian (Kashmiri) *santūr* is the only one with exactly hundred strings. According to him, contemporary Persian experts are unable to explain the 100-stringed name for the Persian instrument, which has only 72 strings. Sharma also finds it interesting that ancient Indian texts have referred to the *śatatantrī* and the *vāna* as being used for accompaniment to the chanting of *mantras* (religious chants/hymns), this being also the purpose for which the instrument is used in the Kashmir Valley.

Construction and Tuning

The contemporary *santūr* used in classical music consists of a trapezoid box, which acts as a rest for the strings stretched across it, as well as the resonator. The box is 60 cm long, 60 cm wide at one end, tapering to 30 cm width at the other. The tapering width has 30 bridges for strings, 15 on each side, over each of which passes a set of three/four strings. The strings are fixed to iron pegs, which are turned for tuning. Sound activation is done by the hammering action of two sticks of walnut wood (mallets), curved at the striking end. The grip of the sticks is shaped for optimal impact control under manipulation by the thumbs and the index fingers (Deva, 2000).

There are two tuning systems in practice. The traditional system tunes the string-sets to the scale of the *rāga* to be performed. This poses a problem of retuning the instrument for each *rāga*. This problem is compounded by the fact that the *santūr* has four strings for every pitch. Retuning even three *svar*s across three octaves implies retuning thirty-six strings. As a solution to this problem, chromatic tuning has now gained popularity. This solution limits the use of abrasion as a technique of melodic execution, but is otherwise efficient.

Being a polychord, the *santūr* activates the sound and executes the melody simultaneously. The three categories of mallet impact in use are: (a) primary impact, (b) secondary impact, and (c) abrasive action.

The dominant technique consists of staccato melodic execution, using the primary impact of a vertical or near-vertical hammering action of the mallet on the desired string-set. The secondary impact of the mallet stroke is used to prolong the activation of a particular pitch in a progressive fade-out. In this kind of action, the musician allows the mallet to bounce on the particular string-set until it has lost momentum. When the musician desires a continuity of sound activation across different pitches in order to shape a melodic contour, he uses abrasive action similar to the bowing action on a bowed instrument.

As an acoustic machine, the *santūr* permits a partial manipulation of volume and timbre, and a reasonable approximation to the melodic continuity characteristic of Indian music. At the present stage in the evolution of its idiom, the *santūr* is therefore best understood as a melodic instrument performed percussively, and whose melodic potential is still in a state of evolution.

Evolutionary Perspectives

Pt. Shivkumar Sharma was ideally suited for his pioneering role because he had received early training in vocal music, and had established himself as a *tablā* player of eminence before deserting it for the *santūr*. His mastery over melody and rhythm enabled him to develop a balanced melodic-rhythmic idiom, which astutely exploits the essential rhythmicality of the instrument, while also neutralizing it.

Sharma took up the *santūr* upon the insistence of his father, Pt. Umadatta Sharma, a *tablā* exponent of the Punjab Gharānā and a vocalist trained in the Benares tradition under the celebrated Guru, Bade Ramdasji. During his tenure as chief producer of music on Kashmir Radio, Pt. Umadatta heard the *santūr* and saw in it a challenge worthy of his son. The instrument Shivkumar inherited from the *sūfiānā* tradition was incapable of delivering contemporary *rāga*-based music in an electronically engineered acoustic environment. However, that was the very instrument on which Shivkumar practised, and made his debut as a *santūr* exponent. While the popular music industry was swept off its feet by the novelty and charm of the sound, the world of classical music was unenthusiastic about its future because of its obvious limitations in the handling of continuous melody and microtonal nuances. This triggered off Sharma's efforts at re-engineering the instrument and developing an idiom aimed at exploiting its unique character, while also enhancing its melodic capabilities.

Sharma first altered the tuning system. The *santūr* of *sūfīānā mauṣiqī* was tuned to Bilāwal scale of Hindustani music, with only *śuddha svars*. The steel string-set raised to the right delivered the middle octave, while the brass string-set raised to the left delivered the lower octave. On both octaves, two additional *svars* were available on each side of the octave. This system was adequate for *sūfīānā mauṣiqī* but lamentably wanting against the demands of *rāga*-based music. Shivkumar replaced this system with chromatic tuning similar to the harmonium with *śuddha svars* on the right side, and the *komal/tīvra svars* on the left side. He adopted this as the stable system, to resort occasionally to *rāga*-scale tuning.

The second major effort was the re-engineering of its acoustic output. He experimented briefly with mallet design, but decided finally to leave it alone, and concentrate on the ergonomics of the *santūr* art. The traditional (*sūfīānā*) method of handling the instrument was to place it on a triangular wooden platform in front of the musician without direct contact between the instrument and either the musician's body or the floor. This was efficient for slow melody typical of *sūfīānā mauṣiqī*, rendered before intimate gatherings and without electronic amplification. Sharma found that, in high-density melody (*tāns*) delivered through microphones, this created a blurred melodic contour. Shivkumar placed the instrument on his lap so that half of the instrument was in contact with his thighs, while the other half was suspended in midair. This provided an "earthing" to the acoustic output without muffling it. Incidentally, this also allowed the musician an upright posture, enhancing the overall ergonomic efficiency of performance. For ideal results, this solution required the *santūr* performer to be — like Sharma — at least 6 ft tall. But, at that stage, Sharma did not need to think beyond his own needs.

The placement and posture solution did not entirely work out the acoustic problem. So, he reviewed the standard four-string set for each *svar*. After some experimentation, he settled down to a three-string set for the middle and higher octaves and a two-string set for the lower octave. In addition, he devised an original *chikarī* (drone) set — conceptually distinct from the conventional *chikarī* set used on the *sitār* and the *sarod*. His *chikarī* is modelled after the extra set Ustad Ali Akbar Khan uses on the *sarod*, which is tuned to the dominant *svar*s of the *rāga*. With these changes, the instrument acquired a satisfactory output for the contemporary acoustic environment, while also reinforcing its distinctive acoustic character.

The desire for superior control of timbre and volume led him next to standardizing the ergonomics of performance. Drawing on the principles of stroke classification (*da/ra*) on the *sitār* and *sarod*, Sharma standardized the impact protocol for different categories of phrases. The combination of mallet-choice and impact-points became the basis for a notation system uniquely designed for the instrument. Sharma perfected this combination in his performance, and adopted it as the basic pedagogical tool for his disciples.

These developments in the design and technique of the *santūr* were inspired by, and synchronous with, the growth of Sharma's musical vision, and the content of music he wished to execute. Beyond the purely ergonomic and the acoustic, his primary concern has been to enhance the capability of the *santūr* for melodic continuity, without denying its essentially percussive character. The issue of melodic continuity pertains to two melodic effects — the elongation of intonation on a single *svar*, and a smooth melodic transition from one *svar* to another — both challenges on an instrument designed for staccato melodic execution.

To the basic technique of using the primary impact for melodic execution, Shivkumar made an early addition of secondary impact. In his early recordings, we hear the use of this secondary impact technique for a *tremolo* effect caused by the bouncing of the mallet on the same string-set for elongated intonation. According to Sharma, he found the results of this technique limited in usefulness, and also "alien" to Hindustani music. He therefore drifted towards the abrasion technique. With this simulation of bowing, which also required a modification of the mallet-grip, he could obtain continuous melody for unlimited durations. This development not only helped the refinement of the melodic facet of his music, but became especially important for executing the delicate ornamentation typical of his renditions in the semi-classical and folk genres. This was a breakthrough because a non-impact technique for a mallet-driven instrument amounted to transcending the intrinsic character of the instrument, without denying it. Because abrasion was possible only within a narrow physical space, Sharma increased the frequency with which he resorted to the *rāga*-scale tuning of the instrument, abandoning the chromatic tuning.

Shivkumar Sharma's Music

Sharma's approach to music can be analysed in four facets — *rāga*-grammar, architecture (*rāga* presentation protocol), sculpture (tonal patterning), and the balance between melodic and rhythmic elements of his music.

Sharma's stature has been substantially determined by his unimpeachable *rāga*-grammar. Without doubt, this has also contributed significantly to the stature of his instrument. The present author has had several occasions to compare the rendition of the same *rāga* by the most respected names in contemporary music with the documented forms of the mature *rāga*s. With respect to seemingly non-controversial *rāga*s like Ahīr Bhairav, as well as the rare *rāga*s like Gorakh Kalyāṇa, Shivkumar Sharma's renderings are amongst the very few which fastidiously follow documented *rāga*-grammar.

Shivkumar's recording of Sohinī, another classic, is rigorous enough on grammar to embarrass a few *paṇḍits*. He treats the middle-octave *gā* as the scale-base, and his rendition of this *uttarāṅga-pradhān rāga,* almost ignores the region below the notional scale-base throughout the rendition, except as a reference point for tonality.

Sharma modelled the architecture of his music after the dominant idiom of the *sitār* and *sarod* in the 1950s with a substantial dependence on *tīntāl bandiś*es. He adapted the stroke-craft component of *sitār/sarod* music to suit the technique and acoustic capabilities of his instrument. In his early music, he also relied heavily on *tihāī*s and *chakradār*s, as was commonly done in *sitār/sarod* music. However, he soon realized that the *santūr* idiom would find respectability in the Hindustani mainstream only if he could save the melodic element from being swamped by the rhythmic element, which was magnified by the intrinsic rhythmicality of his instrument. By his own admission (Interview of 21 June 2004), he adopted the philosophy of "melody not at the cost of rhythm, and rhythm not at the cost of melody".

In his search for a distinctive as well as balanced idiom, Shivkumar later banked increasingly on *jhaptāl* and *rūpak.* Both *tāl*s have asymmetrical beat structures and, therefore, an explicit rhythmicality. With this level of basic rhythmicality, Sharma could concentrate on melody. Progressively, he reduced his reliance on *tihāī*s and *chakradār*s and began replacing them with *gāyakī*-style *āmad*s.

In the sculpture department, Sharma veered more towards the language of the *sarod* than the *sitār*. This was natural because the *sarod* is a semi-polychord of percussive-melodic character, whose immediate ancestor was the Afghan *rabāb*, an instrument meant for playing martial music. *Sarod* music of the 1950s and 1960s provided an appropriate backdrop to the emergence of the *santūr*'s melodic evolution. In its search for a distinctive language, the *sarod* had broken through the traditional barrier of melodic (*chalan / rāga* phraseology), geometric and symmetric tonal patterning. Ali Akbar Khan introduced the dazzling kaleidoscopic approach to tonal patterning to exploit the semi-polychord character of his instrument. At the same time, Radhika Mohan Maitra, was adapting the *rabāb*'s percussive-melodic idiom to the *sarod*, permitting the rhythmic element to drive the melodic. Though without conscious adoption, both these tendencies are reflected in Sharma's *santūr* idiom. This combination of musical elements is consistent with the unique character of his instrument.

The role of kaleidoscopic patterning in the *santūr* idiom, highlighted in Sharma's music, deserves special attention because it has accelerated the process of instrumental music seeking a distinctive language of expression, liberated from its traditional reference point in the vocal expression. The *santūr*'s evolutionary achievement in the hands of Sharma, a highly trained *tablā* exponent, is magnified by the fact that it has also resisted the lure of the percussion idiom.

Shivkumar Sharma's contribution has woven the music of the instrument intimately into the fabric of modern Hindustani music, while also shaping an independent genre for it. This genre has clear reference points in the music of the plucked lutes. With Shivkumar's refinement of the instrument's melodic capabilities, the genre can also claim reference points in the modern vocal genres — *khyāl* and *ṭhumrī*. These reference points not withstanding, it is a genre arising uniquely from the character of the instrument, and comparable to none other.

The Santūr after Shivkumar Sharma

Sharma's rise to the peak of the profession attracted a sizeable inflow of fresh talent to the instrument. The first generation of converts was obviously self-taught, and came from amongst struggling *tablā* players, and performers on the near-extinct instruments like the *jal-taraṅga* and *vichitra-vīṇā*. The physically undemanding character of the instrument, and the misconception about the instrument being easy to master, attracted the second generation. The booming demand for *santūr* training led the second generation of aspirants to a large number of teachers who probably qualified as musicians, but not as *santūr* players. Shivkumar Sharma denies having formally initiated or accepted a single disciple. This leaves his son, Rahul, as the only *santūr* player with known access to his *santūr* expertise and musical wisdom.

Not surprisingly, therefore, the *santūr* has yet to witness the emergence of a significant successor to Sharma. Significance, in this context, can only mean an acknowledged contribution to evolution, which is rooted in the present, but also reveals a clear vision of the instrument's unique destiny as defined by its distinctive acoustic and ergonomic character, though not without regard to its limitations.

Sharma's approach to music represents a fine balance between the melodic and rhythmic elements. He has exploited the rhythmic potential of the instrument astutely, without allowing it to interfere with his parallel refinement of its melodic capabilities and expressions. The rhythmicality of his music is intrinsic to the character of the instrument, and validates its claim to a unique place on the contemporary music-scape. His approach to melodic patterning has stayed within the traditional Indian concept of melody and the exploration of tonal geometry within its confines. At any given time, both his mallets are engaged in executing the same, single, melodic idea. His mallets are, almost always, operating either individually, or in alternating action. Rarely, if ever, are they engaged in simultaneous impact on different string-sets.

The succeeding generation of *santūr* players has,

interestingly, developed a special fondness either for semi-classical/*ṭhumrī rāgas*, and for *rāgas* imported recently from the Carnatic tradition into Hindustani music. The semi-classical *rāgas*, in their very nature, permit a libertarian interpretation of grammar, while most Carnatic *rāgas* have yet to acquire a stable melodic personality in Hindustani music, and therefore are not accountable to any yardstick of grammatical propriety. This freedom from accountability towards the legitimacy of the melodic experience allows the younger *santūr* players to undertake their daring explorations into the instrument's extra-melodic potential. Their basic architecture remains rooted to modern *sitār/sarod* music. Beyond this, the music is obsessed with the percussive-rhythmic possibilities of the *santūr*, and an exploration of the acoustic experience beyond melody. The next generation has begun flirting with pitch-activation routines hitherto alien to Hindustani music, such as harmony, heterophony, and polyphony. As a minor element, younger *santūr* players even interrupt mallet-based music to strum or pluck the strings as on a harp, or to execute short melodic passages on a bass string as on a slide-guitar. The epidemic combination of audacity and technical virtuosity has resulted in some young *santūr* players — with only two mallets in their grips — harbouring delusions of competing with a piano.

These directions have implications for the integrity of the *rāga* experience, which may yet be difficult to assess. They also appear to imply a view of the melodic canvas as a set of unconnected acoustic variables, rather than a frequency-calibrated continuum. Such a view implicitly isolates the acoustic meaning of *svar*s from their cultural meaning rooted in the principle of tonality. Although these directions do not explicitly defy the principle of tonality fundamental to Indian music, they certainly suppress the listener's awareness of melodic progression as practised in Hindustani music. This combination of a splintered melodic experience, and an enlarged acoustic experience, defines a new, perhaps alien, musical culture. Not surprisingly, the second generation of competent *santūr* players is far busier on the international concert circuit than the Indian.

Essentially, Sharma's successors are exploring two principal directions for the instrument — the percussive-rhythmic direction derived from percussion/the *tablā* and the harmony-polyphony-heterophony direction inspired by keyboard-based polychords/the piano. The *tablā* direction grossly underutilizes the melodic potential of the *santūr* while the piano direction demands far more from the *santūr* than it can ever deliver. Viewed from where the *santūr* is today, the former direction seems like a regression, while the latter, a dead-end street. The *santūr*'s attempts at mimicking either of these instruments amounts to a denial of its own distinctive character as hitherto revealed. In addition to issues of aesthetics and cultural meaning, neither of them can, therefore, be said to constitute an evolution in consonance with contextual relevance and specificity.

An evolutionary vacuum, or worse, experimental chaos, following on the heels of a pioneering contribution, is a familiar pattern. It is, for instance, also evident in respect of the Hawaiian guitar, introduced to Hindustani music by Brijbhushan Kabra around the same time as Shivkumar's launch of the *santūr*. Any instrument acquires a propensity for self-generating evolution after several generations of musicians, of different backgrounds, have contributed to the development of its technique and idiom. Shivkumar Sharma picked up an obscure regional instrument, and gave it stature on par with more mature instruments in Hindustani art music. Even if the immediate post-Sharma directions appear bewildering, the *santūr* is now firmly established in Hindustani music.

5.6

THE ŚEHNĀĪ*

THE *śehnāī* could qualify as the single most widely-heard instrument in India, having become an integral part of the tribal, folk, ceremonial and religious traditions of the sub-continent (India/Pakistan/Bangladesh/Sri Lanka). In India, it is proclaimed the *maṅgal vādya*, the auspicious instrument. *Śehnāī* music leads religious processions, sanctifies marriages, announces the opening of temple doors to the public every morning, inaugurates major cultural events and welcomes dignitaries to public functions. It is only in the latter half of the twentieth century that the instrument was elevated to the art-music platform, singular credit for which goes to the formidable musicianship of Ustad Bismillah Khan of Varanasi.

Organology

The instrument belongs to the Oboe family of beating-reed aerophones. Instruments answering to this description, and of near-identical construction, are found in all parts of India, though known by different names. This fact makes the *śehnāī* yet another unresolved mystery in Indian organology. Many of its names are of Sanskrit derivation suggesting ancient Indian origins. Others indicate Perso-Arabic etymology, suggesting Middle-Eastern or Central Asian origins. Some names allude to processions, assemblies and courts, thus referring to their ceremonial function under feudal patronage. And, still others are merely descriptive of either its physical form, or its piercing sound, pointing towards untraceable folk and tribal origins. Organologist, B.C. Deva (2nd edn., 1987) appears to favour the theory of indigenous origin and evolution of the instrument.

Design

The main body of the instrument is a conical bore of wood, ideally teak (*Tectona grandis*). *Śehnāīs* made of gold, silver, and even soapstone are known to exist. The body has four to seven holes punched into it. The musician covers and uncovers these holes to manipulate the melody. The narrow end of the bore is fitted with a mouthpiece (staple), to which are affixed two winnow-shaped reeds, about 1 cm in length. The reeds are made either of marsh-grass or special leaves. The reeds merely regulate the flow of air into the body by beating against the wall of the mouthpiece, but play no role in the manipulation of the pitch. The broad end of the bore, the output end, is fitted with a metallic cup, made usually of brass, but occasionally also of other metals (ibid.).

Śehnāīs are made to a specific pitch in terms of tonality. An average *śehnāī* player manages a melodic canvas of an octave and a half on the instrument. A maestro can, however, coax two octaves out of it, without producing unmusical sounds. Varanasi and Lucknow have been the principal centres of *śehnāī* manufacture. In recent years, however, research-oriented enthusiasts in Nashik, about 150 km from Mumbai, have made the city another major supplier of quality *śehnāīs* (Shailesh Bhagwat, "Saaz-e-śehnāī", *Nāda-brahma,* Marathi Quarterly, Bombay, Issue of January 1996).

Idiom and Repertoire

Being a breath-driven instrument, its natural musical output is continuous melody. The intermittent or rhythmic stopping of the airflow by the action of the tongue is, however, used for creating melodic discontinuities of the staccato variety. Logically, therefore, the *śehnāī* has adopted the idiom of the vocal genres. In the art-music segment, *śehnāī* music borrows its *rāga* presentation protocol from the *khyāl* genre, while in the semi-classical and light segments, it borrows its melodic–rhythmic material from the *ṭhumrī, kajrī, chaitī,* and similar regional genres. Within the predominantly vocalized expression of these genres, however, *śehnāī* music increasingly incorporates staccato expressions simulating the music of the plucked lute family, principally, the *sitār*.

The repertoire of the *śehnāī* acknowledges the fact that its performers make their livelihood primarily in the ceremonial and religious segment of the music market. In this segment, the repertoire must assume that its audience is involuntary and inattentive. It must also assume that the vast majority of the audience is uncultivated in art music. The *śehnāī* player's repertoire is, therefore, dominated by popular, folk and regional music. This dominance also influences the idiom of the *śehnāī* player in his handling of art-music. Even in the idiom of the most acclaimed *śehnāī* players on the art-music stage, the connoisseur will observes the breaching of the boundaries of art music with a drift into folk and popular elements. This tendency has allowed the *śehnāī* to achieve immense popularity on the concert platform, while straddling several other categories of music within Indian musical culture.

Probably for the same reason, the *śehnāī* has been the most successful instrument in the *jugalbandī* (duets) segment of the art-music market. Ustad Bismillah Khan's duets with *sitār* maestro, Ustad Vilayat Khan, have become the stuff of legend.

But, even moderately accomplished *śehnāī* players have been able to produce eminently charming, and even saleable, music in collaboration with partners of compatible stature.

Since the elevation of the instrument to the concert platform by Ustad Bismillah Khan, the *śehnāī* has contributed several maestros to the art-music world. Notable amongst them are Ali Ahmed Hussain of Calcutta, Baburao Khaladkar and Shankar Rao Gakewad, both deceased, of Pune, and Anant Lal of Delhi. Amongst the younger generation of musicians, Shailesh Bhagwat of Mumbai has recently acquired some stature.

Genres in Śehnāī Music

On the concert platform, the repertoire and the idiom of the *śehnāī* have been influenced almost entirely by the towering presence of Ustad Bismillah Khan, spanning over six decades. If, therefore, one has to refer to *gharānā*s of the *śehnāī*, there is probably only one *gharānā* on the art-music scene — the Bismillah Khan Gharānā. He has adopted the *khyāl* genre as his principal inspiration for the presentation of *rāga*-based music, and the regional melodies popular in his home in Varanasi, and its environs as the source for his semi-classical and popular repertoire. The most important amongst these are the *bol-banāo ṭhumrī*, and seasonal songs such as the *kajrī*, *chaitī*, *phāgun* and *sāvan*.

Śehnāī players from other regions have tended to follow this pattern, although *śehnāī* players from the western state of Maharashtra (Mumbai/Pune) do include local folk and regional music, such as *lāvaṇī*s and *nāṭya-saṅgīta* in their presentations. These are also poetry-dominant forms, and are subjected to the same kind of transformation in their *śehnāī* presentation as the *kajrī/chaitī* category of north Indian genres do.

The Ensemble for Śehnāī Performances

The traditional ensemble for *śehnāī* performance has been determined by its role as an outdoor instrument, played in public virtually as background music, and without amplification. In this role, the supporting ensemble was a *sur-śehnāī*, and a pair of *tāśā/nagāṛā* drums. The *sur-śehnāī* is a single-pitch drone, on which no melody can be played. The *sur-śehnāī* performed a role comparable to a *tānpūrā* in vocal music, filling the silences. The *tāśā* or *nagāṛā* are pairs of kettledrums, played with sticks, and commanding an idiom of their own, though less sophisticated than that of the *pakhāwaj* or the *tablā*.

In the concert context, the *śehnāī* ensemble has become more elaborate. Lead *śehnāī* players are now frequently accompanied by a supporting *śehnāī* player, who allows them periodic respite. For a drone, they frequently replace the *sur-śehnāī* with a *tānpūrā*. And, the traditional *tāśa* is frequently replaced by the *tablā*. These deviations from the traditional ensemble recognize the existence of a superior acoustic environment, and the availability of electronic amplification.

The Disappearing Śehnāī

The meagre supply of *śehnāī* musicianship to the art music stage is explained by the socio-cultural reality. Very few *śehnāī* players have either the motivation or the training in art-music to qualify for the concert platform. Even fewer can hope to make a living exclusively as art musicians. More fundamentally, however, the supply of talent to the *śehnāī* profession itself is dwindling because of shifting preferences in its mainstay market segments. The ceremonial and religious market in the cities is shifting to pre-recorded music, electronic synthesisers, and brass bands. The film-music industry, once a significant user of the *śehnāī*, has gone almost entirely electronic. On the concert platform, therefore, the art of the *śehnāī* could risk a growing shortage of quality musicianship in the future.

Interestingly, a similar fate confronts the *sāraṅgī*, yet another instrument believed to be of entirely indigenous origin and evolution, and enjoying a similar presence across the art, tribal, popular, and folk traditions. The *śehnāī* and the *sāraṅgī* appear to be victims of a larger phenomenon in Hindustani music, which is phasing out some indigenous instruments, and enthusiastically adopting instruments of foreign origin, such as the *santūr* and *sarod*. Implicit in these trends is the decline of the music of melodic continuity, and its substitution by the music of melodic discontinuity.

5.7

THE SĀRAṄGĪ*

THE *sāraṅgī* belongs to the bowed chordophone family of short-necked fretless lutes. It is found in various forms all over the Indian subcontinent. The *sāraṅgī* family originated as folk instruments, and now include the sophisticated acoustic machine used in classical music. Instruments of this family represent a wide range of design, from the single-string tribal instrument called *dhodro banam* to the classical *sāraṅgī*. Throughout its history, the *sāraṅgī* has been used for accompanying vocal music. It made its debut as a solo instrument on the art music scene in the early twentieth century and has, since then, enlarged this presence considerably, though only sporadically.

Unlike several other popular instruments in Hindustani music today, the *sāraṅgī* family is believed to be entirely of Indian origin and evolution, with virtually no trace of foreign influence or inspiration. It is related to the *pinākī-vīṇā* and the

Acknowledgement: The perspective on the historical, technical, and sociological facets of the *sāraṅgī*, draws generously upon the pioneering work of Joep Bor of the Rotterdam Conservatorium, Netherlands, published under the title "The Voice of the Sāraṅgī" in the *Journal of the National Centre for the Performing Arts*, Bombay (vols. XV and XVI, nos. 3, 4, 1 September-December 1986 and March 1987).

rāvaṇahasta, two instruments encountered in Hindu mythology. There is evidence, though not conclusive, of their use for accompanying folk and religious music during the eleventh and twelfth centuries. Clearer evidence exists, from the early seventeenth century, of its use as a classical instrument. The classical *sāraṅgī*, as we know it today, evidently evolved around 1850, with Meerut, in the vicinity of Delhi, as the principal centre of manufacturing.

Construction, Design and Tuning

The classical *sāraṅgī* is carved from a single block of wood, ideally *tun* (*Tuna ciliata roem*), which has been seasoned for a year, and treated with *geru* (red ochre) dissolved in water in order to restore its natural colour and sheen.

The instrument is 64-67 cm long with a belly hollowed out in front. The head consists of two peg-boxes, hollowed out from behind. Thus, the instrument consists of four separate chambers. In the partition between the belly and the neck, there is a large hole at the back, which is often used for keeping the bow during transportation. The walls of the *sāraṅgī* shell have to be 7-10 mm thick in order to withstand the tension of thirty-five sympathetic strings and three heavy gut strings for melodic execution.

The instrument is tuned in the pitch range of C sharp to F sharp. The best acoustic output is obtained by tuning the first string to D sharp or E. Unless the *sāraṅgī* player decides to use separate instruments for accompanying male and female vocalists, the tuning of the pitch needs to be varied as required by the vocalist. However, there have been *sāraṅgī* players, like Abdul Lateef Khan (1928–2003) who kept the instrument tuned to the same pitch, irrespective of the fundamental at which the vocalist was singing. His logic, as reported to the present author, was that the instrument sounds best at a certain pitch, and he preferred to vary his playing to maintain the quality of the acoustic output. The three melodic strings are tuned to *sā-pā-sā* or *sā-mā-sā*. Of the two sets of sympathetic strings, the main set is tuned chromatically starting with *komal dhā* or *komal nī* in the lower octave, while the subordinate set is tuned to the scale of the *rāga* for solo playing, and chromatically for accompaniment to obviate retuning for change of *rāga*s.

Playing Technique

Melodic execution is done by the left hand. Pressing the fingernails sideways against the melodic strings activates the desired *svar*s. Some *sāraṅgī* players use the skin above the cuticles for this purpose, with the fingertip touching the fingerboard. Talcum powder is used as a lubricant. The technique of melodic execution involves sliding or articulating separate *svar*s using a systematic fingering technique. The traditional fingering technique uses all the four fingers. Increasingly, however, musicians now use only three fingers, with a selective use of the fourth finger for special effects. There are four distinct schools of fingering.

The sound activation is done with the bow held in the right hand. The shaft of the bow is a straight length of a hard wood, preferably ebony. The shaft is 70 cm long, round in section, which bends when strung with a hank of horse hair from the tail of a stallion. Resin is applied periodically to the playing surface for retaining its abrasive action for sound-activation.

The bow is held in an underhand grip. The first two fingers positioned on the shaft regulate the pressure, while the other two, or three, embrace the nut. In order to elicit the desired acoustic response from the instrument, the bow needs to engage the melodic strings close to the bridge.

The Role of the Sāraṅgī in Music

Throughout history, the *sāraṅgī* has been the instrument on which wandering bards and minstrels in India accompany themselves. At some stage, the more talented and ambitious amongst them were attracted by the glamour of city life, and drifted towards the feudal courts to make a living as accompanists to courtesans. In this role, the *sāraṅgī* emerged as a significant instrument in art music, enlarging it in later years to become the preferred melodic accompaniment for female as well as male singers.

As accompanists to female vocalists, *sāraṅgī* players were involved with the entire range of music performed in the salons of the courtesans, which catered to the needs of genteel society until the end of the nineteenth century in northern India. The instrument soon became an integral part of the vocalist's ensemble — from the lowbrow music performed in establishments verging on the flesh trade, to the middlebrow *ṭhumrī* and *ghazal*, the devotional *qawwālī*, to the highbrow *khyāl* form. Performers of the *dhrupad* genre, however, have kept away from any form of melodic accompaniment, preferring to sing accompanied only by the *tānpūrā*.

By the early nineteenth century, *sāraṅgī* players had become formidable repositories of *rāga* knowledge and compositions, and were recognized as maestros in their own right. Their art had become a part of the system of hereditary musicianship, giving rise to several distinguished families of *sāraṅgī* players. In the salons of the courtesans, *sāraṅgī* players became tutors of female singers and custodians of the vocalist arts, with a share in its revenues. This institution of courtesans operated, understandably, on the fringes of genteel society. An association with it gave *sāraṅgī* players, and the instrument, a stigma that it could not shed until it was too late.

In the early twentieth century, Victorian morals imposed by India's colonial rulers, and social reformist movements launched by the Indian bourgeoisie, pushed the institution of courtesans to the brink. Although art music was not their target, their impact severely dented the future of the *sāraṅgī*, which serviced all genres of vocal music, but depended largely for its sustenance on the world of courtesans. The deathblow, however, came from the harmonium, invented in Paris (1840), which caught on speedily as a replacement for the *sāraṅgī*.

The Harmonium Challenge and the Response

The harmonium's tempered scale made it singularly unsuitable for Hindustani music. However, it was untainted by social stigma, and had several practical advantages. Being a keyboard instrument, the mastery of intonation on it did not require as arduous a training as it did on the bowed and fretless *sāraṅgī*. A harmonium accompanist was also far less likely to bruise a vocalist's ego by challenging his musicianship on the concert platform. Being an easier instrument to master than the *sāraṅgī*, the harmonium also created an ample supply of accompanists, who were cheaper to hire. For performers in the lighter genres, the harmonium was an even greater boon because the vocalist could herself master the instrument, thus dispensing with the accompanist altogether.

Towards the end of the nineteenth century, the declining fortunes of the *sāraṅgī* gave rise to two significant developments. Some exceptional *sāraṅgī* players abandoned the *sāraṅgī* in favour of a career as vocalists. Legendary twentieth-century vocalists — Ustad Abdul Kareem Khan, Ustad Abdul Waheed Khan, Ustad Bade Ghulam Ali Khan — had all begun their careers as *sāraṅgī* players. Another landmark vocalist, Ustad Ameer Khan, belonged to a distinguished family of *sāraṅgī* players and, according to some historians, had also started life as a *sāraṅgī* player. The other significant development was the emergence of the *sāraṅgī* soloist. In the 1920s, spurred by the emerging gramophone record industry, Ustad Bundu Khan (d. 1955), the greatest *sāraṅgī* player of the period, started recording 78 RPM discs of solo performances. In later years, several other *sāraṅgī* players also published solo recordings.

In the post-Independence period, Pt. Ramnarain (b. 1927) has been the most significant *sāraṅgī* player to bid farewell to accompaniment, and to perform exclusively as a soloist. Interestingly, the maestro has received as many years of training from vocalists, as from *sāraṅgī* players. He is largely responsible for creating an international constituency for the *sāraṅgī,* and reviving interest in the art amongst scions of the *sāraṅgī* playing families. At the time of writing, however, the ageing wizard of the Indian fiddle is still the only member of his tribe with an economically viable career as a soloist.

Pt. Ramnarain's individual achievement does not, evidently, symbolize anything like a revival in the fortunes of the *sāraṅgī.* The population of competent *sāraṅgī* players, estimated currently at about 250, is shrinking along with the demand for their art. The accompaniment market has been lost to the harmonium. The government-owned broadcast media, which helped the *sāraṅgī*'s survival for several decades by banning the harmonium, have now lifted the ban. The popular music industry, once a significant user of *sāraṅgī* talent, has shifted almost totally to electronic music.

By way of alternative career models, Pt. Ramnarain has demonstrated the viability of a soloist career. In the succeeding generation, Sultan Khan, a distinguished accompanist and soloist, is attempting a revival of the original model of the bards and minstrels on the art music platform, by turning vocalist and accompanying himself on the *sāraṅgī.* The Sultan Khan model is open only to the rare musician endowed with a trained voice along with formidable talent as an instrumentalist. The soloist model of Pt. Ramnarain might hold greater promise for the *sāraṅgī,* provided the art can attract talent with the required training, innovativeness, and tenacity.

The most significant accomplishment of the few eminent soloists has been the sculpting of a distinctive musical experience, which exploits the soloist's freedom from the vocalist vision, while exploiting the basic acoustic character of the instrument within the broad framework of the *khyāl* and *ṭhumrī* genres. Paradoxically, therefore, the emergence of great *sāraṅgī* soloists could depend on the revival of the demand generated by the accompaniment market. Such a scenario is no longer conceivable.

Quality solos available to contemporary audiences are, therefore, predominantly of *sāraṅgī* players who have distinguished themselves as accompanists. Their calibre as soloists rests on the soundness of their basic training in music, and a musical vision that is not constrained by subordination to a diversity of vocalists performing different styles and genres.

The Sāraṅgī : As the Second Fiddle and the First

The role of the *sāraṅgī* (or harmonium) as an accompanist to vocal music has been amongst the more intractable documentation problems in Indian musicology. This is primarily because, beyond its basic functionality, the role depends on the level of musicianship represented by the two partners in music-making, and the chemistry between them. Since there is no clear tradition of stable partnerships or of prior rehearsals, the chemistry itself is volatile.

The basic contribution of the *sāraṅgī* is to enhance the average acoustic density (sound bytes delivered per unit of time) of the aural experience in a vocal performance. The function has value because the human voice, driven by the breathing cycle and subject to its limitations, is susceptible to involuntary discontinuities in voice production. The melodic accompaniment (*sāraṅgī* or harmonium) is intended to fill up the silences that a vocal rendition creates. Beyond this, the function is aesthetic and, therefore, amenable to a bewildering variety of descriptions. Mature *sāraṅgī* players most frequently describe their accompaniment role as that of "following" or "supporting" the vocalist. Central to these descriptions is the primacy of the vocalist as the architect of the concert, and the subordination of the accompanist to the vocalist's musicianship.

As a solo artist, the *sāraṅgī* player has no vocalist to follow or support. Despite this, he is obliged to work within the framework of vocalism because his instrument is designed explicitly as an acoustic match for the human voice, and as a worthy vehicle for the modern genres of vocal music. These realities impose handicaps, and also offer some advantages.

The handicap lies in having to render a genre of vocal music without the spoken word. In their vocal manifestation, the *khyāl* and the *ṭhumrī* forms use three different categories of articulation — literary verse, *sargam* (enunciation of solfa symbols), and *ākār* (the *ā* vowel). Collectively, these articulations permit a vocalist to (a) cement the structure of the melodic and rhythmic elements, (b) reinforce/enhance the communication of the *rāga*'s emotional content, and (c) impart a phonetic and textural richness to the aural experience. Performing a vocal genre of music without the articulations poses a challenge to the attention-holding power of a *sāraṅgī* solo.

As a soloist, the *sāraṅgī* player compensates for the handicap by focusing his musical energies on exploiting the technical capabilities of his instrument. Contemporary *sāraṅgī* solos appear to follow a combination of two approaches for this purpose. One approach is to stretch the melodic complexity and *svar* densities of typically vocal movements to a level which a vocalist is either unable to match, or will not attempt out of fear of becoming un-musical. The other approach is to incorporate musical ideas and movements borrowed and adapted from the plucked instruments (*sitār / sarod / rudra-vīṇā*), guided by the limitations of musicality. This latter approach is evident in the solo *sāraṅgī* renditions of the young maestro, Dhruva Ghosh.

With its continued anchoring in the *khyāl* and *ṭhumrī* genres of vocal music, the *sāraṅgī* cannot be said, yet, to have evolved a distinctive language for solo performance. However, even at the present stage of its evolution, a solo by a mature *sāraṅgī* player can be a memorable musical experience.

5.8

THE INDIAN CLASSICAL GUITAR*

THE Indian classical guitar is an adaptation of the Hawaiian slide-guitar, one of the several foreign instruments that the assimilative Indian mind has incorporated into its musical traditions. In most cases, the shell of the instrument is an Fhole guitar, acoustically and structurally enhanced to support the multitude of strings.

The design of the instrument is far from standard yet, with several variants in vogue. The commonest variant has a total of twenty-one strings. The melody is executed on five melodic strings. The five strings are tuned, respectively, to the tonic (base *sa=D*), the lower octave *pa*, the lower-octave *sa*, the ultra-lower *pa*, and the ultra-lower *sa*. This provides a melodic canvas of four complete octaves. At the same level as the melodic strings, are strung four supporting strings. Two of these are *chikarī* drones, tuned to the upper-*sa*, while the other two are tuned to the dominant *svar*s of the *rāga* to provide an ambient reinforcement of the *rāga*'s tonal geometry. Running parallel to the melodic strings, and at a lower level, are twelve sympathetic strings tuned to the scale of the *rāga*.

The sound activation is done by the thumb, forefinger, and the middle finger of the right hand, all equipped with

---

metal or plastic picks. The forearm of the right hand rests at the base of the chamber-resonator, with the forearm and palm muscles providing the motive power for the strokes. The melody is executed by a cylindrical or semi-cylindrical metal bar, held in the left hand, either stopping or sliding over the strings along the stem of the instrument. The playing technique is identical to the Hawaiian slide-guitar.

The Hawaiian slide-guitar entered Hindustani music about four decades ago. As such, the instrument is still the subject of considerable experimentation and divergence in terms of acoustic design, technique and, indeed, musical idiom and style.

Evolutionary Perspectives

The slide-guitar came to India before Second World War through the recordings of Sol Hoopii, and Joe Kaipo, with Jimmie Rodgers and others. Touring Hawaiian troupes inspired local imitators. Calcutta's Aloha Boys Band, formed in 1938, was often heard on All India Radio. Within a generation, the Hawaiian guitar had become an integral part of Indian film scores. The sound of the slide-guitar penetrated India's musical consciousness with the prelude to the epoch-making semi-classical song (a *bandiś ṭhumrī*) *bāṭa chalat nayī chunrī raṅga ḍārī* in the film "Ladki" in 1953 (Mark Humphrey, *The Hindustani Slide*, www.IndusLive.com).

By the early 1960s, the Hawaiian guitar had found a secure home in the musical culture of Calcutta, and the state of Bengal, the most prolific nursery of instrumental music talent in the country, and also home to the leading composers of film music until late into the twentieth century. Within Bengal, the instrument became immensely popular for solo renderings of classico-modern genres such as *Rabindra Sangeet* (the compositions of Nobel Laureate Rabindranath Tagore), and folk genres such as *baul* and *plligīti*. The melodic intricacy of these genres produced a vast and mature resource of musicianship on the instrument, and paved the way for its acceptance by the broadcast media, and finally, for its entry into classical music.

Although the immediate inspiration for an Indianized slide-guitar came from North America, the instrument is the heir to an Indian technique of melodic execution. There is, in fact, some basis for speculation that the ancient Indian slide technique for the plucked lute family of instruments may have played a role in the early development of the Hawaiian instrument. There exist accounts of one Gabriel Davion, born in India, and kidnapped by a sea captain to Honolulu in the late nineteenth century, as being the first guitarist to use the slide technique to execute melody on a single string. It is conceivable that this Davion brought the technique of Indian slide-activated melody to Hawaii.

The *ghoṣak* described in Bharata's *Nāṭyaśāstra* (200 BCE – CE 200), and the *ektantrī-vīṇā* repeatedly referred to in musicological texts from the eleventh century CE, are both plucked instruments, on which melody was executed by sliding a hard and smooth mechanical device along the strings, rather than by stopping the strings as on a fretted instrument. In more recent times, the slide principle of melodic execution was represented, in the Hindustani tradition, by the *vichitra-vīṇā*, a fretless zither and, in the Carnatic tradition, by the *goṭṭu vādyam*, a fretless lute — both instruments of considerable antiquity (B.C. Deva, 2nd edn., 2000). Despite their current rarity on the concert platform, both these instruments have resisted total extinction.

It is significant that the *vichitra-vīṇā* and the *goṭṭu vādyam* are, in their respective traditions, near-identical in construction and design to their fretted counterparts. It may therefore be surmised that the slide-principle of melodic execution on these fretless *vīṇās* defined a distinctive musical capability and role. It is interesting that, while the fretted *vīṇās* in both the traditions are present as accompanists to vocal music and also as solo concert instruments, the fretless slide *vīṇās* are more predominantly encountered in solo performance. In a tradition that considers the vocal expression as the validatory model even for instrumental music, it is reasonable to surmise that the fretless slide *vīṇā* was allowed a more predominant solo role because of its closer-to-vocalism capability.

The Vichitra-vīṇā Legacy

In the Hindustani tradition, the decline of the fretless *vichitra-vīṇā* has been virtually simultaneous with that of the fretted *rudra-vīṇā*. Their decline is only partially explained by the decline of the medieval *dhrupad/dhamār* genre of mainstream music, of which the two instruments were an integral part. The major reason for their decline would appear to be their cumbersome ergonomics, and an acoustic quality unsuited for the contemporary environment, governed by electronic amplification and manipulation of musical output.

The Hawaiian slide-guitar appeared to solve both these problems simultaneously while offering the distinctive quality of the fretless slide *vīṇā* — the ability to reproduce every nuance of Indian classical vocalism with minimum interference from the sound-priming (plucking) activity. Admittedly, the slide-guitar was inferior in this role to the *sāraṅgī*, a bowed instrument. But, within the plucked lute family, it could have no peer as a mimic of the vocal expression. Because of this advantage, the Hawaiian slide-guitar offered a much wider range of stylistic options than the *sitār* and *sarod*, both of which required a much higher frequency of plucking.

The only trigger the Hawaiian slide-guitar required for slipping into the *vichitra-vīṇā*'s role in Hindustani music was towering musicianship, which could demonstrate its musical potential, especially relative to the *sitār* and *sarod*. The instrument found its pioneering champion in Brijbhushan Kabra (b. 1937).

Kabra's Guitar

Brijbhushan came from a business family with a deep involvement in music. His father had studied the *sitār* under the legendary Ustad Enayet Khan, the father of Ustad Vilayat Khan. Brijbhushan's elder brother, Damodarlal, had studied under the celebrated Ustad Ali Akbar Khan, and was a distinguished *sarod* player. In defiance of acute cynicism within the family, Brijbhushan said "no" to the *sitār* as well as the *sarod*, and accepted the challenge of elevating the slide-guitar to a level of parity with them under the tutelage of Ustad Ali Akbar Khan.

There was a historical as well organological inevitability about Kabra going along with the established musical approach, and the *rāga* presentation protocol of the major plucked lutes, the *sitār* and *sarod*. The first step in this direction was the introduction of *chikarī* (drone) strings. As on the *sitār* and the *sarod*, his *chikarī* set is mounted on a post-midway up the stem of the guitar on the bass (inward) side. His repertoire includes a three/four-tiered *alāp-joḍa-jhālā* movement, slow tempo compositions primarily of Masit Khani format in *tīntāl*, medium tempo compositions in *rūpak* and *jhaptāl*, and fast tempo compositions in *tīntāl* followed by a *jhālā*. As with the *sitār* and *sarod*, light and semi-classical compositions in a variety of *tāl*s became an important part of a comprehensive repertoire to satisfy contemporary audiences.

Despite the benefit of guidance from a giant amongst musicians, Kabra had to rely on his own resourcefulness for technique. Kabra's musical vision is deeply entrenched in vocalism. It might even be said that, in the melodic content of his music, he has pitted his instrument against the *sāraṅgī*, rather than the *sitār* or *sarod*. He places the highest premium on the capabilities of the slide-guitar for delivering the melodic continuity and microtonal subtleties of Hindustani vocalism. This logically meant the development of an idiom and technique that would minimize the frequency of strokes, and maximize the melodic density achievable under the impact of each stroke. These became the guiding principles of Kabra's musical endeavours.

Within the *rāga* presentation format of the plucked lutes, Kabra's musical vision, and the instrument's capabilities, led Kabra to develop the anarhythmic and melodically rich *alāp* form as his forte. In order to pack the maximum power into each stroke, Kabra dispensed with the picks conventionally used by slide-guitarists, and opted to play with wire plectra (*mizrāb*s) used by sitārists.

Once he had harnessed additional stroke power with *sitār* plectra, he could achieve the desired manipulation of timbre, volume, and sustain without the addition of sympathetic strings. In a private interview with the present author, Kabra expressed the view that the slide-guitar is so rich in the delivery of microtonal values and melodic continuity, that the *sitār*/*sarod* model of acoustic design is irrelevant for the instrument. Kabra also argued that the sympathetic strings, which support only the discrete *svar*s in the *rāga* scale, have the effect of drowning out microtonal subtleties. As a result, the delivery of melodic value is limited, rather than enhanced, by the sympathetic strings.

In order to minimise the melodic discontinuity in his music, Kabra reduced the role of multiple-string execution by opting, once again, for a *sitār*-style solution — of using the first string as the main melodic string, and tuning the second and third strings also in the *sitār* style (lower-octave *pa* and lower-octave *sa*). This enabled him to execute melody across two full octaves on the main string, requiring the second and third strings only for the lower octave. In his interviews to the American press, he has argued that Hindustani music, with its vocalist model, does not require a melodic canvas larger than three octaves.

Kabra established himself and the slide-guitar in Hindustani music at a time when three giants — Ustad Vilayat Khan, Pt. Ravi Shankar, and Ustad Ali Akbar Khan — were in the prime of their trailblazing careers. In such an environment, the mere novelty of the slide-guitar could not have assured the instrument a future in Hindustani music. His success was a victory of his perception, and exploitation, of the distinctive musical value that the Hawaiian slide-guitar had to offer.

After Kabra

In response to the changes in the environment of Hindustani music, Kabra's successors on the slide-guitar scene, including his own disciples, have drifted away from the technical and stylistic choices he made. Most of them have chosen a stylistic direction with a much higher stroke density than Kabra's, and an extensive use of multiple-string execution as an important element in their music. The slide-guitar idiom is now drifting closer to the semi-polychord idiom of the *sarod*, but surpassing it in dazzling potential, thanks to the slide-guitar's superior ergonomics. The technical decisions of the younger guitarists are consistent with these directions.

A melodic canvas spanning four octaves, and across five strings, is now in favour. Sympathetic strings have now become a stable feature of the Indian classical guitar. The emphasis is now on kaleidoscopic tonal patterning and dazzling virtuosity, rather than elaborate *rāga* presentation and melodic richness. Strokes therefore need ergonomic facility more than depth or power. To this end, guitar-style picks have replaced Kabra's *mizrāb*. Some guitarists have also found it efficient to shift the *chikarī* drones to the treble (outward) side of the instrument.

Whether as an acoustic machine, or as the presenter of a well-defined style of instrumental music, the Indian classical guitar is still in a state of dynamic evolution. With the enthusiastic response the instrument has evoked amongst audiences in North America and Europe, its future could well be shaped as much by the global music market as by the Indian mainstream.

5.9

THE TĀNPŪRĀ AND SVARMAṆḌAL

THEY are ubiquitous. Tall pillars mounted on large bulbous bases. You have seen two of them behind every Hindustani vocalist — sometimes four. They are *tānpūrā*s. Some call them *tambūrā*s. Far less frequently than the pillars, you may have seen the laptop that vocalists use during a concert. It is called a *svarmaṇḍal*. The instrument either lies horizontally in the vocalist's lap, or stands upright across his chest. Neither of these instruments produces any melody or rhythm. And, it is fair to ask why they are there.

The Tānpūrā/Tambūrā

The word *tānpūra* derives from two components: *tān* (melodic phrase) + *pūrak* (that which completes or complements). The name describes the function of filling the silences, and providing continuity to the musical experience. Neither the word *tānpūrā*, nor its scientific nomenclature (drone) can, however, do justice to the hallowed position it enjoys, and the importance of its role.

The *tānpūrā* evolved from the idea of supporting a vocal rendition with the *ādhār svar* — the foundation note or scale base to which the musician is singing. The sustained presence of the foundation note helps him to achieve a higher degree of pitch-precision in his recital. But, more importantly, melodic music — such as Hindustani music, in fact, Indian music in general — acquires its meaning only with reference to the foundation note. The support of the foundation note is therefore crucial to delivering the musical meaning of the performance to its listeners.

But, if this was all a vocalist wanted, it was not necessary to have so complicated an instrument as the *tānpūrā*. The folk and tribal traditions have for long used simple instruments which have done this job pretty well in their environments. Some of these instruments are fairly refined in their acoustic design, though falling far short of the contemporary *tānpūrā*. The beauty of the *tānpūrā*'s output is that it remains unobtrusive while aiding the music-making process. At its best, the sound of a perfectly tuned *tānpūrā* is a near-mystical experience — it transports the musician into a trance-like state, and focuses his energies on the process of creation.

The present-day *tānpūrā* represents a maturation of two streams of evolution. One is a folk stream of instruments which have existed in India from times immemorial. Many of them, like the *ektār* (single-stringed instrument), can still be heard all over India, with bards and minstrels singing to its accompaniment. The second stream of evolution is traced to the *tambūrā*, an instrument that came from Persia in the eleventh century CE.

The *tambūrā* from Persia was a fretted instrument on which melody was played. It became an important part of its musical activities at the Delhi court from the thirteenth century. However, by the early seventeenth century, two types of *tambūrā*, similar in structure, were being used — a fretted one on which melody could be played, and a fretless one which played no melody. The fretted one may have been a forerunner of the *sitār*, and the fretless version could have been a nascent *tānpūrā*.

The *tānpūrā* development obviously answered an emerging musical need. Once the need was recognized, the instrument was progressively refined to achieve higher levels of sophistication. Physicists, starting from Sir C.V. Raman, have long been intrigued by the *tānpūrā*'s acoustic qualities, and have invested a great deal of experimental effort into it.

The present-day *tānpūrā* has four strings (sometimes five or even six), which are plucked sequentially. Despite this, the output of the strings is not sequential. It flows out in overlapping harmonic waves, which are in acoustic consonance with one another. In effect, what the *tānpūrā* generates is a rhythm-neutral and cyclical harmonic ambience, compatible with the chosen foundation note, without delivering the foundation note itself. This acoustic phenomenon is created by the design of the *tānpūrā* frame, the special technique of fine-tuning the platform on which the strings are set, the fingering technique, and the acoustic properties of the *tumbā*, sourced ideally from Pandharpur in Maharashtra. The *tānpūrā* is, in fact, acknowledged by the music world as a uniquely Indian masterpiece of acoustic design.

The eminent musicologist, Ashok Ranade, suggests that the need for such an instrument may have surfaced with the ascendancy of *khyāl* vocalism, with its dominant role for the improvisatory process, and vast scope for individual creativity. Little wonder then that the greatest vocalists of the twentieth century worked closely with *tānpūrā* makers of Miraj (southern Maharashtra) to help upgrade the acoustic quality of the instruments made in that city.

With the growing travel needs of musicians, the search began for portable and convenient alternatives. Smaller *tānpūrā*s, called *tānpūrī*s, were in existence, and had a small following — mainly among instrumentalists. A more portable alternative was attempted with the box *tānpūrā*, designed by

Bishandas Sharma of Delhi. The box *tānpūrā* has four strings mounted atop a rectangular wooden box less than half the height of a conventional *tānpūrā*. Another convenience to emerge in this segment was a south Indian innovation — the *śruti* box, a bellows-driven drone about half the size of an executive briefcase. It is sound-primed intermittently like a harmonium. In recent years, the *śruti* box has gone electronic, and electronic *tānpūrā*s have arrived, thus providing hands-free options. Each of these substitutes is being re-engineered constantly in the hope of dislodging the conventional *tānpūrā* from the concert platform, but with only limited success so far.

The Svarmaṇḍal

The influential users of the *svarmaṇḍal* in recent years have been Bade Ghulam Ali Khan and Kishori Amonkar. Though their example has inspired several other vocalists, the instrument is still a rarity in India. Pakistani vocalists, however, appear to use it more widely than Indian vocalists do.

The *svarmaṇḍal* is a harp, most probably of Indian origin. Some authorities equate it with the *mattakokila,* a string instrument mentioned in pre-Christian literature. By the thirteenth century, the *svarmaṇḍal* had become an important accompaniment instrument in Indian music. It is a trapezoid wooden box, with twenty-one to thirty-six metal strings strung across its top. The strings are tuned to the scale of the *rāga* being performed, and plucked with the help of a wire plectrum worn on the fingers.

Although it is capable of playing formal music as much as any harp is, it has been used primarily for occasional strumming to fill the silences in a vocal music rendition. While every vocalist has his or her style of playing this instrument, hardly anyone tries to do more with it than filling silences. This is understandable because most vocalists have a *sāraṅgī* or a harmonium providing melodic accompaniment.

Since the *tānpūrā* and the *svarmaṇḍal* are used together and are both silence fillers — amongst other functions — a comparison between them deserves attention.

The *tānpūrā* is played continuously during a rendition, while the *svarmaṇḍal* is played only intermittently and briefly at each activation. The *tānpūrā* is normally tuned to two fixed points — the scale base and the mid-octave point, while the *svarmaṇḍal* is tuned to the scale of the chosen *rāga* across almost three octaves. The *tānpūrā* does not deliver notes in perceptible sequence, while the *svarmaṇḍal* does. Because of its acoustic design, however, the musical experience of the *svarmaṇḍal* is more a suggestion of melody than melody itself. These features of the two instruments make both instruments unobtrusive, and non-competitive with each other and also with respect to the principal musician's melody. It is therefore possible for a vocalist to derive additional musical value from a *svarmaṇḍal*.

What if a vocalist wants to use a *svarmaṇḍal* but cannot find a competent *tānpūrā* accompanist? Once again, Bishandas Sharma provided a solution. He enlarged the width of his box *tānpūrā* to mount a limited *svarmaṇḍal* type assembly on one side and a full-fledged *tānpūrā* assembly on the other. On this hybrid, called a *svarsaṅgam*, a vocalist can play the *tānpūrā* with one hand, and the *svarmaṇḍal* with the other.

The great *dhrupad* vocalist, Nasir Aminuddin Dagar, once described his pair of *tānpūrā*s as his *māī-bāp* (mother and father). This observation could justify the space devoted to this seemingly unimportant musical instrument, and the time you have invested reading this introduction. The *tānpūrā* is, in fact, so fundamental to Hindustani vocal music, that you cannot imagine its present-day sophistication without its support. The *svarmaṇḍal*, on the other hand, is an optional enrichment of the musical experience, without which a vast majority of Indian vocalists — and their audiences — seem quite happy.

5.10

THE VIOLIN

THERE is one musician whom Lord Yehudi Menuhin, the iconic Western violinist, never failed to meet and hear during his trips to India — the violinist, M.S. Gopalakrishnan. Interestingly, Gopalakrishnan commands equal stature amongst Carnatic and Hindustani connoisseurs. His musical persona virtually sums up the story of the violin in Indian art music.

How It All Began

The violin came to India with European colonists — the French in Pondicherry, the Portuguese in Goa, and the British in Bengal. It was introduced to Indian art music by Baluswamy Dikshitar (1786–1858), a brother of the legendary Carnatic composer, Muthuswamy Dikshitar. Baluswamy heard the violin in a British band, noted its acoustic closeness to the human voice and thought it well suited for accompanying Carnatic vocalism. His father sent Baluswamy as well as Muthuswamy to study the violin under the band master at Fort William. In 1884, Vadivelu, a disciple of the Dikshitar family, introduced the violin to an enthusiastic response at the Travancore court. Around the same time, the Marāṭhā princes of Tanjore also discovered the promise of the instrument, and encouraged its adoption. Since then, several generations of violinists have worked to make the violin a major instrument in Carnatic music.

The instrument entered Hindustani music in the 1930s through the initiatives of Allauddin Khan (Baba), Vishnu Digambar Paluskar, S.N. Ratanjankar, and Gajananrao Joshi.

Amongst the several instruments he had mastered, Baba had also studied the violin under Mr Lobo, the conductor of the Eden Gardens Band in Calcutta. Baba published the first ever violin recording of Hindustani music on a 78 RPM disc, thus heralding its arrival in the Hindustani mainstream. In later years, his disciple, Timir Baran, introduced the violin to film industry orchestration, and another disciple, V.G. Jog, emerged as a towering violinist.

Around the same time, Vishnu Digambar invited Parur Sundaram Iyer, an eminent Carnatic violinist (the father of M.S. Gopalakrishnan) to teach at Gandharva Mahavidyalaya, India's first music university. A few years later, S.N. Ratanjankar, the principal of the Maris College of Music at Lucknow (now Bhatkhande University), invited V.G. Jog to teach at the institution. The feudal chieftain of Aundh in Maharashtra virtually ordered Gajananrao Joshi, an eminent vocalist of the Gwalior Gharānā, to master the violin — which he did without a teacher, and later groomed several young violinists.

Not Really a Foreign Instrument

The violin has its origins in the Indian subcontinent. The instrument belongs to an ancient family of bowed lutes traced to the Rāvaṇhasta, featured in Indian mythology. This family includes a large number of folk and tribal instruments, as also the sophisticated *sāraṅgī*. Remarkably violin-like instruments are depicted amongst the sculptures of the Mallikarjuna Temple (Vijayawada, tenth century), and the Naṭarāja Temple (Chidambaram, twelfth century). The ancestor of the contemporary violin travelled from India to Europe through the Middle East and Central Asia.

Until the acceptance of the bowed instruments in art-music, the Hindustani and Carnatic traditions both gave pride of place to the *vīṇā* as an accompanist to vocal music. Once violin accompaniment partially replaced the *vīṇā*, it was also able to emerge as a solo instrument in Carnatic music. When the violin entered Hindustani music — almost three generations after its Carnatic debut — the *sāraṅgī* was the preferred accompaniment, but fast losing ground to the harmonium. Hindustani music thus ended up reserving the violin for solo performance, and only sporadically as an accompaniment.

For evolving into a mature instrument for Indian art-music, the violin has thus had much more time and much wider exposure in the Carnatic tradition, than in Hindustani music. Little wonder then that Hindustani music remains indebted to Carnatic music for the art of the violin.

The Violin in Hindustani Music

Gajananrao Joshi (1911-87), the pioneer of the violin in Maharashtra, performed predominantly as a vocalist. However, he groomed several younger violinists, amongst whom Shridhar Parsekar (1920-64) built a formidable reputation. Parsekar died young, and Joshi's other disciples either became teachers or made a living in the popular music industry. As a result, the Gajananrao lineage of violinists is no longer represented on the art music platform.

Amongst Hindustani violinists, V.G. Jog (1922–2004) enjoyed the longest innings at the top of the league. Jog had his early training with S.C. Athavale, Ganpatrao Purohit, Vishweshwar Shastry, and S.N. Ratanjankar. He later trained with Allauddin Khan, and took a degree in music from the Maris College of Music. From 1953 till retirement, Jog served on the staff of All India Radio.

Jog performed in the vocal *khyāl* and *ṭhumrī*, as well as the *tantakārī* idiom — the idiom of the plucked instruments, the *sitār* and *sarod*. His *khyāl* style was a mix of Gwalior, Agra and the eclectic Bhaskarbuwa Bakhle styles of vocalism.

In the next generation, the most venerated violinist is M.S. Gopalakrishnan (b. 1931), popularly called MSG. He studied the violin in the Carnatic and Hindustani traditions with his father, Parur Sundaram Iyer. After his father's demise, he studied Kairana Gharānā (Hindustani) vocalism with Guru Krishnananda. He also took an eight-month course in the Western violin technique at the Musee Musicale at Madras.

He exploded onto the Hindustani music scene in his early youth, accompanying leading vocalist like Omkarnath Thakur, D.V. Paluskar and Bade Ghulam Ali Khan. His trajectory in Carnatic music was equally sensational. Despite a less frequent presence on the Hindustani platform, his name spells magic amongst connoisseurs in both the traditions.

MSG presents Hindustani music in the *khyāl* style as well as the *tantakārī* idioms. He is respected for the neatness of architecture, and authentic treatment of musical material in both the traditions. In addition, MSG is revered for his flawless bowing technique, on par with the best in the world.

In the same generation as MSG, the Paluskar tradition of the violin is represented by D.K. Datar (b. 1932). He studied the violin under Vighneshwara Shastry, and vocal music under his uncle, D.V. Paluskar. Expectedly, Datar has remained faithful to the vocalized idiom of the Gwalior Gharānā during his long career as a violinist.

The Carnatic tradition continues to lead the Hindustani art through N. Rajam (b. 1938). She studied Carnatic music under her violinist father, Narayana Iyer, and the famous vocalist, Musiri Subramaniam Iyer. While still in her teens, she became a concert performer and accompanist to the tallest Carnatic vocalists, including M.S. Subbulakshmi.

When her family moved to Bombay (now Mumbai), she enrolled as a private (off campus) student for a degree from the Banaras Hindu University (BHU), where Omkarnath Thakur headed the Faculty of Music. She began intermittent training with him during his visits to Bombay. Soon, she began accompanying him regularly. Later she joined BHU as a lecturer, and flowered as a performer, teacher, and academician under her mentor's supervision. She no longer performs Carnatic music.

Omkarnath publicly acknowledged that Rajam understood his music best and followed it most faithfully. This is significant, because his was an emotionally charged style, rich in the manipulation of timbre and volume. In Omkarnath's music, the highly-evolved technique of Carnatic violinists found a fresh challenge, which Rajam conquered. In this, and several other respects, Rajam is credited with bringing the Hindustani violin idiom and technique closer to the experience of vocalism than ever before.

This overview suggests that the violin started in Hindustani music as an exponent of the vocal idiom (Gajananrao Joshi and Parsekar), was tempted — like the flute and the *sāraṅgī* — to venture into the *tantakārī* idiom (Jog and MSG), and has now returned to the vocalised idiom (Datar and Rajam). Despite the immense influence of Rajam, hers may not be the final verdict on the idiomatic destiny of the instrument in the Hindustani tradition. As we have seen (see chapters on the *bāṅsurī* and the *sāraṅgī*), rival idioms do hold some appeal for performers on the bow and wood-wind instruments.

The Hindustani Violin Today

Rajam is acknowledged as the foremost Hindustani violinist today. In the next generation, the significant Hindustani violinists are both Rajam's disciples — her daughter, Sangeeta

Shankar, and her niece, Kala Ramnath, who later became a disciple of the distinguished vocalist, Jasraj. In a sense, quality Hindustani musicianship on the violin is presently the domain of Carnatic expertise.

Is it then to be expected that future generations of outstanding Hindustani violinists will also emerge from the Carnatic tradition? Not necessarily, says Sangeeta Shankar, who is also an authority on the history of the violin in Indian art music (interview with the author on 15 July 2011). She admits that Carnatic violinists have a head start because of their superior technique, evolved over a longer history of involvement. But exceptional musicianship, she argues, will always create a place for itself. And, fine musicians could emerge from anywhere. As possible nurseries, she points towards Maharashtra and Bengal, both of which have a visible base of students pursuing the art, and even towards a small group of Western violinists seriously pursuing Hindustani music.

Sangeeta's observations — valid as they are — need to be considered against the absence of a "violin culture" which can nurture quality musicians for Hindustani music.

To begin with, the bowed instruments — as a category — now occupy only a small corner on the Hindustani music platform. Even at the top, the "market" for the violin does not have enough room to support full-time performing careers. The government-owned broadcast media, once significant employers of violinists, are shrinking avenues. The popular music industry, a major source of livelihood for violinists till recently, has gone electronic. Very few schools, colleges or universities outside south India employ violin teachers.

The Hindustani tradition has not adopted the violin as standard accompaniment to vocal music. Thus, an important avenue of livelihood and an irreplaceable aid to artistic maturation has been denied to Hindustani violinists. Adding to these factors is the cost of owning a concert quality instrument, which far exceeds the costs of the more popular instruments like the *sitār* and the *sarod*. These realities define an eco-system not particularly conducive to a steady supply of quality violinists.

Considering its musical value and its achievements so far, it is not reasonable to dismiss the violin as a mere footnote in the history of Hindustani music. It is, of course, also difficult to identify forces that can propel it forward. Violin enthusiasts hope that Hindustani music will continue to attract quality violinists from the Carnatic culture at least for a few more generations.

5.11

THE BĀṄSURĪ

THE *bāṅsurī* (the bamboo flute) enjoys such formidable status on the current musical scene, that one would imagine this has always been so. In reality, despite Lord Kr̥ṣṇa's blessings bestowed upon it several millennia ago, the instrument was elevated to the concert platform only in the mid-twentieth century. The development was pioneered by Pannalal Ghosh (1911-60), and consolidated by subsequent generations of flautists.

The *bāṅsurī* is easily the most widely played instrument in India. Starting in the pre-Christian era, it has been present in all segments of the musical culture. Even in the art-music segment, where it had a negligible presence till recently, it has enjoyed a large base of amateur musicianship. The reasons for its popularity are obvious. It is an instrument of simple construction with no moving parts, made from easily available materials, and has fixed holes for the notes, thus making melody reasonably easy to handle. In addition, it is portable, immune to climatic variations, and does not require maintenance or periodic overhaul by expert craftsmen. And, finally — this too matters — even a professional quality flute is a relatively inexpensive proposition. This brings access, and a basic level of competence within widespread reach. Elevating it to the concert platform in its historical context, however, took a lot more than this.

The Context

The bamboo flute is so pervasive, comes in many different sizes and designs, and is known by many names, that its authoritative history is impossible to construct. Fragments of information are, however, available for tracing its trajectory.

In the Vedic era, the bamboo flute was an important accompaniment to religious rites and rituals. Up to the thirteenth century, musicological literature has given detailed descriptions of the instrument, its design, construction, and playing technique. Till this period, it would appear, the instrument enjoyed considerable currency for solo performance and accompaniment. Its fortunes declined probably during the Mogul period.

Amongst the instruments, Akbar's chief musician, Miya Tansen, was partial to the string instruments — the *rudra-vīṇā* and the *rabāb*. During Jehangir's reign, there was one solitary report of a flautist having been honoured at the court. Highbrow music admitted a wood-wind instrument in the seventeenth century, when the *śehnāī* became an integral part of court ceremonies. During the eighteenth and nineteenth centuries, Tansen's descendants remained influential, and propagated the string instruments. The trend continued under the titled aristocracy in British India. Feudal patronage was important in that era because the courts were the only institutions where a large number of musicians interacted, and validated each other's art. Thus, for more than 500 years, the *bāṅsurī* remained isolated from the mainstream of highbrow music.

During Akbar's reign, but independently of the Mogul court, the *bāṅsurī* received a huge impetus from the Bhakti movement. Poets of the movement wove the *bāṅsurī* intimately into the romance of Rādhā and Kṛṣṇa. This resulted in an explosion of popular interest in the *bāṅsurī*. But, it only strengthened the *bāṅsurī*'s presence in middle-brow and low-brow territory. As a result, when Pannalal Ghosh launched his career as a soloist in the 1930s, he was confronted with a folk instrument — at best an amateur instrument — of shrill sound and limited melodic capability.

Pannalal Ghosh

Pannalal Ghosh started playing the *sitār* and the *bāṅsurī* at a young age, with a stronger interest in the *bāṅsurī*. Forced by economic necessity, he joined the film music industry at the age of twenty-three. Alongside his profession, he studied the harmonium with Master Khushi Muhammad, vocal music with the legendary Girija Shankar Chakravarty, and launched himself as a solo flautist. He soon found it difficult to juggle his profession with his passion. At the age of 36, he quit films and became a disciple of Allauddin Khan, a master of several instruments, though a performer on the *surod*. Pannalal's grooming thus gave him a solid foundation in the major genres. His musical vision now required a worthy vehicle. So, he worked systematically on the design of the instrument.

He experimented with a variety of materials — steel, brass, chrome, wood, bamboo, and even polymers. He finally settled on bamboo from India's *north-east* for its acoustic properties. He then enhanced the length of the flute substantially, with a corresponding enlargement of the diameter. He increased the total number of holes on the tube from seven to eight. This gave him a comfortable range of two-and-a-half octaves. For deep lower octave melody, he designed a bass flute, larger and wider than the regular instrument. To manage these innovations, he also had to devise a new fingering technique. The pair of flutes he designed is now virtually the "industry standard".

With this equipment, he was able to spearhead the flute renaissance in Hindustani music. He was the first significant musician to introduce the *sitār*-style *alāp-joḍ-jhālā* form to the flute idiom. He was equally competent in the obvious idiom of the wood-wind instruments — *khyāl, ṭhumrī,* and folk music. His versatility of style and content was passed on to his principal disciples.

The Bāṅsurī after Pannalal Ghosh

In the next generation, Devendra Murdheshwar (Ghosh's disciple) and Vijay Raghav Rao (a disciple of Ravi Shankar) were the leading flautists. They brought the flute idiom closer to the *sitār/sarod* idiom. This trend continued in the third generation, primarily with Raghunath Seth and Hariprasad Chaurasia.

Hariprasad Chaurasia (b. 1938) studied the flute first under Bholanath Prasanna at Allahabad, and qualified as an empanelled artist on All India Radio (AIR). Thereafter, he joined the staff of AIR, Cuttack, where his duties included accompanying a variety of artists in light and folk music. When he moved to AIR Bombay, the world of film music welcomed him enthusiastically because of his technical command over the instrument, and stylistic versatility. He could soon quit his AIR job to make headway as an art-music soloist, while continuing his involvement with films. His potential as an art-music flautist was honed and unleashed in Bombay by his last Guru, Annapurna Devi, and daughter of Allauddin Khan. With this grooming, Chaurasia catapulted himself and the *bāṅsurī* onto the global concert platform.

Stylistic Directions

Chaurasia's last Guru, Annapurna Devi, belongs to a lineage specializing in the string instruments, and is herself an outstanding surbahār player. Her father had trained Pannalal Ghosh, Ali Akbar Khan, Ravi Shankar, and Nikhil Bannerjee, amongst others. A significant consequence of Chaurasia's apprenticeship with her was that the influence of the *sitār*/*sarod* idiom over the flute now became even stronger.

It has been argued that legitimate idiom of a breath-driven instrument is continuous melody, and not the discontinuous melody produced on the plucked instruments. But, you cannot argue with success. The drift towards the *sitār*/*sarod* idiom did, indeed, help the emergence of Pannalal Ghosh, and its reinforcement has paid rich dividends to his successors and the flute. This trend warrants a brief re-look at history.

The wood-wind instruments, as a category, have for long enjoyed only a small share of the classical music market. The causes for this phenomenon are partly historical. For over half a millennium, the princely courts neglected the wood-wind instruments. The *śehnāī*, the more fortunate of the two, had only an inferior status as a provider of background music to ceremonies, and not that of a concert instrument which commands an attentive audience.

The string instruments — beneficiaries of prolonged feudal patronage — became even more dominant after the advent of the microphone, to the extent of surpassing vocal music in popularity and stature. By the time of Pannalal Ghosh's arrival, instrumental music had become almost synonymous with the *sitār*/*sarod*. In such an environment, it is easy to appreciate why Ghosh and his successors have been rewarded for plugging their music into the dominant "model" of instrumental music.

A similar story might be unfolding in the bowed instruments — specifically the *sāraṅgī* and the violin. These instruments are also designed for melodic continuity, and the vocal idiom is their "natural" habitat. They too have had a small share of the market. Consider, for instance, the directions chosen by contemporary maestros of the bowed instruments — Dhruva Ghosh, the *sāraṅgī* virtuoso, and N. Rajam, the veteran violinist. Their music suggests that the bow instruments are also moving — in their own distinctive manner — closer to the idiom of the *sitār* and *sarod* in order to avert further marginalization.

These observations point towards the awesome strength of the homogenizing forces operating within the musical culture. Stylistic diversity now appears to risk audience rejection not only within the realm of each instrument, but even across instruments. This cannot augur well either for this individualistic art or its rich legacy of musical instruments.

5.12

THE PAKHĀWAJ AND TABLĀ

EVERY musician in India wants Zakir to accompany him. Every assembly of Indian connoisseurs wants to hear a Zakir solo. Every Kathaka dancer wants Zakir to add sizzle to her footwork. Every world music ensemble wants Zakir as the lead percussionist. And, every student of the *tablā* wants to be a Zakir. This is, undoubtedly, the triumph of a charismatic genius called Zakir Hussain. But, it is also the victory of the Indian art of percussion, and of rhythm as a musical expression sufficient unto itself.

Zakir Hussain is a product of the north Indian art-music tradition of transforming geocentric time into musical time, which began with the *pakhāwaj* several millennia ago, and continues with the *tablā*.

Pakhāwaj

The *pakhāwaj* (originally known as *mr̥daṅg*) is a venerated instrument. The *mr̥daṅgam* of Carnatic music belongs to the same family. Mythology attributes the *mr̥daṅg*'s origination to Brahmā, the creator of the universe. Such notions often suggest indeterminate antiquity and untraceable origins.

Up to eighteenth century, the *mr̥daṅg/pakhāwaj* was the dominant rhythmic accompaniment for art music and even Kathaka dance. Today, its presence is largely limited to the *dhrupad* genre. The Hindustani mainstream now prefers the *tablā* across all modern genres of music. The *pakhāwaj*, no doubt, still enjoys immense prestige as the originator, developer, and preserver of the rhythmic science and percussion art.

The most widely cited derivation of its name is from Sanskrit: *pakṣa* (side) + *vādya* (instrument). The *pakhāwaj* is a horizontal wooden barrel-drum, asymmetrical on one side. Its forearm-powered open-palm playing technique gives its sound a booming resonance and sonorous dignity. In addition to accompaniment, the *pakhāwaj* also has a solo tradition for connoisseurs of rhythm.

Having been a resident of the Vaiṣṇava temples along with *dhrupad*, the *pakhāwaj* cultivated its art most assiduously in the Mathura/Vrindavan region. From there, it travelled to the Mogul court with *dhrupad*, and continued its forward march. The landmark figure in *pakhāwaj* history was Lala Bhagwandas, a product of the Mathura/Vrindavan tradition, and an esteemed musician at Akbar's court (sixteenth century). His disciples spearheaded *pakhāwaj* traditions in several parts of the country — Punjab, Uttar Pradesh, Maharashtra, Madhya Pradesh, Gujarat, Rajasthan, and Bengal.

When *dhrupad* was declared a "museum piece" in the early years after Independence, this description did not apply to the *pakhāwaj* because, even at that stage, it claimed a substantial resource of quality musicianship. After European and US markets warmed up to *dhrupad*, starting from the 1960s, gathering steam in the 1980s, the *pakhāwaj* scene also got a shot of adrenalin. The instrument now shares the fruits of the *dhrupad* revival.

The *pakhāwaj* now appears to be on the threshold of a new market — the global market for Indian and cross-cultural ensembles. Several Hindustani and Carnatic percussion instruments have entered this segment since the 1980s. The entry of the *pakhāwaj*, though late, is hardly surprising. Any instrument which speaks the language of rhythm with such grace and authority had to, one day, find a global audience.

To this day, the world of the *pakhāwaj* continues to be more vibrant than either *dhrupad* vocalism or the *rudra-vīṇā*. On request, Uday Bhawalkar, the *dhrupad* vocalist, and Akhilesh Gundecha, the *pakhāwaj* exponent, compiled for me a list over twenty contemporary *pakhāwaj* players of concert quality. Aneesh Pradhan, a percussionist and music historian, suspects that many of these twenty could be better soloists than accompanists. Good accompanists, he fears, might still be too few. He attributes the comfortable supply of *pakhāwaj* players to the additional talent available outside art-music — in the devotional music traditions, where the instrument is well entrenched and relatively insulated from market forces.

Tablā

The origin of the *tablā,* the vertical drum pair, is a puzzle that defies solution. Its name has a Persian ring to it; but this is not considered evidence of its origin. The instrument came into prominence during the fifteenth century at the dawn of the modern era in Hindustani music. The era began when the *khyāl* started challenging the supremacy of *dhrupad*. In later years, lighter vocal genres like the *ṭhumrī* and *ṭappā* also became immensely popular. The ponderous *rudra-vīṇā* yielded its pre-eminence to the sprightly *sitār*. Hindustani music now needed a percussion partner of greater agility, delicate playing technique, and softer output. The *tablā,* already a mature instrument by then, steadily enlarged its role on the emerging music-scape, to finally replace the *pakhāwaj* by the eighteenth century.

Historic developments in the *tablā* idiom took place during the reign of Emperor Muhammad Shah of Delhi (1719-48), whose court was also host to the launch of the *sitār*, and the maturation of *khyāl* vocalism. The musician responsible for the percussion revolution was Siddhar Khan Dhadhi.

Siddhar Khan was an accomplished *pakhāwaj* player, who translated the forearm-powered open-palm *pakhāwaj* idiom into the wrist-and-fingers idiom of the *tablā*, thus creating an entirely new percussion language. His students spread to other major centres of music, and adapted the style to respond to local influences and aesthetic values. As a result, the world of the *tablā* now recognizes six major styles, known by the names of the centres where they evolved.

1. *Delhi*: In recent times, Inam Ali Khan and Lateef Ahmed Khan have been the most distinguished exponents of this *gharānā*.

2. *Ajrada*: Habibuddin Khan was the most distinguished percussionist of this style in recent memory.

3. *Lucknow*: Afaque Hussain Khan was the most recent distinguished percussionist of this lineage.

4. *Farrukhabad*: This tradition produced three luminaries in the same generation: Ahmed Jan Thirakwa, Shamsuddin Khan, and Ameer Hussain Khan.

5. *Benares*: This pedigree again produced three outstanding percussionists in the same generation — Shamta Prasad, Kishen Maharaj, and Anokhey Lal.

6. *Punjab*: This style produced the superstars of late twentieth-century music — Allahrakha Khan, and his son, Zakir Hussain. Though masters of their own traditional idiom, the Punjab lineage maestros have enriched it with ideas from several other sources.

The stylistic distinctions between these lineages are, obviously, not as evident in accompaniment, as they are in solo performance, because an accompanist needs to respond spontaneously, free from *gharānā* preferences.

The Tablā as Accompanist and Soloist

Percussion accompaniment for contemporary Hindustani music can be categorized into three levels of presence — supportive, interactive, and competitive.

In accompanying vocalists, whose art is melody-dominant, the *tablā*'s presence is primarily supportive, though it may become mildly interactive in the brisk movements, and the light and semi-classical genres. With the wind and bow instruments, the percussionist's role is similar because these instruments, by and large, follow the vocal idiom.

The equation changes substantially in the case of string instruments like the *sitār*, *sarod*, and *santūr*. These instruments are either plucked or struck. In the process of activating the sound, they create a rhythmic pattern. This gives the *tablā* an opening for an interactive and even competitive relationship with the instrumental idiom.

In order to exploit this potential, instrumentalists have steadily heightened the rhythmic complexity of music, and encouraged percussionists to match it with stroke-craft improvisations. As a result, the collaborative musical effort has become far more engaging, and enlarged the audiences for instrumental music. Progressively, as the string instruments strengthened their hold over the concert platform, they enabled the *tablā* to enhance its visibility. This trend also permitted *tablā* players to acquire an independent following.

The true test of a percussionist's following is the *tablā* solo — a comprehensive and systematic display of mastery over different levels of stroke-density and rhythmic complexity. In the absence of truly towering percussionists, the last quarter of the twentieth century saw a sharp decline in the audiences for *tablā* solos. Thanks to today's enhanced visibility for percussion, the solo is now making a comeback, and drawing young listeners. Sadanand Naimpalli, a respected percussion *guru*, describes this as "The Zakir Effect".

In terms of aesthetic cultivation, today's audiences for *tablā* solos cannot, obviously, be compared to mid-twentieth century audiences. But, the phenomenon does signify a revival of interest in the percussion art, independently of its role as an accompanist. Maybe, it was Zakir Hussain who made it a "happening". But, it is not restricted to Zakir alone. So, the happening was possibly waiting to happen anyway.

5.13

HARMONIUM

TAGORE called it the "bane of Indian music". The All India Radio banned it for several decades. After a brief involvement, Carnatic music rejected the instrument. In Hindustani music, the *dhrupad* genre ignores it. Serious *khyāl* vocalists express grave reservations about its suitability to art music. When pushed, every professional harmonium player turns defensive about his instrument. Attempts to establish it as a solo instrument have failed. Despite the ongoing debate over its musical value, the harmonium holds sway over vocal accompaniment not only in Hindustani art-music, but in all musical genres of northern India. It could be the most widely owned and heard instrument in the country, and claim an enormous base of amateur and professional musicianship.

The harmonium began replacing the *sāraṅgī* towards the end of the nineteenth century, and now appears firmly entrenched. The instrument mechanized the acoustically standardized execution of notes, which *sāraṅgī* or violin players achieve only after years of practice. Satisfactory melodic execution came within easier reach of an unprecedented number of musicians. This became the driving force of the instrument's popularity.

The Instrument

The harmonium belongs to a family of keyboard-based wind instruments which includes a variety of organs, and various types of accordions. The design of the harmonium was patented by a Frenchman, Alexander Dubain in 1840. His design, as it came to India, had the keyboard and reed-panel mounted on a pedestal, primed by foot-pedals for activating the bellows. The instrument was originally played much like a piano with all ten fingers, and with the player sitting on a chair.

The instrument came to India with Christian missionaries, and was probably first heard in the churches of the three presidencies — Calcutta, Bombay and Madras (now Kolkata, Mumbai and Chennai respectively). It entered Indian music in the 1880s through the regional theatre, where it became a sensation. Interestingly, Marāṭhī theatre continued to call it an "organ" much as the churches did. Its main advantage was the volume of the output, richness of its sound and — unlike the string instruments — the convenience of not requiring retuning during a performance. In the theatre of the pre-amplification era, the harmonium probably also enabled the engagement of a smaller orchestra, thus bringing down costs.

The precise timing of the harmonium's entry into art music is not known. The direction was, however, to be expected because of its practical advantages (see chapter on the *sāraṅgī*). It also helped that the regional theatre had, by then, nurtured a substantial base of competent players with a reasonable foundation of *rāga*-grammar. Outside the theatre, however, the instrument faced an initial hurdle.

The concert platform was not willing to accept an accompanying instrument whose player sat on a chair — a level above the vocalist. The problem was solved around 1890 in consultation with the patent-holders and Indian musicians. The result was a compact and portable harmonium with its bellows mounted at the rear. The harmonium player could now sit on the floor, and pump the bellows with one hand, while the other hand executed the melody. With this change, the vocalist could also choose to accompany himself/herself.

After this modification, the instrument took north Indian music by storm. By 1910, the harmonium had reached the remotest corner of India and entered all segments of north Indian music — folk, devotional, semi-classical, and popular. By then, it was also easing the *sāraṅgī* off the stage in art-music. When imports from Europe were disrupted during the Second World War, booming domestic demand gave birth to a sizeable base of Indian suppliers. Prices tumbled and sales soared.

Landmark Personalities

The harmonium wave was stimulated in Bengal and Maharashtra by the stature of a few iconic personalities. Their profiles demonstrate the instrument's early linkages with the worlds of theatre and semi-classical music.

The instrument became a contender for the art music space with Bhaiyya Ganpatrao (1852–1923), a member of princely establishment of Gwalior, who lived mostly in Calcutta. He was trained in *dhrupad, khyāl,* and the *rudra-vīṇā,* but fell in love with the *ṭhumrī* genre, and the newly-arrived harmonium. He became a formidable harmonium player, and also groomed some of the most outstanding *ṭhumrī* singers of the era. In the next generation, the harmonium received a huge impetus in Maharashtra through the person of Govindrao Tembe (1881–1955). Tembe was a brilliant self-taught harmonium player, and a vocalist trained by the redoubtable Bhaskarbuwa Bakhle (1869–1922). Tembe was actively involved in Marāṭhī theatre as a composer, and is credited with memorable compositions, especially in *ṭhumrī* style. Tembe also emerged later as a respected man of letters.

From the middle of the twentieth century, the harmonium's stature was boosted by Gyan Prakash Ghosh in Bengal, and P.L. Deshpande in Maharashtra.

Ghosh was a versatile genius — *tablā* exponent, harmonium player, and composer. The list of his students, covering all segments of musical activity, reads like a Who's Who of music in Bengal. He reportedly supervised the design developments undertaken by Dwarka & Sons, a leading harmonium manufacturer in Calcutta. P.L. Deshpande in Maharashtra was, likewise, much larger than the harmonium he played with distinction. He was a towering literary personality, also highly respected in theatre circles.

In subsequent generations, Bengal and Maharashtra — the most prolific nurseries of musical talent — have continued to produce outstanding harmonium exponents, as well as eminent vocalists who excelled as harmonium players.

The Harmonium and Art-Music

Semi-classical and light music — the *ghazal* and the *ṭhumrī* — admitted the harmonium before art music did. This happened perhaps because the instrument was adequate for the requirements of these poetry-dominant genres while also being very practical. The issue became tricky in the context of a *rāga*-bound and melody-dominant genre like the *khyāl*.

The harmonium is widely acknowledged as being unsuitable for accompanying Hindustani vocal music. Its critics point towards two facets of its design. The basic problem lies with the twelve fixed notes within each octave. To do justice to Hindustani music, an instrument needs to deliver twenty-two notes, including fractional notes. The secondary problem lies in the keyboard-based design. A keyboard instrument cannot faithfully execute every kind of intervallic transition that is used in Hindustani vocalism. When compared to bowed alternatives like the *sāraṅgī* and the violin, it falls short on musical value.

The proponents of the harmonium argue that both these problems are exaggerated. They insist that, with astute control over the pumping and fingering, a competent player can deliver all the melodic nuances of Hindustani vocalism. They contend that an expert player can even create an illusion of the fractional notes which are missing from the instrument's acoustic design.

As an ambitious response to the challenge of fractional notes, innovators have now developed a *śruti* (microtone) harmonium, which can explicitly execute twenty-two notes. This innovation has yet to register its presence on the concert platform.

Why the Harmonium Reigns

Considering that its musical value remains controversial a century after its adoption, we need to explain the harmonium's monopolistic position.

The foremost factor is economics. The harmonium has spawned such a large resource of musicianship that either alternative — *sāraṅgī* or violin — would be several times more expensive to hire. The second factor arises partially from the first. A huge base of musicianship inevitably throws up a few outstanding musicians, whose engagement rates may be higher, but are not prohibitive. And, indeed, the harmonium has produced several such musicians, primarily in Maharashtra and Bengal. They have become preferred accompanists to the leading vocalists, and also attracted exceptional talent as students.

When a quality service is available at a sensible price, the system will tend to resist change — until the consumer revolts. Audiences — as a class — seem to be in no mood to revolt, even if a small minority is dissatisfied. A broadly similar situation prevails amongst vocalists. Serious vocalists continue to lament the demise of the *sāraṅgī*, and the compromised musical values of the harmonium. And, yet, they live with it because, though not entirely acceptable, the harmonium is not insufferable.

To be fair, some leading vocalists of earlier generations are known to have preferred the harmonium to the *sāraṅgī* precisely because it cannot match the vocalist's melodic sophistication. Some eminent vocalists of the past have even refused first-rate *sāraṅgī* accompaniment when it was available because they saw it as distracting, intrusive or competitive. Such attitudes are no longer encountered in the musical culture. Today's vocalists work with the harmonium in a spirit of realism.

The semi-classical, popular, devotional, and partially even folk music professionals are, in fact, plunging deeper into keyboard territory, with electronic organs accompanying them. The *khyāl* platform has, however, accepted only the electronic *tānpūrā* so far — that too as an adjunct to an acoustic *tānpūrā*. For the present, therefore, art music appears to be a safe haven for the harmonium.

The only stress-point in this situation is that harmonium players are paid poorly in relation to their musicianship. Increasingly, trained exponents of the instrument are pursuing other professions, and treating the art music stage as a hobby. Fewer young musicians are training to become harmonium players. A part of the trained talent is mastering electronic keyboards, and drifting towards the popular music industry. Over the next few decades, therefore, harmonium accompanists for art music could become less plentiful, and need to be paid much better. It is difficult to predict how the major players in the business will respond to such a situation.

Implications for Hindustani Vocalism

The harmonium culture has struck deep roots in non-peninsular India. It is normal for students of vocal music to be first taught to play the harmonium, and then to sing to its accompaniment in order to achieve pitch perfection. This dependence on the harmonium lasts several years, till the student is ready to sing accompanied by the *tānpūrā*.

During these years, three things have most likely happened. First, the singer's intonation has been perfected for twelve notes, and not for all the twenty-two required of a complete art music performer. Second, the singer's vocalization organs and melodic imagination have been programmed to function with only twelve notes. As a result, *rāga*s that require intonation beyond the twelve notes of a harmonium either tend to get neglected, or are rendered clumsily. Third, the vocalist's treatment of melody has begun to reflect the harmonium's limitations in sculpting and ornamentation. These infirmities acquired in the most formative years are not easily reversed later because the concert platform imposes the harmonium on the vocalist once again — now as an accompanist.

A few of today's vocalists have, indeed, risen above the aesthetic indoctrination inherent in the harmonium culture, and achieved eminence as musicians. The instrument cannot, therefore, be held wholly responsible for the widespread depletion of melodic subtleties observed in *khyāl* vocalism. However, having dominated Hindustani vocalism for three or four generations, could the harmonium have contributed to this loss by legitimatizing melodically handicapped music?

GLOSSARY

Abhaṅga : *Abhaṅga* is a Sanskrit adjective meaning "indestructible". The word defines a specific genre of devotional folk poetry written in Marāṭhī, the principal language of the western state of Maharashtra. The term gained currency after Chundarasa, the thirteenth-century Kannaḍa poet (Kannaḍa is the principal language of the neighbouring southern state of Karnataka) described his deity, Viṭṭhala, a manifestation of Lord Viṣṇu, as "Abhaṅga Viṭṭhala". The verse of the *abhaṅga* genre is written in the metre of "Ovi", an older poetic format in Marāṭhī literature, encompassing three different sub-formats within the genre.

The term *abhaṅga* is used specifically to describe poetry written by the poet-saints of the Bhakti movement in Maharashtra during the mediaeval period — mainly Sant Nāmdev, Sant Tukārām and the solitary lady saint, Bahinā Bāī. The genre is of high literary merit and also enjoys great popularity. The poetry is generally encased in simple folk-based melody, often corresponding to popular *rāga*s, and set to *kehervā*, the ubiquitous eight-beat rhythmic cycle in all of non-art-music. Its rendition on the art music platform as the tailpiece of a *khyāl* concert is of recent origin. In this context, the renditions remain anchored to the poetic and emotional content of the poetry, with a negligible role for improvisations. [Also see: **Maharashtra, Bhakti**.] See Chapter 4.3.

Abhinaya : The word is Sanskrit for the act of artistic communication with the aid of bodily movements. The language of dance consists of three vehicles for non-verbal communication — the language of the eyes and the facial muscles, the language of the torso, and the language of footwork. The term *abhinaya* refers specifically to the language of the eyes and the facial muscles — the element of mime in dance, with a negligible role for the torso and footwork.

Ābhoga : The term derives from the Sanskrit *bhoga* = satiation/ contentment. The *ā* vowel prefix in Sanskrit connotes "in the direction of/towards". The *ābhoga* is the fourth and valedictory phase of *rāga* exposition in any movement. Like the *sañchārī*, it has now been dropped from *dhrupad* and post-*dhrupad bandiś*es. Its relevance is now limited to the prefatory *alāp* and the improvisatory movements of *bandiś* rendition. The melodic–aesthetic function of this phase is to fold back the melodic canvas which was fully unfolded in the first two phases, and on which, in the third phase, the *rāga*'s distinctive melodic personality is detailed. Though a few musicians do still render a distinct *ābhoga*, especially in the *alāp*, each musician has his own approach to winding up an improvisatory movement with a distinct valedictory phase of exposition. [Also see: **Dhrupad, Bandiś, Sthāī, Antarā, Sañchārī.**] Refer Chapter 2.1.

Adbhut : See **Rasa/Navarasa**.

Addhā Ṭhekā : See **Tīntāl/Tritāl, Ṭhekā**.

Āḍā Chautāl : *Āḍā chautāl* is a *tāl* (rhythmic cycle) of fourteen beats in seven equal sub-divisions of two beats each. Though not very popular in contemporary music, it is amenable to rendering across a wide range of tempi — from slow to moderately fast. It is encountered more frequently in vocal music of the *khyāl* genre than in any other vocal genre or in instrumental music.

Ākār : *Ākār* is derived from *ā* = the uttered vowel *ā* + *kār* = process. It is an important articulatory device deployed in *khyāl* performance. It is found most suited for the delivery of low-density and high or even ultra-high density melody. Of the three articulatory devices used in Hindustani (north Indian) art music, the full-throated *ākār*, arising from the navel, is regarded as having the greatest psycho-phonetic impact, and also the greatest self-illuminating and personality-transforming potential. These qualities relate to the neuro-acoustic triggers of this form of vocalization, and the demands this form of articulation makes on the deployment of lung-power. These facets of vocalization are well understood in the Indian mystical tradition, and yogic practice of *prāṇāyāma*. [Also see: **Khyāl, Yogic, Prāṇāyāma**.]

Alaṁkār : The strictest meaning of the Sanskrit *alaṁkār*, derived from its semantic meaning, is adornment, embellishment, decoration. In this sense, all modes of intonation and intervallic transition in Hindustani music, other than staccato, would fall under the category of *alaṁkār*. In contemporary usage, however, the term has emerged as a generic description of the host of symmetric practice exercises that are given to music students with the aim of cultivating their technical excellence in the handling of melody. [Also see: **Alaṁkār Tāns**.]

Alaṁkār Tāns : The word *alaṁkār* stands for the perfectly symmetrical practice exercises that are given to students of music for cultivating their technical competence in handling melody. These patterns, when deployed as *tāns* — an improvisatory movement — require little melodic imagination. They do, however, appear conspicuously, and often unimaginatively, in contemporary music because of their ability to dazzle with their speed and clarity. [Also see: **Tāns**.] Refer Chapter 4.2.

Alpatva/Bahutva : *Alpatva* is an abstract noun (Sanskrit) for the quality of brevity. Bahutva is its antonym. The *alpatva / bahutva* parameter in *rāga* grammar deals with the explicitness with which each of the permitted tones / *svars* of the *rāga* can be intoned, relative to others. Most tones / *svars* in a *rāga* will receive "normal" weightage. A few may, however, be prescribed either for subliminal or imperceptible intonation, or for prolonged intonation. This is a special and selective dimension of *rāga*-grammar, not universally relevant to all *rāgas*. [Also see: **Rāga**.] Refer Chapter 3.1.

Alāp : The word derives from Sanskrit *alāp* = dialogue / conversation. The aesthetic implications of this word are appropriately translated in the *alāp* movement in Hindustani (north Indian) art music. The *alāp* is a leisurely, deliberate, almost conversational, exposition of the *rāga*'s melodic form aimed at achieving, for it, the highest possible level of intelligibility. This intelligibility is achieved by conformity with traditional principles of melodic progression. Within this general definition, the word describes different categories of movements in different genres of vocal music, and on the different instruments.

Alāp/Joḍ/Jhālā : See *alāp* on the plucked instruments and the *santūr*.

Alāp in Dhrupad : In the *dhrupad* genre of art music, the word *alāp* describes a three-tiered prefatory movement rendered without percussion accompaniment. The first tier of the movement, called "*vilambit* (slow tempo) *alāp*", consists of anarythmic melody presented in the prescribed progression. The second tier called "*madhya laya* (medium tempo) *alāp*", presents melody with a pulsation at about two beats per second, once again in the prescribed progression. The third tier called "*drut* (fast tempo) *alāp*" raises the rate of melodic pulsation to four beats per second or higher. In the third tier, however, melody adopts a broad-span approach, with the laws of progression being considered less binding than in the first two phases of the *alāp*. [Also see: **Alāp**.]

Alāp on the plucked instruments and the Santūr : In terms of melodic–rhythmic structuring, the major plucked instruments of Hindustani music — the *rudra-vīṇā, sitār* and the *sarod* — and the struck polychord, the *santūr*, all follow the three-tiered *dhrupad* protocol for the prefatory *rāga* exposition, and present it without percussion accompaniment. They differ only in name. The first stage of anarythmic melody is called the *alāp*. The second stage of mild pulsation of melody is called *joḍ*. The third stage of accelerated pulsation of melody is called the *jhālā*. The differing nomenclature is also explained by the fact that these instruments use *chikarī* (drone) strings for achieving the pulsation, and perforating the flow of melody, thus adding an acoustic element to the treatment of the three tiers. [Also see: **Alāp, Alāp in Dhrupad**.]

Alāp in khyāl and on wind and bow instruments : The prefatory low-density *alāp* movement is identical in *khyāl* vocalism and on the wind and bow instruments because, being instruments capable of melodic continuity, these instruments have traditionally presented music in the *khyāl* format. The *khyāl* format presents the *alāp* as a percussion-accompanied movement. It is the first improvisatory movement in the *vilambit* (slow-tempo) *khyāl* rendition. The *alāp* in the *khyāl* format consists of rounds of low-density anarhythmic melodic improvisation, in the prescribed progression, woven around intermittent returns to the pre-composed form of the *bandiś*. In the vocal manifestation, the *alāp* of the *khyāl* format may deploy either the poetic form, or vowel forms as articulatory devices.

Note: In recent years, some performers on the wind and bow instruments have adopted the *dhrupad* format for presenting the *alāp*. [Also see: **Alāp, Bandiś, Khyāl, Alāp in Dhrupad**.]

Āmad : The word is probably colloquial for the Sanskrit verb *āgaman* = to arrive. The *āmad* in a *bandiś* is the last phase of either the *sthāī* or the *antarā*, which terminates just before the rendition can return to a rendition of the *mukhḍā* of the *sthāī*. [Also see: **Bandiś, Mukhḍā, Antarā, Sthāī**.]

Antarā : The term is an abbreviation of the Sanskrit *antara-dhātu* = "intermediate material". In the *bandiś*, *antarā* is centred in the upper half of the melodic canvas. It ascends categorically from the mid-octave region of the middle octave to the upper-tonic, provides a climactic and reposeful pause at the upper-tonic, ascends into the higher octave, and then descends in deliberate steps to base-*sa* (the tonic/fundamental). The *antarā* of the improvisatory movements is identical in its progression logic to the pre-composed *antarā* of a *bandiś*. Collectively, the *sthāī* and the *antarā* provide a complete coverage of the melodic canvas. [Also see: **Bandiś, Sthāī, Sañchārī, Ābhoga**.] Refer Chapter 2.1.

Aṅga : See **Aṅga/Apaṅga**.

Aṅga/Apaṅga : *Aṅga* is Sanskrit for limbs. A limb being a facet of the human body, the term is also used metaphorically to describe a facet of an aesthetic endeavour. *Apaṅga* (common noun) is Sanskrit for a cripple, and derives its meaning from *aṅga*, denoting a compromised/defective/missing limb. In aesthetics, *apaṅga* is used metaphorically to describe the unintended and displeasing results of creating or emphasizing a particular facet of an aesthetic endeavour. A cripple, being an object of derision or pity, there is a satirical pun implicit in such usage, as its implications tread the borderline between its literal and metaphorical meaning. Refer Chapter 2.2.

Aṅga [Gāyakī, Tālvādya, Tantakār/Tata] : *Aṅga* is Sanskrit for limbs. A limb being a facet of the human body, the term is also used metaphorically to describe a facet of an aesthetic endeavour. In such metaphorical use of the term, the idiom of each category of musical endeavour is metaphorically described as a facet of the totality of musical experience. The Hindustani tradition recognizes three primary *aṅga*s of musical expression — *gāyakī* (vocalism or the idiom of melodic continuity), *tantakāra / tata* (plucked instruments, or the idiom of melodic discontinuity), and *tālvādya* (percussion instruments or the atonal idiom of rhythm). These idioms are derived from the design, ergonomic and acoustic features of the respective sound producing mechanisms. The human voice is regarded as the most authentic exponent of the musical idea. For this reason, the *gāyakī aṅga* is traditionally recognized as the reference point, and ideal of all musical expression.

Aṅga Prādhānya : The term derives its meaning from Sanskrit *aṅga* = limb/facet + *prādhānya* = dominance. This term refers to classification of *rāga*s on the basis of the region of the melodic canvas in which their centre of gravity falls. In this context, the octave is divided into three overlapping regions (*aṅga*s or limbs). The lower tetrachord (*sā, re, gā, mā*) is called the *pūrvāṅga* (*pūrva* = early + *aṅga* = limb / region). The mid-octave region (*gā, mā, pā, dh*) is called the *madhyāṅga* (*madhya* = middle + *aṅga* = limb / region). The upper tetrachord (*pā, dh, nī, sā*) is called *uttarāṅga* (*uttara* = north = *aṅga* = limb / region). The awareness and observance of this parameter of *rāga* grammar ensures that the musician invests a substantial part of his musical energies in the appropriate region of the melodic canvas, and thus maximizes the probability of achieving the psycho-acoustic goals of *rāga* exposition.

Anuchit : See **Auchitya/Uchit/Anuchit**.

Anuraṇan : See **Svar/Tone**.

Aprasiddha : The word is Sanskrit for "not famous". In music, it is used primarily for classifying *rāga*s into *aparasiddha* = rare/not widely recognized, or *prasiddha* = common/popular/widely recognized. These classifications are dynamic, as *rāga*s move freely between popularity and rarity from generation to generation.

Artha-Bhāva : The term derives from Sanskrit *artha* = semantic meaning + *bhāva* = emotional meaning. The *bol-banāo ṭhumrī* is also called the *artha-bhāva ṭhumrī,* because it uses song-texts as a platform for luxuriant and leisurely melodic ornamentation, with the purpose of making the words come to life. [Also see: **Ṭhumrī, Bol-banāo Ṭhumrī, Nāyikā Bheda.**] Refer Chapter 4.3.

Āroha : Ascending melodic motion.

Āroha pradhān : See **Diśā prādhānya**.

Auchar : The term refers to an anarhythmic prelude, rendered without percussion accompaniment, preceding a *khyāl* presentation. The *auchar* has no clearly defined melodic movements, though it does follow an ascending–descending progression. It remains generally in the lower half of the melodic canvas, does considerably more than merely identifying the *rāga* and aims at creating its atmosphere. [Also see: **Rāga vākya**.]

Auchitya/Uchit/Anuchit : *Auchitya* is an abstract noun, derived from the Sanskrit adjective *uchit* = proper, the antonym for which is *anuchit* = improper. *Auchitya* is Sanskrit for the sense of propriety. In its very nature, the meaning and significance of the term relates to history, geography and specificity, and is, therefore, contextual. In the present context, it is an important yardstick by which oriental societies judge the conduct of individuals, especially those in positions of power and influence. *Auchitya* is, admittedly and explicitly, an elitist criterion of conduct. In each field of human activity, the yardstick is applied by, and from the perspective of, peers and others qualified to sit in judgement over those being judged. For passing muster on this criterion, individual conduct requires social acceptability. But, *auchitya* neither begins nor ends with such acceptability. In the field of culture, the application of the *auchitya* yardstick functions as a mechanism for preventing art from drifting towards populist titillation. Refer Chapter 2.2.

Auchitya bhaṅga : The term is derived from Sanskrit *auchitya* = propriety + *bhaṅga* = breach. *Auchitya bhaṅga* is the act or process which breaches the limits of propriety. [Also see: **Auchitya/Uchit/ Anuchit.**]

Auḍav : The word describes pentatonic *rāgas* (those that deploy five tones/*svars*). The description does not double-count a tone/*svar* if the *rāga* uses the natural as well as its suppressed or enhanced microtones. In this classification, the ascent and the descent are considered together. However, *rāgas* may be described by dual classifications such as *auḍav-sampūrṇa* if, for instance, they are pentatonic in the ascent and heptatonic in the descent. [Also see: **Chatusvar, Ṣāḍav, Sampūrṇa.**]

Aurangzeb : Aurangzeb was a Mogul emperor of ascetic temperament (seventeenth century) and the only one in the lineage who disapproved of the performing arts as immoral and incompatible with the tenets of Islam. Since then, the term "Aurangzeb" has come to symbolize individuals in positions of power and influence conspicuously lacking in interest in, or affinity to, the performing or fine arts.

Avanaddha : *Avanaddha* is one of the five primary classifications of musical instruments in Indian organology. It represents instruments, which are covered with membranes, mainly animal skin. This category describes percussion instruments such as the *pakhāwaj*, *tablā*, and other drums.

Avaroha : Descending melodic motion.

Avaroha pradhān : See **Diśā prādhānya**.

Avatār : Common noun derived from the Sanskrit verb *avataraṇ* = to manifest/to incarnate. The allusion is to the Hindu belief in reincarnation. It hypothesizes that individual souls manifest themselves repeatedly in different bodies, and in different eras, while maintaining a continuity of relationships and unfinished tasks through their eternal journey. The journey is believed to end when an individual dies without any emotional attachments and unfinished tasks. The word *avatār* is used more specially to signify manifestations/reincarnations of Lord Viṣṇu or Lord Maheśa/Śiva, in either human or alternate divine form, appearing with the purpose of relieving humanity of the tyranny of evil forces. [Also see: **Brahmā, Viṣṇu, Maheśa.**]

Baḍā Khyāl : The word derives its meaning from the Hindī *baḍā* =

major/big/large/expansive + *khyāl* = vision/imagination. The term denotes the slow-tempo rendition of vocal music in the *khyāl* genre of Hindustani (north Indian) art-music. In such meaning, it represents the pre-composed element (the poetic–melodic–rhythmic shell of the rendition) along with prescribed improvisatory movements. [Also see: **Khyāl**.] Refer Chapter 4.2.

Baḍhat : The word is Hindi for evolution/progression/growth, and is derived from the Sanskrit *vr̥ddhi*, an abstract noun of identical meaning. In Hindustani (north Indian) music, it refers to the melodic progression prescribed for the improvisatory movements. The prescription is relevant only for the first two phases of *rāga* exposition protocol — *sthāī* and *antarā* — and not to the remaining two phases — *sañchārī* and *ābhoga*, which are free from the progressive logic, and whose rendition varies considerably. [Also see: **Sthāī, Antarā**.]

Baḍhat Tāns : The word *baḍhat* stands for a sense of melodic progression. *Baḍhat tāns* are clusters of high-density melodic runs, which correspond to a notion of deliberateness and disciplined sequencing of ascending and descending melody in the coverage of the melodic canvas. [Also see: **Baḍhat, Tāns**.] Refer Chapter 4.2.

Bandiś [also called Chīẓ or Gat] : The word derives from the Sanskrit verb *bandhan* = to bind. A *bandiś* is that which is bound, encased, pre-composed. The word refers to the pre-composed element in Hindustani (north Indian) vocal or instrumental music. In vocal music, it refers to the pre-composed poetic–melodic–rhythmic shell, which constitutes the nucleus around which the improvisations revolve. In instrumental music, it refers only to the melodic-rhythmic shell. In art music, a *bandiś* is composed in a specific *rāga*, is set to a specific *tāl*, and conforms to traditional rules of composition. [Also see: **Rāga, Tāl**.]

Bandiś Ṭhumrī : The *bandiś ṭhumrī* is the older of the two sub-genres of the *ṭhumrī* genre of semi-classical vocal music. The word *bandiś* in this context signifies its reliance on the pre-composed poetic–melodic–rhythmic form. The word *ṭhumrī* signifies its origins as accompaniment to Kathaka dance, and its continued association with it. Having evolved from older traditions of dance-related musical forms, the *bandiś ṭhumrī* achieved a mature form by the eighteenth century, touched its zenith by mid-nineteenth century, and had become near-extinct as an independent musical genre by late twentieth century. Its evolution into a sophisticated genre was synchronous with the emergence of the princely state of Awadh (Lucknow) as the cultural capital of northern India. Stylistically, the *bandiś ṭhumrī* is a lively piece of music, performed primarily in medium tempo, and composed in the popular *tīntāl* / *tritāl*, along with its stylized variants. The *bandiś ṭhumrī* exerted considerable influence over the evolution of the idiom of the modern plucked-lute family of musical instruments — principally, the *sitār* and the *sarod*. [Also see: **Bandiś, Ṭhumrī, Bol-banāo Ṭhumrī**.] Refer Chapter 4.3.

Bānī : *Bānī* is colloquial for Sanskrit *vāṇī* = speech/language. The reference is to the various styles of performing *dhrupad* that existed in mediaeval times, which were originally also associated with the different dialects in which their lyrics were written. During the period of Miya Tansen's influence over *dhrupad* vocalism (sixteenth century), the different *bānī*s merged their identities into the Senīya tradition. Though this merger did not eliminate the stylistic diversity immediately, the subsequent decline of the *dhrupad* genre has had this consequence. [Also see: **Dhrupad, Miya Tansen, Senīya**.]

Behlava : The word is Hindi, and has connotations of a leisurely quality, informality and indulgence. It is used to describe the anarhythmic *alāp* of certain stylistic lineages of *khyāl* vocalism. The *behlava* form is characterized by the use of the poetic form as the articulatory device, and its relative informality of progression. The *behlava* approach in *khyāl* vocalism has inspired a similar movement in the rendition of slow-tempo *bandiś*es on the *sitār* and *sarod* [Also see: **Khyāl, Alāp in Khyāl, Bandiś**.]

Beṅgālī/Bengal : Adjective derived from "Bengal", a region of undivided India on the east coast, now bifurcated into the nation state of Bangladesh and the Indian state of West Bengal. Beṅgālīs are residents of either part of undivided Bengal, whose mother tongue is Beṅgālī (also called Bāṅglā), written in the Beṅgālī script. In the latter half of the twentieth century, the Indian state of West Bengal emerged as the primary resource of instrumental musicianship simultaneously with the western Indian state of Maharashtra emerging as the most prolific nursery of talent in *khyāl* vocalism.

Bhajan : The word derives from the Sanskrit verb *bhaja* = to serve/to worship. A *bhajan* is a song based on devotional poetry, and owes its influence to the literary flowering triggered off by the Bhakti movement. These songs were originally performed in the temples, and moved from there into people's homes as solo or choral expressions. They are composed typically in folk tunes, or based on a handful of classical *rāga*s. The advent of the gramophone record gave a tremendous boost to their popularity and standardization in rendering. The infusion of classicism into their rendition, and their adoption as repertoire for the concert platform is a twentieth-century phenomenon. In the latter context, the *bhajan* has steadily replaced, and displaced, the *ṭhumrī* and *ṭappā* genres. [Also see: **Bhakti, Ṭhumrī, Ṭappā**.] Refer Chapters 4.3 and 4.4.

Bhakti : The word is Sanskrit for "devotion/surrender", and derives from the verb *bhaja* = to serve/to worship. As a backdrop to the literary and musical culture, the term refers to the movement (the Bhakti movement) in Hindu society starting from around the eighth century. The movement revolted against the power of the clergy over the spiritual lives of the laity, and espoused a direct emotional relationship between the devotee and God. The movement found its most potent symbol in the legend of Lord Kr̥ṣṇa, an incarnation of Lord Viṣṇu, the preserver of the universe in Hindu mythology. The mischief of the infant Kr̥ṣṇa became a stimulus for the maternal/parental instinct, while his dalliances with his paramour, Rādhā, became a powerful trigger for the romantic sentiment. By imagining himself/herself as Kr̥ṣṇa's mother or paramour, the human devotee could establish an emotional bond with Lord Kr̥ṣṇa. Depicted in mythology as a Machiavellian warrior, a worldly philosopher, and a Casanova, Kr̥ṣṇa is "human," while also being divine. This combination of accessi-bility and inaccessibility has provided infinite momentum to the cult of Kṛṣṇa, and dominated the literary, musical, and choreographic culture of northern India during the second millennium. All the major genres of Hindustani (north Indian) art-music — *dhrupad, khyāl,* and *ṭhumrī* — and the Kathaka genre of classical dance, are imbued with the thematic content of the Bhakti cult.

Bhaya : See **Rasa/Navarasa.**

Bībhatsa : See **Rasa/Navarasa.**

Bīn : See **Rudra-Vīṇā**. Refer Chapter 5.1.

Bīnkār : A musician who performs on the *rudra-vīṇā/bīn* [Also see: **Rudra-Vīṇā.**]

Bol : The word is Hindi for "articulated sound / speech". In the context of Hindustani (north Indian) art-music, it refers to the use of the poetic form as the vehicle for the delivery of music. As a vehicle for the communication of musical meaning, the poetic form enjoys the highest premium in the *bol-banāo ṭhumrī* genre, followed by *dhrupad,* and finally by *khyāl.* Being a device equipped with vowels, consonants, as well as semantic and syntactical meaning, the poetic form lends itself to any combination of poetic, melodic and rhythmic manipulation. As such, it is the most versatile articulatory device across a wide range of tone densities. Moreover, it is far less demanding than pure vowel devices, to which the vocalist perforce resorts for delivery of ultra-high density melody. These considerations make the poetic form (*bol*) the most popular articulatory device in contemporary art music. [Also see: **Khyāl, Dhrupad, Bol-banāo Ṭhumrī, Ākār, Sargam.**]

Bol-alāp : When the *alāp* of the *khyāl* genre is presented using the poetic form as the articulatory material, it is called *bol-alāp* [Also see: **Bol, Alāp, Rūpakālapti, Alāp in Khyāl** and on wind and bow instruments.]

Bol-banāo : *Bol-banāo* is the leisurely process of using musical expression to convert the semantic meaning of a song-text into emotional meaning. This mode of musical communication is considered appropriate only in the romanticist *ṭhumrī* genre of semi-classical music. The aesthetics of *bol-banāo* aided the erotic allurement of a courtesan. The process is artistic, takes place in public and fulfils the requirements of decorum worthy of genteel society. Within these constraints, it has to achieve an intimacy not available to the classicist genres, because it is aimed at obtaining the highest price for the courtesan's favours. *Bol-banāo* represents vocal expression of explicitly manipulative intent, traditionally rendered to the accompaniment of mime and gesture. The mode of musical communication relies heavily on ornate melodic embellishments and seductive manipulations of volume and timbre considered inappropriate in the classicist genres — *dhrupad* and *khyāl*. [Also see: **Ṭhumrī, Bol-banāo Ṭhumrī, Dhrupad, Khyāl.**] Refer Chapter 4.3.

Bol-banāo Ṭhumrī : The *bol-banāo ṭhumrī* is the more recent of the two sub-genres of the *ṭhumrī* genre of semi-classical vocal music. The prefix *bol-banāo* describes the leisurely process by which the sub-genre uses musical expression to convert semantic meaning into emotional meaning. The suffix *ṭhumrī* refers to its origins as accompaniment to Kathaka dance, and its continued association with it. The *bol-banāo ṭhumrī* evolved and flourished primarily in the city of Benares, and reflects a considerable influence of folk traditions of the neighbouring districts. This *ṭhumrī* sub-genre reached its zenith during the nineteenth century, and began to loose ground in the early twentieth century when it moved out of the salons of the courtesans and into the concert halls. At the time of writing (December 2003), the genre claims only a handful of significant performers. Besides the *khyāl* vocalists who perform the *bol-banāo ṭhumrī*, only two specialist performers of the genre remain — Girijadevi and Shobha Gurtu. The genre now faces extinction as an independent musical genre. [Also see: **Bandiś Ṭhumrī.**]. Refer Chapter 4.3.

Bol-bāṇṭ/Laya-bāṇṭ : The terms are derived from *bol* = poetic form (or *laya* = tempo) + *bāṇṭ* = distribution. They are forms of improvisation in the vocal genres of Hindustani music, the distinctions between them being ill-defined with respect to vocal renditions. *Bol-bāṇṭ* alters the relationship between the poetic and rhythmic elements in the pre-composed form of the *bandiś* without substantially disturbing the melodic element. *Laya-bāṇṭ* (temporal redistribution) is a similar improvisation, but may also encompass the melodic component. The term *laya-bāṇṭ* may also be used for comparable improvisations in instrumental music, which do not have the poetic form for manipulation. Both forms are generally practiced in medium melodic density. [Also see: **Bol, Laya, Bol-laya**.]

Bol-laya : The term is derived from *bol* = the poetic form + *laya* = tempo. *Bol-laya* is the name given to the medium density movement, sequentially the second improvisatory movement, in contemporary *khyāl* rendition. It involves improvisations utilizing the poetic form as the articulatory device, with melody adopting an explicit rhythmicality in the rendition. This movement may include elements of *bol-bāṇṭ/laya-bāṇṭ*. Some musicians may, however, choose to replace — either partially or entirely — the poetic form with the *sargam* (solfa symbols) as the articulatory material for this second, medium-density movement. This represents a "logical" progression from the preceding *alāp* movement, which involves only an anarhythmic treatment of low-density melody. [Also see: **Alāp, Alāp in Khyāl, Bol-bāṇṭ, Bol, Bol-alāp**.]

Bol-tān : The term derives from *bol* = the poetic form + *tān* = high-density melodic runs. When *tāns* are rendered in *khyāl* vocalism with words and phrases from the song-text as the primary articulatory device, rather than the alternatives available, the *tān* form is called a *bol-tān*. This form of *tān* may also be occasionally encountered in *bandiś ṭhumrī* rendition, and is routinely adopted in *ṭappā* singing. [Also see: **Tān, Bol, Ṭappā**.]

Brahmā : The Creator of the Universe in Hindu mythology. [Also see: **Trimūrti**.]

Bṛhat Kinnarī : See **Kinnarī/Kinnarī-Vīṇā**.

Chañchār : See **Dīpchaṇḍī, Charcharī**.

Chaitī : The word is derived from the name of the Chaitra month of the Hindu calendar (spring). The *chaitī* is a genre of folk songs from the eastern part of Uttar Pradesh (Northern Provinces) and its adjacent districts. Its signatory feature is verse in which poetic lines end with *ho rāma*. The songs are generally of two stanzas each, and of standard melodic construction, which does not correspond to the art music definition of *sthāī-antarā* progression. The thematic content of the poetry is primarily romantic, and deals with the pangs of separation from the beloved, as narrated by a female protagonist. It is a poetry-dominant genre, possessing limited scope for melodic elaboration and improvisation, and set to a 7-beat or 14-beat rhythmic cycle common in *ṭhumrī*-related folk genres. The courtesans of Benares and neighbouring Gayā elevated the *chaitī* songs to the status of a semi-classical art form. The genre is regarded as one of the allied genres of the *bol-banāo ṭhumrī*. [Also see: **Bol-banāo Ṭhumrī**.] Refer Chapter 4.3.

Chakradār : The word derives from Sanskrit *chakra* = circle, and is Hindi for a circular pattern. The *chakradār* is an expanded version of a *tihāī*. There are many patterns available for expanding a *tihāī* into a *chakradār*. However, the most common is one that renders the same *tihāī* three times to culminate at the *sama*. [Also see: **Tihāī, Sama**.] Refer Chapter 2.4.

Chalan : The word derives from the Sanskrit *chal* = to walk or Hindi *chāl* = gait/demeanour. A *rāga*'s distinctive melodic personality is outlined by a set of characteristic phrases, which incorporate a substantial part of its grammar. This set of phrases — generally not more than eight or ten in number — are collectively called the *chalan* of the *rāga*. [Also see: **Rāga**.] Refer Chapter 3.1.

Charcharī : *Charcharī* is the name of a north Indian dance form of folk origin. It is an erotic dance, accompanied by song and instrumental music. *Charcharī* is also the name of a *tāl* (rhythmic cycle) to which the accompanying music of the dance form is composed. The *charcharī* dance form, along with the associated musical content, has been identified as an important source for the modern *ṭhumrī* genre of semi-classical music. The beat-pattern of *charcharī tāl* is also called *chañchār* or *dīpchaṇḍī*. This *tāl* is used exclusively in the *bol-banāo ṭhumrī* genre, and may be considered its most important *tāl*. [Also see: **Chañchār, Dīpchaṇḍī, Ṭhumrī**.] Refer Chapter 4.3.

Carnatic/Hindustani music : The word derives from the name of the

"Karnāṭ" region of India, approximately covering all of peninsular India south of the Vindhyachal range of mountains. A unified Indian tradition of art music underwent a bifurcation starting in the early part of the second millennium. The north of the country came under increasing middle eastern (mainly Perso-Arabic) cultural influence consequent to a series of invasions, while south India remained relatively insulated from such influences. This bifurcation was probably magnified by art-music responding more explicitly to the regional musical cultures of the north and south, and to the differing predilections of its patrons. These forces gave rise to two parallel art music traditions — the north Indian tradition, called Hindustani music, and the south Indian tradition, called Carnatic music. The two systems have similarities as well as dissimilarities, and follow their independent evolutionary paths. However, there is evidence of growing cross-fertilization of musical ideas and practices between the two traditions after Independence (1947).

Chatusvar : The word is derived from the Sanskrit *chatur* = four + *svar* = tone. The term describes a *rāga,* which utilizes only four tones/*svar*s. In this classification, the ascent and the descent are considered together. Quadratonic *rāg*s are very few in Hindustani (north Indian) music, five tones/*svara*s being considered the minimum required to form the basis of an aesthetically satisfying musical rendition. However, *rāga*s may be described by dual classifications such as *chatusvar-sampūrṇa* if, for instance, they are quadratonic in the ascent and heptatonic in the descent. [Also see: **Auḍav, Ṣāḍav, Sampūrṇa**.]

Chauguṇa/Chaturguṇa : The word derives from *chau* = four + *guṇa* = multiple. When any melody is performed at a melodic (tone) density four times the beat density (tempo) of accompanying percussion or the base-tempo of the *bandiś,* the expression is called *chauguṇa/chaturguṇa*. The highest ratio of tone-density to beat-density practiced in Hindustani music is eight times. [Also see: **Bandiś**.]

Chautāl [loosely also called Dhrupad] : *Chautāl* is a *tāl* (rhythmic cycle) of twelve beats in six equal sub-divisions of two beats each.

It is the primary *tāl* of the *dhrupad* genre of mediaeval art music, and is generally performed in medium tempo.

Chhūṭ Tāns : The word derives probably from *chhūṭ* in Hindi = "abandon/release". When a melodic motif, once defined, is abandoned or released, it escapes/flees/leaps. The *chhūṭ tān* conveys such an impression by leaping to different regions of the melodic canvas, while retaining the tonal geometry of the basic motif. The totality of the aural image is a collage of similar patterns strewn across the melodic canvas, generally in ascending and/or descending sequence, though not necessarily so. [Also see: **Tāns**.] Refer Chapter 4.2.

Chhoṭā Khyāl : The word derives from the Hindī *chhoṭā* = minor/small + *khyāl* = vision/imagination. The term denotes the fast-tempo rendition of vocal music in the *khyāl* genre of Hindustani (north Indian) art music. In such meaning, it encompasses the pre-composed element (the poetic–melodic–rhythmic shell of the rendition) as well as the conventional architecture of the rendition with respect to the improvisatory movements. Compared to the *baḍā khyāl*, the architecture of a *chhoṭā khyāl* presentation is informal. [Also see: **Khyāl**.] Refer Chapter 4.2.

Chīẓ : See **Bandiś**.

Dādarā : *Dādarā* is a *tāl* (rhythmic cycle) of six beats in 3+3 sub-division. The *tāl* is generally used in medium and fast tempi. However, the term also refers to a genre of folk-based semi-classical genre of vocal music allied to the *bol-banāo ṭhumrī*. This genre, originating in the musical traditions of the districts around the city of Benares, is performed not only in the *dādarā tāl*, but also in a couple of other *tāls*. The dividing line between the *dādarā* and *bol-banāo ṭhumrī* is blurred. The significant feature of the *dādarā* vocal genre is the heightened rhythmicality of rendition, relative to the subdued rhythmicality of the *bol-banāo ṭhumrī*.

Dhamār : *Dhamār* is a *tāl* (rhythmic cycle) of fourteen beats with an irregular/asymmetrical 5+2+3+4 sub-division. It is an integral part of the repertoire of the *dhrupad/dhamār* genre of art-music, and is ideally suited for medium tempo rendition. *Dhamār* is one of the very few *tāls*, which does not begin on an accentuated beat.

For this reason, and also because of its irregular sub-division of beats, *dhamār* is considered an enigmatic *tāl* of reluctant rhythmicality.

In the *dhrupad / dhamār* genre, poetry composed to the *dhamār tāl*, irrespective of the *rāga* in which it is composed, is related predominantly to the Holī (also called Horī) the spring festival of colours. This makes the *dhamār tāl*, along with its associated poetic element connected with Holī/Horī, a distinct sub-genre of the *dhrupad* genre. Subsequent to the *dhrupad* revival in the last quarter of the twentieth century, many instrumentalists, especially *sarod* players, have begun to occasionally perform post-*dhrupad* music in the *dhamār tāl*.

Dhrupad [Also called *dhrupad-dhamār*.] : The word derives from sanskrit *dhruva* = fixed / immutable + *pada* = verse. It refers to a genre of *rāga*-based music, which dominated the Hindustani (north Indian) tradition between the fifteenth and eighteenth centuries. The genre evolved as an art form consequent to the transportation of the devotional music of the Vaiṣṇava temples to the secular environment of feudal courts. The genre places a high premium on the integrity of its poetic element in rendition and is, therefore, predominantly a genre of vocal music. Its primary instrumental manifestation is the *rudra-vīṇā* (also called *bīn*). After the decline of its strongest patron, the Mogul Empire, in the early nineteenth century, *dhrupad* progressively surrendered the mainstream platform to the modern *khyāl* genre, taking the *rudra-vīṇā* along with it on the downhill path. *Dhrupad* was near extinct by mid-twentieth century, but experienced a minor revival in the last quarter of the century, primarily supported by audiences and scholars in Europe and the US. [Also see: **Vaiṣṇava, Rudra-Vīṇā, Khyāl**.] Ref. Chapter 4.1.

Dīpti : See **Svar/Tone.**

Dīpchaṇḍī : *Dīpchaṇḍī* is a *tāl* (rhythmic cycle) of fourteen beats in 3+4+3+4 sub-division. It is related genealogically to *chañchār / charcharī tāls* associated with the *ṭhumrī* genre of semi-classical vocal music, and is virtually indistinguishable from them. *Dīpchaṇḍī* itself is also encountered exclusively in the *bol-banāo* *ṭhumrī* genre. Like the *dhamār tāl* (also of 14 beats) the *dīpchaṇḍī tāl* is also associated with songs celebrating the spirit of Holī/Horī, the spring festival of colours. This sub-genre of the *bol-banāo ṭhumrī* is occasionally referred to as *horī-dīpchaṇḍī*. [Also see: **Ṭhumrī**.]

Diśā Prādhānya : The term derives its meaning from Sanskrit *diśā* = direction + *prādhānya* = dominance. This term refers to a classification of *rāgas* on the basis of the direction of melodic motion in which the *rāga*'s distinctive melodic personality is most significantly expressed. *Rāgas* are classified as either *āroha pradhān* (*āroha* = ascending melodic motion + *pradhān* = dominant) or *avaroha pradhān* (*avaroha* descending melodic motion + *pradhān* = dominant). Awareness and observance of this parameter of *rāga* grammar encourages the musician to invest a substantial part of musical energy in melodic thrusts in the appropriate direction, thus maximizing the probability of achieving the psycho-acoustic goals of *rāga* exposition.

Duguṇā/Dviguṇā : The word derives from *dvi* or *do* = two + *guṇā* = multiple. When any melody is performed at a melodic (tone) density twice the beat density (tempo) of accompanying percussion, or the base-tempo of the *bandiś*, the expression is called *duguṇā*. The highest ratio of tone-density to beat-density practised in Hindustani music is eight times. [Also see: **Bandiś**.]

Drut [or Drut laya] : An adjectival phrase derived from the Sanskrit *drut* = running/galloping + *laya* = tempo. It describes a rendition in fast tempo. The notion of tempo (slow/medium/fast) is relative and dynamic. It differs between generations, between stylistic lineages, between different genres of vocal music, and between vocal and instrumental music.

Ektantrī-Vīṇā : The word derives from the Sanskrit *ek* = one/single + *tantrī* = string + *vīṇā* = stringed instrument. The *ektantrī-vīṇā* is described in musicological texts from the eleventh century CE. Evidently, it was a long-necked fretless lute with a single string, on which melody was executed by sliding a hard and smooth mechanical device along the strings, rather than by stopping the strings with the bare fingers. This instrument may also be regarded as an ancestor of the *vichitra-vīṇā* and the slide-guitar. [Also see:

Ghoṣak, Vichitra-Vīṇā, Indian Classical Guitar.] Refer Chapter 5.1.

Ektāl : *Ektāl* is a *tāl* (rhythmic cycle) of twelve beats in six equal subdivisions of two beats each. The *tāl* is immensely popular for slow as well as fast tempo renditions in the *khyāl* genre of vocal music. It is amenable to rendition in a wide range of tempi, from below twenty beats per minute to over 240 beats per minute. Its use in medium tempo *khyāl* rendition is rare. The use of this *tāl* in instrumental music is restricted to performers on the wind and bow instruments, who generally render *khyāl* genre compositions.

Fāgun : *Fāgun* is a genre of folk songs, which derives its name from the month of Fālguna in the Hindu calendar (early spring). The genre belongs to the eastern districts of Uttar Pradesh (Northern Provinces), and evolved as an ally of the *bol-banāo ṭhumrī* performed by courtesans of Benares. In the Indian literary and musical tradition, spring is most clearly associated with man's romantic urges. Hence, the lyrics of *fāgun* songs are dominated by romance. The explicit reference to the month of Fālguna is generally found in *fāgun* songs. The songs are normally rendered with emotive embellishment of the poetic element, but without substantive melodic improvisation. [Also see: **Bol-banāo Ṭhumrī**.] Refer Chapter 4.3.

Gamak : The term derives from the Sanskrit verb: *gam* = to go. In the strictest musicological sense, the word is generic to all intervallic transitions in Indian music, classified according to the melodic contours they respectively define. In contemporary Hindustani usage, however, the word has come to denote one specific category of *gamak* — the *tribhinna gamak* — which creates a vibratory melodic contour. It is a contextual intonation of a tone/*svar*, conveying the impression of being repeatedly attacked from an adjacent tone/*svar*. The effect may be compared with a magnified *vibrato* in Western music. The *gamak* is practised in vocal as well as instrumental music.

Gat : See **Bandiś**.

Gat-toḍ : The term derives from *gat* = composition/*bandiś* performed on the plucked lute family of instruments + *toḍ* = complex rhythmic patterns. The *gat-toḍ* is a medium density improvisational movement in the traditional idiom of the *sītār* and the *sarod*. It involves the rhythmic manipulation of melody, accompanied by complex bi-directional stroke patterns mimicking the idiom of percussion. This form is akin to, and a modern successor of, the *tar-paraṇ* form of improvisation practised on the *rudra-vīṇā* in *dhrupad* music. [Also see: **Bandiś, Tar-paraṇ, Paraṇ, Dhrupad**.]

Gāyakī Aṅga : See **Aṅga [Gāyakī, Tālvādya, Tantakār/Tata]**.

Ghan : *Ghan* is one of the five basic classifications of musical instruments in Indian organology. These classifications are independent of the technique of sound activation and technique of melodic execution.

Ghan, in Sanskrit, means solids. Such instruments are mainly percussive or percussive-melodic in character. The *kāṣṭha taraṅga*, (the Indian xylophone) now extinct, was the last instrument in this category to be performed in Indian art music. [Also see: **Kāṣṭha Taraṅga**.]

Gharānā : The word derives its meaning from the Hindi *ghar* (Sanskrit *gr̥ha* = house). *Gharānā* is a collective noun meaning a group, which shares the same homestead. In the era of hereditary musicianship, the term came to represent a lineage, which cultivated a distinctive style of rendering music over successive generations. Once kinship ceased to be the primary criterion for entry into the music profession, the term was redefined to denote a stylistic lineage. As a stylistic lineage, a *gharānā* is characterized by three critical features — (a) a long period of rigorous training and aesthetic indoctrination of each aspirant under an authorized *guru* of the lineage, (b) acquisition of the art through aural transmission, and (c) a sworn loyalty of each member to the music-making philosophy and style of his mentor/lineage. The decay of the *gharānā* phenomenon began in the second quarter of twentieth century and is now almost complete. The *gharānā* model of continuity and change has been replaced by alternative models, yet to be conceptualized. Refer Chapter 1.6.

Ghasīṭ/Sūta : The word derives from the Hindi *ghasīṭ* = to drag, and Sanskrit *ghr̥ṣṭa* = abrasion. The explicit reference here is to an intervallic transition achieved on the plucked string instruments, by dragging a finger of the left hand over a large melodic span under the impact of a single right hand stroke. This process defines a linear, rather than curvilinear melodic contour. Such a transition, when executed in vocal music, is called a *sūta* or *syūnta*.

Ghaẓal : The word is Persian for "addressing a lover in poetic form". The term defines a poetry dominant genre of music imbued with the romantic sentiment. Its poetic structure derives probably from the *kasīdā* form in Persian literature. The Islamic Sufi sects adopted the *ghaẓal* form early during their presence in India, making the love of God an important thematic element. *Ghaẓal*s were originally written in Persian. When the form was adopted in Urdu literature, its thematic content was substantially enlarged, to encompass *ishq* (love), *ashq* (tears) and *maut* (death). *Ghaẓal*s were originally sung in a very simple, repetitive, melodic structure, with no improvisation. In the nineteenth and twentieth centuries, its melodic approach began to drift towards that of the *bol-banāo ṭhumrī*. The genre, however, continues to accord an autonomous status to the poetic element, far more categorically than the *ṭhumrī* genre does. [Also see: **Urdu, Bol-banāo Ṭhumrī**.] Refer Chapter 4.3.

Ghoṣak : The word is derived from the Sanskrit verb *ghoṣaṇ*, meaning announcement. In the present context, the term refers to a fretless stick-zither of the plucked variety, described in the ancient text on dramaturgy, Bharata's *Nāṭyaśāstra* (200 BCE – CE 200), on which melody was executed by sliding a hard and smooth mechanical device along the strings, rather than by stopping the strings with the bare fingers. This instrument, along with the *ektantrī-vīṇā*, is considered the ancestor of the *vichitra-vīṇā*, and the Hawaiian slide-guitar. [Also see: **Ektantrī-Vīṇā, Vichitra-Vīṇā**.] Refer Chapter 5.1.

Gītkīrī : The word is colloquial and partially onomatopoetic. There is no consensus on its definition. It is frequently used to signify a short, crisp, brisk melodic passage, across adjacent tones/*svar*s, without loops or angularities. It warrants a nomenclature when inserted, for dramatic effect, into either low-density or convoluted/zigzag melodic movements. The presence of this expression is most prominent in the *ṭappā* genre of semi-classical music, though it is also deployed by some lineages of *khyāl* vocalism. [Also see: **Ṭappā, Khyāl**].

Gopāla : The word is derived from Sanskrit *go* = cows + *pāla* = one who breeds/nurtures/protects. The word *gopāla*, though defensible as a generic description of all cowherds, is normally mentioned reverentially as a name for Lord Kṛṣṇa, the Divine Cowherd. This facet of his persona is especially important because of his popularity with *gopīs*, the women of the cowherd community in which he grew up. This nexus with the community constitutes the thematic material for the cultural manifestations of the Bhakti movement in non-peninsular India. [Also see: **Bhakti**.]

Guru : See **Guru-śiṣya Paramparā.**

Guru-śiṣya Paramparā : The term derives from Sanskrit *guru* = teacher/mentor/guide + *śiṣya* = disciple/ward/student/aspirant + *paramparā* = tradition. The term refers to the traditional relationship between a teacher and his students, which forms the basis of the transmission of all forms of knowledge, including musical knowledge. The salient features of this relationship are total subordination of the personality of the student to that of his teacher, in return for which the teacher accepts total responsibility for the grooming of the disciple in the chosen field of education. The two-way unconditionality and totality of commitment characteristic of this relationship is critical to its success because of the aural mode of transmission and the personality-transforming goal of education. In this tradition, therefore, the *guru* is accorded a status on par with God. [Also see: **Gharānā.**]

Harmonium : A member of the keyboard based family of free-reed aerophones. Although such instruments have existed in India and other parts of Asia for centuries, Christian missionaries probably introduced the harmonium to India from Britain in the eighteenth century, as accompaniment for choirs in churches. The original import was a platform mounted pedal-primed version, which was later replaced with a portable hand-pumped variant with thirty-seven keys. Despite the incompatibility of its tempered scale with Indian intonation practices, the instrument is now the most widely used melodic accompaniment to all genres of vocal music — other than *dhrupad/dhamār* — and has replaced the *sāraṅgī* in this role. Attempts to establish it as a solo instrument have met with only limited success. [Also see **Sāraṅgī**.].

Hāsya : See **Rasa/Navarasa**.

Hindustani music : See **Carnatic/Hindustani music**.

Hindustani slide-guitar : See **Indian Classical Guitar**.

Holī/Horī : Semi-classical genres of vocal music associated with Holī, the spring festival of colours, but more particularly with poetry describing the mischief the infant or adolescent Lord Kṛṣṇa played on the occasion with the womenfolk of his village. They are set primarily to the *dīpchaṇḍī* and *dhamār tāls*. [Also see: **Dīpchaṇḍī, Dhamār**]

Hopping Tāns : These are, as the name suggests, melodic patterns that hop across alternating tones/*svars*, often repeating each hop, and most commonly in ascending formation. Only a few stylistic lineages of *khyāl* vocalism practice this form of *tāns*. [Also see: **Tāns**.] Refer Chapter 4.2.

Horī-Dīpchaṇḍī : See **Dīpchaṇḍī, Holī/Horī**.

Indian classical guitar/Hindustani slide-guitar : The Indian classical guitar/Hindustani slide-guitar is an adaptation of the Western F-Hole Hawaiian slide-guitar, modified to meet the requirements of Hindustani (north Indian) art-music. The instrument was introduced to Hindustani music in the 1960s by Brijbhushan Kabra, a disciple of the *sarod* maestro, Ustad Ali Akbar Khan. In terms of technique of melodic execution, the Indian classical guitar and the Hawaiian guitar are both heirs to the ancient Indian fretless stick-zithers, the *ektantrī-vīṇā*, the *ghoṣak*, and the *vichitra-vīṇā*. The technique of these ancient instruments evidently travelled to Hawaii with one Gabriel Davion, kidnapped from India to Honolulu by a sea captain in the nineteenth century. The technique gave birth to the Hawaiian guitar, and returned to India before Second World War through the recordings of American guitarists, Sol Hoopii and Joe Kaipo. [Also see: **Ektantrī-Vīṇā, Ghoṣak, Vichitra-Vīṇā**.] Refer Chapter 5.8.

Jal Taraṅga : The word is derived from Sanskrit *jal* = water + *taraṅga* = waves. The term describes an ancient Indian polychord of the struck variety, consisting of twelve/fifteen china-clay bowls of different sizes, which are tuned to a *rāga*-scale by filling them with appropriate quantities of water. Sound activation is done by beating the cups with sticks akin to sticks used for drums used in popular Western music. The instrument receives mention in musicological texts only from the late seventeenth century and is now nearly extinct, appearing occasionally in orchestral ensembles. Refer Chapter 5.5.

Jamjam/Zamzam : The word is colloquial and partially onomatopoetic. There is no consensus on its definition. It appears to signify a repetitive and deliberate intonation of pairs of tones/ *svar*s in quick succession. Though used in the context of instrumental as well as vocal music, it appears to be more applicable to the idiom of the plucked instruments.

Jhālā : See **Alāp/Joḍ/Jhālā**.

Jhaptāl : *Jhaptāl* is a *tāl* (rhythmic cycle) of ten beats in 2+3+2+3 sub-division. This *tāl* is suited for slow to medium tempo rendition.

Jhūmrā : *Jhūmrā* is a *tāl* (rhythmic cycle) of fourteen beats in 3+4+3+4 sub-division. It is ideally suited for slow and ultra-slow rendition in the *khyāl* genre of vocal music. The *jhūmrā* tempo rarely exceeds 20 beats per minute.

Joḍ : See **Alāp/Joḍ/Jhālā**.

Jugalbandī : The term derives its meaning from Sanskrit *jugal/yugal* = a couple + *bandī* = linked/tied/locked. The term describes duet performances of music by two lead musicians in collaborative effort. The total ensemble for a *jugalbandī*, including supporting musicians, can go up to six people. Being an improvisation-dominant art form, Hindustani music is not particularly amenable to collaborative efforts, except under rare conditions conducive to compatibility. *Jugalbandī*s (duets) are, however, a popular format. Refer Chapter 2.3.

Kajrī/Kajlī : The word is derived from Hindī *kājala* = kohl, representing the black colour, darkness. The name of this genre of poetry-dominant vocal music probably alludes to the cloudy skies, and the ambient darkness associated with the rainy season (July to September) in which this genre is performed. It is performed by women, and accompanied by circular dance. Like the *chaitī* genre of seasonal songs, this genre belongs to the folk tradition of Uttar Pradesh (Northern Provinces) and was elevated to the status of a semi-classical art form by the courtesans of Benares. The genre is regarded as one of the allied genres of the *bol-banāo ṭhumrī*. [Also see: **Chaitī, Bol-banāo Ṭhumrī**.] Refer Chapter 4.3.

Kalāvant/Kalāvantī Khyāl : The word derives from Sanskrit *kalā* = art + *vanta* = owner. Literally, the word denotes the practitioner of any art. In the present context, the term refers to a mediaeval community of *dhrupad* vocalists. *Kalāvantī* is an adjective derived from *kalāvant*. The *kalāvantī khyāl* was presumably distinguished from its other variants by virtue of its practitioners having been groomed in the stylistics of the *dhrupad* genre. [Also see: **Dhrupad, Khyāl**.]

Kaṇ/Sparśa : The word is Sanskrit for "grain/microscopic particle". When a tone/*svar* is intoned after — but almost simultaneously with — the fractional intonation of an adjacent tone/*svar*, the incidental tone/*svar* is called a *kaṇ svar*. This embellishment of intonation is used in vocal as well as instrumental music. In instrumental music, this form of embellishment is executed by the consecutive — though near simultaneous — use of two fingers. It involves no more than a summary touch of the incidental tone/*svar*. This is why, it is also called *sparśa*, Sanskrit for "touch."

Karuṇa : See **Rasa/Navarasa**.

Kāṣṭha Taraṅga : The word is derived from Sanskrit *kāṣṭha* = wood + *taraṅga* = waves. The term describes an ancient polychord of the struck variety, an Indian version of a xylophone. Sound activation is done by impacting wooden strips of different sizes with sticks with rounded heads. The instrument is nearly extinct, now encountered occasionally in orchestral ensembles. Refer Chapter 5.5.

Kathaka : Kathaka is the name of the principal genre of classical dance in the north Indian performing arts tradition, closely linked to its musical and poetic traditions. The word derives from Sanskrit *kathā* = story + *kār* = narrator. Kathaka is also the name of an ancient community of story-tellers, who specialized in the narration of episodes from the major Hindu epics through mime and vocal-instrumental accompaniment. By religious orientation, the Kathakas were devotees of Lord Kṛṣṇa, an incarnation of Lord Viṣṇu. Members of this community, and their religious and artistic traditions, have shaped the modern Kathaka genre of dance, as well as the modern *ṭhumrī* genre of semi-classical music, both of which revolve around the legend of Lord Kṛṣṇa. [Also see: **Ṭhumrī, Viṣṇu.**] Refer Chapter 4.3.

Khervā : *Kehervā* is a rhythmic cycle of eight beats in 4+4 subdivision. It is generally performed in medium tempo.

Khyāl : The term derives its meaning from the Perso-Arabic word *khyāl*, meaning idea, imagination, subjectivity, individuality, or impression. It represents a confluence of *rūpakālapti*, an ancient genre of Indian art music (eighth/ninth century), and Perso-Arabic music, encouraged by the landmark poet-musician, Amir Khusro (thirteenth century). *Khyāl* is the modern genre of vocal music, which replaced *dhrupad* as the mainstream genre starting in the early nineteenth century. *Khyāl* is an improvisation-dominant genre, compared to its predecessor, *dhrupad*, which had a strong tendency towards being a pre-composed genre. The *khyāl* is characterized by its linear architecture, involving a progressive intensification of melodic and rhythmic density and complexity. A *khyāl* rendition generally consists of two parts — a slow tempo rendition called the *baḍā* (major) *khyāl* and a medium-to-fast tempo rendition called *chhoṭā* (minor) *khyāl*. [Also see: **Rūpakālapti, Dhrupad, Baḍā Khyāl, Chhoṭā Khyāl.**] Refer Chapters 4.2 and 2.1.

Khaṭakā : The word is colloquial and partially onomatopoetic. Its definitions vary considerably. The word has two connotations — of a jolting quality, and of a forceful, audible impact. A generally acceptable definition would be the intonation of two neighbouring, though not necessarily adjacent, tones/*svar*s in quick succession, generally staccato, in which the first tone/*svar* is intoned with considerably greater force and impact than the second. The *khaṭakā* description is also appropriate for melodic expressions involving sudden drops across a distance of three or four tones/*svar*s specifically required by the grammar of some *rāga*s.

Kinnarī/Kinnarī-Vīṇā : The word *kinnarī* is an adjective derived from the Sanskrit *kinnar*, meaning a category of celestial being. *Kinnar* also denotes a community of professional musicians. The word *kinnarī* may be construed either as an adjective derived from *kinnar*, or translated as as "female *kinnar*". In the present context, it refers to an ancient instrument, a member of the fretted stick-zither family, which is considered the ancestor of the *rudra-vīṇā*. *Kinnarī-vīṇā*s were of two varieties: the *bṛhat* (great/major) *kinnarī*, and the *laghu* (small/minor) *kinnarī*. The *laghu kinnarī* is believed to be the direct parent of the *rudra-vīṇā*. [Also see: **Rudra-Vīṇā**.] Refer Chapter 5.1.

Kīrtan : *Kīrtan* is the verb associated with the Sanskrit abstract noun *kīrti* = glory/praise. A *kīrtan* is a song sung in praise of, or dedicated to the glory of someone, principally God. In thematic content, the *kīrtan* is similar to the *bhajan*, the distinction between them often being no more than semantic. *Kīrtan*s are, generally, shorter forms of poetry than *bhajan*s. *Kīrtan*s are written in all Indian languages and in every dialect of them. Its poetic form varies from region to region, as does its mode of rendition. As a piece of devotional music often sung in a choral modality, it is poetry-dominated, makes modest demands on musicianship and has no role for deliberate improvisation. In the Carnatic (south Indian) art music tradition, the *kīrtan* is a very definite compositional form, and is rendered in accordance with prescribed rules. [Also see: **Bhajan, Carnatic**.]

Komal [with respect to svar/tone] : The word derives from Sanskrit *komal* = soft. The Hindustani scale consists of seven natural tones, plus mutations representing either suppressed or enhanced frequencies of five of the seven tones. The seven natural tones are called *śuddha*, the suppressed tones are called *komal*, Sanskrit for "soft", while the solitary enhanced tone is called *tīvra*, Sanskrit for "Sharp." The Hindustani scale deploys *komal*/suppressed mutations/frequencies of the 2nd, 3rd, 6th, and 7th degrees (*re, gā, dhā, nī*) and a *tīvra*/sharp mutation of the 4th (*mā*). [Also see: **Śuddha, Tīvra**.]

Kṛti : The word is used generally as a common noun, meaning "artefact" [the product of a creative endeavour], though derived from the Sanskrit *kriyā* = action. In the context of art-music, the term refers to a specific category of songs performed in the Carnatic (south Indian) art music tradition, which follow certain rules of composition. [Also see: **Carnatic/Hindustani music**.]

Krintan : The term is colloquial and partially onomatopoetic. It is especially suited to the technique of the *sitār*. *Krintan* requires the dexterous movement of two fingers over the frets. The first *svar* executed with a right-hand stroke supporting one left-hand finger resting on the fret-board. The subsequent *svar*s of the phrase are executed with the second finger hitting the appropriate fret in a hammering motion, but without further right-hand stroke support. With this technique, a phrase of up to four *svar*s can be executed.

Laḍīguthāva Tāns : The term is a compound of two words: *laḍī* = chain + *guthāva* = knitting. This pattern progressively weaves an intricate web of interlocked patterns along its melodic path. [Also see: **Tāns**.] Refer Chapter 4.2.

Laggī : *Laggī* is a lively *tablā* solo which, in most cases, heralds the end of a *bol-banāo ṭhumrī* rendition. This form appears to be an early twentieth-century innovation. The *laggī* is always performed in an eight-beat or sixteen-beat rhythmic cycle, irrespective of the *tāl* (rhythmic cycle) in which the *bol-banāo ṭhumrī* is rendered. The beat-density of the *laggī* rendition is normally twice that of the preceding *bol-banāo ṭhumrī* rendition. [Also see: **Bol-banāo Ṭhumrī**.] Refer Chapter 4.3.

Laghu Kinnarī : See **Kinnarī/Kinnarī-Vīṇā**.

Lāsya : *Lāsya* is an interpretative dance form described in Indian texts dating back to the pre-Christian era. It is a solo female dance form, accompanied by female singers and an orchestra. In the dance, the dancer utilizes mime to interpret the accompanying song, which describes her lover, and complains about his conduct. The musical content and context of this ancient dance form makes *lāsya* the earliest identified ancestor of the modern *ṭhumrī* genre of semi-classical vocal music. [Also see: **Ṭhumrī**.] Refer Chapter 4.3.

Lāvaṇī : The word derives from Sanskrit *lāvaṇya* = seductive grace/ charm of a woman. *Lāvaṇī* is the name of a titillating folk dance form popular in the rural areas of southern Maharashtra. The songs that accompany the dance enjoy immense popularity independently of the dance form. Mirroring the emergence of the *bol-banāo ṭhumrī* from a decelerated version of the *bandiś ṭhumrī* in northern India, the *lāvaṇī* form also evolved *baiṭhakī-chī-lāvaṇī* — literally, the sitting *lāvaṇī*. This is presented with the musician seated on the floor. In this format, music is presented at a slower tempo, and the dance element is restricted to mime and gesture. In this variant of the *lāvaṇī*, the emphasis is on emotive poetic-melodic communication. This is a sophisticated romanticist genre which has remained a regional genre, primarily because of lyrics written in a regional language. [Also see: **Maharashtra, Bandiś Ṭhumrī, Bol-banāo Ṭhumrī**.]

Laya : *Laya*, Sanskrit for tempo, is the time interval between the equidistant beats of a *tāl*, when rendered. It represents a linear calibration of the flow of time, while the *tāl* is a cyclical calibration of it. *Laya* may be expressed as a number of beats per minute, while the *tāl* is defined, amongst other criteria, by the number of beats within a cycle. In performance, a *tāl*, rendered in a particular *laya*, may be defined by number of seconds per cycle. [Also see: **Tāl**.]

Laya-bāṇṭ : See **Bol-bāṇṭa/Laya-bāṇṭ**.

Layakārī : The word derives from Sanskrit *laya* = tempo + *kārī* = expertise/craftsmanship. When a musician, either a percussionist or a lead-musician, indulges in a display of rhythmic craftsmanship or artistry, deviating from the standard or pre-composed melodic, rhythmic, or melodic-rhythmic form, the resultant musical experience is called *layakārī*. [Also see: **Laya, Tāl**.]

Madhya Laya : An adjective derived from the Sanskrit *madhya* = medium + *laya* = tempo. The notion of tempo (slow/medium/ fast) is relative and dynamic. It differs between generations, between stylistic lineages, between different genres of vocal music, and between vocal and instrumental music.

Madhya Saptak : The term derives from Sanskrit *madhya* = middle +

saptak = a group of seven tones / *svar*s. The term describes the middle octave of the melodic canvas. While the Western tradition considers the scale as consisting of eight points, the Indian system treats the same distance as consisting of seven frequency intervals. Hence, the reference to the scale as seven, rather than eight. This highlights a fundamental cultural difference. The act of music making in Indian music is focused on the handling of tonal intervals and transitions rather than the tonal point themselves.

Madhyāṅga-pradhān : See **Aṅga prādhānya**.

Mādhurya Rasa : See **Viraha Rasa/Mādhurya Rasa/Vātsalya Rasa**.

Mahārājā/Nawāb/Zamīndār/Sultān : *Mahārājā* (*mahā* = great + *rājā* = king), *nawāb* (Feudal Lord or Nobleman, generally Muslim), and *zamīndār* (*zamīn* = land + *dār* = owner of), *sultān* (Persian for *mahārājā*). These terms denote different levels / categories of power and influence in feudal-agrarian India. Under colonial rule, the *mahārājā*s, *nawāb*s, *zamīndār*s, *sultān*s were guaranteed military protection of British armies in return for a share of land revenue. This aristocracy became a significant patron of the fine and performing arts. Its support was largely responsible for the emergence of the *gharānā*s in Hindustani (north Indian) art-music, and for ushering in the Golden Age of Hindustani music. [Also see: **Gharānā**.]

Maharashtrian/Maharashtra : Adjective derived from "Maharashtra", the name of the Indian state on the west coast. Maharashtrians are residents of Maharashtra, whose mother tongue is Marāṭhī, a Sanskrit-based language, written in Devanāgarī (Sanskrit) script. In the latter half of the twentieth century, Maharashtra emerged as the most prolific nursery of talent in *khyāl* vocalism, simultaneously with the emergence of the eastern Indian state of West Bengal as the primary resource of instrumental musicianship.

Maheśa/Śiva : The destroyer of the universe in Hindu mythology. [Also see: **Trimūrti**.]

Mandra Saptak : The term derives from Sanskrit *mandra* = lower + *saptak* = a group of seven tones / *svar*s. The term describes the lower octave of the melodic canvas. The octave below the lower octave is frequently described as the *ati-mandra* (the ultra-lower) *saptak*. While the Western tradition considers the scale as consisting of eight tonal points, the Indian system treats the same distance as consisting of seven intervals. Hence, the reference to the scale as seven, rather than eight. This highlights a fundamental cultural difference. The act of music-making in Indian music is focused on the handling of tonal intervals and transitions rather than the tonal point themselves.

Maṅgal Vādya : The term derives its meaning from Sanskrit *maṅgal* = auspicious + *vādya* = musical instrument. It is an epithet accorded, amongst Hindustani [north Indian] instruments, only to the *śehnāī*. [Also see: **Śehnāī**.]

Mañjh : The term is colloquial for Sanskrit *madhya* = middle. The term refers to a section of the *bandiś*, not necessarily found in all *bandiśes*, and often also indistinct — between the *sthāī* and the *antarā*. Although its melodic structure is not standardized, it always fails to qualify as an *antarā*. It may therefore be viewed as the composer's attempt at an unusually comprehensive mapping of the *rāga*'s melodic personality within the confines of the pre-composed element. [Also see: **Bandiś, Sthāī, Antarā**.]

Mata : *Mata* is Sanskrit for opinion/ideology/doctrine. At different stages in the history of Indian musicology, different schools of thought have emerged, called *mata*s, each with its own classification and codifications of *rāga*s. These classifications ostensibly reflected a diversity in the melodic entities they handled, and in the manner of their treatment in performance. *Mata*s are now only of academic/historical significance. This evidence is cited in support of the view that the Indian musical tradition has always been replete with, and tolerant of, diversity. This diversity was, in later years, reflected in the *gharānā*s of Hindustani music. Refer Chapter 1.5.

Matta Tāl : *Matta tāl* is a *tāl* (rhythmic cycle) of eighteen beats, in nine subdivisions of two beats each. It is a minor *tāl* of the *dhrupad/dhamār* genre. When performed, it is generally performed in medium to fast tempo.

Mīṇḍ : *Mīṇḍ* is the primary mode of intervallic transition in Hindustani music — vocal as well as instrumental. It describes a transition, akin to a traction, which literally "stretches" a tone/*svar* in order to reach another tone/*svar*, defining a curvilinear path. It is the opposite of a staccato transition.

Mirāsī : *Mirāsī* is the name of a community of Muslim musicians who accompany courtesans on various musical instruments, mainly the *sāraṅgī* or *tablā,* and teach them music. Being a professional classification, the term also came to be used, though rarely, for Hindu musicians in similar professions. Hereditary musicians residing in Punjab have also been called *mirāsī*s. Traditionally, members of this profession claimed a share of the income of the salons to which they were attached. The profession has been viewed with some reservations in art music circles. A career in the courtesan districts had "second grade" connotations in an era when feudal patronage was the most coveted certification of musicianship. Secondly, accompaniment is/was seen as a compromise forced upon those who are/were not good enough to become lead performers. Thirdly, accompanists are/were not expected to be able to retain/cultivate a clear musical vision. And, finally, the music of the courtesan districts is/was not viewed as "pure" art music. These factors led to an image of *mirāsī*s as unreliable teachers for "pure" music. On the other hand, it cannot be denied that some very respected names in twentieth-century *khyāl* vocalism came from *mirāsī* backgrounds. Most of these issues have lost their relevance in contemporary music.

Miya Tansen : The word derives from Persian "Miya" = Honourable/Lord + "Tansen" = the sixteenth-century musician who served the court of the third Mogul emperor, Jalaluddin Mohammad Akbar. He was invited to the Mogul court after he had acquired a formidable reputation as a musician in the court of *mahārājā* of Rewa in the Central Provinces. A Hindu brāhmaṇa by birth, his original name was Ramtanu Mishra, which became Tansen upon his conversion to Islam and entry into Mogul service. In addition to his legendary musicianship, Tansen's significance to music also rests on his contribution as manager of the patronage function at the imperial court, and perpetuation of vocal as well as instrumental musical traditions through his direct descendants. [Also see: **Senīya.**]

Mukhḍā : The word derives its meaning from Sanskrit *mukh* = face. The word describes the first phrase (but, occasionally a string of phrases) of the *sthāī* in a *bandiś* — literally its face — which culminates at the *sama*, the first beat of the rhythmic cycle. By implication, the term is not relevant for *bandiś*es which commence on the first beat of the rhythmic cycle. By virtue of being the launch phrase of the *bandiś*, and by also being its most frequently iterated phrase right through the rendition, it qualifies for its nomenclature. The *mukhḍā* is the signature of the *bandiś*, and often contains the *pakaṛ* (the catch-phrase or signature) of the *rāga*. The best-composed *mukhḍā*s are able to build and release aesthetic tension within a very short span of time. For this reason, the composition and rendition of the *mukhḍā*s is accorded great importance in the musical arts. [Also see: **Bandiś, Sthāī, Pakaḍ, Rāga.**]

Murkī : The term is colloquial, though probably related to the Hindi verb *maroḍanā* = to twist. The *murkī* is a special type of *mīṇḍ*, where the phrase involves a twisted / wrap-around execution with a jerky motion. This melodic expression is encountered in vocal music as well as instrumental music. [Also see: **Mīṇḍ.**]

Nagāṛā/Nakkārā : See **Tāśā/Nagāṛā.**

Nāṭya-saṅgīta : The term derives from Sanskrit *nāṭya* = theatre + *saṅgīta* = music. The term refers to a modern genre of *rāga*-based music from regional theatre, which dominated the entertainment of bourgeois society in the western state of Maharashtra during the nineteenth and early twentieth centuries. The Marāṭhī theatre movement was an important manifestation of the nationalist renaissance in both respects — culturally as well as politically. Its leaders had close links with nationalist leaders like Balgangadhar Tilak and Savarkar, and deployed drama astutely to provoke public sentiment against India's colonial rulers. Marāṭhī theatre participated in the nationalist movement as a covert insurgency, utilizing historical and mythological themes as metaphors for the prevailing socio-political reality. The musical and choreographic component of the productions perhaps helped camouflage the insurgent undercurrents, while also providing entertainment through an additional expression of "Indian-ness" at a time when it was severely threatened.

The music in Marāṭhī theatre was presented in monologue, conversational as well as choreographic contexts, and was almost always based on classical *rāga*s, though also occasionally on folk melodies. In its balance between poetic, melodic and rhythmic elements, and in the relative weightage to pre-composed and improvise elements, the predominant *rāga*-based segment of *nāṭya-saṅgīta* falls between the *chhoṭā khyāl* and *bandiś ṭhumrī* genres of art music. It therefore demands a high level of musicianship.

The theatre movement maintained close links with the stalwarts of the Hindustani art music tradition, enlisting many of them as composers, teachers, singer-actors, and accompanists on the instruments. Very successful and prosperous theatrical companies toured the length and breadth of the large Marāṭhī-speaking region of India. Their activity created the most solid regional constituency for the modern *khyāl* genre of Hindustani (north Indian) vocal music, and supported the cultivation of a massive resource-base of musicianship. Since Independence, the touring theatre company, and the musical theatrical production have both succumbed to the onslaught of the feature film and television as the dominant entertainment media. The accumulated asset of *nāṭya-saṅgīta* is, however, still a formidable force in the musical culture of Maharashtra. [Also see: **Maharashtra, Chhoṭā Khyāl, Bandiś Ṭhumrī.**] Refer Chapter 4.3.

Nawāb : See **Mahārājā/Nawāb/Zamīndār/Sultān.**

Nāyikā Bheda : The term derives from Sanskrit *nāyikā* = female protagonist + *bheda* = classification. The lyrics of the modern *ṭhumrī* genre of semi-classical vocal music are dominated by the erotic/romantic sentiment. Even within this broad theme, they portray primarily the agony of a female protagonist separated from her beloved. *Nāyikā bheda* is an eight-way classification of such situations in the amorous relationship (ten, according to some aestheticians). These are not merely academic constructs for the thematic classification of poetry. They aid contextual visualization and guide the auto-suggestive and communicative processes of the performer. These concepts are crucial to the aesthetics of the *bol-banāo ṭhumrī* genre, which uses song-texts as a platform for a luxuriant and leisurely melodic ornamentation, with the purpose of making the words come to life. [Also see: **Ṭhumrī, Bol-banāo Ṭhumrī**.] Refer Chapter 4.3.

Nom Tom : The term refers to the meaningless consonants used as articulatory material in the *alāp* of the *dhrupad* genre of art music. The practice has its origins in the chanting of the names of Lord Viṣṇu — Oṁ, Hari, Ananta, Nārāyaṇa, etc., which later gave way to meaningless consonants (*nom, tom, ta, na, ri,* etc.) encouraged partially by a religious barrier when performed by Muslim musicians, and guided partially by greater articulatory convenience in high-density melody. As a result, the *dhrupad alāp* is often also referred to as *nom tom alāp*. [Also see: **Dhrupad**.]

NRI : An abbreviation for "non-resident Indians". Members of the Indian diaspora, residing primarily in the USA, Europe and the Middle East, but increasingly, also in Australia and New Zealand.

Nyāsa : *Nyāsa* is Sanskrit for "pause/rest/stabilise". *Rāga*-grammar allows only some, and not all, of its permissible tones/*svar*s as termination points for melodic phrasing. These are called *nyāsa svars*. [Also see: **Rāga**.] Refer Chapter 3.1.

Pada : The word derives its meaning from Sanskrit *padya* = verse/poetic form as distinct from *gadya* = prose. The word has, however, come to be more closely associated with devotional poetry. In contemporary music, the term is used to denote, not merely the poetic element, but the entire poetic–melodic–rhythmic shell of compositions in the *dhrupad* genre of art music. A substantial proportion of *dhrupad* verse is no longer of devotional character. However, because of the origins of the *dhrupad* genre in the music of the Vaiṣṇavite temples, the word *pada* has been retained. In the *dhrupad* genre, the word *pada* has the same meaning as *bandiś* in the post-*dhrupad* genres. [Also see: **Bandiś, Dhrupad**.]

Padāśrit : The word derives its meaning from Sanskrit *pada* (*padya*) = verse/poetry + *āśrita* = dependent on. The term describes a genre of music dominated by the poetic element. *Dhrupad* and *ṭhumrī* may both be described as *padāśrit* genres. [Also see: **Dhrupad, Ṭhumrī**.]

Pakaḍ : The word is Hindi for "grip". In Hindustani music, it refers to the signatory phrase or phrases of a *rāga*, which identify it beyond reasonable doubt. [Also see: **Chalan, Rāga**.]

Pakhāwaj [loosely, also called Mr̥daṅga] : The name derives from the Sanskrit: *pakṣa* = sides + *vādya* = instrument for sound production. It dates back to the pre-Christian era, with its origins shrouded in mythology. The *pakhāwaj*, a horizontal two-faced tapering cylindrical drum, was the principal percussion instrument of the Hindustani (north Indian) art-music tradition, until the advent of the *tablā*. Both sides are covered with goat-skin and tuned, at each performance, by laying, in the centre of each face, a fresh paste of wheat-flour. This coating enhances the sustain of its acoustic output. The instrument emits an atonal, bass sound. It remains, to this day, the standard rhythmic accompaniment to performances of the *dhrupad / dhamār* genre, but has no presence in the modern genres of art-music. Other two-faced barrel drums descended from the *pakhāwaj* are, however, still used in popular and folk music. The *pakhāwaj* of the Hindustani (north Indian) tradition corresponds to the *mr̥daṅgam* in the Carnatic (south Indian) tradition, though the two differ marginally in construction and design, and substantially in idiom. [Also see: **Tablā, Dhrupad**.]

Paṇḍit : The word is Sanskrit for a person who commands respect in society by virtue of his knowledge of theory in his chosen field. In the music world, however, the honorific is accorded to any Hindu musician of exceptional attainments as a performer, the knowledge of theory being implicit in his musicianship. A Muslim of comparable attainments is called an *ustād*. In print journalism, it is common to represent the word *paṇḍit* in its abbreviated form "Pt." and *ustād* in its abbreviated form as "Ust.". No formalized framework exists for conferring such honorifics to musicians. They emerge through an informal process of consensus building within the community of musicians.

Paraṇ/Sur Paraṇ/Tar Paraṇ : The *paraṇ* (etymology speculative) is the major compositional form typical of the *pakhāwaj*, the prime percussion instrument of the *dhrupad* genre. A *paraṇ* usually spans across at least two cycles of the *tāl*, and may, or may not, end in a *tihāī*. Unlike post-*dhrupad* music, the *dhrupad* genre allows the principal musician and his percussion accompanist to take-off simultaneously into improvisations/variations on the pre-composed form. The percussionist's primary deviations from the *ṭhekā* are pre-composed *paraṇ*s. They are mirrored/mimicked by the principal musician [vocalist/instrumentalist], who matches them with his own improvisations to ensure that melody and rhythm arrive synchronously at the *sama*. The matching *paraṇ* pattern performed by a vocalist is called a *sur* (melodic) *paraṇ*, while the one performed on the *rudra-vīṇā*, or any other plucked instrument is called a *tār* (string) *paraṇ*. [Also see: **Ṭhekā, Sama, Tihāī, Rudra-Vīṇā, Dhrupad**.] Refer Chapter 4.1.

Paṭhān : A tribe of Muslim warriors hailing from Afghanistan and the north-western districts of Pakistan.

Peśakār : The word derives from the Persian/Urdu *peśa* = to present respectfully. The *peśakār* is the opening movement of a *tablā* solo recital, played in a perceptibly slow tempo. For this reason, it is often called the *alāp* of the *tablā* idiom. It is characterized by a balanced distribution of sound symbols between the bass and the treble drums. It is based on a stylized rendition of the *ṭhekā* of the *tāl*, which is elaborated through various permutations and combinations of sound syllables and beat-densities within the same tempo. Although the basic pattern of the *peśakār* is pre-composed, the musician has considerable scope for improvise variants on the basic pattern. [Also see: **Tablā, Ṭhekā**.]

Prāṇa/Prāṇāyāma : *Prāṇa* is Sanskrit for "the life force". *Āyāma* is Sanskrit for "control/discipline". In Hindu philosophy, the involuntary process of breathing represents the life force. The Hindu mystical tradition prescribes complex breathing exercises, called *prāṇāyāma,* as a means of acquiring control over the life force. Submitting an involuntary act — breathing — to the human will is one of processes prescribed in the practice of *yoga*. Its perfection leads ultimately to salvation, defined as a release from the cycle of death and rebirth. This science is intimately related to the technique of vocalization and intonation in art-music, evolved as a self-illuminating and personality transforming pursuit.

Prabandha gān : The term derives from Sanskrit *prabandha* = organization/structure/format + *gān* = singing/song. The reference is to the genre of vocal music which dominated Hindustani art music between the eleventh and thirteenth centuries. The nomenclature suggests that it was a highly disciplined, probably entirely pre-composed, genre of music. One of the streams of *prabandha gān* is believed to have evolved into the mediaeval *dhrupad* genre, which dominated the mainstream from the fifteenth to the eighteenth centuries. [Also see: **Dhrupad**.] Refer Chapter 4.1.

Prasiddha : The word is Sanskrit for "famous". In music, it is used primarily as a means of classifying *rāga*s into *prasiddha* = common/popular/widely recognized, or *aprasiddha* = rare/not widely recognized. These classifications are dynamic, as *rāga*s move freely between popularity and rarity from generation to generation.

Pukār : The word is Hindi for "calling out". It describes a cry, an appeal, a calling for attention. As a musical expression, it is ill-defined, but is generally used to described an exclamatory expression, which leaps upwards briskly, and across a substantial tonal distance, from a lower tone/*svar* to one much higher and then returns to the starting tone/*svar*. The expression is dramatic, and therefore found more often in the romanticist *ṭhumrī* genre than in the classicist *khyāl* genre. Its use would be frowned upon in the ultra-formal *dhrupad* genre.

Punjābī Ṭhekā : See **Tīntāl/Tritāl, Ṭhekā**.

Pūrvāṅga pradhān : See **Aṅga prādhānya**.

Qawwālī : *Qawwālī* is a poetry-dominant genre of music, with lyrics originally in Persian, and later in Urdu. A controversial theory regards the *qawwālī* as an important influence on the evolution of the modern *khyāl* genre. The Islamic Sufi sects adopted this as a major vehicle for the propagation of their philosophy. Amir Khusro, the legendary thieteenth-century poet-musician and a Sufi, contributed substantially to its evolution and stature. In recent times, however, its thematic content has been enlarged substantially. In its contemporary form, a great deal of *qawwālī* is, in fact, *ghazal* in a different mode of rendition. Another distinguishing feature of the contemporary *qawwālī* is a combination of alternating solo and choral modalities of presentation, and a large ensemble, often including multiple melodic and percussion accompaniments. [Also see: **Khyāl, Urdu, Ghazal**.]

Qawwālī Ṭhekā : See **Tīntāl/Tritāl, Ṭhekā**.

Quaidā : The word is Persian/Urdu for "the law/the principle". The *quaidā* is normally the second movement in a *tablā* solo performance. The *quaidā* is more structured than its preceding movement, the *peśakār*, and has negligible scope for improvisation. The *quaidā* is presented in four well-defined phases, in proper sequence. In the first phase, the unadorned basic motif (the *quaidā*/the law/the principle) of the movement is presented in its unadorned form. In the second phase, the basic motif is broken down into smaller units to facilitate elaboration. In the third phase, the basic motif is interpreted in close adherence to the structure of the *tāl* in which the *quaidā* is composed. In the fourth and final phase, the particular *quaidā* is rounded off with a *tihāī*. [Also see: **Peśakār, Tihāī**.]

Rabāb : The *rabāb* is an instrument of the short-necked fretless lute family, played by plucking. It has a carved wooden body, with the lower half covered by goat-skin, and the upper half with a wooden finger board. It uses catgut strings and, like a mandolin, is plucked with a triangular plectrum. The *rabāb* came to India from two sources. The first *rabāb*, a larger instrument, came from Persia with conquering armies around the eleventh century. The second, a smaller instrument of similar construction, came from Afghanistan with soldiers in the employ of early Moguls. The Persian *rabāb* became a significant performer of the *dhrupad* genre during the Mogul period, while the Afghan *rabāb* participated in the evolution of post-*dhrupad* genres during the nineteenth century. Though extinct now, the two *rabāb*s are significant because they are the ancestors of the contemporary *sarod*. [Also see: **Sarod**.] Refer Chapter 5.4.

Rabābīya : A musician who performs on the *rabāb* [Also see: **Rabāb**.] Refer Chapter 5.4.

Rabindra Sangeet : This is a modern (twentieth century) genre of vocal music named after the Nobel laureate poet-composer, Rabindranath Tagore. His poetry was written in his mother tongue, Beṅgālī. Because of his calibre as a composer, his songs have attained autonomous stature independently of their poetry, and are prized also as pieces for rendition on the instruments. Tagore was well versed in *dhrupad*, *ṭhumrī* and *ṭappā* genres, had studied the art-music tradition of south India, as also the music of the Vaiṣṇava temples. He was conversant with the folk music of his native Bengal, several parts of India, and of many Asian and European countries. His compositions represent a mix of melodic and rhythmic ideas from Indian art music traditions, along with all genres of music from various parts of the world. A lot of his music is *rāga*-based, though not categorically bound by *rāga* grammar. Despite the catholicity of his approach to composition, Tagore's compositions bear the unmistakable and inimitable imprint of his musical vision. In its vocal as well instrumental manifestations, Rabindra Sangeet is performed strictly in its pre-composed form, without any melodic or rhythmic improvisation. Although Rabindra Sangeet enjoys a substantial following outside Bengal, it is primarily a regional genre of modern music. [Also see: **Saṅgīta, Dhrupad, Ṭappā**.]

Rāga : The word, generally used as a suffix, is Sanskrit for "attitude/quality of response/emotional content of a relationship". In music, it has come to denote a melodic idea or framework, associated with a specific quality of emotional response. The notion of *rāga*-ness is, therefore, inseparable from the concept of *rasa* in Indian aesthetics. A *rāga* is a psycho-acoustic hypothesis, which states that melody, created and rendered in accordance with a certain set of rules, has a high probability of eliciting a certain quality of emotional response. The set of rules for the creation and rendition of the melody constitute the grammar of a *rāga*. An awareness of the target response enables a musician to transcend grammar and enter the realm of literature.

As a melodic entity, a *rāga* is neither a pre-composed melody nor a mode or scale. It is represented by a set of rules governing the selection, sequencing and treatment of tones/*svar*s. These rules define a framework, which is tight enough to ensure aesthetic coherence, while also providing sufficient freedom for individual creativity. This approach to guiding the melodic content of music was necessary for a tradition, which combines the role of the composer and performer in the same individual. As a cultural choice, this approach harmonizes the competing demands of continuity within change, and unity within diversity. This enables each performed piece of music to retain a familiarity while giving audiences a substantial access to a novelty and freshness of the musical experience. Every *rāga* is a plausible psycho-acoustic hypothesis because of the accumulated experience of society, and continues to remain plausible by every musician being allowed to test it, and even revise it, at every performance. The hypothesis is perennial and ever-changing, never intending to attain the finality of a theory.

Each *rāga* is shaped and re-shaped by each performance, and has no existence exogenous to this context. The achievement of its emotional goals is accepted as a random event because it is susceptible to a host of variables, many of which may be uncontrollable and even unrelated to the music itself. The names of *rāga*s, and their grammar, are only the starting point of familiarity for contemporary audiences. The music itself is bound by neither names nor grammar, beyond the willingness of musicians and their audiences to accept such a binding. Their interaction has the sole purpose of sharing the experience of literature — a happening — while grammarians struggle to relate the happening to a name, and to document what made it happen. [Also see: **Rasa/Navarasa**.] Refer Chapters 3.1 to 3.4.

Rāga-mālikā : The term is derived from Sanskrit *rāga* = melodic framework + *mālikā* = garland. A *rāga-mālikā* is a presentation format which strings together — mechanistically and sequentially — several *rāgas* for the purpose of telescoped/abbreviated presentation. In such a presentation, each *rāga* retains its melodic identity, without forging either a compound or emulsion of the component *rāgas*. The *rāga-mālikā* format delights primarily by the cleverness with which the musician makes the transitions between sequentially rendered *rāgas*. Refer Chapter 3.2.

Rāga svarūpa : The term derives from *rāga* = melodic framework + *svarūpa* = form/image. *Rāga svarūpa* is a notion of a *rāga*'s distinctive melodic personality enshrined in pre-composed strings of melodic phrases — virtually melodic sentences. This approach, espoused primarily by certain lineages of *dhrupad* vocalism, is more rigid than the *chalan* approach, which permits the musician greater freedom in the sequencing of phrases. [Also see: **Rāga, Chalan**.] Refer Chapter 3.5.

Rāga vākya : The term derives its meaning from Sanskrit *rāga* = melodic framework + *vākya* = sentence. The term describes a string of two or three prefatory phrases — a sentence — rendered before the commencement of a *khyāl* presentation, with no objective beyond identifying the *rāga*. The *rāga vākya* is, in a sense, a cryptic/telegraphic/abbreviated version of an *auchar*. [Also see: **Auchar**.]

Rāsak/Rāsa Līlā : *Rāsak* is the name of an erotic fertility dance of folk origin, accompanied by song and instrumental music. The music is set to *rāsa tāl*, corresponding to the modern *kehervā tāl*. The *rāsak* is closely associated with *rāsa līlā*, a ballet form celebrating the legend of Lord Kṛṣṇa, which shaped the modern Kathaka genre of classical dance. The choreographic, thematic and musical content of the *rāsak* and the *rāsa līlā* has been identified as an important source for the modern Kathaka genre of dance and the modern *ṭhumrī* genre of a semi-classical music. [Also see: **Kathaka, Ṭhumrī, Kehervā**.] Refer Chapter 4.3.

Rāsa Līlā : See **Rāsak/Rāsa Līlā**.

Rasa/Navarasa : The Indian aesthetic tradition views the sensory experience as a pathway to the emotional, and the emotional as a pathway to the spiritual. This reflects the fundamental transcendentalism of Hindu thought. All art is, therefore, validated by a single dominant criterion — its ability to elicit an emotional response. This criterion acknowledges that, at its most intense, the experience of beauty evokes a response that transcends its qualitative aspect, and acquires a mystical quality. This defines the potential of the artistic endeavour, and its reception, for personality transformation and spiritual evolution. At the intermediate aesthetic level, however, the tradition allows for the classification of works of art on the basis of the quality of the emotional response. The name given to these qualities is *rasa*, a metaphorical expression derived from the Sanskrit *rasa* = extract/essence/juice.

Orthodox aesthetic theory, annunciated in pre-Christian texts, recognizes nine basic emotions/sentiments, called *navarasa*, Sanskrit for *nava* = nine + *rasa* = qualities of sentiment/emotional experience. The nine are: (a) Śr̥ṅgār, the romantic sentiment, (b) Karuṇa, the sentiment of pathos, (c) Hāsya, the sentiment of mirth, (d) Raudra, the sentiment of wrath, (e) Vīra, the sentiment of valour, (f) Bhayānaka, the sentiment of fear, (g) Bībhatsa, the sentiment of disgust, (h) Adbhut, the sentiment of surprise/marvel, (i) Śānta, the sentiment of peace. Over the two millennia since this enumeration, critical literature has added several other sentiments, and combinations of orthodox sentiments, to the interpretation of the emotional content of artistic endeavours. [Also see: **Rāga**.]

Rasik : The word is a common noun derived from the Sanskrit *rasa* = the target emotional response of a work/piece of art. The word is loosely translated as "connoisseur", but is unique in its cultural meaning. A *rasik* is a person who is equipped with the knowledge, beliefs and emotional receptivity required to partake of *rasa*. Classical musicological texts have enumerated the qualifications of a *rasik* in considerable detail. In the Hindustani tradition, the listener is not the passive recipient of a unidirectional musical communication. The *rasik* — individually as well collectively — is an active participant in the process that constantly shapes and re-shapes *rāga*s and every other aspect of the musical tradition. By virtue of his connoisseurship, he constitutes one of the pillars of the quality control mechanism in the musical culture, and is as responsible for the trends in the musical tradition, as are the musicians themselves. [Also see: **Rāga, Rasa/Navarasa**.]

Raudra : See **Rasa/Navarasa**.

Rūpak Tāl : *Rūpak* is a *tāl* (rhythmic cycle) of seven beats in 3+2+2 subdivision. Like the *dhamār tāl*, *rūpak* also begins on a subdued beat, and has an irregular cadential structure. For this reason, it is considered ideal for slow and medium tempo rendition in art music. Folk traditions do, however, deploy variants of the *tāl*, which are performed at a brisk tempo, though with a dented beat pattern. *Rūpak* is generally encountered in the *khyāl* genre of vocal music and in instrumental music. A few *ṭhumrī* compositions are also composed in this *tāl*. Contemporary musicians have frequently rendered traditional compositions set to *dhamār* of fourteen beats in *rūpak* of seven beats. [Also see: **Dhamār**.]

Rūpakālapti : The term derives from Sanskrit *rūpak* = definitive form + *ālapti* = conversation / dialogue. As a musical expression, *ālapti* has the same connotation as *alāp*. An *alāp* is a leisurely, deliberate, even conversational, exposition of the *rāga*-form. The Indian musical tradition recognizes two categories of *alāp* / *ālapti*. (a) *rāga-ālapti*, which uses only vowel form as articulatory device, and (b) *rūpak-ālapti*, which uses the poetic form as the articulatory device. This latter form, dating back to the eighth / ninth century, is believed to have been the precursor of the modern *khyāl* genre. Interestingly, the *bol-alāp* in the contemporary slow-tempo *khyāl* corresponds to the definition of *rūpakālapti*. [Also see: **Alāp, Khyāl, Qawwālī**.] Refer Chapter 4.2.

Rudra-Vīṇā [*Also called Bīn*] : A member of the fretted stick-zither family of plucked instruments. A revered instrument with strong mythological and mystical associations. Evolved around the thirteenth century when frets were added to a fretless predecessor. The instrument is associated with the mediaeval *dhrupad/dhamār* genre of music. It was originally used as accompaniment to vocal performances, but later acquired its independent performing domain. The *rudra-vīṇā* is the principal inspiration — acoustic as well as stylistic — for the plucked instruments in contemporary Hindustani (north Indian) art-music. As *dhrupad* receded from centre stage of art music, the *rudra-vīṇā* surrendered its place to later instruments which were ergonomically more efficient, and could adapt themselves to the contemporary environment — acoustic and stylistic. At the time of writing, only five competent performers on the *rudra-vīṇā* are known to exist (December 2003). They are — in descending order of age — Pandharinath Kolhapure, Asad Ali Khan, Shamsuddin Faridi Desai, Hindaraj Diwekar, and Bahauddin Dagar. Only the last two are below 50. [Also see: **Dhrupad**.] Refer Chapter 5.1.

Sacivālaya : The word derives from Sanskrit *saciva* = Secretary + *ālaya* = a building. In India, a *saciva* (secretary) is the seniormost bureaucrat in a government department. *Sacivālaya* is the common noun for the various seats of the state governments and of the central government. The bureaucrat is a symbol of immense power over all aspects of public life — including the cultural — without any accountability either for the bona fides of his decisions, or for the results they deliver.

Sadra : A genre of vocal music composed exclusively in the *jhaptāl* rhythmic cycle of ten beats. It is believed to derive its name from the village of Shahdara near Delhi. The village was home to two brothers, Shivnath and Shivmohan (sixteenth century), disciples of the legendary Nayak Baiju, credited with having developed this genre. Like *dhrupad* and *khyāl* lyrics, *sadra* lyrics are written in Braja Bhāṣā, the dialect spoken in and around the city of Mathura. The *sadra* genre, now almost extinct, is regarded as a transitional genre heralding the decline of *dhrupad* supremacy in art music. [Also see: **Jhaptāl, Dhrupad, Khyāl**.]

Sādhāraṇī Śailī : The term derives from Sanskrit *sādhāraṇī* = common/ ordinary + *śailī* = style. The reference here is to a style of presenting *rāga*-based vocal music, presumably widely practised during the last centuries of the first millennium. One of the presentation formats within this style was the *rūpakālapti* form, which is regarded as the precursor of the modern *khyāl* genre of vocal music. [Also see: **Rūpakālapti, Khyāl**.] Refer Chapter 4.2.

Sama : The word is an abbreviation of the Sanskrit *samāvasthā*, a compound of two words *sama* = equilibrium + *avasthā* = state. It defines the first beat of the rhythmic cycle, at which it releases the aesthetic tension built up by its internal arrangement of beat subdivisions and cadences. The *sama* is also the point at which the *mukhḍā* of the *bandiś* culminates, releasing the aesthetic tension built by its melodic design, and its interaction with the rhythmic cycle. Because it is the focal point for the synchronous release of aesthetic tension by the rhythmic as well as the melodic elements, the *sama* has a magnified cathartic value, and is critical to the aesthetics of Hindustani (north Indian) art-music. [Also see: **Mukhḍā, Bandiś Tāl.**]

Sampūrṇa : The word is Sanskrit for complete / comprehensive, and describes heptatonic *rāgas* (those that deploy seven tones / *svars*). The description does not double-count a tone / *svar* if the *rāga* uses the natural as well as its suppressed or enhanced microtones. In this classification, the ascent and the descent are considered together. However, *rāgas* may be described by dual classifications such as *ṣāḍav-sampūrṇa* if, for instance, they are hexatonic in the ascent and heptatonic in the descent. [Also see: **Chatusvar, Auḍav, Ṣāḍav.**]

Saṁvādī : See **Vādī/Saṁvādī.**

Sañchārī : The term derives its meaning from Sanskrit *sañchār* = dispersion / diffusion. This is the third and penultimate phase in the *rāga* presentation protocol. This segment of pre-composed *bandiśes* is frequently dropped in the contemporary rendition of *dhrupad* compositions (*padas*), and not found in *bandiśes* of the post-*dhrupad* genres. This phase of *rāga* exposition protocol therefore pertains only to the improvisatory movements. As the term suggests, the logic of this phase is freed from ascending-descending progression of the *sthāī-antarā* phases of *rāga* exposition, which are designed to jointly and systematically unfold the *rāga* across the entire melodic canvas. The melodic-aesthetic function of the *sañchārī* is, instead, to summarize the first two phases, while emphasizing those facets of the *rāga*'s melodic personality, which are insufficiently expressed by the progressive logic of preceding phases. It is, in its very character, a free-flowing phase of improvisation. [Also see: **Dhrupad, Bandiś, Sthāī,**

Antarā, Ābhoga.] Refer Chapter 2.1.

Saṅgīta : The word derives its meaning from Sanskrit *sam* = company + *gīta* = song. The term originally referred to the totality of a song, accompanied by instrumental music as well as dance. Gradually, dance was separated from the meaning of the term, which now describes, collectively or individually, the vocal and the instrumental musical arts.

Santūr : A member of the box-polychord family of struck instruments, and related to the hammered dulcimer/cimbalom family of instruments found in several parts of Asia and Europe. Origin most likely in India as *śatatantrī-vīṇā* (*śatatantrī* = 100 strings + *vīṇā* = a stringed instrument) or in Persia as *santūr* (*san/sad* = 100 + *tūr* = strings). It was traditionally performed only in the Kashmir Valley in India as accompaniment for religious chants of the Islamic Sufi sects. In the latter half of the twentieth century, it was re-engineered and elevated to the concert platform as a solo instrument by Pt. Shivkumar Sharma, who remains its most significant exponent. Refer Chapter 5.5.

Sapāṭ Tāns : *Sapāṭ* is Hindi for "flat-out", a straight melodic run pattern with no loops or angularities. *Sapāṭ tāns* can be descending or ascending, and of varying melodic spans. [Also see: **Tāns.**] Refer Chapter 4.2.

Saptak : See **Mandra Saptak, Madhya Saptak, Tār Saptak**.

Sāraṅgī : A member of the short-necked lute family of bowed instruments. An instrument of considerable antiquity and almost certainly of Indian origin. For centuries, the instrument — known by several names, and in several forms — has been used by bards and roving minstrels for accompanying themselves. It entered art-music around the seventeenth century, and has been an accompaniment to the modern genres of vocal music — *ṭhumrī, ṭappā* and *khyāl*. In recent years, it has begun to emerge also as a solo instrument. It is, however, threatened with extinction since the emergence of the harmonium as the more popular accompaniment to vocal music. In the latter half of the twentieth century, the most distinguished exponent of the instrument has been Pandit

Ramnarain, the only exponent to carve out a viable career as a soloist. Refer Chapter 5.7.

Sarasvatī-Vīṇā : The name derives from Sarasvatī, the Hindu goddess of learning and the fine arts, whose iconographic representation invariably shows her holding a long-necked fretted lute. The term *sarasvatī-vīṇā* refers to the fretted lute popular in Carnatic (south Indian) tradition of art music. Though, at one stage, the Hindustani (north Indian) *rudra-vīṇā* — organologically, a stick-zither — was also occasionally called a *sarasvatī-vīṇā*, the two instruments are now clearly associated with their independent respective names. The instruments have near-identical histories, and are of comparable antiquity. Both started as accompaniment to vocal music, and later also acquired solo performance status.

Sargam : The *sargam* derives its name from the first four solmnization/ solfa symbols (*sā, re, gā, mā*) of the Hindustani scale. The use of solfa symbols as an articulatory device in vocal performance is called *sargam*. Such use is well established in the Carnatic (south Indian) tradition. Ustad Abdul Kareem Khan is credited with initiating its use in *khyāl* performance in the early twentieth century. Having been only a pedagogical device until recently, it was frowned upon, by some stylistic lineages of *khyāl* vocalism, as childish. The other major genres of vocal art music — *dhrupad* and *ṭhumrī* — do not deploy this device at all. The *sargam* has proven its aesthetic potential primarily as a vehicle for medium-density melody in the *baḍā* (slow-tempo) *khyāl*. Its use in low-density and high-density melody is limited and acceptable. Its occasional use in ultra-high density melody is pregnant with unmusical results. (Also see: **Khyāl, Baḍā Khyāl, Dhrupad, Ṭhumrī**).

Sarod : A member of the short-necked fretless lute family of plucked instruments. The *sarod* has two identifiable ancestors — a Persian instrument called *rabāb* which came to India around the eleventh century, and the Kābulī (Afghan) *rabāb*, which came to India around the thirteenth century. The art of the *rabāb* received great support from the Mogul court (fifteenth-eighteenth centuries). The present physical form of the *sarod* evolved from the *rabāb* and the *surśṛṅgār* in the early part of the twentieth century. In the latter half of the twentieth century, the most eminent exponents of the instrument have been Ustad Ali Akbar Khan and Pandit Radhika Mohan Maitra. [Also see: **Surśṛṅgār, Rabāb**.] Refer Chapter 5.4.

Sarodīya : A musician who performs on the *sarod* [Also see: **Sarod**.] Refer Chapter 5.4.

Ṣāḍav : The word describes hexatonic *rāga*s (those that deploy six tones/*svar*s). The description does not double-count a tone/*svar* if the *rāga* uses the natural as well as its suppressed or enhanced microtones. In this classification, the ascent and the descent are considered together. However, *rāga*s may be described by dual classifications such as *ṣāḍav-sampūrṇa* if, for instance, they are hexatonic in the ascent and heptatonic in the descent. [Also see: **Chatusvar, Auḍav, Sampūrṇa**.]

Śānta : See **Rasa/Navarasa**.

Senīya : Senīya is an adjective derived from the name of the legendary sixteenth-century musician, Miya Tansen. It is used to describe his genealogical as well as stylistic heirs. The Senīya lineage is represented in vocal music, music of the *rudra-vīṇā*, and also its successors amongst the plucked lutes, the *sarod* and the *sitār*. There are occasional references to a Senīya Gharānā as a distinctive lineage with identifiable stylistic features preserved through several generations of musicians. In the contemporary environment, however, these claims appear untenable. [Also see: **Miya Tansen, Gharānā**.]

Śehnāī : The word probably derives from Persian *śāha* = king + *nāī* = pipe. The instrument played in India is, however, almost certainly of Indian origin. The instrument belongs to the oboe family of beating-reed aerophones. It has the status of the most preferred instrument at religious ceremonies and public functions. As such, it could be the single most widely-heard instrument in India. In this traditional role, the *śehnāī* addresses involuntary audiences of indeterminate profile in terms of aesthetic cultivation. Consequently, its traditional repertoire has been dominated by regional and folk genres of music. In the latter half of the twentieth century, Ustad Bismillah Khan, who remains its tallest exponent, elevated the instrument to the art-music platform. The instrument is heading for extinction, as the ceremonial market moves towards pre-recorded music, brass-bands and orchestral ensembles, and the film/popular music industry — once its major client — goes electronic. Refer Chapter 5.6.

Śiṣya : See **Guru-Śiṣya Paramparā**.

Sitār : A member of the long-necked fretted lute family of plucked instruments. Theory crediting its origins to a Persian instrument called *sehtār* (lit: three strings) and its adaptation in the thirteenth century by Amir Khusro, are no longer tenable. Instruments of this variety have existed all over India for centuries before Amir Khusro. Latest research attributes the systematic development of the instrument to Fakir Khusro Khan (eighteenth century), the brother of Niamat Khan Sadarang, a landmark figure in the evolution of the *khyāl* genre of vocalism. In the second half of the twentieth century, the most distinguished exponents of the *sitār* are: Ustad Vilayat Khan, Pandit Ravi Shankar, Pandit Nikhil Bannerjee, and Ustad Abdul Haleem Jaffar Khan. Refer Chapter 5.2.

Śiva/Maheśa : The destroyer of the universe in Hindu mythology. [Also see: **Trimūrti.**]

Sparśa : See **Kaṇ/Sparśa**.

Śṛṅgār : See **Rasa/Navarasa**.

Sthāī : The word is Sanskrit for "stable/immoveable". The *sthāī* in a *bandiś* functions as the core of the *bandiś* as well as the entire rendition, including the improvisatory movements. It is the nucleus around which the presentation revolves, and is the refrain to which the musician returns intermittently between rounds of improvisation. The *sthāī* is generally anchored either in the lower half of the melodic canvas, or in that region of it, in which falls the *rāga*'s melodic centre of gravity. As the core of the pre-composed *bandiś*, the *sthāī* generally identifies the *rāga* beyond reasonable doubt, though some *sthāī*s are deliberately oblique in this respect. Improvisatory movements also have their *sthāī* and *antarā* sections. In this context, the *sthāī* performs a similar, though not identical, melodic-aesthetic function, as in the *bandiś*. The improvisatory movements follow a linear rather than cyclical logic. Therefore, the *sthāī* does not function as a refrain for intermittent repetition. The improvisatory movements are, instead, subjected to a discipline of progression. The *sthāī* of an improvisatory movement is centred categorically in the lower half of the melodic canvas. It is required to commence with improvisations around base-*sa* (the tonic/fundamental), to descend first into the lower octave, and then ascend to the scalar midpoint in deliberate steps. [Also see: **Bandiś, Antarā, Sañchārī, Ābhoga.**] Refer Chapter 2.1.

Sthāī, Antarā, Sañchārī, Ābhoga : These are names of distinct phases in the *rāga* exposition protocol prescribed for sequential rendition aimed at the satisfactory communication of a *rāga*'s melodic and emotional personality in Hindustani music. In the sixteenth century, the legendary Miya Tansen enunciated them as rules of composition for *dhrupad padas* (*bandiśes*) consisting of four stanzas of verse each. The soundness of their aesthetic logic caused them to be accepted as guiding principles also for the melodic structuring and sequencing of the improvisatory component of art music. These principles are respected, to this day, in the *dhrupad* as well as post-*dhrupad* genres, though with some telescoping of protocol. The last two movements — the *sañchārī* and *ābhoga* — have been dropped from music in the post-*dhrupad* genres. In the *alāp* movement in vocal as well as instrumental music, the four-part protocol is still respected. [Also see: **Miya Tansen, Pada, Bandiś, Sthāī, Antarā, Sañchārī, Abhoga, Alāp**.] Refer Chapter 2.1.

Śuddha [with reference to svar/tone] : The word derives from Sanskrit *śuddha* = pure. The Hindustani scale consists of seven natural tones/*svars*, plus mutations representing either suppressed or enhanced frequencies of five of them. The seven natural tones are called *śuddha*, the suppressed tones are called *komal*, Sanskrit for "soft", while the solitary enhanced tone is called *tīvra*, Sanskrit for "sharp". The Hindustani scale deploys *komal*/suppressed mutations/frequencies of the 2nd, 3rd, 6th, and 7th degrees (*re, gā, dhā, nī*) and a *tīvra*/sharp mutation of the 4th (*mā*). [Also see: **Komal, Tīvra.**]

Śuddha [with respect to rāgas] : The word is Sanskrit for the adjective "pure/unalloyed". The word is used to describe a *rāga*, when performed in consonance with its melodic grammar as currently recognized, without making any deliberate attempt at either its tonal/melodic enhancement, or at introducing melodic features of other *rāga*s into it. A *śuddha rāga* is definitely not either an allotrope of a *rāga*, or a compound or emulsion of more than two or more *rāga*s. Allotropes, compounds, and emulsions have no accepted *rāga*-grammar, and provide considerable creative freedom to the musician. This is the context and rigorous adjectival meaning in which this book has used the term, except when naming *rāga*s with the word *śuddha* prefixed to them. When used as a prefix to a proper-noun, the prefix *śuddha* can have a variety of connotations other than the lexicographic adjectival sense. Refer Chapter 3.2.

Śuṣka Vādya : The term derives from Sanskrit *śuṣka* = dry/lifeless + *vādya* = musical instrument. This epithet is used to describe instruments which are considered incapable of solo performance, and are permitted a role only either as accompaniments to vocal music, or in orchestral ensembles. This classification is not organological, but arbitrary, and valid only in the historical context in which it is given. At one stage (around the sixteenth century), even the venerable *rudra-vīṇā*, the precursor and stylistic parent of the contemporary plucked lutes, was considered a *śuṣka vādya*. Today, in view of the sophistication of the solo idiom of the *rudra-vīṇā*, it is impossible to sympathize with this description. [Also see: **Rudra-Vīṇā**].

Sūta : See **Ghasīṭ/Sūta**.

Sūfīānā Mauṣiqī : The term derives its meaning from Persian *sufiānā* = of the Sufi sects + *mauṣiquī* = music. It defines a genre of music practiced in the Persia/Kashmir/Afghanistan region, is based on the poetry of the Islamic Sufi sects, and is rendered in consonance with the principles enshrined in their philosophy. These renderings are accompanied either by the *rabāb* or by the *santūr*, both instruments of percussive-melodic character. [Also see: **Rabāb, Santūr**.]

Sultāl: *Sultāl* is a *tāl* of ten beats with five equal sub-divisions of two beats each. It is ideally suited for fast-tempo rendition. It is an integral part of the repertoire of the *dhrupad/dhamār* genre of art-music. It is rarely, if ever, heard in other vocal genres or in instrumental music.

Sultān : See **Mahārājā/Nawāb/Zamīndār/Sultān**.

Sur Paraṇ : See **Paraṇ/Sur Paraṇ/Tar Paraṇ**.

Sur Śehnāī : A member of the beating-reed Oboe family of instruments. It is used as a drone accompaniment to a *śehnāī* recital, either along with a *tānpūrā* or even exclusively. In design and construction, it is identical to the *śehnāī*, the only difference being it has only one hole punched into its stem for delivering a single *svar*/tone/pitch, which is the tonic to which the lead-*śehnāī* player's *śehnāī* is tuned.

Surbahār : A member of the long-necked fretted lute family of plucked instruments. The *surbahār* is a bass-*sitār*, near-identical in construction to the *sitār*, though enlarged to scale. The invention of the *surbahār*, around 1825, is attributed variously to Ustad Sahebdad Khan, great grandfather of the contemporary *sitār* maestro, Ustad Vilayat Khan, and to a lesser-known sitārist, Ustad Ghulam Mohammed. The latest research favours the latter attribution. Sitārists conceived the instrument for presenting the prefatory *alāp-joḍa-jhālā* movements, derived from the idiom of the *rudra-vīṇā* (*bīn*). With recent developments in the acoustic capabilities of the *sitār*, the *surbahār* is heading for extinction. The most distinguished exponents of the instrument in the latter half of the twentieth century have been Ustad Mushtaque Ali Khan and Ustad Imrat Khan. [Also see: **Sitār, Alāp, Joḍ, Jhālā**.] Refer Chapter 5.3.

Surśṛṅgār : *Surśṛṅgār* is a member of the short-necked fretless lute family of plucked instruments. It represents a short-lived late-nineteenth century attempt at driving the acoustic and melodic capabilities of the Afghan *rabāb* closer to that of the *rudra-vīṇā*. The most significant version grafted a *surbahār*-style chamber-resonator at the bottom, to a *rabāb*-style fingerboard, along with a *rudra-vīṇā* type chamber-resonator at the top. It was a cumbersome instrument to play and was suited, like the *surbahār*, only for prefatory movements. After surrendering its most promising design features to the *sarod*, the instrument faded into history. [Also see: **Rudra-Vīṇā, Sarod, Rabāb, Surbahār**.] Refer Chapter 5.1.

Suṣīr : *Suṣīr* is one of the five primary classifications of musical instruments in Indian organology. It represents instruments with holes in them. These classifications are independent of the technique of sound activation and technique of melodic execution. The *suṣīr* category corresponds to aerophones in Western organology.

Svar/Tone : The word derives from Sanskrit *sva* = self + *ra* = illumination. *Svar* is, therefore, an utterance expressing the entirety of the practitioner's being, and has the potential for personality transformation. Though an avowedly subjective expression, it necessarily has certain known and measurable acoustic features. However, the Indian musical tradition also identifies two features, which pose conceptual problems. The Sanskrit texts do not define the terms for them, which are almost impossible to translate. The qualities are *dīpti*, loosely translated as luminosity, and *anuraṇan*, loosely translated as a haunting quality. Clarity on these dimensions may have to await either an acoustically meaningful translation of these terms, or their recognition as hitherto unknown/unmeasured acoustic dimensions. This brief etymological-acoustic discussion supports the growing realization that, *svar* in Hindustani music does not correspond efficiently to the Western notion of tone or a pitch-ratio relative to the tonic.

The Hindustani scale has twelve *svar*s, all of which acquire musical meaning only with reference to the tonic, arbitrarily chosen by the musician. These twelve *svar*s have names. But, the existence of standard frequency ratios for eleven of them, relative to the tonic, is debatable. Nor is it clear that their musical values depends upon the existence of such standardized acoustic relationships. There could, in reality, be stronger evidence to support the opposite argument — that their musical value depends precisely on the freedom the musician has to intone them in accordance with aesthetic, rather than acoustic, principles. This is particularly so since, as a rule, Hindustani music eschews staccato intonation.

This is consistent with the crucial difference between the Hindustani and the Western scales. The Western scale is an octave with eight fixed points, while the Hindustani scale is a *saptak* with seven intervals covering the same tonal distance. Music-making activity in Hindustani music is focused on the handling of intervals, while Western tradition focuses its attention on handling the tonal points.

The issue here is, in fact, philosophical and cultural more than acoustic. Any cultural manifestation can be held accountable only to its own goals and values. The primary values of the Indian musical tradition are spiritual, with the aesthetic and the sensory being subservient to it. In the hierarchy of music-making goals, the primary place belongs to the generation of *rasa* at the highest possible level of intensity. A musician shapes and re-shapes *rāga*s in order to achieve the *rasa* goal. In the process, he also arranges and re-arranges relationships between the individual units of melodic expression, the *svars*. The amorphous character of *rāga*s and the floating pitch values in Hindustani music are an essential part of a tradition that gives the musician the combined role of a composer-performer, requiring both these processes to be performed simultaneously. The *rāga* and the *svar* both have only ephemeral validity as the stimuli of an interactive process validated solely by its generation of the target emotional response, the *rasa*. [Also see: **Saptak, Rāga**.]

Svarāśrit : The term derives its meaning from Sanskrit *svar* = tone/ melody + *āśrita* = dependent on. The term describes a genre of music dominated by the melodic element. To a lesser or greater extent, every musical genre is *svarāśrit*. The term acquires greater meaning when in conjunction with other dimensions. The *dhrupad* genre is, for instance, *padāśrit* and *svarāśrit*, while the *tarānā* genre may be considered *svarāśritā* and *layāśrita* [*laya* = tempo + *āśrita* = dependent upon]. [Also see: **Dhrupad, Padāśrit, Tarānā**.]

Svarmaṇḍal : The instrument is a member of the harp family and belongs to the box-polychord variety of plucked instruments. It is used as an accompaniment to vocal renditions of the *khyāl* and *ṭhumrī* genres. Unlike the *sāraṅgī* or the harmonium, on which melody is executed, the *svarmaṇḍal* is only strummed intermittently as a filler of silences. The strumming is done bi-directionally with grown finger nails, or guitar-style metallic or plastic picks. The instrument is not a replacement for a *tānpūrā*, and may be used either in addition to a melodic accompaniment, or exclusively. In the 1950s, the towering vocalist, Ustad Bade Ghulam Ali Khan popularized its use, to be followed on a substantial scale by vocalists of the succeeding generations. The *svarmaṇḍal* is, however, not as universally used for vocal accompaniment as is the *tānpūrā*. Attempts at establishing it as a solo instrument for playing melody have been isolated and futile. [Also see: **Tānpūrā**.]

Tablā : Though the name resembles a middle eastern drum called *tablā*, the *tablā* is a uniquely Indian instrument. The *tablā* came into being when the *pakhāwaj/mṛdaṅga*, the ancient tapering barrel drum, was split half-way in order to make the instrument easier to play. Historicity of event remains vague. The bass drum is played by the left hand, while the treble, by the right. Both drums are covered with goat-skin membranes. Both drums have a coating of iron-filings and carbon permanently affixed on the membranes. This coating is affixed in the center of the treble drum and off-centre on the bass drum. The bass drum is made of metal, while the treble drum is made of wood. The *tablā* is now standard percussion accompaniment to all vocal and instrumental genres of Hindustani [north Indian] music, other than *dhrupad*, folk and some popular genres. [Also see: **Pakhāwaj**.]

Tablā Taraṅga : The term is derived by linking two words : *tablā* = the treble drum of the *tablā* = pair + *taraṅga* = waves. It describes a polychord of the struck variety, consisting of twelve-fifteen treble drums, each tuned to a different tone / *svar* of the *rāga* scale. It is the only Indian instrument to deploy a percussion instrument, or a part of it, to produce melody. Unlike other struck polychords, the *tablā taraṅga* is struck with the bare hands rather than mallets or sticks. The instrument has survived primarily on its rare use in film and orchestral music. Only one living exponent of competence is known to exist (in December 2003).

Tāl : The word derives from the Hindī *tāl* = sound of clapping with the hands. It originated in the ancient practice of keeping time with the clapping of hands, or tapping on the thighs to the accompaniment of recitations of Sanskrit hymns. Such a practice was necessary because the hymns were composed to standard metres prescribed by the literary tradition, and their poetic integrity could be preserved only by recitation at a specific tempo. In musical usage, the same function is performed by a rhythmic cycle performed on percussion instruments. Each *tāl* is a rhythmic cycle defined by its distinctive number of beats, sound symbols for percussion impact and beat-subdivisions representing its cadence. Each *tāl* also has a tempo — or a range of tempi — at which it is appropriately deployed. The *tāl* also defines the metric structure of the *bandiś*, and regulates the cyclical component of the improvisatory movements woven around it. [Also see: **Bandiś**].

Tālvādya Aṅga : See **Aṅga [Gāyakī, Tālvādya, Tantakār/Tata**.]

Tāns : In contemporary usage, *tān* refers to high-density melodic patterns in the *khyāl* genre and post-*dhrupad* instrumental music. A melodic passage may be described as a *tān* only if its *svar* / tone density is at least twice the beat-density (tempo) of the rendition at that particular stage in the presentation of percussion-accompanied music. As a general principle, a melodic run exceeding a *svar* / tone density of four intonations per second can be called a *tān*. In consonance with the prescribed architecture of the modern genres, *tān*s are rendered after the rendition has passed through the presentation of low-density and medium-density improvisatory movements. Even within the high-density *tān*s phase of the rendition, it is considered proper for the musician to observe certain principles of logical sequencing.

Though *tān*s are essentially a display of technical virtuosity, their melodic construction is subject to the constraints of *rāga*-grammar, and their *svar* / tone density is constrained by the requirements of musicality. It is finally the melodic imagination that goes into the construction of *tān*s, rather than their speed, that distinguishes the truly great musician from the merely competent. The imagination works — though with varying degrees of success, no doubt — with a few basic melodic patterns which constitute the raw material of *tāns*. Some frequently recurring patterns in *tāns* are: (a) *baḍhata*, (b) *laḍīguthāva*, (c) *sapāṭ*, (d) *chhūṭ*, (e) *alaṁkār*, (f) hopping. [Also see: **Khyāl, Baḍhat Tāns, Laḍīguthāva Tāns, Sapāṭ Tāns, Chhūṭ Tāns, Alaṁkār Tāns**.] Refer Chapter 4.2.

Tānpūrā : The word derives from Hindi *tān* = a musical phrase/ melodic line + Sanskrit *pūrak* = filler/supplement. This etymology defines its function in Hindustani music. It supplements the aural experience and supports the musician's creative effort. It performs primarily a drone function as an accompaniment to music of all genres of vocal as well instrumental Hindustani art-music. The instrument is standard accompaniment to vocal music, but optional in instrumental music. The instrument is a member of the long-necked family of fretless plucked lutes. In musicological texts, oblique references to it are available from the thirteenth century, while unambiguous references exist from the seventeenth century. The instrument has four, five, or six strings tuned to the middle octave and lower-octave tonic chosen by the musician, along with supplementary strings tuned to corresponding/ dominant pitches as permitted by *rāga*-grammar. Unlike the *svarmaṇḍal*, which is strummed only intermittently, the *tānpūrā* is plucked continuously during a performance. However, like the *svarmaṇḍal*, the *tānpūrā* does not execute melody. Both are designed for a tonally blurred acoustic output, which shapes the acoustic ambience. The *tānpūrā* is, however, valued more for its psycho-acoustic influence on the auto-suggestive and creative processes of the musician, than for the enrichment of the aural experience for listeners. [Also see: **Svarmaṇḍal**.]

Tantakār/Tata Aṅga : See **Aṅga [Gāyakī, Tālvādya, Tantakār/Tata**.]

Ṭappā : The *ṭappā* is a modern semi-classical genre of vocal music. It owes its inspiration to the songs of the camel-drivers of Punjab and India's north-western frontiers. Originally a folk form, later adopted by courtesans, it was accepted in genteel society by the late seventeenth century. The pioneering role in the refinement of the genre is attributed to Ghulam Nabi, a late eighteenth-century vocalist from Lucknow, who composed under the pseudonym

"Shorie Miya". The genre was enthusiastically adopted thereafter by *khyāl* as well as *ṭhumrī* singers. The identifying feature of the *ṭappā* is a vivacious, even mischievous, treatment of melody. The treatment is not only naughty within itself, but also in relation to the beat patterns of the rhythmic cycle. Like the semi-classical *ṭhumrī* genre, the *ṭappā* is also heading for extinction, though it has a better chance of a revival than the former. [Also see: **Ṭhumrī.**] Refer Chapter 4.4.

Ṭap-Khyāl : The *ṭap-khyāl* is a sub-genre of the *khyāl* genre vocal music. It superimposes the mischievous treatment of melody characteristic of the *ṭappā* genre on to *khyāl* compositions, guiding the improvisatory movements towards a similar direction. [Also see: **Khyāl, Ṭappā.**]

Tar Paraṇ : See **Paraṇ/Sur Paraṇ/Tar Paraṇ.**

Tār Saptak : The term derives from Sanskrit *tār* = higher frequencies + *saptak* = a group of seven tones/*svars*. The term describes the higher octave of the melodic canvas. The octave above the higher octave (the ultra-higher) is frequently described as the *ati-tār* (ultra-high) *saptak*. While the Western tradition considers the scale as consisting of eight tonal points, the Indian system treats the same distance as consisting of seven frequency intervals. Hence, the reference to the scale as seven, rather than eight. This highlights a fundamental cultural difference. The act of music-making in Indian music is focused on the handling of tonal intervals and transitions rather than the tonal point themselves.

Tarānā : The *tarānā* (etymology speculative) is a genre of vocal music, which uses meaningless consonants as articulatory material, instead of the poetic form. Though the contemporary *tarānā* falls broadly within the *khyāl* genre, the use of meaningless consonants is much older than the *khyāl* genre. These consonants are drawn primarily from the sound symbols used in the "language" of percussion (*dha, dhin, tirkit,* etc.) and the plucked lute family of instruments (*da, ra, dir,* etc.). The occasional use of *nom tom* phonemes used in *dhrupad* is also encountered in *tarānā* compositions. *Tarānā*s are composed in all *rāga*s and all *tāl*s, and generally performed in medium and fast tempi. The rendition of *tarānās* is much like the *chhoṭā khyāl*, though usually without virtuoso *tāns*. [Also see: **Khyāl, Chhoṭā Khyāl, Nom Tom, Dhrupad, Tāns**.]

Tāśā/Nagāṛā : The *tāśā* and the *nagāṛā* belong to the family of indigenous kettle-drums used as rhythmic accompaniment to the *śehnāī*. The shell of these drums was originally formed on a potter's wheel, but later cast in metal — mainly copper or a copper alloy. The drums come in pairs of pan-like vessels, covered with a membrane of goat skin. Though their sound is atonal, one is a bass drum, while the other — the smaller — is a treble drum. They are struck with sticks. In addition to their role as accompaniment to the *śehnāī*, they have also enjoyed an independent adrenalin-pumping and heralding function in military ceremonies of the feudal era, either on their own, or in conjunction with other ceremonial instruments such as the Indian bugles and trumpets. Though played with sticks, the *tāśā* and *nagāṛā* have evolved a sophisticated idiom, which has also influenced the idiom of the *tablā*, an instrument of far superior musical capability played with bare hands. [Also see: **Śehnāī, Tablā**]

Tata : *Tata* is one of the classifications of musical instruments in Indian organology. The word represents all instruments with strings, irrespective of technique of sound activation and technique of melodic execution.

Tatāvanaddha [also called Vitata] : *Tatāvanaddha* is one of the five primary classifications of musical instruments in Indian organology. The term is derived from the Sanskrit *tata* = stringed + *avanaddha* = covered with a membrane. This category covers a small group of instruments, mainly short-necked lutes of the plucked variety such as *rabāb* and *sarod*, and of the bowed variety, such as the *sāraṅgī*. [Also see: **Tata, Rabāb, Sarod, Sāraṅgī**.]

Ṭhekā : Every *tāl* (rhythmic cycle) played on the *tablā* or *pakhāwaj* is defined by sound syllables representing the strokes on the two surfaces of the drums. These sound syllables and corresponding stroke patterns represent the internal arrangement of sub-divisions and cadences characteristic of the *tāl*. This standard form of the *tāl*, without any improvisation or stylization, is called the *ṭhekā*.

Several *tāls* have *ṭhekā* variants. The immensely popular *tīntāl/ tritāl*, for instance, has stylized variants variously called *addhā ṭhekā*, *punjābī ṭhekā* and *qawwālī ṭhekā*. [Also see: **Tāl, Tīntāl/Tritāl**.]

Ṭhumrī : The word derives from an onomatopoetic expression *ṭhumkā*, signifying the sound of anklet bells of a dancer. The *ṭhumrī* is a modern genre of semi-classical music, which originated as an accompaniment to the Kathaka genre of north Indian dance, and evolved into an independent art form. The genre subsumes two sub-genres — a brisk and lively form called *bandiś ṭhumrī*, and a leisurely sentimental form called *bol-banāo ṭhumrī*. The thematic content of the genre revolves around the mythical romance between Lord Kr̥ṣṇa, an incarnation of Lord Viṣṇu, and his paramour, Rādhā. In the cult of Rādhā and Kr̥ṣṇa, the romance is viewed as a metaphor for the intimate relationship between God, representing the male/active principle, and man representing the female/ passive principle. The *bandiś ṭhumrī* reached its zenith in the mid-nineteenth century and was nearly extinct by the early twentieth century. The *bol-banāo ṭhumrī* acquired the status of a mainstream genre in the early twentieth century, and is now headed for extinction. [Also see: **Bandiś Ṭhumrī, Bol-banāo Ṭhumrī**.] Refer Chapter 4.3.

Tigun/Triguṇā : The word derives its meaning from *tri* or *ti* = three + *guṇā* = multiple. When any melody is performed at a melodic (tone) density three times the beat density (tempo) of accompanying percussion, or the base tempo of the *bandiś*, the expression is called *triguṇā/tigun*. The highest ratio of tone-density to beat-density practised in Hindustani music is eight times. [Also see: **Bandiś**.]

Tihāī : The word derives from the Hindi *tīn* = three. The repetitive iteration of any melodic, rhythmic melodic-rhythmic, or choreographic pattern exactly three times is called a *tihāī*. Its purpose is to create rhythmic interest by building up and releasing aesthetic tension within a very short period of time, normally less than a minute. The triplet form which probably originated in the choreographic art, was mimicked by the percussion art which accompanied it and finally found its way into melodic expression.

The *tihāī* is a rhythmic expression which may be interpreted choreographically, rhythmically, or melodically. The number of iterations in a *tihāī* (three) has a very definite aesthetic significance, which cannot be fulfilled by any other number of iterations of the pattern. [Also see: **Sama.**] Refer Chapter 2.4.

Tilwāḍā : *Tilwāḍā* is a *tāl* (rhythmic cycle) of sixteen beats in four equal sub-divisions. It is suited for slow and ultra slow rendition in the *khyāl* genre of vocal music. The *tilwāḍā* tempo rarely exceeds twenty beats per minute.

Tīntāl [also called Tritāl] : *Tīntāl* is a *tāl* (rhythmic cycle) of sixteen beats in four equal subdivisions. It is the single most popular *tāl* of Hindustani (north Indian) art-music, more particularly in instrumental music. The primary reason for its popularity is its tested amenability to rendition at virtually any tempo — from thirty beats per minute to over 500 beats per minute. Stylized or dented versions of the *tīntāl* — *addhā ṭhekā, qawwālī ṭhekā* and *punjābī ṭhekā* — are used in the *ṭhumrī* genre.

Tīvra [with respect to svar/tone] : The word derives from Sanskrit *tīvra* = sharp/strident. The Hindustani scale consists of seven natural tones, plus mutations representing either suppressed or enhanced frequencies of five of the seven tones. The seven natural tones are called *śuddha*, the suppressed tones are called *komal*, Sanskrit for "soft", while the solitary enhanced tone is called *tīvra*, Sanskrit for "sharp." The Hindustani scale deploys *komal*/ suppressed mutations/frequencies of the 2nd, 3rd, 6th, and 7th degrees (*re, gā, dhā, nī*) and a *tīvra*/sharp mutation of the 4th (*mā*). [Also see: **Śuddha, Komal.**]

Trimūrti : The word derives its meaning from Sanskrit *tri* = three + *mūrti* = manifestation. It refers to the Holy Trinity of Hindu mythology — Brahmā, Viṣṇu and Maheśa/Śiva. They are conceived as a collective entity because they are regarded as manifestations of the Divine Power. Of the three, Viṣṇu enjoys the most frequent and intimate involvement with human affairs, followed by Maheśa, and Brahmā, in that order. [Also see: **Brahmā, Viṣṇu, Maheśa.**]

Uchit : See **Auchitya/Uchit/Anuchit**.

Urdu : A dialect of Hindi, the mainstream north Indian language, with a substantial presence of Persian and Arabic vocabulary, but only minor syntactical influence. The dialect is written in the Persian script. The name derives from the Turkish word "Urd" = the market in a military camp. This suggests its origins amongst settling soldiers from conquering Middle Eastern armies. Unlike Persian, Urdu never became a language of the feudal courts in India. However, the dialect did trigger off a major literary flowering during the colonial era (nineteenth and early twentieth centuries) primarily through the *ghazal* genre. [Also see: **Ghaẓal**.]

Ustād : The word is Persian for a teacher. In the music world, it signifies a Muslim musician of sufficient attainments to qualify as a teacher. A Hindu of comparable attainments is called a *paṇḍit*. In print journalism, it is common to represent the word *paṇḍit* in its abbreviated form "Pt." and *ustād* in its abbreviated form as "Ust.". No formalized framework exists for conferring such honorifics to musicians. They emerge through an informal process of consensus building within the community of musicians.

Uttarāṅga prādhānya : See **Aṅga prādhānya**.

Vādī/Saṁvādī : *Vādī* is derived from the Sanskrit verb *vad* = to speak. Contextually, *vādī* may be translated as "proponent/protagonist". *Saṁvādī* derives from *saṁvād* = dialogue. The *vādī* and *saṁvādī* are the two dominant tones/*svar*s in a *rāga*. The *vādī* is the primary dominant, while the *saṁvādī*, generally in the alternate tetrachord of the scale and in acoustic correspondence with the *vādī*, is the secondary dominant tone/*svar* of the *rāga*. The two, together, form the foci around which the *rāga* exposition revolves. [Also see: **Rāga**.] Refer Chapter 3.1.

Vādya : A common noun derived from the Sanskrit verb *vad* = to speak. *Vādya* = that which can speak/can emit a sound. The term is descriptive of all musical instruments.

Vaiṣṇava/Vaiṣṇavite : Adjective derived from the name of Viṣṇu, the Preserver of the universe in Hindu mythology. It is used primarily to describe the code of conduct and ecclesiastical culture associated with the sects devoted to Lord Kṛṣṇa, one of the ten incarnations of Viṣṇu. Similarly, cults devoted to Maheśa/Śiva are described as Śaiva or Śaivite. [Also see: **Maheśa, Brahmā**.]

Vajrāsana : The word refers to a posture, practised in the science of *yoga*. The word is of Sanskrit derivation. Of its several meanings, the most appropriate in the present context is *vajra* = severe/hard/demanding + *āsana* = posture. The posture involves sitting on the floor with both knees folded tightly together in front, with the soles of the feet facing in the opposite direction, and buttocks resting on the heels. For its ergonomic efficiency, this was — until recently — the prescribed posture for *rudra-vīṇā* players. The posture was probably also considered appropriately reverent for laity in the presence of royalty or in the temples. [Also see: **Yogic**.]

Vāna-Vīṇā : A member of the box-polychord variety of struck instruments. It is an ancient Indian instrument with 100 strings, whose description matches the ancient *śatatantrī-vīṇā* and the contemporary *santūr*. [Also see: **Santūr, Śatatantrī-Vīṇā**.]

Vātsalya Rasa : See **Viraha Rasa/Mādhurya Rasa/Vātsalya Rasa.**

Vichitra-Vīṇā : A member of the fretless stick-zither family, on which melody is executed by sliding a piece of rounded glass, akin to a paper-weight, along the strings. This instrument is a successor to the ancient *ektantrī-vīṇā*, and a precursor of the Hawaiian slide-guitar. The *vichitra-vīṇā* of the Hindustani (north Indian) tradition is identical to the *goṭṭu vādyam* of the Carnatic (south Indian) tradition, now renamed *chitra-vīṇā*. [Also see: **Ektantrī-Vīṇā, Indian classical guitar**.]

Vilambit [or Vilambit laya] : Adjective derived from Sanskrit *vilamba* = delay. In music, it is used to describe slow-tempo rendition. For ultra-slow tempo renditions, the term used is *ati-vilambit* (*ati* = extreme). The notion of slowness, or briskness, is relative and dynamic. It differs between generations, between stylistic lineages, between different genres of vocal music, and between vocal and instrumental music.

Vīra : See **Rasa/Navarasa**.

Viraha Rasa/Mādhurya Rasa/Vātsalya Rasa : Viraha and Mādhurya are two *rasas* — outside of the nine *rasas* in orthodox aesthetic theory — relevant to the lyrics of all the major genres of Hindustani music. *Viraha* is Sanskrit for absence/separation. *Mādhurya* is Sanskrit for the quality of sweetness/tenderness in a human relationship. *Vātsalya* is Sanskrit for maternal/parental sentiment. Conceptually, the three are connected in Indian aesthetic theory.

Viraha Rasa is regarded as a compound of Śr̥ṅgār Rasa = the romantic sentiment and Karuṇa Rasa = the sentiment of pathos. Poetry of the Viraha Rasa deals with the agony experienced by a woman separated from her beloved. Mādhurya Rasa = the sweetness/tenderness of feeling, is viewed as a component of Śr̥ṅgār Rasa. Śr̥ṅgār is a compound of *mādhurya* (tenderness) and *kāma* (physical/erotic desire). Once *mādhurya* has been isolated as an independent emotion, it can be seen as a participant in other compound emotions/sentiments. One such compound is *vātsalya*, the maternal sentiment, of which *mādhurya* is the dominant component. [Also see: **Nāyikā Bheda, Rasa/Navarasa**.]

Viṣṇu : The Preserver of the universe in Hindu mythology. [Also see: **Trimūrti**.]

Yogic : An adjective derived from the Sanskrit *yoga* = union, representing the ancient Indian science of attaining a state of harmony between the body, mind, and soul.

Zamīndār : See : **Mahārājā/Nawāb/Zamīndār/Sultān**.

Zamzam : See : **Jamjam/Zamzam**.

SUGGESTED BIBLIOGRAPHY

Musical Aesthetics

Eisenberg, Evan, 1988, *The Recording Angel — The Experience of Music: From Aristotle to Zappa*, New York: Viking Penguin Inc.

Hanslick, Eduard, 1974, *The Beautiful in Music*, London, New York, Novello, Ewer & Co.

Mathieu, W.A., 1994, *The Musical Life*, Boston: Shambhala Publications.

Meleish, Kenneth (ed.), 1993, *Key Ideas in Human Thought*, New York: Facts on File.

Rao, Suvarnalata, 2000, *Acoustical Perspectives on Raga-Rasa Theory*, Delhi: Munshiram Manoharlal.

Saxena, Sushil Kumar, 2001, *Hindustani Sangeet and a Philosopher of Art Music, Rhythm and Kathaka Dance vis-à-vis Aesthetics of Susanne K Langer*, Delhi: D.K. Printworld.

———, 2009, *Avenues to Beauty: Elight Essays in Aesthetics*, Delhi: D.K. Printworld.

———, 2010, *Aesthetics: Approaches, Concepts and Problems*, Delhi: D.K. Printworld.

———, 2010, *Hindustani Sangeet: Some Perspectives, Some Performers*, Delhi: D.K. Printworld.

———, 2012, *The Winged Form: Aesthetical Essays on Hindustani Rhythm*, Delhi: D.K. Printworld.

Seashore, Carl, 1967, *Psychology of Music*, Mineola, NY: Dover Publications.

Stockhausen Karlheinz, 1989, *Towards a Cosmic Music*, Shaftesbury, Dorset, UK: Element Books.

General (Hindustani Music)

Bhatkhande, Vishnu Narayan (Hindi), *Bhatkhande Sangeet Shastra*, vols. I–IV, Hathras: Sangeet Karyalaya.

Garg, Lakshmi Narayan (ed.), 1989, Hindi, *Nibandha Sangeet*, Hathras: Sangeet Karyalaya.

Jaidev Singh, Thakur, 1995, *Indian Music*, Calcutta: Sangeet Research Academy.

Mehta, R.C. (ed.), 1993, *Composition in Hindustani Music*, Baroda: Indian Musicological Society.

Ranade, Ashok D., 1984, *On the Music and Musicians of Hindoostaan*, Delhi: Promilla & Co.

———, 1993, *Hindustani Music*, Delhi: National Book Trust of India.

Dhrupad/Dhamār

Raja, Deepak & Suvarnalata Rao (ed.), 1999, *Perspectives on Dhrupad*, Baroda: Indian Musicological Society.

Srivastava, Indurama, 1980, *Dhrupada: A Study of Its Origin, Historical Development, Structure and Present State*, Delhi: Motilal Banarsidass.

Khyāl

Deshpande, Vamanrao H., 1973, *Indian Musical Traditions: An Aesthetic Study of Gharānās in Hindustani Music*, Bombay: Popular Prakashan, 2nd edn. 1987.

———, 1989, *Between Two Tanpuras*, Bombay: Popular Prakashan.

Deodhar, B.R., 1993, *Pillars of Hindustani Music*, Bombay: Popular Prakashan.

Nadkarni, Mohan, 1999, *The Great Masters: Profiles in Hindustani Classical Vocal Music*, Delhi: Harper Collins.

Wade, Bonnie C., 1984, *Khayāl: Creativity Within North India's Classical Music Traditions*, London, New York: Cambridge University Press.

Ṭhumrī

Manuel, Peter, 1989, *Ṭhumrī in Historical and Stylistic Perspectives*, Delhi: Motilal Banarsidass.

Sinha, Shatrughna, 1983, *Hindi Ṭhumrī kī Utpatti, Vikās aur Śailiyāṅ*, Delhi: University of Delhi.

Organology and Instrumental Music

Bor, Joep, 1987, "The Voice of the Sarangi", *Journal of the National Centre for the Performing Arts* (vol. XV and XVI, nos. 3, 4, 1; September-December 1986 and March 1987).

Deva B.C., 1977, *Musical Instruments*, Delhi: National Book Trust of India.

Miner, Allyn, 1997, *Sitar and Sarod in the 18th and 19th Centuries*, Delhi: Motilal Banarsidass.

Saxena, Sudhir Kumar, 2008, *Art of Tablā-Rhythm: Essential, Tradition and Creativity*, Delhi: D.K. Printworld.

Journals

Journal of the Indian Musicological Society (English Annual), Ambegaokar Building, Jambu Bet, Vadodara.

Sangeet Natak (English quarterly), Sangeet Natak Akademi, Rabindra Bhavan, New Delhi.

Śruti (English monthly), 10, Kasturi Ranga Road, Chennai.

INDEX